Resisting Change in Suburbia

AMERICAN CROSSROADS

Edited by Earl Lewis, George Lipsitz, George Sánchez, Dana Takagi, Laura Briggs, and Nikhil Pal Singh

Resisting Change in Suburbia

ASIAN IMMIGRANTS AND FRONTIER NOSTALGIA IN L.A.

James Zarsadiaz

UNIVERSITY OF CALIFORNIA PRESS

*The publisher and the University of California Press
Foundation gratefully acknowledge the generous support
of the Lisa See Endowment Fund in Southern
California History and Culture.*

University of California Press
Oakland, California

© 2022 by James Zarsadiaz

Library of Congress Cataloging-in-Publication Data

Names: Zarsadiaz, James, 1985– author.
Title: Resisting change in suburbia : Asian immigrants and frontier nostalgia
    in L.A. / James Zarsadiaz.
Other titles: American crossroads ; 67.
Description: Oakland, California : University of California Press, [2022] |
    Series: American crossroads ; 67 | Includes bibliographical references and
    index.
Identifiers: LCCN 2022010304 (print) | LCCN 2022010305 (ebook) |
    ISBN 9780520345843 (cloth) | ISBN 9780520345850 (paperback) |
    ISBN 9780520975774 (epub)
Subjects: LCSH: Suburbanites—California—San Gabriel River
    Valley—20th century. | Asian Americans—California—San Gabriel
    River Valley—Social life and customs—20th century. | Asian American
    families—California—San Gabriel River Valley—20th century. |
    Immigrants—California—San Gabriel River Valley—20th century.
Classification: LCC HT352.U62 S83 2022 (print) | LCC HT352.U6 (ebook) |
    DDC 307.7409794/930904—dc23/eng/20220521
LC record available at https://lccn.loc.gov/2022010304
LC ebook record available at https://lccn.loc.gov/2022010305

Manufactured in the United States of America

31 30 29 28 27 26 25 24 23 22
10 9 8 7 6 5 4 3 2 1

For my mother, sister,
and the communities of "the 626" and "the 909"

CONTENTS

ILLUSTRATIONS

MAP

FIGURES

TABLES

ACKNOWLEDGMENTS

This book started from a casual curiosity. As someone born and bred in the San Gabriel Valley, I simply wanted to know what attracted Asian Americans to these suburbs of Los Angeles. When I moved to Washington, D.C., for college in the mid-aughts, I explored this question with more nuance—comparing and contrasting the urban form vis-à-vis the suburban, making sense of how varied suburbs can look and feel across the United States, and reading about different histories and patterns of migration. From there, I began what would become a ten-year formal research endeavor.

I attribute much of my interest in the built environment and the Asian American experience to what I learned as an American Studies undergraduate at George Washington University. Tom Guglielmo's immigration history course, Suleiman Osman's post–World War II cities class, lectures by Richard Longstreth, and seminars on cultural criticism shaped my academic path. When I was applying to doctoral programs in 2007, few tenured historians specialized on research about L.A.'s suburbs, let alone a relatively unknown place called the San Gabriel Valley. At Northwestern University, Henry Binford, Kate Masur, and my advisor, Ji-Yeon Yuh, believed in my research from the beginning, continually offering sound advice and food for thought. Thank you to the Smithsonian Institution, particularly Arthur Molella and Konrad Ng, both of whom sponsored me as a research fellow at the National Museum of American History and Asian Pacific American Center.

For the last decade and a half, I have had the good fortune of working and collaborating with scholars in the fields of US History, Asian American Studies, Ethnic Studies, Urban Studies, and Western History. From providing critical feedback at conferences or colloquia to lending professional advice over coffee, I have benefited from the expertise and generosity of

Rick Baldoz, Laura Barraclough, Carolyn Chen, Catherine Ceniza Choy, Margaret Crawford, William Deverell, Jerry Gonzalez, Jinah Kim, Nancy Kwak, Shelley Lee, Matt Lassiter, Willow Lung-Amam, Dawn Mabalon, Nancy MacLean, Martin Manalansan IV, Rhacel Salazar Parreñas, Robyn Magalit Rodriguez, Nitasha Sharma, Tom Sugrue, Linda Trinh Võ, and Janelle Wong. I want to give a special thanks to former and current "SGV" residents Cindy I-Fen Cheng and Becky Nicolaides for their mentorship and for making sure I always remember what is at stake when documenting Asian American and suburban histories.

I am grateful for years of innumerable, stimulating conversations with Joe Bernardo, Genevieve Clutario, Jean-Paul deGuzman, Jennifer Fang, Valerie Francisco-Menchavez, Yaejoon Kwon, Simeon Man, Jan Padios, Mark Padoongpatt, Dana Nakano, Nic John Ramos, Christen Sasaki, Lily Ann Villaraza, and Tessa Winkelmann—all of whom I met as graduate students en route to careers in academia, government, and nonprofit work. Thank you to Ethan Caldwell and Angela Maglasang Caldwell, Patricia Nguyen, Phonshia Nie, Jennifer Sta.Ana, and Kim Singletary for the camaraderie and hearty laughs in or out of Chicago, and to writing mates Sony Coráñez Bolton, Kareem Khubchandani, Tom Sarmiento, and Ian Shin for community and the countless "meme-able" moments we've shared. I also want to express my gratitude to Matt Bliese, John Bonifacio, Peter Byeon, Sarah Collins, Jerome Kare, Jenina Morada, Mike Nemerof, Riki Parikh, and Hayley Richardson for their check-ins, calls, or for standing by me during various stages of this journey.

Since fall 2013, the University of San Francisco has been a terrific home base for an interdisciplinary scholar like me. I am grateful for the range of university support I have received including the Faculty Development Fund, Sabbatical and Post-sabbatical merit awards, and the College of Arts and Sciences, Center for Research, Artistic, and Scholarly Excellence, and faculty-of-color writing retreats. My colleagues in the Department of History, Asian Pacific American Studies Program, Critical Diversity Studies Program, Urban Studies Program, and Yuchengco Philippine Studies Program have fostered a collegial environment, making it pleasure to come to campus. In particular, thank you to Pamela Balls-Organista, Kathleen Coll, Eileen Fung, Candice Harrison, Evelyn Ho, Heather Hoag, Uldis Kruze, Genevieve Leung, Christina Garcia Lopez, Wei Menkus, Julio Moreno, Kathryn Nasstrom, Nadina Olmedo, AJ Purdy, Evelyn Rodriguez, Mary Wardell, and Taymiya Zaman; Annmarie Belda, Danielle Castillo, Janessa

Rozal Chin, Natalie Chu, Cheryl Czekala, Danica Harootian, Liza Locsin, Elonte' Porter, and Stephanie Rose; and to Debbie Benrubi, Sherise Kimura, Carol Spector, and the entire team at Gleeson Library. I also want to thank former students Nell Bayliss, Evan Chan, Malik Lofton, Jazlynn Pastor, and especially Eugenie Mamuyac for their research assistance.

One of the best things about doing fieldwork is meeting people. I truly appreciate the approximately fifty East Valley residents who sat down with me in their homes and workplaces or at parks and cafes to talk extensively about their lives and experiences. Their personal histories added dimension, putting a human face behind every story. I thank the archivists, librarians, and research staff at the city halls of Chino Hills, Claremont, Diamond Bar, Eastvale, Monterey Park, Walnut, and West Covina; County of Los Angeles Hall of Records; County of Los Angeles libraries at Diamond Bar, Hacienda Heights, Rowland Heights, Walnut, and West Covina; Pomona city library; Butler Library at Columbia University; Doheny Library at University of Southern California; Ethnic Studies Library at University of California, Berkeley; Gelman Library at George Washington University; Smithsonian American Art Museum; Art Resource; West Covina Historical Society; Workman and Temple Family Homestead Museum; Hsi Lai Temple; Rowland Unified School District; Walnut Valley Unified School District; and the *Los Angeles Times.* Many thanks to Cecilia Arellano, Bill Bartholomae, Jeane Carse, Lee Cavanaugh, Tara Craig, Ralph Drew, John Forbing, Joyce Fraust, Heidi Gallegos, Allan Lagumbay, Amirah May Limayo, Cheryl Linnborn, Venerable Manching, Dr. Maria Ott, Yvonne Palazuelos, Lydia Plunk, Wei Chi Poon, Marsha Roa, John Rowland V, Peter Schabarum, Carl Schoner, Veronica Siranosian, Paul Spitzzeri, Dace Taube, and Dr. Forest Tennant for helping me locate individuals, navigate databases, retrieve documents, and obtain copyrights.

Thank you to University of California Press for providing a space to tell this story. In particular, thank you to Niels Hooper for seeing this project's potential and for providing sharp insights throughout the process. Thanks also to Naja Pulliam Collins, Jon Dertien, Gary Hamel, Melissa Hyde, and the entire production team for their timely responses, logistical support, and overall efforts in making sure this book came together. And of course, I am deeply indebted to the manuscript's anonymous reviewers. They raised provocative questions and gave detailed, fair, and thoughtful suggestions.

Finally, I thank my mother Myrna, my late father Anastacio, and sister Karen and brother-in-law Phil for their constant love, compassion, and steadiness.

When my tank was running low, their enthusiasm and care provided fuel. Along with my immediate family, my extended family witnessed how hard I've worked on this book. Stretching from Baltimore and San Diego to Sydney, Australia, I thank my Uncle Romy and Aunt Ching, Uncle Jim, Aunt Nancy, Uncle Elmer, and the entire Dy family for cheering me on every step of the way. And to my nephews Liam and Cooper: Once you reach your teenage years, I hope you read this book with a better understanding of your birthplace and mine, the East San Gabriel Valley.

Introduction

IT WAS A QUINTESSENTIAL JUNE AFTERNOON in Southern California: sunny, dry, and so hot that the car steering wheel was too painful to handle. I pulled up to a shopping center in Diamond Bar, a master-planned suburb in Los Angeles's East San Gabriel Valley, also known as the East Valley. I met longtime resident Carl Schoner for an oral history interview in one of Diamond Bar's two Starbucks stores (three, if you include the kiosk inside the Target on the other side of the parking lot). After we ordered iced teas, we got to talking about what living in the area meant to him. I wanted to meet Carl after discovering his self-published books, *Suburban Samurai* (2006) and *When We Were Cowboys* (2009). In the former, he wrote about the "Asian invasion of the San Gabriel Valley," noting it was a "friendly invasion" but "an invasion nonetheless."[1] The latter is a set of stories of the "fondest memories of all young people who were lucky enough to have grown up in the more open expanses of Southern California's San Gabriel Valley back in the good old days of the 1960s and 1970s."[2] Carl's memoirs reflect two strands of how residents and outsiders alike understand the region's past and present: a once-rural place filled with folksy equestrians, farmers, and ranchers, and contemporaneously, a collection of newer suburbs that would later be known for their sizable Asian populations. In both works, Carl eulogizes a life he and thousands of residents experienced before the valley suburbanized and emerged as an Asian immigrant hub. It was a place people like Carl revered and reveled in until it was taken away from them—or so it was felt.

Carl's background is not unlike other East Valley natives or settlers who came of age in the post–World War II years. Born in 1953 to an Italian American mother and German American father, Carl's family resided in the area when it was still rural. They briefly lived in New York City to take care of his

"You know , Hai, it's not normal to prepare
grilled tofu at a western BBQ!"

FIGURE 1. Cartoon image from Carl Schoner's
2006 self-published book, *Suburban Samurai*. Image
courtesy of Carl Schoner.

grandfather until 1961, when they returned to Diamond Bar. For them, the
East Valley was a reprieve from living in the city, a place he and his mother did
not regard as a decent environment for families. One of Carl's earliest memories upon returning was seeing the emerald hills and idyllic ranches he grew
fond of as a kid. He threw himself back into the western lifestyle he missed.
Well into his teenage years, Carl worked at Phillips Ranch "shoveling poop at
the horse stalls," fixing fences, and riding horses.[3] At the ranch, Carl felt most
in touch with nature and himself. It was where he went to escape reality, especially amid the cultural and political turbulence of 1960s America. Before the
ranches and farms were bulldozed to make way for single-family houses, he
claimed the East Valley was true country—open hills, freedom, a community
where cowboys roamed: "It was absolute heaven." But by "the middle 1980s,"
Carl said "it began to change," a sentiment laden with sadness and bitterness
that I heard in nearly all my interviews with homeowners.[4] "Change" denoted
their frustrations with development and density. "Change" was also a veiled,

less provocative way to describe disapproval of the valley's population shifts, particularly the rise of Asian immigrant settlers and their impact on the community. While some folks were outraged, most critics of change—aesthetic, demographic, or otherwise—were simply dissatisfied with disruptions to the status quo. Peoples, cultures, or everyday practices that did not fit a white frontier imaginary challenged their understandings of what it meant to live in L.A.'s countryside.

White families sought a peaceful, "rural" albeit suburban lifestyle, but so did Chinese, Filipino, and Korean immigrants who settled in California after the passage of the 1965 Hart-Celler Act, which relaxed decades-long immigration restrictions from Asia and Latin America.[5] Judy Chen Haggerty, a Chinese homeowner in Rowland Heights, settled in the East Valley with her husband—who is white and originally from Pennsylvania—in the early 1980s. They established roots during the building boom and shortly before the influx of Asian settlement later in the decade. As a new resident, Judy regularly experienced overt and covert forms of racism, including moments with her spouse. To build a support system in the East Valley, she founded the Rowland Heights Chinese Association in 1989, around the time Chinese associations were founded in the neighboring suburbs of Walnut and Diamond Bar.[6] Over time, Judy liked seeing other people who looked like her and appreciated the groundswell of Chinese shops. By 1996, with Rowland Heights as a separate anchor, the "Chinese Golden Triangle" of nearby Hacienda Heights, Walnut, and Diamond Bar contained approximately 1,869 Chinese businesses.[7] By the 2010s, 4,683 Chinese service-sector businesses operated in the area.[8] Retail conveniences and the rising Asian population forged a sense of permanence and community. But critiques about change in L.A.'s hinterland came from Asian homeowners as well. This included Judy: "When we bought the house, there [were] still cows [around town]. It [was] so nice . . . [and] actually, I'm sorta missing it [now]."[9] Like Judy, her father believed it was necessary to speak English, socialize with non-Chinese people, and live in a community that fostered assimilation. As the Asian population rose, some Asian suburbanites—like their white neighbors—asked: Was the East Valley still rural after these transformations?

. . .

One of Los Angeles County's last bastions of wilderness, the East San Gabriel Valley had given way to mass suburbanization by the 1960s. Families

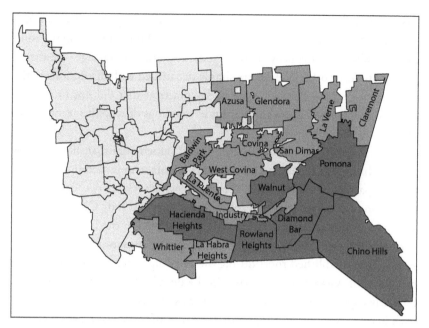

MAP 1. Map of selected suburbs of Los Angeles County's East San Gabriel Valley, including Chino Hills (San Bernardino County). The dark gray–shaded towns denote the six "country living" communities of focus: Diamond Bar, Walnut, Chino Hills, Phillips Ranch (neighborhood in Pomona), Hacienda Heights (unincorporated area), Rowland Heights (unincorporated area). Map created by Malik Lofton.

flocked to the region because planners, developers, builders, and realtors promised buyers a slice of western "frontier nostalgia" or what they commonly called "country living." This referred to a way of life where residents relished the open space, prioritized family time, and cherished the folksiness of small-town America. This idea of country living rested on the myths and lore of an old American West, where rugged individuals appreciated nature, traditionalism, and a republican spirit of independence. Knowing this form of modern agrarianism had cachet, private actors packaged "country living" for upwardly mobile families. It was not organically built. It was a lifestyle reliant on formal or informal methods of social control to regulate "rural" space and culture. Whether one resided in a brand-new home within a master-planned tract or in a decades-old, self-built farmhouse, everyone lived in the "country."

This book is about the suburbanization of Los Angeles's East San Gabriel Valley and how a handful of country living suburbs grappled with spatial, demographic, and political change in the late twentieth and early twenty-first centuries. I argue that myths of American suburbia, the American West, and the American Dream informed residents' expectations. Furthermore, I argue that residents' allegiances to the ideals, rhetoric, and iconography of country living shaped their identities, subjectivities, and perspectives, thus informing how they engaged with civic affairs. Beyond politics, the romance and fantasies of western rurality affected residents' day-to-day lives, from neighborhood aesthetics to where they shopped. For generations across the American West, people created the mythology of country living. East Valley residents made country living tangible, bringing it to life and giving it specific meaning as a unique suburban experience. For over four decades, country living widened residents' opportunities for material gain, social clout, or political power. It influenced how they defined or organized themselves and their towns in relation to the city (i.e., L.A.) and other suburbs, while also narrowing the scope of who or what belonged in these suburbs.

Country living is not just a framework for understanding the East Valley. It is a way to understand why suburbanites across Southern California acted upon or reacted to broader changes in a modernizing, globalizing America. Specifically, for people of Asian descent, engaging with the organizing concept of country living as a culture and a space illustrated the limits of suburban racial inclusion. It forced Asian suburbanites to wield or weaponize their influence in complicated ways because country living suburbia was a landscape not designed for them. Residents often contradicted themselves in how they defined country living and how they lived this lifestyle. For some, "country living" was an all-encompassing term—which I refer to throughout the book—to describe a community's commitment to egalitarianism, humility, neighborliness, and a respect for tradition. These traits rested on Jeffersonian notions of the honest yeoman. For others, particularly settlers of the 1980s and 1990s, country living was about worldliness, sophistication, and exclusivity. In general, residents understood country living as a static landscape reserved for Americans of European origin (i.e., white). Over time, homeowners used this rhetoric in local politics to stave off unwanted development. Critics also used "country living" to express discomforts with the presence of Asian culture—that is, languages, religions, design practices, childrearing methods, and everyday customs. Residents used this seemingly innocuous term to describe not only a lifestyle; it was also a class- and color-blind mechanism for controlling peoples and places. Strategic deployments of the country living ideal were examples of what Eduardo Bonilla-Silva calls "racism lite" in the era of American multiculturalism and diversity.[10] Suburbanites who said they wished to protect country living veiled their intolerance, rage, or fears of the unknown through these modes of subtle prejudice.

Calls to curb change through the politics and language of country living enabled homeowners to conceal discriminatory motivations and allowed policies or attitudes to prevail at a time when social norms discouraged explicit bigotry commonplace before the civil rights movement. Though white homeowners frequently used the term "country living" for political purposes, Asian homeowners adopted it for their interests as well. Like their white neighbors, some Asian residents held racist, classist, and anti-Asian views. They aligned with the political right under the banner of protecting country living to guard their assets as a propertied class. Moreover, by standing with conservative interests, Asian immigrants could claim their worthiness as suburbanites and their willingness to Americanize—a criticism white residents had of their foreign-born counterparts. Asian families were not necessarily seeking white approval. But acceptance made it easier for them to feel a part of a landscape purportedly not designed for them (i.e., suburbs). By embracing local cultures grounded in western frontier nostalgia, Asian immigrants and their children were afforded degrees of privilege and a proximity to the privileges of whiteness their co-ethnics did not receive or experience in lower-middle- or working-class suburbs.

Even when residents expressed a commitment to multiculturalism, diversity, or inclusion in country living, they nonetheless held Asian immigrants to higher standards because their ethnic traditions, practices, and origins were deemed threats to the Euro-American mores of postwar suburbia. Asian families were generally accepted into (and in some cases embraced in) East Valley society as long as they minimized ethnic expression and fit into the mold of the "model minority." By complying with or bending (not breaking) norms, Asian homeowners were able to gain influence as well as cultural capital. As they reached critical mass in the 1990s and 2000s, Asian immigrants—who were once the outsiders—slowly became insiders or part of the political establishment, influencing who and what was allowed in country living.

To be sure, critics' motivations against development or diversity were not always purely based on racism and classism. These were not simple cases of whites versus Asians, middle-class versus rich. It was complicated. In country living, alliances formed and disagreements occurred within and across demographic lines. Residents' feelings and perspectives ran the gamut. And while "country living" evoked a lifestyle and regional aesthetic, it meant different things at different times and held different purposes. Residents weaponized the term depending on what interests were at stake. Their expectations, contradictions, and double standards resulted in a suburban experience where everyone was doing too much or not enough, specifically people of Asian descent.

In the late twentieth and early twenty-first centuries, the East San Gabriel Valley held the promise for families to have it all: a home, a stable quality of life, and social citizenship in what people around the world considered the promised land, Southern California. Thousands of families achieved the American Dream in these frontier-themed suburbs. But through what means? I am motivated by a handful of other questions as well: How influential were myths of the frontier and the old West in motivating families to settle in these suburbs? Why was country living understood as a static, timeless, never-changing place? How did those ideas inform their expectations? What did race, ethnicity, class, generation, and political ideology have to do with the experience of country living? Why was change considered pernicious? Why was it crucial for residents to protect and preserve country living? What was lost or taken away? While their reasons varied, ultimately, the people of the East Valley sought an atmosphere illustrative of their values and in alignment with their expectations of life in postwar L.A.

. . .

Los Angeles is among America's most studied and misunderstood metropolitan areas. As Mike Davis, Michael Dear, Robert Fogelson, and Allen Scott have described, L.A.'s form is what makes it distinct from the likes of New York, Chicago, and the urban Rust Belt.[11] Like its Sunbelt counterparts of Atlanta, Dallas, Houston, Las Vegas, and Phoenix, L.A. is a sprawling collection of lower-density communities that together make a city. Greater L.A. fragmentally extends across the five counties of Los Angeles, Orange, Riverside, San Bernardino, and Ventura. As such, critics bemoan L.A. as a chaotic postmodern metropolitan nightmare of multiple centers in search of a core and an identity; its neighborhoods and suburbs ostensibly lack a clear sense of place or character; and its built landscapes are reproductions or simulations of other locales causing geographers and theorists like Edward Soja to dub such places as "the real fake."[12] Indeed, whether they are well-known "old money" suburbs like Palos Verdes or "new money" suburbs like Calabasas and Coto de Caza, L.A.'s upper-middle-class and well-to-do enclaves were inspired by verdant, quixotic landscapes beyond US borders. Housing, retail spaces, and whole communities were designed as imitations of English country cottages, Mexican plazas, or Mediterranean villages, thus calling into question if L.A. suburbs have organic identities or architectural styles.

L.A.'s sharp contrasts, lack of physical cohesion, and "inauthentic" aesthetics are what makes it a city that fascinates and frustrates. But I am more curious about why metro L.A.'s unknown parts do not capture the public's attention or register in the scholarship of Southern California, particularly the under-the-radar suburbs of the East Valley. I am specifically interested in its modern development, its people, and what "everyday urbanism"—as John Chase, Margaret Crawford, and John Kaliski call it—looks like in country living communities.[13] Rather than solely focusing on race, class, and materiality, I am also curious as to why residents—particularly homeowners—viewed the world the way they did. Some settlers genuinely saw themselves as living a rugged lifestyle akin to the days of the old frontier. Yet many homeowners resided in full-scale, contained, master-planned communities, which they considered markers of refinement, cultivation, and modernity. In country living, disconnect and contradictions are part and parcel of this particular suburban experience. As Karen Tongson notes, "National discourses about the suburbs . . . perpetuate the mythos of its racialized, classed, and sexualized homogeneity." These popular assumptions did not always apply in L.A.'s metropolitan fringe.[14] Pockets of nonwhite, working-class, and queer folks existed. Yet Americans across racial lines sustained these myths because the white, middle-class, heterosexual suburb and suburbanite held social capital. Finally, the scale of upper-income Asian settlement in the East Valley further set these communities apart from comparable towns of the San Fernando Valley, Inland Empire, and Orange County, thus piquing my curiosity in wanting to answer the question: "Why here?"[15]

Resisting Change in Suburbia joins robust fields of research on L.A., post-WWII suburbanization, and post-1965 Asian settlement. I build on nearly three decades of pioneering studies. Despite L.A. County containing thirteen Asian-majority suburbs and several unincorporated areas, there is minimal research in the humanities intersecting these three fields of academic inquiry.[16] In the 1990s, a group of social scientists took an interest in the San Gabriel Valley's demographic turn. They focused on Monterey Park, a West San Gabriel Valley town whose rapidly growing Chinese immigrant population forced the question of immigrants' "rights to the suburbs." In their respective studies, Tim Fong, John Horton, and Leland Saito focus on conflict, political representation, and white antagonism.[17] Fong and Horton examine the impact of resistance toward the Chinese, oftentimes positioning the Chinese as victims of systemic racism and xenophobia. Taking this further, Saito focuses on the ways in which Asian residents built diverse alliances—namely with Latinos and empathetic whites—to reach interracial accord.

Geographers, sociologists, and economists interested in Asian suburbanization continued to prioritize the West Valley well into the 2010s. However, rather than focusing on conflict, researchers examined the impact of local commerce vis-à-vis transnational markets. They sought to explain how globalization "reached" and affected suburban L.A., particularly what Wei Li coins and classifies as "ethnoburbs"—that is, suburban Asian ethnic enclaves whose economic or geopolitical pull extended beyond their municipal boundaries.[18] Li and Min Zhou, for example, illustrate how Chinese banks, import-export firms, and retail made the valley a critical Pacific Rim node. While Li and Zhou acknowledge that racial and spatial politics informed the day-to-day lives of Asian residents, they did not make this a main area of inquiry.[19] Wendy Cheng's study of Monterey Park and three neighboring suburbs—Alhambra, Rosemead, and San Gabriel—places race and racial positionality at the center of Asians' everyday experiences. Unlike Fong, Horton, and Saito (whose studies focus on white and Latino reactions to Asian settlement) and unlike Li and Zhou (who are principally interested in political economy), Cheng focuses on how Asian and Latino residents crafted "regional racial formations."[20] Simply, these two marginalized communities formed ideas about each other based on geography, landscape, and quotidian encounters. Cheng's research provides a useful model for thinking about racial difference and the social dynamics informing interethnic exchange in this part of the valley. Ultimately, these studies are less focused on how class played a role in homeowners' interests, political ideologies, racial attitudes, and intra-Asian suburban identities (i.e., Asians in affluent suburbs versus Asians in working-class suburbs). In the East Valley concept of country living, matters of class intersected with race, thus influencing the texture of everyday life. Controversies over Asian-inspired design on buildings, for example, illustrated this intersectionality because critics believed such aesthetics denoted inelegance and a low-class citizenry.

As a cultural historian, my first and primary point of departure is to understand and locate how myths about suburban life, the American West, and the American Dream shaped residents' expectations and politics in the

East Valley. Early in my research, I noticed a recurring theme in print media and during conversations with residents: the allure and ubiquity of country living. As settlers of the modern American West, foreign- and native-born residents articulated a thirst for a romanticized way of life. They expressed an interest in seeking out a piece of a frontier past that may or may not have been there. The East Valley embodied what Henry Nash Smith refers to as "virgin land." It was a western landscape purportedly ripe for conquest. It was given meaning thanks to myths, symbols, and Americans' constant desire to distinguish "progress" from "primitivism."[21] Here, the agrarian spirit of "Manifest Destiny"—an ideology that has shaped modern American culture since the nineteenth century—was personified in country living suburbia. Over time, residents believed the old West was dying, adding heft to the myth. As Neil Smith notes, "The greater the separation of events from their constitutive geography, the more powerful the mythology and the more clichéd the geographical landscapes expressing and expressed through the mythology."[22] Or, as Roland Barthes suggests, "Myth is constituted by the loss of the historical quality of things."[23] Real or fictional peoples, places, things, or experiences are made more powerful when they disappear or appear to be gone. Ultimately, myths stay alive even when all else has left. With these myths undergirding residents' perspectives, the further away the East Valley moved from its rural heritage, the more its residents worked to protect and preserve country living.

In the East Valley, I suggest that the myth of the American Dream—the belief that anyone no matter their origins and life circumstances can attain stability and success in the United States if they work hard enough—intertwined with myths of suburbia and the western frontier. For to achieve the American Dream with suburban homeownership as the ultimate marker of success, one must toil with grit and tenacity to make it happen—which are among the purported characteristics of true westerners.[24] From the built environment to local culture, frontier imaginaries informed residents' ideas about race, class, and national belonging. White residents and corporate homebuilders alike crafted ideas of California rurality: an isolated landscape of cowboys, agrarians, and untamed land. To be sure, people around the world absorbed cultural representations of an organic frontier filled with such images. These consumers included the valley's Asian immigrants, who—like their white neighbors—often perceived these myths as reality or wanted them to be reality, especially in the early years of suburban development.

As an Asian Americanist, my next point of departure is to explain why the East Valley became a hotbed of Asian suburbanization. Long overshadowed by America's "first suburban Chinatown" of Monterey Park, the East Valley's rapid rate of development and Asian suburbanization in the 1980s and 1990s is worthy of examination since Asian enclaves continued to emerge beyond the West San Gabriel Valley and "the 626."[25] Finally, I illustrate the overall social and political impact Asian immigrants made on these suburbs. In the Northern California town of Fremont, for example, Asian families significantly altered neighborhoods. This was oftentimes measured through their influence in housing and retail. From Asian-owned "McMansions" to Asian strip malls, Willow Lung-Amam claims these "landscapes of difference" became "the focus of new city planning and design policies that tried to manage and mute their difference."[26] Similar actions and responses occurred in the East Valley as early as the mid-1980s amid an influx of Chinese settlement. At the same time, a contingent of affluent Asians sought to keep the aesthetic status quo in place, particularly in well-to-do suburbs or neighborhoods of country living. Consequently, rather than solely focusing on the politics of design and land use, I am equally interested in how Asian residents influenced electoral politics as activists and community leaders. Asian immigrants have played a key role in suburban governance for decades, yet there is minimal attention paid to their impact on civic life. Finally, despite Asian immigrants long being characterized as cryptic and old-fashioned, Asian suburbanites who settled after the 1965 Hart-Celler Act came to symbolize a form of American modernity rooted in transnationality. Their affluence and mobility afforded them a type of social capital based on wealth and cultural exposure. White critics who railed against Asian families increasingly saw well-heeled immigrants as figures of a contemporary world that did not include them, and for some, that was unsettling.

. . .

As a historian interested in qualitative research, I rely on archives, libraries, and digital databases when researching a subject. While there are innumerable materials on Los Angeles, this is not the case for the suburbs of the East San Gabriel Valley. In researching an under-studied region, I had to be creative about obtaining primary and secondary sources. The way I absorbed local histories and gained critical insights on everyday life was to talk with the people who lived there. I conducted approximately fifty oral histories to learn about trends, phenomena, and details not covered by media. The East Valley was often out of the geographical scope and interest of daily urban publications.[27] Even community or regional newspapers with reporters on the beat did not have regular access to city leaders, nor did they thickly describe how residents felt about esoteric neighborhood issues. Oral histories filled in gaps of information not provided in articles, books, city council minutes, or photographs. Oral histories were also useful for getting a sense of how people understood the past and how memory operated (i.e., what people remembered [or chose to remember]). Finally, interviews were helpful in learning about historically marginalized populations (e.g., Asian immigrants) who were peripheralized in print journalism and in the archive.

A majority of oral history respondents were US-born whites, followed by foreign-born Asians of Chinese, Filipino, or Korean ancestry (all but three Asian interviewees were born abroad), and several Black and Latino residents. Whites and Asians received the most attention from local figures and regional or national media because of their visible presence or influence in country living suburbia. Interviewees currently or previously lived in the East Valley suburbs of Diamond Bar, Walnut, and Chino Hills; Phillips Ranch in the city of Pomona; and the unincorporated areas of Hacienda Heights and Rowland Heights. Some interviewees worked in the area as well, though many commuted to jobs in Los Angeles or in Orange County. Most interviewees worked in traditionally white-collar fields and held at least a bachelor's degree. Among white interviewees, professions included public school teachers, doctors, business consultants, government bureaucrats, and stay-at-home mothers. Among Asian interviewees, professions included accountants, bankers, engineers, import-export workers, and entrepreneurs. Interviewees were generally between the ages of forty to seventy-five years old at the time of the interview. To properly trace change over time, I primarily spoke with interviewees who moved to the area no later than the early 1990s.

I encountered several challenges in locating interviewees fully representative of these suburbs' demographics. First, while I identify as Asian American, there were cultural and linguistic barriers between myself and residents of the area's three largest Asian populations (i.e., Chinese, Filipino, Korean). Not being able to speak their native tongue during interviews posed a challenge for immigrants who struggled to articulate their thoughts in English. This deterred some people from participating, which meant I obtained the perspectives of Asian residents whose comfort with English afforded them privileges over their counterparts with a lesser grasp of the language. Immigrants with a stronger command of English were likely privy to information and local knowledge less accessible to others. Second, residents who were key players in regional politics between the 1980s and 2000s felt uncomfortable speaking about recent history fearing retribution, particularly because those whom they mentioned were still alive. The elected or appointed officials I spoke with typically did so on the condition that their identities remained anonymous. Regardless of age or race, interviewees worried their words would offend their neighbors or allies given the intimacy of these communities. Third, it was challenging to find residents able or willing to commit to a whole day (or even an afternoon) for an interview. This is an obstacle researchers encounter when soliciting participants. As a result, interviewees with full-time careers reserved less time than retirees or those without jobs and familial obligations. Together, these logistical reasons made it harder to solicit Asian immigrant voices compared to others. Finally, figures who played major roles in the development and politics of the region prior to 2000 had relocated or passed away. This forced me to rely on a limited archive or the word of living interviewees who knew them.

Though oral histories were a primary source base, I still turned to community and regional newspapers for foundational information. Ethnic- and immigrant-oriented periodicals were useful as well. What Chinese, Filipino, and Korean journalists found newsworthy may not have been the case for the mostly white staff at the *Los Angeles Times, Orange County Register,* or *San Gabriel Valley Tribune*. Beyond newspapers, I sifted through publications such as homeowners association newsletters, chamber of commerce bulletins, and city and county government documents (e.g., planning commission minutes). I also extracted information from developers', builders', or planners' paperwork including iterations of master plans, architectural blueprints, and tract housing advertisements or brochures.

Throughout this book, explanations or recollections of events and how residents responded will seldom make sense. This is not a tidy story. In fact, it is messy and befuddling at times. The things people did or how they reacted were rarely clear, logical, or consistent. Rumors, gossip, and suspicion influenced residents' views on changes in their neighborhood and everything else happening around them. These paradoxes and contradictions exist because residents' views shifted or evolved over time. Moreover, sensitives about race and class made people cautious about what they said, which did not always align with what they believed.

I acknowledge upfront that *Resisting Change in Suburbia* is not a synthesis or comprehensive historical study of the San Gabriel Valley or suburban

L.A. While race and racism are key themes in this story, I do not chart or chronicle relations between all racial groups, particularly whites, Latinos, and Asians—communities that constituted the valley's demographic majority. In taking this approach, I do not suggest people operated in bubbles or lived lives apart from others. Rather, this allows me to delve deeper into the groups who comprised (or would comprise) the racial majorities or pluralities of country living communities and subdivisions (i.e., whites, Asians). Finally, narratives of white-Asian conflict or tenuous white-Asian alliances dominated press coverage and the oral histories I conducted. Much of the concern in media or in community discussions was on the impact of Asian suburbanites. The pace of Asian settlement and scale of property acquisitions across L.A. (mostly purchased by Chinese immigrants with overseas capital) thrust Asians to the front of public debate—and panic—over the valley's changing landscapes.[28] Despite a significant Latino population in the valley, Latinos' impact on country living suburbs was seldom mentioned in oral histories and written sources, presumably because of Asians' "exoticism" and distant points of origin (i.e., across the Pacific). They were what Ronald Takaki calls "strangers from a different shore."[29] This made them extra vulnerable for scrutiny and social policing. Latin—chiefly, Mexican—culture was legible to white Californians. Generations of European and white settlers consumed romanticized ideas of Spanish colonization and Mexican traditions, embodied in regional architecture and simplified folklore about Alta California and the mission system.[30] Finally, I do not cover the intricacies of local history because I am more concerned with how wider trends, phenomena, issues, and cultural beliefs influenced the spatial organization, politics, and daily lives of country living residents.

Lastly, regarding terminology and names: Throughout the book, I refer to Americans of European origin as "white." Numerous oral history interviewees referred to whites as "Anglo," "Anglo American," "Euro-American," or "Caucasian." Asian oral history interviewees sometimes referred to whites as "American." For simplification, I use "white" as a catch-all way of identifying residents of European descent. Moreover, ethnicities within the category of "white" (e.g., British, French, German) carry similar weight when measuring the privileges of whiteness, and thus "white" is most appropriate here. While there are cultural distinctions between foreign- and US-born Asians, I generally refer to people of Asian descent as "Asian" rather than "Asian American." This is to be more inclusive of differences in citizenship and national identity. Moreover, most oral history interviewees used "Asian" more than

"Asian American." It is worth noting that in mainstream press sources I cite, "Asian American" is used as often as "Asian." It is also worth noting that the majority of Asian residents settling in the East Valley between the 1980s and 2000s were immigrants, not all of whom became US citizens. This is still the case in recent years: 67 percent of Asians in the valley are immigrants.[31] Typically, oral history interviewees referred to Asian residents by ethnicity (e.g., Chinese, Filipino, Korean). Unless an ethnic group was specified in my sources or oral histories, they will be referred to as "Asian." To respect the privacy of my interviewees, I have assigned pseudonyms to all who requested it. I also assigned pseudonyms to interviewees whose sensitive content warranted one. Throughout the book, I frequently use the terms *homeowners* and *residents* interchangeably because most interviewees owned a house and because homeowners were at the center of local politics. Finally, the use of *ethnoburb* is widely accepted among scholars to describe suburbs with sizable nonwhite populations, particularly Asian or Latino immigrants. In this book, *ethnoburb* is typically used to distinguish suburbs with an overt Asian cultural presence in the built environment rather than describe a community where Asians constituted a racial majority or plurality.[32] For example, Walnut's population was majority Asian with economic and political ties to the Pacific Rim. But the aesthetics of Walnut's commercial districts were not as explicitly Asian in design as was the case with parts of Rowland Heights or Hacienda Heights—places that residents, interviewees, and scholars considered towns with ethnoburb-like qualities.

. . .

Resisting Change in Suburbia serves as a window into the mindset, perspectives, and lives of typical upwardly mobile suburbanites who believed they lived on the L.A. frontier. Regardless of race or country of origin, homeowners demonstrated through their actions and politics the lengths people went to experience, protect, and preserve their idea of country living. Their motivations and actions illustrate the power of how myths shaped one's expectations and sense of place. As the chapters ahead reveal, East Valley residents sought a lifestyle that was suspended in an era removed from the forces of modernity and globalization. However, change occurred rapidly, particularly the growth of Asian settlement. Some white residents vehemently resisted their Asian neighbors. But many were open to them as fellow suburbanites. That openness, though, came with conditions. While

Asian settlers attempted to negotiate the boundaries created by their white neighbors, most worked within them as a means of achieving acceptance. Asian residents embraced well-intentioned albeit problematic ideas of color-blindness, multiculturalism, and the "model minority" to make suburbia work for them. Taking a moderate or conservative approach to dealing with race or racism and forging class-based alliances with white residents provided Asian homeowners greater opportunities for social and political clout in a setting that did not belong to them as immigrants and people of color. Like their white neighbors, middle-class and affluent Asian homeowners enjoyed the privileges of a desirable zip code. Yet unlike their white counterparts whose whiteness was understood as the default in the suburbs, Asian suburbanites—willingly or through pressure—made additional concessions so they could comfortably call the East Valley their home.

Chapter 1 broadly traces the suburbanization of the East San Gabriel Valley since the 1960s, particularly the towns of Diamond Bar, Walnut, Chino Hills, Phillips Ranch, Hacienda Heights, and Rowland Heights. By the 1980s, these rural outposts-turned-bedroom communities coalesced around a shared aesthetic or theme of western agrarianism, or what were often called country living suburbs or communities.[33] I argue that planners, small- and large-scale developers, builders, realtors, and other figures packaged a life-style predicated on myths of the old West. By promoting these images and ideals, regional actors successfully attracted families to the outskirts of L.A. County, each hoping to experience the romance of a bygone era.

Chapter 2 focuses on the people of the East Valley. Three waves of post–World War II settlers held varying but overlapping views of country living and collectively worked to uphold this lifestyle. While homeowners moved into the region for practical reasons (e.g., initial affordability of houses, distance from work), I argue that the country living ideal was a primary motivator. Moreover, for many residents, ideological beliefs informed where and how they lived; how they engaged in civic life; and how they viewed the role of government in their day-to-day lives. For wealthier Asian immigrants, country living was enticing partly because residing in these trendy suburbs gestured their assimilation into America. Unlike their white neighbors who easily built their lives in suburbia, for Asian immigrants, the process of suburbanization was a test of citizenship too. Developers, builders, and realtors lured Asian buyers to the East Valley through strategic marketing and customized architecture. But their perceived otherness made it difficult for them to integrate and quickly feel at home.

Chapter 3 examines Asian immigrants' impact on the East Valley's built environment. As Asian families exercised their rights to the suburbs, critics questioned their behavior and customs. From the construction of Buddhist temples to the emergence of Chinese supermarkets, some residents believed ethnic spaces disrupted country living and were inherently anti-assimilationist. Even residents who claimed to support diversity and multiculturalism chastised Asian suburbanites. While Asian immigrants' actions were seen as deliberate transgressions, I argue that their integration of ethnic and cultural practices were nominal acts of assimilation. Asian immigrants continued to purchase foreign goods, speak their native tongue, and congregate with co-ethnics. But their investment in western frontier nostalgia and willingness to conform through a variety of measures were actually bold gestures of amenability and assimilation. Furthermore, ethnic spaces generated a sense of place and kinship among immigrants. Ironically, the spaces Asians were criticized for transgressing were typical fixtures of suburbia (i.e., churches, temples, shopping centers). The only difference was that these catered to Asian residents, not whites. In these moments, white critics attempted to frame immigrants as the exclusionists, not the other way around. Particularly on matters of space and land use, Asian suburbanites typically aligned with the local cultures of country living because this lifestyle presented them a range of privileges or an adjacency to white privilege that Asian suburbanites in less prestigious ethnoburbs or working-class towns did not receive or experience.

Chapter 4 focuses on the ways in which Chinese, Filipino, and Korean families were seen as friends and foes of East Valley country living, particularly in the realms of education and politics. They were "model minorities" whose traditionalism and affluence marked them as ideal neighbors. Yet Asian immigrants were simultaneously labeled threats because their perceived exoticism undermined the whiteness of these western suburbs. I argue that while Asian residents perennially stood in this "in-between" zone, at times they leveraged this position in ways to materially or politically benefit them in the long haul. By aligning with the right in numerous local issues, Asians demonstrated that they too could be good suburbanites and, by extension, good Americans. Moreover, by playing up their status as "model minorities" in school and in civic life, they gained community trust and cultural capital. As Asians reached critical mass, they wielded their influence over the white establishment (also known as the "Old Guard") or built strong, class-based interracial alliances with each other in the collective spirit of protecting country living. This was possible because Asian immigrants took a third lane to keep the peace. That is, they subscribed to parts of assimilationist ideas and rejected others, and they acquiesced to as well as ignored pressure from white residents as they saw fit. These strategies ultimately conferred on Asian immigrants varying degrees of power even when white homeowners thought they remained in full control. By meeting in the middle, Asian immigrants claimed a space for themselves in the suburbs.

Chapter 5 situates the "Slow Growth" movement in relation to broader concerns about change in the East Valley. Homeowners worried that country living was coming to an end amid rising densities. As mass suburbanization continued well into the 1990s, residents believed they needed to curb development and harness control from out-of-touch politicians or bureaucrats. Concurrently, residents' pleas to stop change happened amid sharp demographic turns (i.e., Asian settlement). Taken together, critics feared shifts in the peoples, places, and politics of the region disrupted country living. I argue that the Slow Growth movement and synchronous calls to incorporate were not just about residents' fears about development and the death of country living. These were movements meant to minimize the presence and influence of Asian immigrants.

Chapter 6, which builds off the previous chapter, focuses on the reasons for and legacies of cityhood. Throughout the 1980s, 1990s, and 2000s, residents in Diamond Bar, Chino Hills, Hacienda Heights, and Rowland Heights urged their neighbors to back incorporation for the sake of civic autonomy. Advocates believed city councils and commissions ensured greater local control. Particularly in the late 1980s and 1990s, as development continued to sweep across the valley, pro-cityhood forces (along with Slow Growth activists) promoted incorporation as a key strategy for safeguarding country living. In some communities, however, arguments for or against incorporation were tinged with xenophobia and anti-Asian motivations. The simultaneous rise of Chinese settlements in places like Hacienda Heights generated fears of an Asian takeover, which included the arena of suburban politics. I argue that over time, activists' efforts to incorporate (or not incorporate) became more about the need to limit Asian influence and less about the need to protect country living. By keeping the East Valley low density and mainstream (i.e., white), the myths of suburbia, the American West, and the American Dream that residents were wedded to remained intact. For residents across racial lines, that was the goal.

. . .

The East San Gabriel Valley has a distinct past from other regions of greater Los Angeles. Country living was the heart of its aesthetic, cultural, and political identity. Through vignettes of local history, *Resisting Change in Suburbia* illustrates how residents' allegiances to myths and popular ideas informed their perceptions of time, place, and the people around them. For native- and foreign-born families alike, expectations did not always match lived experiences. Through their actions and rhetoric, homeowners tried as much as possible to align their dreams with reality. Desires to experience, protect, and preserve country living coupled with pressures to achieve the suburban American Dream encouraged homeowners to make calculated decisions. Beyond myths, class interests played a key role in influencing why residents did what they did and how they interacted with each other. Homeowners acted in ways that benefitted them at the expense of others, thus limiting opportunities for community building that did not center around material gain or the protection of privilege.

Meanwhile, under the guise of promoting tolerance and diversity (i.e., color-blindness, multiculturalism), suburbanites across demographic lines supported degrees of racial liberalism as a means of opening up country living. While these ideas and social attitudes made it easier for Asian immigrants to feel at home in suburbia, concurrent pressures to assimilate into the Euro-American mainstream encouraged Asian families to acquiesce in ways that curtailed their freedoms of ethnic expression. Interestingly, many Asian homeowners publicly or passively supported calls to restrict "Asian-ness" because it did not fit the country living model and that restrictions purportedly served the greater good. Protecting western rurality protected people's status—something important to all suburbanites including immigrants who wished to distinguish themselves from their poorer co-ethnics. Ironically, exclusion and promoting a white suburban West served as a source of neighborhood unity for the largely white and Asian communities of country living. Ultimately, what bound these disparate groups together was a collective fear that change undermined the myths and ideals that brought them to the East Valley to begin with. The families who had attained the privileges of country living homeownership believed nothing should stop them from experiencing a lifestyle they worked hard to achieve.

ONE

———

Constructing "Country Living"

IN 1991, Shawn Dunn moved from Oregon to Diamond Bar. Raised by a white father and Korean immigrant mother, Shawn quickly noticed the East San Gabriel Valley's growing ethnic diversity. As a mixed-race Asian, suburban Los Angeles was a sharp contrast to his rural upbringings in the Pacific Northwest. Though his neighbors considered Diamond Bar and nearby suburbs as pockets of untouched pastoralism, Shawn held a different view. For Shawn, the East Valley was far from authentically rural. These were simulations of a romanticized American West devised by his neighbors and predecessors: "[These communities were] kind of going for the Western/ Country Western theme . . . and gracious country living. [But] it's just standard suburban sprawl. . . . These [are] modern tract houses with earth-tone colors. There are sidewalks. There are trails. But the trails are paved. The grasses are all green. There's no biodiversity."[1]

Among the neighborhoods that best embodied these frontier fantasies was Snow Creek. In summer 1984, Walnut welcomed the master-planned subdivision named after a meandering stream in the village. Families purchasing a Snow Creek home, the *Los Angeles Times* claimed, would "automatically become part of a new lifestyle that revolves around the friendly, small-town atmosphere."[2] It was "a place where families can ride horses along scenic equestrian trails or take early morning jogs just minutes from their front doors."[3] Like other builders in the region, Shea Homes promised Snow Creek residents a lifestyle that blended agrarian charm with contemporary amenities suitable for a professional class. One Shea executive stated, "Snow Creek is the hometown we all left behind. It provides a peaceful, country-like setting to raise children, and has the added benefit of being within one of the state's top-rated school districts."[4] Indeed, Snow Creek's meticulously manicured landscape appealed to young families who sought a retreat from urbanism and a piece of the suburban good life. Owning one of these tasteful single-family homes included access to high-performing public schools, state-of-the-art recreational facilities, close proximity to shopping malls, and an abundance of open space. But settling into "country living" also meant one obtained the privileges of suburban homeownership and the bragging rights of having achieved the American Dream, East Valley style.

Rather than seeing country living as an organic landscape and lifestyle, I argue that developers, builders, realtors, and adjacent actors (e.g., boosters, civic leaders, media) created this model because of an interest among buyers to experience a way of life suspended in time: an idyllic California removed from the forces of modernity. Regardless of whether these frontier imaginaries were real, imagined, or both, myths of the West influenced regional cultures, architecture, and the identities of its residents. Since the 1960s, East Valley suburbanites embraced the mantra and package of country living. They worked to protect this way of life, particularly amid fears that rurality was coming to an end as development and demographics transformed around them. Residents' desires to experience and maintain forms of Western frontier nostalgia shaped how they made sense of place and responded to change. For homeowners, these ideals influenced how they voted and what politics to support; informed their interactions with neighbors; and set the parameters of what was respectable or normative in their communities.

FROM HINTERLAND TO COUNTRY LIVING SUBURBIA

The San Gabriel Valley has been home to the indigenous Tongva (later Gabrielino) peoples for seven thousand years.[5] Upon Spanish colonization, indigenous communities were exposed to European diseases, exploited, and displaced from their lands. Forcibly proselytized into Christianity, the Tongva were pivotal in the construction of the San Gabriel Mission (founded in 1771). Among the goals of the Spanish mission system was setting up *ranchos* for agricultural development, cementing a European presence in local farming cultures. The system enabled generations of European, white, and Mexican settlers to raise cattle and grow grains, fruit, and other crops. This would continue for nearly a century after secularization in 1830. Settlers received land grants well into the 1840s and attracted another wave of nonindigenous settlement. Prominent ranchers, farmers, and land owners like John Rowland, William Workman, Ygnacio Palomares, Ricardo Vejar, Jose de la Luz Linares, Louis Phillips, and Elias "Lucky" Baldwin would bestow the names of towns, boulevards, and emblems across the San Gabriel and Pomona Valleys, accentuating a long history of settler colonialism.[6]

Agricultural suburbs (or "agriburbs") sprang up along major railways and arteries in the nineteenth century, connecting the valley to other parts of the nation.[7] As Matthew Garcia notes, the valley was the heart of the "citrus belt" and was more heterogeneous than post–World War II settlers believed. Ethnically diverse *colonias*—sizable agricultural communities with predominantly Latino, Asian, Black, and working-class white workforces—developed in the late nineteenth and early twentieth centuries, yet its overall landscape remained rural.[8] With mile-upon-mile of citrus groves and cattle ranches, farming communities like Pomona, Covina, San Dimas, and Claremont crystallized the East Valley's small-town identity well before the 1940s. Residents held tight to the valley's pastoral roots even as mass suburbanization enveloped the land.[9]

Following World War II, Los Angeles County developed into what would become the most populous county in the United States. Buoyed by a growing military-industrial complex and a high concentration of Pacific Rim businesses in later decades, thousands of families settled in new tract houses throughout greater L.A. generating a significant economic boom. In 1940, 2.7 million people resided in the county. By 1960, the population soared to 6 million, and by the turn of the century, the figure rose to 9.5 million.[10] But it was not only the globalizing Cold War economy fueling this rate of new settlement. From homebuilders' advertisements to Hollywood films, Americans widely promoted a golden California lifestyle across the nation and around the world. Cultural tropes of perennial sunshine, sprawling properties, and the prospect of living out the suburban American Dream attracted people to L.A.

In the second half of the twentieth century, master-planned communities grew trendy throughout the United States, particularly suburbs that evoked rural nostalgia. This included The Woodlands (Houston), Ashburn (Washington, D.C.), Peachtree City (Atlanta), and Porter Ranch (L.A.), among others. Since the 1960s, planners and builders in Southern California embraced a model of replicating real and imagined pasts with the conveniences and amenities of the modern era. Across greater L.A.'s newly developed suburbs, street names, neighborhood signage, monuments, and vernacular architecture visually or rhetorically paid homage to California's bucolic heritage.[11] What is unique about the East Valley was residents' longtime affinity for a romanticized, oftentimes ahistorical frontier devoid of racial diversity and violent conquest. Planners, developers, builders, and realtors promoted exaggerated or alternative histories of a bygone era comprised of picturesque farms, quiet meadows, and friendly townspeople. Homeowners adopted these Eurocentric narratives and images of the West, understanding the valley as a place where cowboys and Spanish or Mexican aristocrats quietly luxuriated among the hills. Even as the valley reached buildout, local actors continued to promote embellished histories of what they called "old California."[12] These cultural fictions were baked into the public imagination for generations.

To be sure, the appeal of country living or reproductions of American rurality were not entirely new or novel. Americans' distaste for and distrust of cities has been part and parcel of American thought since the Early Republic and the Gilded Age.[13] From the early 1800s through the 1920s, American writers, architects, and builders took aesthetic and cultural inspiration from the English countryside.[14] They transported these ideals across the Atlantic, shaping communities from New England to the Upper Midwest.[15] Intellectuals, designers, landscape architects, and horticulturalists like Catharine Beecher, Andrew Jackson Downing, Frederick Law Olmsted, and Calvert Vaux hailed the virtues of a country lifestyle, associating rurality with refinement and morality.[16] The individual, single-family cottage, farmhouse, or villa embodied upper-class Christian respectability, while easy access to nature for the urban sort reinforced the idea that the countryside was a critical neutralizer from the perils of the city. Jeffersonian and Turnerian ideas about the frontier—that is, a form of rurality centered around piety or boundlessness and opportunism, respectively—informed the motivations of Southern California's earliest settlers, many of whom were gentleman farmers or moneyed pioneers of the West. They helped set a foundation for country living in eastern L.A. County. These towns were similar to what Laura Barraclough classifies as "rural urbanism" in the northern part of the county: "In the San Gabriel and San Fernando Valleys, rural urbanism took the form of gentleman farming, which was envisioned as the foundation of a middle-class white settler society."[17] These models of modern agrarianism, rooted in eras of conquest and European colonialism, appealed to white families. Whether it was called "country living" or "rural urbanism," whites' allegiances to Western frontier myths consolidated the force of whiteness in Southern California suburbia into the twenty-first century.

Developed concomitantly with the East Valley, Irvine in neighboring Orange County emerged as a prototype of the ideal Sunbelt suburb, featuring elements of the country living lifestyle found in towns like Diamond Bar.[18] Hailed for its tidiness and aesthetic continuity, Irvine sought to be the anthesis of postwar urbanization and suburbanization. Planners went "away from the grid."[19] Instead, they embraced a village model, a landscape of circuitous roads and cul-de-sacs meant to encourage intimacy. In the 1960s and 1970s, planners and architects including William Pereira wanted a fashionable, middle-class oasis evocative of California's idyllic past. Developers initially pitched Irvine as a suburb that embraced nature, rejected sprawl, and prioritized pedestrians over automobiles. As Stephanie Kolberg notes, "Whereas some have viewed master-planned communities as attempts to retreat from modern life, Irvine's marketers frequently touted the advantages of modernity and the progressive nature of development, as the new city was to utilize the best-available tools of contemporary society in order to create a more nature-infused rational order."[20] But by the 1990s, Irvine's citizenry abandoned earlier ideals and emerged as an exemplar of an urbanized suburb. Leaders favored large-scale development but presented it as "smart growth." Moreover, they remained reliant on private transit and became a culpable contributor to the sprawl Irvine's founders sought to prevent. By the end of the decade, Irvine's trajectory mirrored suburbanization occurring across the metropolitan Sunbelt.[21]

Much like the Irvine example, the East Valley's master-planned communities started off, in principle, as a fresh alternative to city living and the typical postwar suburb. Over time, they too became denser and busier than originally intended. At residents' behest, builders added more shopping and recreational options, thus increasing density in the 1970s and 1980s. Suburbs needed a commercial tax base to pay for community services and infrastructure even though critics claimed these forms of development marred the idyllic environment they wished to preserve. In essence, homeowners wanted to have their cake and eat it too. All the while, residents insisted they could maintain a rural ambiance if developers and governments acted accordingly. This included a greater emphasis on homeowners associations (HOAs) to police space under the guise of protecting property values and their suburban lifestyle. Individual tracts had HOAs, but so did entire communities where homeowners were automatically made members.[22]

Suburbs across Southern California were gunning to be what Joel Garreau calls "edge cities." With more jobs and businesses than residents, these were full-fledged cities posing or broadly seen as typical suburbs.[23] Edge city boosters held ambitions to become the next great American city, oftentimes taking inspiration from Anaheim and other Disneyland-like forms of (sub) urbanism.[24] Boosters of the East Valley's master-planned tracts did not aim to be corporate, nor did they encourage the type of vertical growth typical of edge cities like Irvine, Pasadena, Glendale, or Burbank. Ironically, in their attempts to be anti-cosmopolitan, the East Valley's country living suburbs became trendy, highly sought-after communities in the 1980s and 1990s.

The version of western Americana promised to homeowners was an up-market, au courant version of an antiquated lifestyle. Large-scale land acquisitions by national and multinational developers like Shea, William Lyon, and Kaufman & Broad (KB) provided a blank slate for them to reimagine the hinterland, thus allowing the idea of an endless, eternal frontier to thrive. In turn, the country living aesthetic was cohesive and thematically uniform across East Valley suburbs, neighborhoods, and tracts thanks to the wide availability of non- or less-developed land. Residents promoted the virtues of pastoral Southern California and saw themselves as settlers of the frontier, even as these suburbs reached populations upwards of fifty thousand. People across age and generation of settlement embraced country living but varied by how they defined it, particularly when confronted with perceived economic threats. Nevertheless, residents shared common goals resting on the need to preserve, defend, and experience this lifestyle. As L.A. transformed before their eyes, native- and foreign-born homeowners alike bemoaned change begot by modernity and globalization. They believed it was up to them to protect country living for all.

SIX MODELS OF EAST VALLEY COUNTRY LIVING

Chino Hills, Diamond Bar, and Walnut are incorporated communities with their own city councils and governments. Hacienda Heights and Rowland Heights are unincorporated areas of Los Angeles County. Both towns are Census Designated Places (CDPs) overseen by a county supervisor and residents' or homeowners associations with limited governing authority. Phillips Ranch is a contained country living neighborhood within the city of Pomona without a formal representative body beyond HOAs; Pomona governs the hamlet. Each of these suburbs, CDPs, and neighborhoods had unique yet overlapping stages of post–World War II growth. Collectively, their individual histories and identities as agrarian outposts forged a regional identity of country living.

Diamond Bar: An Exemplar of the East Valley Picturesque

A visit to this serene, conveniently located community, tucked snuggly away from the frantic hubbub of the city, leaves no room for conjecture as to why Diamond Bar's success has been so great. Not only does the individual homeowner have pride in his new property, but in the community as well. . . . Diamond Bar is planned for permanent convenience and lasting values—and that includes a touch of the peacefulness, even separateness, that makes this lovely community what it is. At last . . . Diamond Bar is open![25]

Diamond Bar is . . . kid country, family country, fun country, freeway country . . . it's California country. [In] Diamond Bar, there's room to live. And there always will be.[26]

[Diamond Bar is] the home of gracious country living . . . [and is a] community rich in heritage and holding promise for a thriving tomorrow.[27]

[Diamond Bar is] a beautifully master-planned community, nestled in the charming rural countryside of eastern Los Angeles County.[28]

[Diamond Bar] is a city of the future being born today, at a time when Americans have unanimously re-affirmed the traditional values of our rural heritage and are seeking a way of life which preserves them, without sacrificing the amenities of modern civilization.[29]

Among the East Valley's most desirable postwar suburbs was Diamond Bar. Boosters promoted the rural virtues of the master-planned community. From branding to landscaping, Diamond Bar epitomized country living. Diamond Bar's image as an agricultural hamlet goes back to the nineteenth century. In 1837, Mexican governor Juan Bautista Alvarado gave a twenty-two-thousand-acre parcel of land to Ygnacio Palomares and Ricardo Vejar. Three years later, Jose de la Luz Linares was granted a parcel as well. They, including California transplants William "Uncle Billy" Rubottom of Arkansas and Frederick E. Lewis II of New York raised livestock in present-day Diamond Bar and Phillips Ranch (Pomona).[30] The community was named after Diamond Bar Ranch's diamond-shaped branding irons, which were used to stamp cattle for easy identification should they wander away. Diamond Bar and Phillips Ranch were also known for breeding Arabian horses, attracting horse breeders and equestrians from across the United States.[31] By

COUNTRY LIVING CLOSE TO TOWN   DIAMOND BAR

FIGURE 2. Diamond Bar promotional brochure, ca. late 1970s/early 1980s. Image courtesy of City of Diamond Bar, CA.

the 1920s, local breeders were critical suppliers for Hollywood movie studios who borrowed horses for globally exported western films.

In the late 1950s, Quinton Engineers Ltd. prepared the Diamond Bar Master Plan.[32] Envisioned as a "twentieth century city, complete with all the essential elements," Diamond Bar was on path to becoming the county's largest master-planned community.[33] Planners and developers promised to right the wrongs of unplanned suburbanization elsewhere in L.A. In 1956, Christiana Oil Corporation and Capital Company (a subsidiary of Transamerica Corporation/Transamerica Development Company) purchased Diamond Bar Ranch. The eight-thousand-acre property housed one of the West Coast's leading producers of commercial beef. William A. Bartholomae, president of Bartholomae Oil Corporation—whose holdings included oil production, gold mining, and real estate across California, Nevada, and Alaska—owned the ranch and sold it for $10 million.[34] At the time, Diamond Bar was reported to be the "largest single piece of pastoral land" left in the county. To local farmers, Bartholomae's decision to sell signaled suburbanization was on its way.[35] Residents, most of whom lived in remote areas, feared mass development would ruin the frontier lifestyle they cherished.

Builders long avoided Diamond Bar, citing its hilly topography as an expensive and challenging undertaking.[36] Following World War II, local boosters—comprised of business owners and wealthy proprietors—lobbied county bureaucrats and property owners to develop the area. These pressures, coupled with growing demands for housing, changed opponents' minds knowing there was potential for significant profit. Upon Diamond Bar Ranch's acquisition, agricultural operations ceased to make way for a master-planned suburb of "country villages where open space was the rule, not the exception." Boosters championed Diamond Bar's mantra of rustic elegance through the language of country living. But they also claimed that one of Diamond Bar's numerous advantages was its location. Transamerica boasted that Diamond Bar was "near the city, yet isolated—and protected—from the suburban sprawl that was blighting much of Southern California."[37] Innumerable brochures, advertisements, and publications pointed out Diamond Bar's rural qualities as within a commuter's reach. One builder said Diamond Bar was a "trend-setter" in suburban planning: "At Diamond Bar, we have created a new concept of living within an environment dedicated to preservation of the surrounding natural beauty." In essence, boosters claimed they offered a fresh, modern, and accessible approach to the old-fashioned rural ideal.

Diamond Bar was not the only community ballyhooing and marketing the region's country living setting. To meet consumer demand, developers and builders across the East Valley erected tracts comparable to the Diamond Bar model hoping to lure buyers seeking this lifestyle.[38] Diamond Bar residents saw themselves as part of a unique concept and claimed they were ahead of their time. Developers dubbed Diamond Bar a "modern city" organized with "a plan based on forethought and modern engineering" to deliver the perfect suburb.[39] At the same time, Diamond Bar was a place that claimed to respect its bucolic past.[40] Throughout the 1960s and 1970s, newspapers joined the chorus of praise of Diamond Bar's ingenuity as a forward-thinking planned community. One of the valley's largest periodicals advertised that "country living comes naturally" in Diamond Bar and that this was a lifestyle apt for young and established families alike. The East Valley's "heritage of haciendas and hospitality," one marketer said, was a new, welcoming place for people seeking a taste of old California before sprawl destroyed its idyll.[41]

One of Diamond Bar's major selling points was the suburb's attention to spatial regulation. Transamerica zoned all land for specific purposes. Carefully delineated boundaries encouraged clear neighborhood identities and cohesion throughout. Though the majority of land was dedicated to residential and limited retail or industrial property, a large slice of the community was reserved for open space. This visually reminded residents that they lived in the country. The Diamond Bar Master Plan stated that "the topography will dictate the neighborhood residential units, which will logically be developed in the valleys and on the ridges."[42] Multifamily buildings were to be concentrated "near commercial zones," situating cheaper housing to busier areas (e.g., near strip malls).[43] This kept density or signifiers of urbanism (i.e., apartments, condominiums, townhomes, shopping centers) concentrated along major thoroughfares. Planners believed this type of spatial organization was rational. Crucially, this plan covertly delineated which residents were considered worthier of the total country living experience. Single-family homes for upper-income families were generally set closer to greenbelts and hills, away from commercial activity to ensure higher property values. Builders embraced the Master Plan with gusto, believing this was on the cutting edge of suburban planning: "The feeling of open country, the careful preservation of natural beauty in and around neighborhoods, the respect for the land" were guaranteed to be protected thanks to the Master Plan.[44]

Boosters, developers, and builders appealed to buyers through gendered rhetoric, suggesting Diamond Bar's amenities, architecture, and order were conducive for raising respectable heterosexual families. As the presumed breadwinners, men could enjoy themselves at the community golf course and country club. Beyond these refined venues, ads suggested Diamond Bar's easy access to the wilderness turned boys into men; wide open spaces encouraged rugged, masculine behavior and cultivated the virtues of proper manhood.[45] Advertisers fashioned separate spheres in brochures by highlighting a selection of shopping centers tailored for stay-at-home mothers.[46] While men took advantage of the leisurely opportunities all over town, women maintained the home front and kept the heterosexual nuclear family intact through their domesticity. From built-in washer-dryer units to chef's kitchens, promoters claimed Diamond Bar homes were designed with the "modern woman" in mind—including those who also worked outside the house and appreciated the suite of amenities at their fingertips.

In 1963, amid the rush of new home sales, Transamerica's developers promised Diamond Bar residents an "18-hole public golf course with country club facilities, private equestrian center with indoor and outdoor show facilities, private 132-acre equestrian park, 50-acre natural park, 2 neighborhood parks, roping/riding/boarding equestrian facility, 7 private recreation clubs," as well as schools and churches within the next two decades.[47] Builders fulfilled many of those amenities until 1977 when Transamerica pulled away from maintaining Diamond Bar, leaving additional landscaping and construction duties to the county and homeowners associations. Transamerica's departure also meant Diamond Bar would be sold to multiple developers (who sub-divided the land) well before Transamerica implemented all aspects of the Master Plan. Unlike Transamerica, Los Angeles County officials were less attentive to improvements, and they did not fully enforce the Master Plan. As the boom continued, developers and builders proceeded with minimal concern for maintaining Diamond Bar's rural ambiance. Residents grew im-patient with the county, thus spurring movements to incorporate and adopt Slow Growth measures in subsequent years.[48]

At the height of Diamond Bar's growth in the 1980s, boosters like the Diamond Bar Development Corporation reaffirmed Diamond Bar's contra-dictory identity of being both rugged and civilized. That is, they insisted the Jeffersonian ideal of a simple agrarian lifestyle did not have to disappear in the late twentieth century. Rather, this commodified version of rurality was one that embodied how to properly "do" agrarianism in a modern capital-ist republic. One specific neighborhood, The Country, was built with these ideas in mind. In its earliest brochures, promoters declared,

> There is a promise here that cannot be denied. It is reflected in the glint of early sunlight on fresh meadows and old trees. Its voice is heard in the song of the meadowlark, in the faint murmur of the wind. It beckons those who really want to escape the monotony and mediocrity of urban life, urban pres-sures. Possession of the land is not beyond the means of those who work in the city, who need to rest in the country. Possession of the land awaits those who truly deserve to own a part of it.[49]

The original Diamond Bar Plan earmarked land for The Country. At the time of its unveiling, the twelve-hundred-acre community featured thirty-three ranch-style tract homes. Empty plots were reserved for custom-built homes set on properties ranging from three-quarters of an acre to four acres.[50] Boosters heralded Diamond Bar as an end-to-end pastoral suburb with The Country standing as its marquee community. Envisioned as a gated equestrian village, planners hoped to entice families by advertising The

FIGURE 3. Diamond Bar Country Estates (The Country) brochure, ca. late 1960s/early 1970s. Image courtesy of City of Diamond Bar, CA.

Country as the pinnacle of timeless, rustic elegance. Residents handsomely paid for "costly homes amid rugged terrain" intricately designed for discerning buyers seeking an abundance of space.[51] But like other country living subdivisions, despite its veneer of carefree, undisturbed living, The Country was a tightly regulated community.[52] Bordered by white wooden fences and

FIGURE 4. Custom-built homes and mansions located inside The Country, Diamond Bar, CA, May 2012. Photo taken by James Zarsadiaz.

protected by private security officers, The Country promised the literal freedom of the countryside yet was shielded from elements beyond its confines. Gated communities like The Country afforded homeowners a feeling of physical and emotional security—a plus for privacy-conscious buyers distrustful of the outside.[53]

Inside The Country, equestrians enjoyed a number of amenities. This included bridle trails and a championship riding arena dubbed "the largest covered show ring of its kind in the Western United States."[54] Adjacent to the riding arena stood an exhibit house that provided "the feeling of strength and security reminiscent of the Old Southwest, yet updated to provide view, convenience and charm in a contemporary manner."[55] Additionally, the facility's "stucco, heavy timbers, wood and stone" were intended to evoke an "indigenous" character likened to a "house of the Old West."[56] Architects believed the facility easily blended into the natural landscape and reinforced the valley's rural heritage.[57] Developers noted that even homeowners without horses could still relish the "breezy countryside with its park-like plateaus and gentle valleys."[58] Furthermore, they claimed "nature lovers" would

FIGURE 5. Custom-built home located inside The Country, Diamond Bar, CA, May 2012. Photo taken by James Zarsadiaz.

"find contentment in the rich natural vegetation. Especially rewarding were the countless meadows of knee-deep grass" demarcated by builders, legitimizing its rural albeit master-planned milieu.[59]

Developers, builders, and advertisers frequently called The Country "horse country" and alluded to its setting as a space for exploration, combining rhetoric of the wild Western frontier with romanticized notions of white settler colonialism.[60] Crucially, The Country's bucolic environs reminded homeowners of simpler times, divorced from the social turbulence of the era—that is, the civil rights movement, second-wave feminism, and wars in Southeast Asia. The semirural setting evoked conservative innocence, a sellable commodity to whites disenchanted with the overall direction of a seemingly destabilizing America. As the state diversified in the 1970s and beyond, white suburbanites and rural dwellers doubled down on the need to protect L.A.'s pastoral (read: Euro-American) past. In the San Fernando Valley, for instance, white residents bemoaned a loss of rural purity and tried to preserve reimagined histories of an Anglo California through spatial policing. As Laura Barraclough notes, their attempts to regulate built and natural environments through "rural land-use activism" in the San Fernando Valley were responses "to the city's changing political, economic, and demographic dynamics."[61] Their constructions of whiteness through land sought to uphold a community devoid of ethnic or racial diversity.

The Country, along with the rest of Diamond Bar, was a product imagined by planners, developers, builders, and realtors. They created landscapes combining the best of both worlds: rural and urban. Unlike the city, country living was not meant to be democratic. They were gracious suburbs that one had to earn their way in. By the 1980s, Asian immigrants were able to penetrate these exclusive towns through their wealth, illustrating how money—particularly capital acquired through a globalizing marketplace—provided them that access, not necessarily whiteness nor whites' desires for suburban diversity.

. . .

Five other East San Gabriel Valley communities developed in similar fashion to Diamond Bar, each borrowing planning and design elements from their neighbors. Along with Diamond Bar, the communities of Walnut, Chino Hills, and Phillips Ranch were entirely or predominantly masterplanned country living in style. Upheld through municipal codes and social control, these communities were typically uniform in design and scale. This was generally less the case in the unincorporated areas of Hacienda Heights and Rowland Heights. Their earlier phases of development and older housing stock made it less possible to build new large-scale subdivisions like those in Walnut. Nevertheless, the popular demand for country living resulted in pockets of similar residential or commercial development in both towns.[62]

Walnut: An Enclave of Rural Refinement

After the secularization of San Gabriel Mission in the 1830s, John Rowland and William Workman purchased approximately fifty thousand acres of land known as Rancho La Puente. Rowland, a native of the Mid-Atlantic and then the Midwest, and Workman, a Missourian by way of England, met as business partners in New Mexico before moving to Alta California. Together, they attracted farmers and cattle ranchers to the valley. Over time, rural outposts across the ranch cohered into communities. This included what would become Walnut, along with present-day Hacienda Heights, Rowland Heights, Industry, La Puente, West Covina, Covina, and San Dimas.

Like Diamond Bar and Rowland Heights, Walnut was once known as a horse-friendly community. Residents with modest or middle-class backgrounds were able to raise horses on their properties thanks to the area's abundant land and limited industry. Since the 1800s, a small group of families from the Midwest and East Coast as well as France, Spain, Mexico, and Armenia owned and operated horse, hog, citrus, wheat, grain, and walnut ranches throughout town.[63] L.A. moguls owned weekend ranch houses including Bullocks department store co-founder J. P. Winnett. His ranch, which contained Brookside Equestrian Center, was a hub for Southern California's professional equestrians including US Olympians. The ranch was also the setting of the 1944 film, *National Velvet*, starring Elizabeth Taylor.[64]

In 1959, Walnut incorporated when the cities of Industry and West Covina threatened to annex the community. Unlike Diamond Bar and Chino Hills—which were envisioned as completely master-planned country living suburbs early on—Walnut developed into a suburb of master-planned rural-themed subdivisions and neighborhoods that, over time, visually melded into a singular country living suburb. Walnut leaders modeled its General Plan after Los Altos Hills, a tony Northern California suburb lauded for its open space and stately homes.[65] After incorporation, Walnut's founders envisioned a suburb of about sixty to ninety thousand people.[66] But leaders quickly scrapped those plans in the mid-1960s and 1970s after noticing residents' consistent oppositions to townhomes, duplexes, and apartments. Thus, leaders and homeowners established a culture of "slow growth" well before it became a local mantra in the 1980s. Its longtime reputation as a hotbed of NIMBY (Not In My Back Yard) activism helped keep Walnut a "bedroom community" with a so-called "rural atmosphere."[67] Officials happily claimed Walnut had "the strictest open-space requirements of any city around," which was a point of pride for homeowners who scoffed at L.A.'s older, denser suburbs.[68]

Developers and builders long overlooked Walnut because of its hilly terrain and isolation from Los Angeles. Until the 1960s, they focused on L.A.'s inner-ring suburbs because of its flatter landscapes and because Walnut lacked the infrastructure.[69] Thus, compared to its established neighbors like Covina and Glendora whose development occurred along state highways or historic rail lines, Walnut's mass suburbanization happened later. As demands for new housing increased, developers and builders who previously avoided Walnut saw its potential. Their targeted demographic of middle- and upper-middle-class families sought higher elevations for top-dollar views and physical distance from less affluent residents residing on the flatlands. Until the 1990s when Walnut moved towards buildout, new settlers equated Walnut's sweeping vistas and untamed wilderness to the magical realism of a Hudson River School painting. These romanticized visions heightened Walnut's prestige. Upon his reelection to the city council in 1981, Bill Daley said Walnut's "open spaces, the quality of homes being built in the area, [and] the idea of wanting to live in the last virgin city in the county of Los Angeles" were reasons families flocked to the suburb and why country living needed to be protected for its future.[70] Boosters touted that these previously untouchable lands were now open to those who wanted a piece of the old West.

Walnut's boom period of growth between the 1970s to 1990s witnessed the development of agrarian-themed tracts including The Willows, Hunter's Hill, and The Knolls, to name a few. Developers promoted the valley's verdant charms as well as its vast selection of what advertisers classified "executive homes." Local and multinational builders like J.M. Peters, KB, Lewis, Marlborough, Shea, Transamerica, and William Lyon hoped to attract dual-income families with Walnut's executive homes, which were trendy options in new tracts across the region. Executive homes were substantially larger than typical postwar suburban tract houses, ranging from two thousand to three thousand square feet.[71] Most were built with sizable front- and back-yards for children and entertaining. Top-of-the-line plans at Snow Creek, Timberline, and similar subdivisions featured a range of "domestic bling" including three- to four-car garages, security systems, "country kitchens," bathrooms with "Roman-style tubs," lofts, bonus rooms, wet bars, and "retreats"—all tailored for professionals seeking additional space and bragging rights.[72] Some houses included dens or home offices designed for telecom-muters or entrepreneurs with flexible schedules. As Barbara Kelley argues, post-WWII suburbs like Levittown set the cultural and physical foundation of the proper, modern American home, which featured all the trappings of domesticity.[73] Over time, in-home amenities became more elaborate thanks to new technologies. Theater-style movie rooms, heated jacuzzies, and in-home gyms were increasing commonplace. By the 1970s and 1980s, new homes in Walnut and elsewhere in the East Valley became larger, wider, and more compartmentalized—all of which denoted luxury. But these designs also encouraged privatism and individualism over togetherness. Ironically, contemporary country living was antithetical to the family-centric, quaint lifestyle boosters encouraged.

FIGURE 6. Snow Creek (Walnut, CA) new tract homes advertisement, *Los Angeles Times*, September 22, 1985. Image courtesy of *Los Angeles Times*.

Advertising for new homes in East Valley suburbs like Walnut became critical sources of regional identity formation. Buyers placed themselves in family-friendly representations of country living. In dozens of Snow Creek ads, Shea Homes' marketing team played up rural nostalgia and wholesomeness. In one *Los Angeles Times* advertisement, Shea Homes suggested families seeking an "old-fashioned" way of life would thrive in Snow Creek. It was a slow-paced neighborhood where family life and "yesterday's values" were prioritized in a "fast-changing world."[74] Another ad showcased a white family picnicking in a park, suggesting the valley's salubrious sunshine was amenable to perennial outdoor living.[75] One Snow Creek ad displayed a young white family strolling hand-in-hand amid wild brush and Walnut's twenty-six miles of bridle trails.[76] It profiled three subdivisions within Snow Creek (River Run, Glenbrook, and Countrywalk), all extolling the virtues of a rural-themed master-planned suburb: "Snow Creek is a brand new community that's designed to give you country charm and urban sophistication."[77] In Snow Creek's Countrywalk tract, developers highlighted what they dubbed "master-planned family living," a way of life where children could have "a place to play ball," a room to call their own, a "place to spend time with the family," and a "home close to the fun places" like shopping malls, movie theaters, Disneyland, Knott's Berry Farm, and Dodger and Anaheim stadiums.[78] These forms of marketing encouraged families to assume a particular identity upon ownership—that is, a resident who respects tradition yet is built for modern times.[79] Advertisers hoped to appeal to families disenchanted with city living. Indeed, neighborhoods like Snow Creek resonated with white-collar professionals who worked in L.A. and associated poverty, grit, and diversity as characteristics of a globalizing inner city. L.A. was unlike the "main streets" or quaint villages of their childhood, purportedly vice-free places ostensibly frozen in time. For residents, country living served as an escape from the urban vices and disorder they encountered during the 9-to-5 workday. Establishing roots in a suburb like Walnut provided commuters a sense of permanence and relief. Brochures and advertisements touted master-planned suburbs as sensible choices for smart buyers. Shea Homes, for instance, said builders' "planning and attention" put into every Snow Creek neighborhood had the "country in sight and the family in mind," unlike other suburbs whose founders and architects lacked vision and skill.[80] These attitudes, rooted in Progressive Era "civilization" projects and then revived under the guise of "urban renewal" in the 1950s and 1960s, made their way to the suburbs.

Walnut's appeal rested on the myths its boosters, developers, and builders sold. Residents believed these subdivisions were the closest to Western rurality possible in an urbanizing L.A. They were drawn to Walnut because of its image as a rugged, agrarian landscape. Yet Walnut's sophistication and tidiness were equally enticing. Cultivated, curated wilderness served as a guiding principle in how Walnut residents understood and controlled space, especially as more Asian immigrants settled across the East Valley in the late twentieth century.

Chino Hills: Rebranding a Sordid Place

Located in San Bernardino County, Chino Hills developed in similar fashion to its Los Angeles County neighbors of Diamond Bar, Walnut, and Phillips Ranch because of its proximity and the residents they attracted. Chino Valley—comprising Chino and Chino Hills—was an agrarian community of farmers and cattle ranchers. Beyond its agricultural past, Chino

Hills carried an unsavory and colorful reputation for much of the twentieth century. In the 1920s, Chino Hills was a wet colony during Prohibition. Residents claimed illegal drinking, gambling, prostitution, and gang activity plagued Chino Valley well into the 1930s. Between the 1950s and 1970s, the area was home to beatnik, hippie, and artist communes seeking nature and isolation from densely populated cities.[81] Chino Hills' proximity to Chino correctional facility—one of the region's largest state prisons—further marred its reputation.[82]

Chino Valley boosters pressured land owners and county officials to suburbanize. From their perspective, Chino Hills' proximity to Los Angeles and Orange counties—with their growing number of suburban office parks—meant Chino Hills was an ideal location. Despite investors who worried its inland geography turned off commuters, others believed it was primed for growth. Boosters anticipated resistance from established residents who enjoyed Chino Valley's isolation. Longtime homeowners believed suburbanization would ruin one of the few authentically rural places left in greater L.A. In the early 1970s, suburbanization advocates claimed growth was not only inevitable; development in Chino Hills was a sign of progress and something "residents . . . private builders and government officials . . . can't sidestep."[83] Nevertheless, pro-development forces wished to retain the area's bucolic character, which they believed was possible if county leaders and planners designated ample open space in their vision of a master-planned community. Because of its location at the nexus of three counties, creating the suburb of Chino Hills involved the cooperation of multiple governmental agencies between L.A., Orange, and San Bernardino counties.[84] In 1973, San Bernardino County revised a 1966 land use plan that permitted developers to build on two-thirds of Chino Hills' 28,300 acres of open space. Orange County, which bordered the Chino Hills range, marked 21,300 acres of open space a "priority greenbelt project" to prevent over-development and to help sustain Chino Valley's agrarian landscape. Developers and county leaders envisioned the master-planned suburb to be divided into eight separate but interconnected villages, all of which shared comparable amenities and design elements.

In 1976, Kaufman & Broad (KB) Homes began grading land, ushering in Chino Hills' era of mass suburbanization.[85] One of Chino Hills' principal villages was Carbon Canyon Village, created in 1986. The village concept was designed so residents would not have to leave their neighborhood. Planners hoped these would be self-sustaining places and create village-based identities. Carbon Canyon Village's Ranch Oaks tract, for example, featured three tennis courts, a swimming pool, and a community clubhouse. Ranch Oaks had 225 acres of open space complete with corrals, a training ring, a tack room, and bridle paths for equestrians. Grocery stores and strip malls were strategically placed between the villages to minimize vehicular travel, thus encouraging residents to walk. Beyond the villages' amenities and intricate layout, builders boasted Chino Hills' accessibility to regional shopping centers, country clubs, and parks, including San Dimas' Bonelli Regional Park and Chino Hills' own state park. Together, these features rounded out Chino Hills' image as a modern "rural" suburb.

Meanwhile, developers, builders, and other actors actively worked to erase Chino Hills' lowbrow reputation. They downplayed its sordid history and adjacency to the prison by promoting its tracts as tucked away residential gems.[86] One builder urged buyers to "discover the hidden beauty" of the "new" Chino Hills, a community that retained its pastoral qualities yet was wholly suburban, orderly, and family-friendly.[87] In a larger effort to rebrand itself, in 1991, as the community inched toward incorporation, voters considered changing its name to Canyon Hills.[88] By removing "Chino," residents hoped to expunge any seedy connotations of its past.

During the 1990s and 2000s, Asian realtors worked to change Chino Hills' image as well. They emphasized its competitive housing values and rural aesthetic akin to tonier communities like Walnut. And unlike white boosters who emphasized Chino Hills' distance from L.A. or the nearby penitentiary, Asian agents stressed its "close but not too close" location to the Asian strip malls of Rowland Heights, Hacienda Heights, City of Industry, and West Covina. They hoped to entice Chinese, Filipino, and Korean buyers seeking access to Asian businesses. Furthermore, Asian realtors and community leaders emphasized Chino Hills' high-performing public schools and newer facilities. This convinced buyers to choose Chino Hills over suburbs with well-known award-winning school districts like Diamond Bar, Walnut, Arcadia, and San Marino—communities that were legible to moneyed families across the Pacific. As one Taiwanese television station noted, Chino Hills' learned citizenry was "an indicator of an outstanding population" and that "high grades among Asian Pacific Islander students has caused many Chinese families to move into the area." They added: Chino Hills was a "great space to live one's life due to its rural feel," "big, sturdy trees," "rolling hills," and "low crime rate." The town was "immaculate," "vigorously green," and contained "landscapes of majestic gold," the perceived hallmarks of East

Valley life.[89] In the span of two decades, residents, including its Asian population, remade Chino Hills into a prestigious, transnational suburb.

Phillips Ranch: Country Living in an Urbanized Place

The community of Phillips Ranch is located within Pomona. One of the oldest municipalities in Los Angeles County, Pomona was named after the ancient Roman goddess of fruit.[90] In the late nineteenth and early twentieth centuries, Pomona and surrounding agriburbs produced and distributed citrus across the country. Water from the Coachella Valley, along with vital access to transcontinental railways allowed the regional citrus industry to thrive. Since the 1940s, working-class white and Mexican migrant labor ensured handsome profits for agribusiness. Many of these workers lived in the area's agriburbs, resulting in relatively diverse communities.[91]

One of the largest parcels Pomona acquired was Phillips Ranch. Founded by Louis Phillips in 1862, the idyllic ranch was known for grazing sheep and cattle.[92] Instead of protecting Phillips Ranch as a public preserve, Pomona leaders and developers saw the ranch as an economic opportunity. In 1964, Louis Lesser Enterprises Inc. purchased Phillips Ranch for $17.5 million.[93] Local leaders envisioned a master-planned suburb similar to the type of development occurring next door in Diamond Bar. By creating a "new" Phillips Ranch with "decent, safe, and sanitary housing," they hoped to destigmatize Pomona's reputation.[94] Ultimately, boosters wanted a rural, upmarket hamlet that felt as though homeowners were on "permanent vacation."[95]

Pomona officials and planners promised to develop Phillips Ranch "cognizant of the environmental surroundings," with housing positioned "to fit the natural contours of the land as much as possible."[96] Residing in the planned community was to be reminiscent of the old Phillips family ranch. Unlike the density and disorder of L.A., boosters claimed Phillips Ranch would develop into a suburb with a "sense of wide open spaces, of unlimited horizons, of the freedom of the old west."[97] Another developer boasted, "There is a chance here to lead the full life, a life simultaneously complemented by rural and city qualities." Builders promised prospective buyers they would deliver a balanced suburban lifestyle, offering the best of town and country: "Louis Phillips' old homestead has been transformed into perhaps the most spectacular master-planned community ever created in Los Angeles County—the new Phillips Ranch. . . . A completely self-contained community of carefully conceived proportions, an environment that encourages family life. . . . Quiet cul-de-sacs and wide streets replace crowded noisy boulevards."[98] Planners, developers, builders, and Pomona officials made the Phillips Ranch brand clear: this was an agrarian-themed community. Its logo and insignia of blue skies and green hills coupled with its motto of "Sophisticated Country Living Near the City" was ubiquitous in brochures, street signs, and the flags that stood on vast lots signaling new tracts.[99] Boosters deployed metaphors of the old West and rural nostalgia to sell homes. One advertisement exclaimed, "Join the Great Los Angeles Land Rush," evoking the spirit of frontier settlement.[100] Phillips Ranch's numerous "Tudor, French, Mediterranean, Cape Cod, ranch, and contemporary" homes set "against a backdrop of majestic snow-capped mountains and "picturesque plains, hills, and valleys" were marketed as sound investments, especially amid the "rush" to buy in Los Angeles County's "undiscovered" hinterland.[101] This housing "rush"—harkening back to the language of Manifest Destiny—convinced prospective buyers to settle now before they lost their slice of the West to faster-moving suburban pioneers. Pomona leaders further anticipated Phillips Ranch's proximity to colleges and universities (e.g., Mt. San Antonio College, Cal Poly Pomona, University of La Verne, Claremont Colleges) and employers like General Dynamics—a key producer of missiles during the Cold War—would attract an educated population of scholars, engineers, and scientists.[102]

During the 1970s and 1980s, Phillips Ranch developers, builders, and local officials banked on attracting upwardly mobile white families to soften Pomona's image as a blue-collar town plagued with "inner city" problems. The *Los Angeles Times* claimed Pomona was a "quiet citrus community built by conservative Anglo farmers that woke up one day to find that it had become a multiracial, multicultural manufacturing center with all the urban woes of downtowns across the country."[103] By emphasizing an imagined Euro-American pastoralism of yesteryear, Phillips Ranch boosters inscribed rural whiteness onto the landscape, attempting to erase its contemporary form and population makeup. Subdivisions like Country Park Villas, Country Wood, Falcon Ridge, Meadow Ridge, Phillips Meadows, and Sun Country were intended to evoke an old, bucolic American West—not of an urban place.[104] One of Phillips Ranch's higher-end tracts, Diamond View Estates, was designed by famed L.A. architect Robert Earl, which boosters hoped would dispel Pomona's unsavory reputation. The community's 400 three-, four-, and five-bedroom homes featured different exteriors including "Cape Cod, Country English, Country French, Country Gable, Country Manor, English Estate, English Tudor, French

A Sophisticated Country Setting

It is the Ranch's country charm and closeness to all the advantages of urban living that make it such a special community. Some of the finest shopping, educational, cultural, and recreational facilities in the world are nearby. Yet the Ranch itself is so full of quiet spaces, of hills to walk, of untouched terrain, that it seems a place apart. There is a chance here to lead the full life, a life simultaneously complemented by rural and city qualities. Phillips Ranch is the best of both worlds.

FIGURE 7. Phillips Ranch (Pomona, CA) promotional brochure, Westmor Development Co., ca. early 1980s. Image courtesy of City of Pomona, CA Library.

Chateau, French New Orleans, Italian Valley, New English Cottage, Spanish Colonial, Spanish Monterey, and Williamsburg," all resembling a rural European or American style.[105]

Boosters thought these aesthetic and marketing strategies would curb white flight. Boosters also hoped these moves would attract new wealth. In Pomona's Specific Area Plan, leaders expected Phillips Ranch to "attract higher income housing and bring in new families and additional 'buying power' to Pomona while encouraging incumbents to remain."[106] Planners said, "Single family housing in the Phillips Ranch [community] will be designed to appeal to the upwardly bound, white collar family with children." They anticipated these tactics would make "the ranch" a competitive option for families considering comparable suburbs.[107]

The targeted marketing of planners, developers, builders, and other actors worked. They helped create a clear suburban class consciousness among Phillips Ranch residents as they did not see themselves as part of its parent city, Pomona. Rather than being clumped with their working-class "urban" neighbors, residents deliberately distanced themselves as sophisticated country living suburbanites. When a *Los Angeles Times* reporter asked Cindy Morris, a new homeowner, why her family settled in Pomona, Morris corrected them: "This is not Pomona, this is Phillips Ranch."[108]

Hacienda Heights and Rowland Heights: Country Living before "Country Living"

Among the six country living communities, the unincorporated areas of Hacienda Heights and Rowland Heights are closest in proximity to L.A.'s city limits. Before the emergence of themed subdivisions like Phillips Ranch or full-scale master-planned country living suburbs like Diamond Bar, Hacienda Heights and Rowland Heights provided a taste of the western idyll to people who wished to escape the hubbub of L.A. In both communities, the earliest-built houses sat near freeways and thoroughfares linking L.A. to the valley's agricultural zones. Houses were generally modest, situated on flatlands, and typically constructed between the 1950s and 1970s. Because of their remote location, both towns were less dense than prewar industrial suburbs like South Gate and immediate postwar suburbs like Lakewood.[109] Since Hacienda Heights and Rowland Heights residents did not have their own city councils and commissions, they lacked local oversight. This resulted in less uniformity in development and design. By the 1990s, Hacienda Heights and Rowland Heights embodied what critics described as the tragedies of country living gone wrong. While builders erected new rural-themed subdivisions in the 1980s and 1990s, neither community was entirely master-planned nor featured predominantly master-planned tracts. Thus, their earliest settlers prided themselves in being "true" rural dwellers. They believed mass-produced houses and neatly packaged communities lacked authenticity. Residents chided developers and builders for erecting what they saw as insultingly saccharine versions of western living.

The modern development of Hacienda Heights began in 1913, when Edwin Hart—a native Ohioan—bought a ranch from land baron Lucky Baldwin.[110] Formerly known as North Whittier Heights, Hacienda Heights offered homesites suitable for gentleman farmers as early as the 1920s.[111] The community was known for its verdant landscapes and avocado and citrus groves. Following World War II, Hacienda Heights attracted working- and middle-class families who preferred a sparsely populated environment but were still within commuter's distance to L.A. Earlier settlers typically lived in self-built, ranch-style houses. Development picked up around 1970 when direct freeway access to and from L.A. reached Hacienda Heights. Additional highways and arteries to and from the city steadily extended eastward into Rowland Heights, Walnut, Diamond Bar, Phillips Ranch, and Chino

Hills, spurring development in areas otherwise primarily reachable through local access or country roads.

Single-family homes constructed by small-scale builders emerged in the early 1960s. Hacienda Heights remained predominantly white until the 1970s when middle-class Mexican American families settled in the area in greater numbers. For upwardly mobile Mexicans moving from L.A., Hacienda Heights was the "Chicano Beverly Hills."[112] After the opening of Hsi Lai Temple in 1988, Hacienda Heights became a magnet for Chinese immigrants. By the early 1990s, the community was roughly one-third white, one-third Latino, and one-third Asian (mostly Chinese).[113] In the early 1970s, more developers started building on Hacienda Heights' higher-elevated hills. Once considered untouchable zones, hills were less controversial as building sites due to consumer demand. Unlike the modest homes situated on flatlands, developers erected luxury homes on hilly areas mirroring the type of growth occurring in neighboring master-planned suburbs like Diamond Bar and Chino Hills. These newer subdivisions embraced a "shabby chic" image. For example, newspaper features describing the Countrywood subdivision suggested its "California ranch or contemporary theme . . . carried out in the exterior of the homes using wood siding materials such as stained, rough-cut wood, stucco, and masonry" was a trendy western aesthetic.[114] Boosters suggested these tracts featured details tailored for buyers with discriminating taste and a penchant for an outdoor-focused lifestyle. Hacienda Heights' bucolic setting encouraged families to revel in nature amid their everyday routines. In assessing a new subdivision in Hacienda Heights, a *Los Angeles Times* reviewer noted a key detail embodying these principles: "To capitalize on California outdoor living, many of the homes have a pass-through service counter from the kitchen to the outdoor areas," blurring the edges between indoor and outdoor, civilization and wild à la Frank Lloyd Wright.[115] The idea was of balance—with the environment woven into things like eating (e.g., dining al fresco in the backyard overlooking the valley), relaxing (e.g., gardening, swimming), and exercising (e.g., going on hikes). For new homeowners, these amenities and design elements epitomized the unique flavor of Sunbelt suburbia.

Anticipating further development, the Los Angeles Regional Commission approved Hacienda Heights' Community General Plan in 1978, projecting a 28 percent growth rate over the next two decades.[116] Amid pressures to suburbanize, longtime residents and leaders worked with county officials on land use policies ensuring Hacienda Heights remained low density. Similar to the community plans of Phillips Ranch and Diamond Bar, the Hacienda Heights General Plan said its priority was to "preserve the community as a predominantly single family bedroom area," a lifestyle that kept its "country" identity intact.[117] The plan included policy recommendations such as minimal alterations to Hacienda Heights' "natural hillsides," the need for additional park facilities, a "system of equestrian trails," and continuous plans to "improve traffic circulation" whenever new homes were built.[118]

By the 1970s, Hacienda Heights evolved from a rural town into a postwar suburb. Since its master-planned neighbors like Diamond Bar emerged as fashionable communities in the 1980s and 1990s, Hacienda Heights' newer families demanded more amenities from Los Angeles County officials to replicate the "modern" master-planned way of life. Rather than embracing the ruggedness its earliest postwar residents cherished, their demands included facilities and aesthetics typical of planned communities: paved sidewalks, uniform street furniture and signage, children's playgrounds, customized hiking and equestrian trails, and other manicured facilities of a leisure class. At the end of the twentieth century, Hacienda Heights' landscape was a patchwork of older ranch houses, middle-income townhomes, modest tracts, and newer country living subdivisions—the latter generally comprising of wealthier Asian immigrants. To many East Valley residents, Hacienda Heights' promise of the agrarian ideal did not survive the pressures to develop. As a result, residents could not claim the same form of upmarket country living like their neighbors in Walnut or Chino Hills because Hacienda Heights lacked local control. They did not have a city council and municipal commissions to create and enforce codes under the banner of protecting residents' quality of life and property values.

Hacienda Heights' neighbor to the east, Rowland Heights, also retained its rural landscape for much of the twentieth century. Its earliest postwar settlers were drawn to the quiet, bucolic setting.[119] Equestrians fondly recalled days of galloping the hills before mass suburbanization. As early as the 1960s, developers started promoting a planned concept of frontier nostalgia in Rowland Heights. In 1966, Del Crest Homes advertised a new tract appealing to families seeking to leave the hustle and bustle of L.A. Del Crest promised a "non-congested country style living." The extensions of the 60 Freeway in the 1970s helped put Rowland Heights on the map for new housing. Rather than taking local roads to access highways to and from L.A., the freeway now allowed easy access to the city, as well as justification for developers to build further inland.[120]

In 1979, the Rowland Heights Coordinating Council in conjunction with the County of Los Angeles (its governing body) approved a General Plan. Enacted in 1981, residents said they wanted to protect Rowland Heights' "typical suburban bedroom community" feel with "very little land in industrial use." They believed the "preservation of natural hillsides and vegetation and the maintenance of livestock keeping areas" would "maintain the rural atmosphere of the community." The General Plan stressed residents' desires to keep Rowland Heights' "established rural community character," particularly under the specter of mass development. By the 1980s, Rowland Heights' new subdivisions were aesthetically on par with sister developments in master-planned country living suburbs and neighborhoods. This was especially true along Rowland Heights' southern hills where newer, pricier development occurred. Builders, realtors, and homeowners alike took advantage of the area's higher elevations knowing homes perched above the valley translated into higher property values. Ads for tracts like Rollingwood, Suncrest, Indian Springs, Country Hollow, North Country, South Country, and Rancho El Dorado—all built between 1973 and 1984—promised the conveniences and luxuries of modern single-family homes set in the hinterland.

Rowland Heights remained a predominantly white community until Asian families settled in greater numbers during the 1980s. Amid these demographic shifts, pressures to protect Rowland Heights' pastoral environment grew louder. Critics suggested Chinese, Filipino, and Korean newcomers urbanized the area. Their "foreignness," along with Asian business owners' purported lack of respect for Euro-American design, English signage, and low-density development frustrated critics who read their actions as anti-assimilationist, non-suburban, and therefore un-American. Critics accused Asians of refusing to conform to the mainstream and for going against the General Plan's country living fundamentalism. For residents lamenting change in both Hacienda Heights and Rowland Heights, the perceived decline of Western rural culture was attributed to these demographic shifts.

Hacienda Heights and Rowland Heights symbolized how minimal local control and unregulated growth put communities at risk of urbanization. By the 1990s, residents claimed both towns were a far cry from their agrarian roots. Once regarded as authentic pastoral villages, Hacienda Heights and Rowland Heights became poster children of how not to do country living. Unlike their neighbors—namely, Walnut, Diamond Bar, and Chino Hills— Hacienda Heights and Rowland Heights were unable to stop development partly because of their unincorporated status. Residents felt they could no longer claim an independent rural identity because, ironically, they were not afforded the tools, mechanisms, and political clout of an autonomous city. Their lack of local control resulted in a varied landscape unaligned with their tonier master-planned counterparts whose rural identity relatively stayed intact. For critics, the towns' Asian storefronts dotting the retail landscape illustrated the need for tightening land use and design rules. At the same time, master-planned suburbs—despite holding Asian racial pluralities by the 1990s—still felt and looked more "country" because Asians in suburbs like Diamond Bar supported an invisible ethnic presence in the built environment. Notably, master-planned suburbs like Walnut emerged as solid models of rural authenticity, not communities like Hacienda Heights. Though they were able to maintain some semblance of agrarianism through zoning, both Hacienda Heights and Rowland Heights were no longer read as such to residents by the 1990s. In other words, a suburb's ability to minimize density and ethnic expression—that is, Asian culture—validated its claims to having a country living profile. As Hacienda Heights' and Rowland Heights' population and built environment shifted, they were less qualified to claim a country identity.

. . .

The pursuit of country living brought families to the edges of greater Los Angeles. Whether they settled in the years following World War II or during the closing decades of the twentieth century, East Valley residents sought an environment evocative of a timeless American West. Before mass suburbanization, homeowners experienced a way of life where remote pastures, two-lane roads, and horses galloping the fields were the norm. Through word of mouth and masterful advertising, developers, builders, realtors, and other actors successfully branded a type of "rural" suburbia purportedly blending town and country, modern and rustic. For those who invested in this packaged version of western agrarianism, this too was authentic country living. Over time, fears of an impending end to the valley's idyll rallied homeowners together even if they at times disagreed on what constituted "country." Despite the differences of these six communities, residents shared common expectations and desires. They wanted to experience, protect, and preserve cultural myths of frontier nostalgia in a rapidly changing L.A.; this was a unifying set of motives shaping how residents forged relationships and engaged with the politics of race, space, and change.

TWO

———

The People of "Country Living"

IN THE CLOSING DECADES of the twentieth century, commentators, pundits, and the press declared greater Los Angeles the "Gang Capital of America."[1] They believed drugs, gangs, and violence made it a place to be avoided at all costs; the inner city itself was reminiscent of a war zone. In contrast, L.A.'s outer-ring suburbs were sanctuaries from the perceived disarray of the metropolis. For families who agreed with these critiques, investing in an East San Gabriel Valley home held the promise of a future that was a return to a static, simpler past. In "country living" suburbs, communities, and tracts, homeowners enjoyed the advantages of postwar technology, design, and infrastructure.

At the same time, residents likened the region to life in a pleasant, provincial West. It was open, traditional, family-focused, and untouched by the perils of modernity or the downsides of American urbanism. These myths—imagined, exaggerated, or both—informed how suburbanites understood their lives in a transforming California. Planners, developers, builders, realtors, and other actors promoted these contradictory images and ideals. But it was residents themselves—native- and foreign-born alike—who consumed, believed, and perpetuated such notions even before moving in.

Whether it was the 1960s or 1990s, regardless of when families put down roots, homeowners sought forms of frontier nostalgia because it was antithetical to the status quo of urban and suburban America. The East Valley's landscape and local culture embodied the tenets of an anti-urban class skeptical of a liberalizing, changing society. Sentiments to preserve country living and its associations with an old American West grew stronger as L.A. became denser, busier, and more diverse. This chapter focuses on the people of the East Valley and their motivations for establishing lives in the region's

TABLE 1 Median Household Income, 1980–2010.

	1980	1990	2000	2010
Chino Hills (CDP before incorporation)	N/A	$58,030	$78,374	$106,347
Diamond Bar (CDP before incorporation)	$30,799	$60,651	$68,871	$99,083
Hacienda Heights (CDP)	$30,029	$51,837	$59,485	$85,953
Pomona (including Phillips Ranch)	$15,392	$32,132	$40,021	$60,598
Rowland Heights (CDP)	$22,911	$46,404	$52,270	$75,587
Walnut	$30,215	$64,333	$81,015	$108,669

Data from 1980 Census, 1990 Census, 2000 Census, US Bureau of the Census; 2010 Census "Quick Facts," US Bureau of the Census.

country living suburbs or master-planned tracts. Though residents bought their homes for practical reasons, I argue that the appeal of country living was a major attraction. These communities reinforced a range of ideological beliefs and cultural myths, especially those of suburbia and the Western frontier. Furthermore, for married couples, an investment in a single-family home meant one achieved an important benchmark in the American Dream. Regardless of race and class, country living informed homeowners' perspectives, politics, and sense of identity. Their attachments to the lifestyle illustrate how they positioned themselves as suburbanites and as Americans against the backdrop of the Cold War and a globalizing California.

In 1959, Patricia Bowler met her husband, John, a commander with the Los Angeles County Sheriff's Department. Four years later, they married and started their lives together in the San Gabriel Valley town of Whittier. There they met another young couple, Art and Carol Herrera. Both couples hit it off as friends, partly because Art also worked for the Sheriff's Department. In 1966, the Bowlers and Herreras each bought homes sixteen miles east of Whittier in the newly developed community of Diamond Bar. The two couples moved with one truck and settled in the same tract. The Bowlers and the Herreras were among Diamond Bar's suburban pioneers. For the Bowlers, knowing John's fellow law enforcement colleagues considered Diamond Bar a choice suburb appealed to them. Most convincing, for Patricia at least, was its country living aesthetic. She had long known about Diamond Bar, associating the area with tranquil greenbelts, sweeping vistas,

TABLE 2 Race/Ethnicity, 1980.

	White	Black or African American	Hispanic or Latino (of any race)	Asian	Total Population
Chino Hills (CDP before incorporation)	12,246 90.42%	182 1.35%	N/A N/A	174 1.28%	13,543
Diamond Bar (CDP before incorporation)	23,259 82.93%	1,436 5.12%	3,937 14.03%	1,681 5.99%	28,045
Hacienda Heights (CDP)	38,697 78.29%	673 1.36%	13,047 26.39%	5,472 11.07%	49,422
Pomona (including Phillips Ranch)	58,164 59.50%	17,609 18.01%	28,287 28.94%	2,362 2.41%	97,742
Rowland Heights (CDP)	22,002 77.87%	834 2.95%	7,078 25.05%	2,307 8.16%	28,252
Walnut	9,635 75.58%	498 3.90%	2,562 20.09%	1,300 10.19%	12,748

Data from 1980 Census, US Bureau of the Census. Note: unable to retrieve Hispanic or Latino (of any race) data for Chino Hills, CA.

TABLE 3 Race/Ethnicity, 1990.

	White	Black or African American	Hispanic or Latino (of any race)	Asian	Total Population
Chino Hills (CDP before incorporation)	20,382 73.82%	1,381 5.00%	4,527 16.39%	3,724 13.48%	27,608
Diamond Bar	34,252 63.81%	3,036 5.65%	8,839 16.46%	13,293 24.76%	53,672
Hacienda Heights (CDP)	31,001 59.21%	1,215 2.32%	16,328 31.18%	14,207 27.13%	52,354
Pomona (including Phillips Ranch)	75,400 57.24%	18,963 14.39%	66,589 50.55%	8,825 6.69%	131,723
Rowland Heights (CDP)	23,093 54.14%	2,148 5.03%	12,576 29.48%	12,433 29.15%	42,647
Walnut	14,008 48.12%	1,396 4.79%	6,704 23.03%	10,271 35.28%	29,105

Data 1990 Census, US Bureau of the Census.

TABLE 4 Race/Ethnicity, 2000.

	White	Black or African American	Hispanic or Latino (of any race)	Asian	Total Population
Chino Hills	37,656	3,697	17,151	14,744	66,787
	56.38%	5.53%	25.68%	22.07%	
Diamond Bar	23,103	2,680	10,393	24,066	53,919
	42.84%	4.97%	19.27%	44.63%	
Hacienda Heights (CDP)	21,797	825	20,320	19,174	53,122
	41.03%	1.55%	38.25%	36.09%	
Pomona (including Phillips Ranch)	62,419	14,398	96,370	10,762	141,986
	43.96%	10.14%	67.87%	7.57%	
Rowland Heights (CDP)	14,206	1,268	13,748	24,432	48,553
	29.25%	2.61%	28.31%	50.32%	
Walnut	8,513	1,259	5,803	16,728	30,004
	28.37%	4.19%	19.34%	55.75%	

Data from 2000 Census, US Bureau of the Census.

TABLE 5 Race/Ethnicity, 2010.

	White	Black or African American	Hispanic or Latino (of any race)	Asian	Total Population
Chino Hills	38,035	3,415	21,802	22,676	74,799
	50.84%	4.56%	29.14%	30.31%	
Diamond Bar	18,434	2,288	11,138	29,144	53,387
	34.52%	4.28%	20.86%	54.59%	
Hacienda Heights (CDP)	21,873	743	24,608	20,065	52,294
	41.82%	1.42%	47.05%	38.36%	
Pomona (including Phillips Ranch)	71,564	10,924	105,135	12,688	149,058
	48.01%	7.32%	70.53%	8.51%	
Rowland Heights (CDP)	11,506	772	13,229	29,284	48,993
	23.48%	1.57%	27.00%	59.77%	
Walnut	6,913	824	5,575	18,567	29,172
	23.69%	2.82%	19.11%	63.64%	

Data from 2010 Census, American Fact Finder (2006–2010 American Community Survey 5-Year Estimates), US Bureau of the Census.

and horse ranches. Compared to L.A. and its inner-ring suburbs, Patricia believed Diamond Bar "looked like a nice place to live, to raise children. . . . [It was] a clean, healthy environment." The Bowlers' first Diamond Bar home was backed up against rolling hills. The dead end of their street, Ambushers Lane, was "wilderness . . . [and] was country living" in her eyes. In the early years, Patricia said waking up in the middle of the night to hear "a hoot (from an) owl (sitting) in the trees . . ." was nature in its purest form.[2] For the Arkansas native, Diamond Bar's landscape was redolent of her rural Southern upbringing.

Patricia's praises of Diamond Bar's agrarian qualities were not exceptional. Her neighbors saw the East Valley as an idyllic, utopian-like place—a contrast to the drab austerity or vice-filled landscape of Los Angeles. Along with their critiques of the city, residents believed country living firmly stood against the suburban trends of the 1940s and 1950s. That is, unlike the Levittowns of the East Coast or L.A.'s older suburbs like South Gate, Huntington Park, and Lakewood, the East Valley's newer tracts—particularly those in master-planned neighborhoods—took open space and buyers' desires for roominess into greater account. Homeowners praised planners, developers, and builders for not putting houses close together and for providing basic landscaping that did not distract from the area's natural surroundings. For earlier settlers including the Bowlers, minimal infrastructure was a plus, leaving homeowners with the democratic independence to customize their properties within reason. East Valley boosters claimed that the typical eyesores and inconveniences of other postwar suburbs would not be an issue in master-planned towns like Diamond Bar because these were modern, thoughtfully conceived communities.

Along with Diamond Bar, the suburbs of and subdivisions within Walnut, Chino Hills, Phillips Ranch, Hacienda Heights, and Rowland Heights attracted families from around the United States. With the promise of country living, homeowners who purchased their properties in the 1960s and 1970s believed they moved in when the valley was authentically rural despite its suburban infrastructure. The later wave of residents—that is, buyers who moved in during the 1980s and 1990s (many of whom were Asian immigrants) also believed they were moving to the countryside. Whether they were white residents hailing from the Midwest and South or immigrants from Asia, homeowners believed the East Valley offered an innocent, unparalleled way of life in L.A. Its verdant and almost-phantasmal setting was a marked difference from the city and its inner-ring suburbs. Moreover, residents believed the area exemplified a dignified Victorian past, a sentiment that resonated with homeowners concerned about cultural and demographic changes in the closing decades of the twentieth century. While there was general agreement in wanting to protect country living, how people interpreted and qualified "rural," "Western," and "country" differed at times, with race, class, and generation informing one's definition(s). Residents held varying beliefs in what should (and should not) be in their towns or subdivisions. The main unifier, though, was a collective desire to experience the good life in the hinterland, with frontier nostalgia serving as the aesthetic, cultural, and political glue holding together three waves of settlers.

THE FIRST SUBURBAN WAVE: 1960S TO LATE 1970S

Despite its agrarian heritage, the East Valley was not removed from the city of Los Angeles. Its farming towns and *colonias* played an integral part of Southern California's economic expansion for decades. Accessible by rail and local roads, settlement in what were otherwise rural and agricultural communities was possible for non-farming families, though less friendly to daily commuters to and from L.A. This, however, did not bother numerous families. In fact, the East Valley's distance and faraway feel enticed families disillusioned with L.A. in the era of "urban crisis."[3] Many residents of this generation were part of the valley's "Old Guard," a moniker referring to older, usually white, lower-middle- and middle-class residents who had political clout or held critical leadership roles. They were generally wary of change, held conservative views, and disliked urbanism and growth.

Remoteness was one reason Bill and Laura Richardson moved to Hacienda Heights from L.A.'s Boyle Heights neighborhood. After marrying in 1966, they followed the advice of Bill's coworker who suggested heading east for more affordable, larger homes. Serendipitously, an acquaintance was selling their house in Hacienda Heights, which they purchased for $26,000 in 1969. Their first home sat surrounded by lush hills and a mixture of modest and jerrybuilt houses, constructed by small builders or the landowners themselves. Both born into Black families of the Depression Era South, the Richardsons quickly acclimated, citing the East Valley's country landscape as a plus. After several years in Boyle Heights, Laura was anxious to leave: "I came from a very, very small town (in Arkansas). I was scared to death in Los Angeles. I was ready to get out of there. It was too big. . . . It was too big to conceive that anybody could live there."[4] Laura despised the city so much she started her own in-home accounting business in the early 1980s so she no longer needed to travel to L.A. for accounting jobs. For Bill, along with its rural landscape, Hacienda Heights was an ideal community because the recently extended 60 freeway provided access to his office in Downtown L.A. Yet Hacienda Heights remained physically, culturally, and psychologically far from the city. Though he utilized the freeway for commuting, once Bill exited, he and others took dimly lit roads to get home. Limited accessibility heightened the country feel, which Bill believed was what made Hacienda Heights a "picturesque [and] idyllic" town.[5] A native Texan, Bill loved living among cows, horses, and wildlife. These elements were what made the East Valley—as he described it—"rustic, quiet, and very peaceful."[6] For the Richardsons, seeing their equestrian neighbors riding horses along the hills throughout the day kept them closer to their roots. A local agrarian culture reinforced their affinities for a simpler, slower pace.

The Richardsons suggested their political views pushed them out of L.A. as well. As longtime Republican Party activists, Bill and Laura considered themselves self-made individuals who did not rely on the government to achieve economic stability. They embodied the "rags-to-riches" story embedded in color-blind, conservative ideals of meritocracy and hard work as the ticket to success. They associated indulgence and vice in urban America as telltale signs of liberalism's failures. Rather than aligning with their Black identities, they stressed how their rural heritage informed how they engaged with neighbors and understood the world around them. Active in charitable work, the Richardsons believed their down-to-earth nature and penchant for volunteerism were rooted in the standards of a bygone era. The Richardsons and their contemporaries subscribed to Jeffersonian notions of the ideal American. That is, of the yeoman: an agrarian whose toil, servitude, honesty, and faith in God helped keep society afloat and pious. Particularly for older homeowners, rural communities embodied the godliest of settings and contained the purest of Americans. They were wary of modernity and rebuffed impositions of state power. Residing in the East Valley ensured those ideals remained front and center of their family life amid a rapidly changing California.

Similar to the Richardsons, Janice Stewart felt the East Valley's landscape allowed her to live what she called a "rustic lifestyle." Born in 1938, Janice grew up in a self-built home in the West San Gabriel Valley suburb of Montebello, ten miles east of downtown L.A. She and her second husband

Richard moved to Diamond Bar in 1976. For $79,900, they bought a two-year-old single-story tract house in north Diamond Bar. Janice believed Diamond Bar's reputation as a conservative town was an appropriate fit for a lifelong libertarian. Lovers of the outdoors, Janice and Richard enjoyed the metaphorical freedom of less-developed towns. When they settled in Diamond Bar, it was an unincorporated area. This appealed to them because it suggested minimal governance, less intrusion, and greater autonomy.[7] Janice was a "Goldwater Girl," a believer in Barry Goldwater's brand of Sunbelt conservativism. In the late 1950s, Janice read the writings of Goldwater, William F. Buckley, and the *National Review*, which shaped her perspectives on the role of government in Americans' day-to-day lives. "I want to live in a meritocracy," Janice said, and not in a society where people relied on "handouts" or big government. The cultures and geography of country living embodied and emboldened her philosophies on liberty and egalitarianism.[8] In this spirit, city living was far from desirable:

> [The] West Side (of L.A.) is not my lifestyle. . . . Plus, all my [college] friends [from the University of Southern California] were in Orange County [or] Pasadena. . . . I did not want a two-story house. I wanted something with a porch. . . . I wanted something that was California bungalow, ranch, or craftsman [in style]. I mean, that's what I wanted. When I saw this porch and then the kitchen—a big, open, tiled kitchen—that was it! [And] the view. . . . Plus, I liked it was rural [in Diamond Bar and the East San Gabriel Valley].[9]

The East Valley's unpretentious lifestyle reflected Janice's roots as a child of blue-collar Quaker parents and Richard's background as a Midwesterner: "[Rural living] is what I grew up with. [And Richard] was born in Joplin, Missouri. Of course, [Joplin is] all rural . . . still is all rural."[10] Janice and Richard looked at homes in inner-ring suburbs closer to L.A., but their experiences visiting relatives or friends living there persuaded them to move east and inland: "We looked near Huntington Park . . . and my dad's sister lived in South Gate—and we were like 'nuh-uh!'"[11] The Stewarts avoided houses built in the immediate postwar period, considering them run-down, dilapidated, or located in cramped communities too similar to city living. While the towns they explored—South Gate and Huntington Park—are suburbs, to Janice, they were not "country" or conservative enough. Diamond Bar country living delivered what they wanted. The Stewarts of Diamond Bar and the Richardsons of Hacienda Heights rejected urbanism because it did not afford them the literal and metaphorical freedoms found in the country.

Moreover, the Stewarts and the Richardsons were of a generation reared on the values of what James Gregory calls "plain-folk Americanism," a set of beliefs and characteristics rooted in the Great Depression.[12] This especially applied to Californians from Southern and Interior states like Oklahoma, Texas, Arkansas, and Missouri. They prided themselves as inherently resourceful, resilient, and patriotic.

Rowland Heights homeowners Dave and Cathy Johnson married in 1963. They briefly lived in Long Beach and then bought a home for $17,500 in Hollydale, a section of present-day South Gate. Besides its proximity to Dave's job, Hollydale's intimate feel lured them in: "Hollydale was like a little Midwestern island that was kinda rural-ish. The home we had was in a tract that was up against the [Los Angeles] River. On the east side was an undeveloped area with a guy who had three acres with horses. . . . The kids got into horses because of that [neighbor]. It was a real folksy area, country-ish type of people there—a sense of a small community."[13] Over time, the Johnsons sought a bucolic setting and felt a need to settle farther away from L.A. With the intention of building their own home, they originally purchased a lot in The Country in Diamond Bar, a gated equestrian community of ranch-style and custom-made homes. During escrow, the Johnsons got cold feet. As a young couple raising two children, Dave and Cathy worried about the stress of building a house from the ground up. They backed out of the deal in 1968 and instead purchased a ranch-style house in Rowland Heights in 1970 thanks to a tip from Dave's coworker at County-USC Hospital, where Dave was a pharmacist. They liked that the home was affordable, included a barn house, and was accessible to L.A. via the 60 freeway which recently extended into Rowland Heights.[14] Like their neighbors, the Johnsons owned a number of farm animals. Though they had a taste of small-town life in Hollydale, Rowland Heights had more open space. As parents with young kids, this made the country living experience feel especially wholesome and authentic.

The Richardsons, Stewarts, and Johnsons shared similar desires to live a rural lifestyle. They believed raising children in pastoral settings resulted in humble, God-fearing families unmolested by the cultures and material temptations of the city. They felt unadulterated knolls and greenbelts were not only picturesque, but access to them also facilitated a healthier state of being. Finally, for this earlier wave of postwar settlers, the valley's sylvan landscape and overall milieu represented the tenets of an old-fashioned American life: freedom and traditionalism. They understood these values and characteristics as inaccessible or increasingly under attack in a rapidly urbanizing L.A. In the following decades, their new neighbors moving into master-planned communities and subdivisions sought these ideals too. But settlers of the second wave wanted an upmarket version of country living. Rather than pursuing a life à la *Little House on the Prairie*, these younger families chased modern—and in some cases, glamorous—versions of the western idyll.

THE SECOND SUBURBAN WAVE:
LATE 1970S TO MID-1980S

Beyond its pastoralism, residents of the second suburban wave were drawn to the East Valley because of the affordability and availability of luxurious country living houses. Access to high-performing public schools and the master-planned layout of most new tracts were plusses. For these residents, country living was stylish because popular culture of the era celebrated western fashion (e.g., chaps, boots, denim, "cowboy" couture), western architecture (e.g., ranch-style, Spanish colonial), western landscapes as seen on television (e.g., *Dallas, Dynasty, Knots Landing, Falcon Crest*), and a western president (i.e., Ronald Reagan), all emblematic of Americans' fascination with the western frontier since Spanish exploration in the late 1700s.

In 1986, the *Los Angeles Times'* Ted Leibman and Caltech professor Bruce Cain mapped the Southern California electorate and broke down voter characteristics by region. Their compilation played to popular stereotypes: worldly yuppies on L.A.'s West Side, young bohemians in Hollywood, and a tableau of middle-class or new money suburbanites in the East San Gabriel Valley. Leibman and Cain classified Hacienda Heights as a community of "furs and station wagons" where "well-educated, affluent, mobile professionals with teen-age children" revel in "far from city life" suburbia.[15] They labeled Rowland Heights and Walnut as "young suburbia," places where "white-collar families with money and young children" live the good life.[16] Politically, they considered the East Valley safe Republican territory. However provocative and droll their analyses, Leibman and Cain understood the region drew in people with similar backgrounds and interests. These were families who railed against urbanism. They happily left L.A. or its adjacent suburbs fearing crime, violence, and—for many—growing racial and class diversity that made them uncomfortable. On the whole, they sought a country

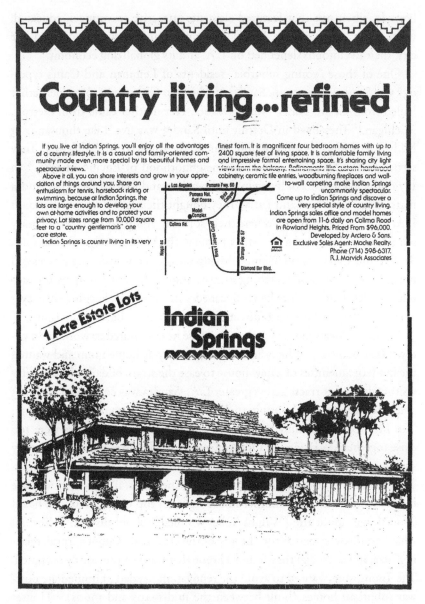

Country living...refined

If you live at Indian Springs, you'll enjoy all the advantages of a country lifestyle. It is a casual and family-oriented community made even more special by its beautiful homes and spectacular views.

Above it all, you can share interests and grow in your appreciation of things around you. Share an enthusiasm for tennis, horseback riding or swimming, because at Indian Springs, the lots are large enough to develop your own at-home activities and to protect your privacy. Lot sizes range from 10,000 square feet to a "country gentleman's" one acre estate.

Indian Springs is country living in its very finest form. It is magnificent four bedroom homes with up to 2400 square feet of living space. It is comfortable family living and impressive formal entertaining space. It's sharing city light views from the balcony. Refinements like custom hardwood cabinetry, ceramic tile entries, woodburning fireplaces and wall-to-wall carpeting make Indian Springs uncommonly spectacular.

Come up to Indian Springs and discover a very special style of country living.

Indian Springs sales office and model homes are open from 11-6 daily on Colima Road in Rowland Heights. Priced From $96,000.

Developed by Arciero & Sons.
Exclusive Sales Agent: Macke Realty.
Phone (714) 598-6317.
R.J. Marvick Associates

1 Acre Estate Lots

Indian Springs

FIGURE 8. Indian Springs (Rowland Heights, CA) new tract homes advertisement, *Los Angeles Times*, June 11, 1978. Image courtesy of *Los Angeles Times*.

lifestyle, albeit one that featured elements attractive to younger, educated, white-collar professionals. While newcomers distrusted and disliked the city, their livelihoods depended on L.A. and its globalizing economy.

One of those "young suburbia" residents of Leibman and Cain's typology was Sandra Thompson. Sandra was born in Chicago in 1947. Her father hailed from Grand Forks, North Dakota. Her mother came from Detroit, Michigan.[17] They lived in Detroit until Sandra was five. Like thousands of Midwestern families after World War II, they moved to California. They settled in the San Fernando Valley neighborhood of Encino in 1952.[18] In 1979, after a few years of living in San Francisco and Marina Del Rey, Sandra married her then husband Larry. They bought their first home in the south L.A. city of Hawthorne. When their son was about to enter elementary school, they purchased a two-story home in the Walnut Ridge tract in 1987. Sandra and Larry found Walnut driving on the freeway during a weekend house hunt, a common searching strategy among this wave of upwardly mobile couples. Families hit the road armed with print ads, keeping their eyes peeled for flags or billboards directing them to freshly built subdivisions.[19]

For Larry, location was a priority because he commuted to work in downtown L.A. Sandra, on the other hand, was a stay-at-home mom and wanted the modern amenities of a new house to ease the strain of daily chores. After visiting dozens of tracts across greater L.A., Sandra was convinced Walnut's ambiance, layout, and housing stock had a type of charm unseen elsewhere: "[In Moorpark and Simi Valley in Ventura County], the homes were too close together. . . . [Irvine in Orange County was] master-planned, but they were just so close to each other. That's the thing we just loved about Walnut. The openness . . . the whole community is. These lots, like the way we have here . . . you don't have another house right on top of you. Plus, we heard good things about the [Walnut Valley Unified] school district."[20] Beyond what Sandra described as the "beauty of the area" and Walnut's "rural, relaxing" feel, it was crucial they found a home that was not previously occupied. The Thompsons wanted to avoid the renovation needed of immediate postwar suburban homes (built between the mid-1940s and 1960s).[21] Houses like those of the San Fernando Valley or South Bay were typically older, smaller, and not necessarily built to last. Following World War II, builders quickly erected homes to accommodate a housing shortage, a baby boom, and returning veterans looking to buy (facilitated by loans via the 1944 GI Bill). Over time, these communities—which were class and ethnically diverse (that is, largely of European origin)—became poorer and more racially diverse.[22] East Valley homeowners like Sandra suggested that as L.A.'s inner-ring suburbs aged, the reputation of these communities declined. This included places like her hometown, Encino: "I'd say the San Fernando Valley changed for the negative. [It's] dense. It's overpopulated. Here [in Walnut], I saw open space and relaxation."[23] Unlike other parts of suburban L.A., the East Valley's generally newer and larger housing stock with a range of built-in features ensured a higher-income population. Sandra also praised Walnut's Master Plan and claimed the meticulous landscaping and building regulations kept neighborhoods desirable: "Any other community would've had the walls of my back fence right on the street, [on] the sidewalk. . . . In Simi [Valley], Moorpark, [and] Irvine . . . they all had these teeny-tiny backyards unlike here."[24] Sandra—who once served on Walnut's Planning Commission—claimed the suburb's housing setbacks and codes protected greenbelts and limited density. These aesthetic rules minimized signifiers of urbanism keeping Walnut both "rural" and orderly. Though Sandra did not view Walnut as authentically country, she thought the town's idyllic settings and slower pace of life embodied the wholesome lifestyle she and her neighbors desired.

Like the Thompsons, Sharon and Ken Smith believed their family needed to reside in a place that resembled a traditional middle-class lifestyle.[25] When Ken accepted an engineering position in Pomona in 1979, they "took a protractor and drew a ten-mile circle around Pomona and found Diamond Bar."[26] The Smiths bought their first Diamond Bar home in 1979 and moved to a newer, larger house, also in Diamond Bar, in 1986. A native of nearby Whittier, when Sharon attended her high school senior winter formal at the Diamond Bar Golf Course, she fell in love with the area. She considered it a "dream suburb" and one of L.A.'s "reach communities."[27] To Sharon, "the hillsides, the recreational opportunities, the sheer physical beauty of the place was very attractive to us."[28] Ken thought Diamond Bar was a refreshing departure from the older, denser communities of Bellflower, Lakewood, and Torrance, suburbs he lived in prior to marrying Sharon. The Smiths felt their second Diamond Bar home was particularly special because of its elevated and secluded location from the town's main thoroughfares, keeping them away from anything remotely busy. Sharon noted, "My husband liked the smell of the chaparral because to him it was like going on vacation. . . . And Ken had a friend [in the neighborhood], [who was originally] from Taiwan actually . . . and he just fell in love with the neighborhood. . . . He liked that it was a little bit newer [and] liked the three-car garage—very appealing to him."[29]

An active gardener and lover of the outdoors, Sharon said access to nature was a hallmark of East Valley living. This was what sold them on Diamond Bar. Along with the landscape and lifestyle, Sharon believed Diamond Bar had civic pride because families held similar demographic profiles or world views. Beyond her domestic obligations including raising their two sons, Sharon was tapped into local politics. She founded Diamond Bar Republican Women Federated to help bolster GOP activism across the valley. She was the first woman to serve on Diamond Bar's Parks and Recreation Commission and was later appointed to the prestigious Planning Commission. While in office, she created recreational services like public basketball courts and a concerts-in-the-park series to uphold the founders' spirit of having a suburb that kept up with the times yet remained devoted to its origins of being an agrarian, outdoor- and family-focused community. Sharon suggested her public service and the grassroots activism of her contemporaries helped preserve Diamond Bar's rural integrity because this wave of settlers fully understood its master-planned heritage.

While the first suburban wave enjoyed scant development and a sparse population, the second wave, people with disposable income, wanted a range of amenities. New or updated infrastructure, public works, manicured landscaping, recreational centers, running paths, lit street signs, and tidy horse trails (which equestrians deemed pointless because they needed wide open spaces for proper riding) were musts. Younger families expected convenience or extravagance in their private worlds too. This included three-car garages, professional kitchens, minibars, spas, greenhouses, and sprawling backyards suitable for outdoor entertaining apropos of a leisure-oriented Sunbelt lifestyle—many of these were integrated in what builders sometimes called "executive homes."[30] Gated communities were increasingly trendy as well, since some upper-income buyers equated fencing and private security as markers of exclusivity. Walnut, however, banned gated communities because they were "too elitist" or anti-western. Old Guard homeowners like Tom Sykes said, "A gate is a gate, and that isn't really the philosophy of this community," which prided itself for its physical openness as a rural-themed town.[31]

By the mid-1980s, younger families of color started to gain a foothold in country living suburbs, joining their white counterparts of the first and second wave. Though a modest number of Latinos and a smaller cohort of Black residents lived in these suburbs, Asian residents quickly outnumbered them and surpassed whites in Diamond Bar, Walnut, and Rowland Heights by the end of the 1990s, constituting the racial majority or plurality in each

FIGURE 9. Backyard and surrounding tract homes in Diamond Bar, CA, 1980. Photo by Joe Deal. From the Los Angeles Documentary Project. Image courtesy of Smithsonian American Art Museum.

town.[32] Among Walnut's newest residents of color was William Choctaw. He moved to California in the 1970s for a medical internship after receiving his MD from Yale University. Raised by a single African American mother in what he called a "poor, rural part of Nashville, Tennessee," William sought economic opportunity elsewhere.[33] After graduating from Tennessee State University, he landed a Robert Wood Johnson Foundation fellowship, which was tailored for people of color so they could attend medical school. He claimed Yale exposed him to a "different world" of privilege and access. Going to New Haven was his first time traveling out of the Deep South. It was also his first time on an airplane. When he relocated west for an internship at the University of California, Davis, he met fellow medical intern

Patrick Travis, who was from Los Angeles and was one of the few Black students in the program. "When I moved [to L.A.], I looked him up and they [Patrick and his spouse] showed me parts of the San Gabriel Valley. I liked the homes, the neighborhoods, and it was in my price range."[34]

In 1978, William joined the medical faculty at USC and settled in West Covina. A few years later, he decided to set up a private practice nearby, to which his friend Patrick joked, "Why? There are no Black people in the San Gabriel Valley."[35] William cited race did not get in the way of deciding where he should work or live, alluding to being unfazed by areas with few Black residents. He opened his office in Walnut in 1983. Two years later, he bought a home in an equestrian-themed tract situated on Branding Iron Road. He believed Walnut was an ideal place to rear children, partly because of its master-planned rural identity:

> There was a lot of open space, animals . . . [and] orange trees—before they were built out and developed. It was really the open space [I admired most]. It just seemed like a very, very nice area. Sorta slow-moving, [a] nice place to raise kids—just the whole area [felt that way]. . . . I liked the horse trails, and it was upscale . . . the greenery, a lot of trees, a very elegant type of place. And I really liked that. I like all the parks for the kids, and that sort of thing. My kids were big time soccer people.[36]

Like his neighbors, William believed Walnut's country living aesthetic evoked an innocence of yesteryear despite its new infrastructure and modern amenities. Moreover, William thought the people of the East Valley shared his Southern family values. He believed in a meritocracy and felt hard work—not government handouts—was the key to a stable life. For William, regardless of race, one could achieve the American Dream with ambition and drive.[37] Though he supported diversity, he suggested America would be better off as a country if it moved toward a color-blind society. Outside of private practice, William served on Walnut's Parks and Recreation Commission. He then sat on the Planning Commission in 1988, which he considered a stepping stone to the city council. He said it was the "most powerful commission in the city" because it helped keep Walnut structurally and aesthetically in order.[38] The Planning Commission was particularly important in making sure the suburb stayed true to its country living identity. In 1989, William was elected to the city council. He claimed he would protect Walnut's small-town feel. Over time, his role as a public official expanded to include matters of race relations between native-born whites and the rapidly growing foreign-born Asian population. As a person of color on the white-majority city council, he was expected to stand as the cultural broker between whites and nonwhites. At the same time, despite his allegiance to striving for a post-racial world, William wanted to help Asians integrate to suburbia—or, at the very least, assist in cultivating a civic culture respectful of diversity.

William, Sharon, and Sandra embodied the generation of "young suburbia" Leibman and Cain described. They were solidly middle- or upper-middle-class homeowners whose retreat to country living was out of a desire to escape the city. Like the first suburban wave, this generation was also reared in small towns or in more conservative parts of the United States. Country living suburbs provided them a middle ground between urban and rural. The growing sophistication of regional infrastructure coupled with in-home and community amenities made country living a place that met their desires as upwardly mobile families seeking a rustic flavor. The cultures, symbols, and signifiers of Western rurality surrounding them shaped residents' understandings of what it meant to live away from L.A. and all its problems. By the end of the 1980s, suburbanites found that country living spoke to immigrants as well, namely Asian families who would predominate the next wave.

THE THIRD SUBURBAN WAVE: MID-1980S TO LATE 1990S

Among the three suburban waves, these settlers were richer and disproportionally Asian. This resulted in a palpable shift in the area's demographic profile. On the whole, post-1965 Asian immigrants arrived in the United States with significant global capital or attained middle- or upper-middle-class status within years of settling. They came with the intentions to own a single-family home, preferably a new property situated within a reputable school district. These factors helped keep the regional housing market robust amid regional or national economic downturns. A spate of recessions in the early 1980s and 1990s impacted Southern California real estate, yet country living tracts fared well because of diasporic Chinese families. In the early 1990s, new homes in master-planned tracts were typically priced in the low to mid-$100,000s. By decade's end, new houses started in the high-$200,000s to over $500,000. The surge of young families from Hong Kong and Taiwan as well as Mainland China, the Philippines, South Korea, and India continued well into the twenty-first century.[39]

This cohort of Asian immigrants settled directly into the valley, skipping the traditional urban-to-suburban pathway of their pre-1965 immigrant counterparts.[40] In turn, Asian families arriving after the 1970s had weaker ties to Chinatown, Filipinotown, Koreatown, and Little Tokyo. Between 1980 and 1990 alone, the Asian population soared 119 percent in L.A. County, with most residing in the San Gabriel Valley.[41] Between 1990 and 2000, the county's Asian population continued to climb. Specifically, in the valley, the Asian population jumped another 20 percent, with the biggest jumps occurring in the East Valley suburbs of Walnut and Rowland Heights.[42]

Thanks to developer Fred Hsieh, the San Gabriel Valley was legible across the Pacific. In the 1970s, Hsieh promoted the West Valley suburb of Monterey Park as the "Chinese Beverly Hills" in advertisements throughout Asia.[43] Dubbed "America's first suburban Chinatown," Monterey Park introduced Asian immigrants to California and widened their imaginations in fulfilling the American Dream. As competition stiffened for single-family homes in Monterey Park and in nearby suburbs like Arcadia and San Marino, communities on the eastern side of the valley—once considered too far away from L.A.—were increasingly popular. In the mid-1980s, Hacienda Heights and Rowland Heights were hot housing markets among Chinese and Korean immigrants and their families. Soon after, Diamond Bar, Walnut, and then Chino Hills would join the list, creating another stream of Chinese and Korean settlement in the valley, with the latter two communities especially popular among Filipinos.

A critical factor in drawing in Asian residents to the East Valley was the role of direct advertising. Homebuilders and realtors targeted Asian buyers interested in country living suburbia. One of the earliest marketing materials explicitly soliciting Asian buyers was a 1983 ad for the North Country tract. It featured a multiethnic trio of married couples. Based on their surnames— the Lees, the Brownings, and the Jungs—this trio of Chinese, white, and Korean homeowners resided in one of the newest country living subdivisions of Diamond Bar and Rowland Heights.[44] Not only did the tract sit against the backdrop of a pristine pastoral setting, but also its homes were affordable, due in part to low interest rates, enticing young families to settle east. Paid newspaper articles began showcasing Asian families, thus generating greater interest in the East Valley. In a 1990 *Los Angeles Times* feature, William Lyon Co. highlighted the success of an upper-middle-class Filipino family. They lived in a new Timberline tract home set amid "panoramic views of . . . [the] hills and valleys" of Walnut and Diamond Bar. In the

FIGURE 10. North Country (Diamond Bar, CA & Rowland Heights, CA) new tract homes advertisement, *Los Angeles Times*, February 5, 1983. Image courtesy of *Los Angeles Times*.

piece, Alfonso and Linda Ancheta hailed Timberline's location as "close to everywhere," making it ideal for "family outings."[45] As baseball fans, their proximity to Dodger and Anaheim stadiums, as well as other recreational sites—parks, Orange County beaches, and Lake Perris—were among the benefits of homeownership in Walnut. As an architect, Alfonso appreciated what he deemed the "outstanding" construction quality of their home. Despite the Anchetas' unassuming, assimilated ways, they were a transnational family who "still retain[ed] their ties with their Mother Land" through Filipino provincial associations and charitable groups working in the Philippines.[46] Even with their global connections, paid features like this stressed the race-neutral, "all-American" nature of country living, attempting to paint immigrant families who occupied them as largely stripped of their ethnic heritage and happily navigating their lives as suburban homeowners.

Builders, realtors, advertisers, and other actors were increasingly attuned to the cultural particularities involved when Asian buyers—particularly Chinese families—searched for property. Terrence Hanna, president of the L.A. division of J.M. Peters Co., said builders producing houses in the East Valley recognized "that a white, two-child two-parent family is not the only market anymore." In new subdivisions like J.M. Peters's Walnut Estates tract, they were "targeting an affluent Asian executive family" who wanted a traditional suburban home but with Asian-friendly touches.[47] Corporate builders altered their design and marketing strategies with Asian buyers in mind. Model homes were staged to help immigrants imagine their lives in the suburbs. This included Chinese cookbooks displayed in the kitchen, red silk slippers in the master bedroom, and "good luck" cat statues or money trees in the foyer. Photographs on the wall of sales offices were of Asian families relishing in the suburban good life. Builders offered pamphlets in English, Mandarin Chinese, and Korean and emphasized the East Valley's wholesome, sylvan ambiance. The influx of Pacific Rim capital pressured multinational homebuilders like Shea Homes to hire bilingual Chinese and Korean sales agents for their East Valley tracts. Asian agents received corporate training on customer service. These agents also educated their white employers and coworkers about cultural traits, habits, and sensitivities. This included the propensity for haggling or holding frank, less-than-chummy conversations.[48] These strategies worked. One *Los Angeles Times* piece acknowledged the shift of Asian immigrant settlement, moving inland and to the outer reaches of L.A. County: "Neighborhoods [in the San Gabriel Valley] are in transition. A recent influx of immigrants, mostly from Pacific Rim countries, is gradually changing the ethnic makeup. . . . Families from Taiwan and Hong Kong, once concentrated in the western San Gabriel Valley cities of Alhambra, Arcadia, and Monterey Park, are drifting eastward to Hacienda Heights, Walnut and Diamond Bar, where schools are considered better, land is cheaper and houses are newer."[49]

Many Asian suburbanites came from or previously lived in dense cities like Taipei, Hong Kong, Shanghai, Manila, and Seoul. Even for immigrants who preferred an urban lifestyle in Asia, like their white neighbors, the prospect of living in an American city was not a viable option. From New York to L.A., American cities were seen as places infested with drugs, crime, gangs, homelessness, and rampant violence, with much of these vices or problems stereotypically associated with African Americans and the urban poor. Moreover, the unreliability or perceived lack of safety of public transit coupled with L.A.'s devotion to the private automobile deterred Asians accustomed to well-funded, high-functioning transport systems like those of Hong Kong. Immigrants were attuned to such perceptions of American urbanism as consumers of internationally disseminated news and media in the mid- and late twentieth century.[50] In contrast (and simultaneously), the ubiquity of golden California living in popular culture informed their reasons to suburbanize once in L.A. No matter their origins, the East Valley epitomized a modern American lifestyle. Yet because of its rural aesthetics, it evoked a type of traditionalism and familiarity buyers sought as well. In parts of Hong Kong and Taiwan, for example, English-language textbooks for overseas Chinese kids promoted American suburbanization as the symbol of assimilation. Illustrations depicted suburban landscapes as normative, respectable, and aspirational.[51] To be sure, these were ideas Asian families already in America also absorbed, including those who were able to penetrate California's white suburbs before the 1970s. During the early Cold War, white residents in L.A. and Bay Area suburbs gradually accepted Asian families because they were seen as non-threatening minority neighbors as well as proxy allies during US interventions in the Pacific.[52] Some politicians even claimed that the admittance of Asian families in suburbia was an example of why America was not a racist society, attempting to counter communists' and civil rights advocates' criticisms.[53]

Asian immigrants believed a home to call their own was a hallmark of the American Dream, a legible concept to many families before touching ground in the United States. As Nancy Kwak notes, American hegemony in postwar geopolitics widely promoted homeownership as a universal want.[54] Providing access to homeownership was a key part of US international aid initiatives because homeownership was understood as a bulwark against communism. Across South and Southeast Asia, for example, American experts including United Nations officials assisted in state-based programs advancing "homeownership for all," an ideal that government leaders and civilians alike embraced as a symbol of modernity.[55] For Asian immigrants, suburban homeownership served as a signifier of social citizenship and meant one achieved a critical stage of Americanization. These were things their white neighbors did not have to prove or think about because they were the racial default of postwar suburbia. As Eric Pido argues, the idea of "being American" and experiencing the American Dream for Asian families—particularly Filipino families—was "intrinsically tied to property ownership in suburban neighborhoods."[56] Filipinos practiced "homeownership as a way of performing citizenship" in a society that rendered Asian families unfit for citizenship and alien to the suburban way of life.[57]

Beyond these reasons, one lesser known but important catalyst in attracting Asians to East Valley suburbia was the emergence of *feng shui* homes. From the outside, these houses looked like typical single-family residences. But they were built with distinct features attractive to—if not necessary for—families who followed *feng shui*. Entire tracts or house models were designed in accordance with the principles and rules of the ancient Chinese tradition. *Feng shui* homes were ubiquitous in the region yet their ethnic-specific characteristics were invisible to the naked eye. A homeowner who complied with *feng shui* guidelines welcomed positive *chi* (energy) and financial prosperity. For example, if a home faced a "T-junction," placing an octagonal mirror above the front door prevented negative energy from ramming through the entrance. If a house had an indoor staircase in front of a door, this meant family fortunes would flow out. Placing large plants or a vase of fresh flowers in between facilitated the circulation of positive *chi*, remedying this design flaw. *Feng shui*'s appeal cut across class lines in the Chinese community, but the tradition—or for some, the superstition—was also practiced among other Asian groups (e.g., ethnic Chinese from the Philippines or Vietnam) who believed *feng shui* brought households good luck.[58]

Lewis Homes and Kaufman & Broad (KB) Homes were among the first companies to hire *feng shui* consultants or masters, a business strategy that began in the San Gabriel Valley during the 1980s. *Feng shui* consultants advised architects, landscapers, and interior decorators on how to entice discerning Chinese customers in the valley's popular housing markets. For example, consultants suggested planting red flowers around tracts to signify and invite good luck. They recommended not placing master bedrooms directly above kitchens since it symbolized the burning of a family's bed, which put heterosexual marriages in danger. Beyond *feng shui* itself, consultants were cultural ambassadors. They provided architectural suggestions based on the needs of East and Southeast Asian families. A typical *feng shui* home included staircases away from the front and back doors, choice window placement, fully equipped kitchens with gas stoves and strong ventilation amenable for wok cooking, larders able to accommodate provisions for multigenerational households, and sizable cabinets to "store 50-pound bags of rice."[59] Some builders offered models up to eight bedrooms to accommodate extended families (8 being a lucky number for Chinese families), while others customized foyer cabinetry for storing footwear since Asian families generally considered wearing shoes indoors a serious faux pas.[60]

Over time, developers in the East Valley consulted *feng shui* experts as a practice. This prevented the construction of unsellable houses. One of Lewis Homes' master-planned communities in Walnut served as a cautionary tale. In 1988, Lewis Homes unveiled their model homes for The Terraces and The Summit at Walnut Ridge. Houses ranged from 1,679 to 2,708 square feet and were priced from $320,000 to well over $400,000.[61] While these homes sold at a quick pace, Lewis executives noticed one of their plans was harder to sell, particularly among Chinese buyers, who were a significant share of the market. Puzzled at the model's weak sales, corporate executives asked their sales representatives about this trend. According to Lewis Homes staff, prospective buyers from Hong Kong and Taiwan rejected this specific model because of the exposed wooden beam, a critical design element that deterred good *chi*. Lewis Homes swiftly removed the open beams in unsold models. The decision paid off, and all updated models sold as quickly as the other plans. According to Randall Lewis, Lewis Homes yielded to immigrants' demands because "paying attention to Chinese superstitions is no different than designing for the varying housing needs of childless couples."[62] And after years of wondering why they struggled to tap into the market of wealthy Asian buyers, Lewis figured it was time to learn about *feng shui*. Ever since, they have integrated *feng shui* design as a regional strategy to ensure quicker sales.[63] Small- and large-scale developers—most of whom were run by white executives—were unaware of these cultural customs. Executives such as Mark Beiswanger, a division president of KB Homes, considered these beliefs odd, yet he recognized their power in real estate: "If it's a predominantly Asian market and people believe in it, and it's very important . . . we will plot houses in particular directions, change interior parts, the landscaping and where you put it."[64] Selling homes was the primary objective, and since wealthy Chinese immigrants purchased houses in full and in cash, builders were happy to oblige.

The *feng shui* readiness of an East Valley home emerged as a serious deal-breaker. Some immigrants abided by the principles so strictly that even one design flaw was enough to rule out a property or an entire neighborhood. Valerie Yu, the project manager at Walnut's Belgate Estates tract, witnessed dozens of Chinese clients walk away from expensive deals should *feng shui* consultants mark homes unlivable. They might lose a nonrefundable deposit, but they considered it worth the financial hit if it meant their long-term well-being.[65] One customer lost a $15,000 deposit because a *feng shui* master said the house was inauspicious. Though builders still profited from failed deals, it was worse to not be able to sell houses at all. Builders increasingly implemented preventative measures by creating units guaranteed to sell.[66] Catering to this niche market was lucrative. In the late 1980s and early 1990s, when home sales slowed down across the state, existing and new homes in the valley continued to sell at a steady rate due in part to Asian buyers. Developers realized the Asian consumer was a vital demographic for successful profits. When asked why the Southland housing market was strong in select parts of L.A. and Orange counties, Randall Lewis claimed foreign investment and Asian immigrants kept sales strong: "By foreign investment, I don't mean just Japanese, but the whole Pacific Rim, including Chinese, Koreans, and Filipinos," with the latter three groups prioritizing the East Valley.[67]

Beyond aesthetics, *feng shui* consultants and cultural liaisons advised builders and city planners to exclude the number 4 in home addresses. Traditional Chinese buyers considered 4 a "bad luck" number since it sounds similar to the Chinese word for "death." In new country living tracts, builders often omitted 4 from their roster of addresses while integrating 8 in disproportionate amounts.[68] For those who could not overlook a 4, homeowners paid city and county governments to alter their addresses. Initially, municipalities did not charge property owners to change their home or business address. Eventually, cities picked up on a trend of wealthy Chinese buyers willing to shell out money for this service.[69] By the 1990s, cities with substantial Chinese populations (20% or more) charged among the highest fees in the region. West Valley ethnoburbs Monterey Park and Arcadia charged $500 to change an address while San Gabriel charged $750. In the East Valley, Walnut charged $450 while Diamond Bar charged about $375 (on top of a required $1,000 deposit). In contrast, suburbs with low Chinese populations (0–10%) charged double-digit fees or made the changes gratis.[70] In Monterey Park, officials claimed the fees were justifiable. As the first valley suburb to institute an address change fee in 1986, city leaders and bureaucrats claimed they were being inconvenienced even though most of the critical, logistical work took place at the county or post office level.[71] Asian leaders and civil rights advocates accused suburbs like Diamond Bar, Walnut, San Gabriel, and Monterey Park of implementing exorbitant fees to take advantage of their new, oftentimes affluent Chinese neighbors. Critics claimed local leaders dismissed these as trivial superstitions yet benefitted because the fees were a cash cow for city governments. By the mid-1990s, rather than have Chinese families hassle with address changes (and because it helped sell homes) numerous builders opted out of the 4 for everyone's sake.

These seemingly innocuous, culturally specific design elements and modifications to single-family houses—all of which were subtle and invisible to folks from the outside—made a tremendous impact on the built environment. Moreover, developers' targeted strategies and desires to sell homes resulted in a major turn in the region's demographics. Race did not matter to profit-driven actors as much as money. Asian immigrants made it possible for builders and realtors to put up sold signs every day. Families of the third wave had the global capital and interest in owning a country living home. Imperceptible touches of ethnic expression like *feng shui* design sweetened the deal and helped make the East Valley a hub of Asian America.

. . .

> Many [Asian] immigrants have come to Walnut. Asian people value education and good living conditions. Just like [me] in the 1980s. . . . Asians have decided that this place is well-suited to inhabit . . . since we have mountains, bodies of water, nature, and forests. Walnut is extremely cozy.
>
> —M A R Y   S U, Walnut homeowner and city council member[72]

> Chino Hills has thirty-eight different parks, all very pretty. There are mountains and water to see at one's desire. The scenery at night is also particularly beautiful. There are benefits to living in Chino Hills. Chino Hills has never changed . . . Since the city's inception, there were clear plans and rules in developing the city. As a result, our streets are nice and wide. Our houses are new and pretty. So in this regard, Chino Hills is a very comfortable place to live . . . In Spanish, "Chino" itself means China. Therefore, Chino Hills really means China Hills.
>
> —W E I M I N G   L I A O, Chino Hills homeowner and president of Chinese American Association of Chino Hills[73]

Among this third wave of settlers was Joaquin Lim. Originally from Hong Kong, Joaquin moved to Walnut in 1986 citing its affordability for new single-family homes. While Joaquin called himself a "city man" accustomed to the hubbub of urban life, he wanted to raise his two daughters in the suburbs. He cited crime, gangs, and drug use as reasons to avoid Los Angeles.[74] He initially wanted to buy a home in San Marino, a tony West Valley suburb renowned for its stately mansions, elegant thoroughfares, and high-performing schools. At the time, home prices in San Marino were $30,000–35,000 over his budget, an amount he was not willing to pay since the houses were older and smaller than what he could get by moving east into the county. The move-in condition of a typical Walnut house was a plus for recently arrived immigrant families who immediately started new jobs upon arriving to the United States. Thanks to aggressive marketing from Chinese realtors in Asia and in Southern California, immigrants like Joaquin heard through word of mouth that other parts of the valley had good schools including Walnut and Diamond Bar. Access to a solid public K–12 education was a major factor in his decision to buy in Walnut, so Joaquin purchased a single-family home in the master-planned tract of Snow Creek. An economist and business consultant, Joaquin's white-collar background fit the bill of what developers imagined as their primary clientele.

Joaquin believed Walnut's country living milieu ultimately sold him and others to the East Valley: "I think the majority of people I know in Walnut . . . think [of Walnut as a] pastoral community. . . . Those parks, those open spaces, those are the things that have drawn them to Walnut in addition to the school district."[75] Indeed, Chinese-language media agreed and painted country living suburbs as desirable commodities for well-to-do immigrants, thus helping intensify the demand. In a real estate and travel series by an L.A.-based Taiwanese television station, the narrator remarked Walnut's "relaxing walkways . . . fields full of rural greenery . . . ninety acres of parks, exercise space, and trails . . . gives a deep impression of [a] European village." Thus, "Walnut has long been a model American city . . . [and] as such, many Chinese people have made the decision to take root" in the master-planned town.[76]

Joaquin's appreciation for Southern California traces back to his upbringing in Asia. While attending international school in Hong Kong, he was exposed to British and American media throughout his youth. He watched globally distributed American films and television shows, listened to American music, and read American magazines such as *Time, Life,* and *Mad.* The motion picture industry was particularly influential in exporting ideas and images of a happy, perennially sunny L.A. As John Findlay notes, "The movies . . . promoted Los Angeles around the world, helped form the city's identity and style, and made it into the first American cultural hearth west of the Mississippi River."[77] Popular culture idealized the West Coast and its manicured suburbs as a glamorous standard of modern American living. Those ideas circulated from Hollywood to Hong Kong. Joaquin thought places like Walnut epitomized the ideal suburban lifestyle he admired during his childhood: "[America] was paradise" and it was "exactly what I wanted."[78] Furthermore, Joaquin thought American meritocracy provided freedoms unheard of in British colonial Hong Kong. Homeownership, to him, was accessible and achievable if one worked hard enough. Joaquin suggested suburban homeownership was the ultimate symbol of fulfilling the American Dream. In numerous ways, Joaquin measured his assimilation by the fact that he owned property in a fashionable L.A. suburb.

Echoing Joaquin's sentiments, Walnut homeowner and Filipino immigrant Bella Cristobal did not understand the appeal of urbanism. After living in L.A. and then in the working-class suburb of South Gate during the late 1970s, Bella and her husband Chris happily fled to the East Valley. They settled in West Covina in 1979 because "a lot of young people" were purchasing homes in the booming suburb.[79] They were also uncomfortable in L.A. and South Gate, which they believed were dangerous places. Bella recalled the race of securing an East Valley home: "During that time when my husband and his friends tried to buy a house [in West Covina], there were only like sixty-four houses for sale [in a new tract]. So, they announced and said, 'Okay, on Saturday we will be selling houses.' . . . But on Friday, people were already [in] line . . . staying overnight even."[80] The Cristobals were so anxious to leave South Gate they had no qualms about standing in long queues on their free time. In 1985, they moved to the neighboring town of Walnut, which they considered an upgrade. Bella found Walnut's newer housing stock, higher-performing public schools, and its reputation as a country living suburb an attractive alternative. She believed living in Walnut—with its strawberry patches, lemon groves, and cattle ranches—was the closest thing to residing on a farm in Los Angeles County. Its bucolic settings were warmly familiar since she grew up on a large family compound in the Philippine countryside. At the same time, Bella joked, "We weren't looking for *country* country!" She still wanted the conveniences of a freshly built master-planned community. Walnut's idyllic character was icing on the cake.[81] She also noted that unlike L.A. and its inner-ring suburbs, the East

Valley's far-flung distance ensured her physical safety and a layer of protection from urban vice. Walnut's manicured environment suggested order, calm, and a "civilized" citizenry: "It's peaceful [in Walnut]. You [can] go to the park [and not] be scared of crimes being committed [unlike in L.A. or South Gate]. You know you feel safe. You're not scared that there [are] people [here] who will hurt you."[82]

Like Joaquin, Bella cited the influence of popular culture as one of the reasons she pursued country living. She said, "[In the Philippines] we see the picture[s] of how Americans have these big houses, OK? You see the movies . . . movies where you have the country and a lot of people love country [living]. [Filipinos] love the country setting."[83] Agrarianism—whether in the Philippines or in their new home of America—appealed to Filipinos regardless of their class or geographic upbringing. While pastoral provinces in the Philippines were far from affluent, the cultural innocence of the countryside resonated with immigrants, including those who grew up in some of Asia's densest cities (e.g., Manila). The Cristobals' motivations to leave L.A. and buy a cheaper home brought them to the East Valley. But their quest to experience country living further encouraged them to settle outside city limits. Positive perceptions of rural and suburban landscapes in both Philippine and American culture coupled with their negative experiences in urban or "urban-like" suburbs made towns like Walnut the ideal place to build a life as Americans.

For Walnut homeowner Ivy Kuan, neighborhood ambiance and proximity to work mattered in deciding where to live. Originally from Taiwan, Ivy moved to Boston in 1974 to attend college. After receiving undergraduate and graduate degrees in engineering, she contemplated a position at Kodak in Rochester, NY. However, Ivy sought to leave the Northeast. Her sister lived in Southern California and urged her to consider Los Angeles. In 1980, Ivy hired a recruiter to help her find a job. She resided in the San Fernando Valley neighborhood of Canoga Park for a few years. When she married her then husband Miles, also a Taiwanese immigrant, they moved to the South Bay suburb of Torrance. In 1989, Ivy wanted to be near her new job in Monrovia, a West Valley suburb. Following the advice of her Taiwanese friends, they planned to buy a home in Arcadia. Despite its prestige, they were unconvinced Arcadia was a good place to invest since the housing stock was older and costlier than elsewhere in the region. When Ivy was about to start a new job in the East Valley suburb of San Dimas, she consulted with her sister-in-law who was a local realtor; she suggested Walnut.

In 1990, Ivy and Miles found a two-story house in the Meadowpass neighborhood, an area comprised of upscale mansions as well as modest houses zoned for rearing small animals and horses. Though Ivy liked the home, she initially had mixed feelings about the community. "In the beginning," Ivy said, "I thought Walnut was a little bit far.... [But] I heard about [its] good school district ... and the newness of the house mattered."[84] Ivy disliked the neighborhood's minimal infrastructure (e.g., dirt roads, limited street lighting), which she did not know until later was intentional. Older Meadowpass homeowners—most of whom resided in smaller dwellings (built before the new housing boom of the 1980s and 1990s)—enjoyed the rustic feel and railed against formal landscaping or aesthetic modifications.

Ivy recalled reading a leaflet listing the unique rules of her neighborhood: "The brochure said the good part [about living in Meadowpass was that] you can have horses, sheep, raise chickens, stuff people usually cannot [raise]" in typical subdivisions.[85] For her family, the allowance of small farm animals in their backyard was neither a priority nor desired, and that it was "too country" for their liking. One of the least appealing aspects of what Ivy called "Walnut's rural atmosphere" was in front of and alongside their home: a heavily trafficked horse trail.[86] She did not mind horses and their owners riding the paths. But Ivy found the piles of manure left behind and equestrians peering into their lot an annoyance. Her family preferred concrete sidewalks typical in newer tracts around town. After several years of homeownership in Meadowpass, Ivy and Miles wrote a petition asking the city to pave over or reroute the trail. About thirty neighbors signed the petition. Longtime white equestrians, especially those from Walnut's Old Guard, believed Miles, Ivy, and the signatories did not fully appreciate Walnut's "rural" lifestyle. They suggested Walnut's newcomers—a significant portion of them being affluent Asian immigrants—were disrespectful of the area's heritage. They expressed confusion as to why homeowners like Ivy claimed they wanted country living but disliked the idea of being among wildlife and other natural elements.[87] For some Asian residents including Ivy and Miles, the qualities and characteristics of country living were best appreciated in distant greenbelts or through symbols in the built environment—not on their yard.

While Walnut's rurality eventually won over early skeptics like Ivy, many Asian immigrants said they chose these East Valley suburbs precisely for their bucolic settings. Those who intentionally sought country living juxtaposed these communities against L.A. and older postwar suburbs that epitomized the failures of poor planning and urbanism. Aging infrastructure, crime, and perceptions of congestion or disorder pushed white-collar immigrants farther away from the city. Diamond Bar homeowner Simon Ha suggested unlike the residents of L.A. or the West Valley ethnoburbs of Monterey Park and Alhambra, the East Valley's landscapes and residents were refined. Originally from Taipei, Taiwan, Simon worked as a ship engineer for Mobil Oil. He met his wife Bonnie, also from Taipei, through his uncle's import-export company. They married in June 1983 and decided to move to the United States that fall. Encouraged by a family friend living in New York City, Simon and Bonnie settled in Harlem off 124th Street and Lenox Avenue. They worked at their friend's Chinese take-out restaurant for six months. They decided to move to L.A. once Bonnie learned she was pregnant with their first child, Maggie. Simon joked, "We didn't know how to cook" and felt it was time to seek other types of work.[88] More importantly, Simon did not see Manhattan as suitable for raising children: "I think if I stayed there, my future . . . (sigh) I [didn't want it to] be like that, [working] in the kitchen. And that area is not good for a family."[89] Bonnie and Simon agreed to find a way to get out of the working-class barrio.

One of Simon's best friends from Taiwan, Jimmy Liu, lived in the South L.A. suburb of Cerritos and encouraged the Has to resettle on the West Coast. Simon was intrigued, having heard about Southern California's salubrious weather through friends and from literature he read in Taiwan. Los Angeles seemed particularly attractive after surviving "a really bad cold" and fever his first month in Harlem.[90] He felt the East Coast was unhealthful and gloomy. Settling in Southern California was a necessary lifestyle change from "everything [being] gray in New York," sentiments Sunbelt transplants have expressed and mythologized since the nineteenth century.[91] Simon praised L.A. for its uplifting surroundings which, in turn, reinvigorated his optimism for the American Dream. Having a friend in L.A. coupled with the growing availability of Chinese retail options eased Simon and Bonnie's decision to move. It also reaffirmed their decision to move to America. Upon arriving to Southern California, they lived with Jimmy for a month and then moved to the City of Commerce, where Simon worked in the swap meet business. The Has moved to Monterey Park in 1985. They ran a pizza shop in nearby San Gabriel and lived behind the pizzeria for a couple years. With a stable business, a growing family, and a desire to leave San Gabriel, the Has looked eastward for a newer, bigger home. Simon hired a Taiwanese realtor he found through *World Journal*, a

US-based Chinese-language newspaper with one of its national headquarters located in Monterey Park.

The Has originally had their eyes set on Hacienda Heights, but that was not rural enough for them. Moreover, they believed Hacienda Heights' homes were dated and not as elegant as those in surrounding towns. After talking with their realtor, Simon had a change of heart: "My agent said 'Why not [try] Diamond Bar? Take a look.' They brought me to Diamond Bar and I said, 'Oh nice! Countryside! Quiet! It's my dream house here . . .' [It's] more country—which is why I moved to Diamond Bar" in 1988.[92] Diamond Bar's idyllic setting suggested a type of calm and order not found in L.A. or the West Valley. They preferred Diamond Bar's orderly, master-planned setup. For homeowners who shared Simon's perspective, tightly controlled "rural" landscapes like Diamond Bar, Walnut, Phillips Ranch, and Chino Hills were, ironically, more authentic. Simon's daughter, Maggie, claimed her father boasted about the spaciousness, grandeur, and novelty of country living. Homeownership in the area symbolized their hard-fought success at making it in America: "He would say, 'We live in the hills! Look how beautiful it is.' We're not crammed in like other people are. . . . He said that while we grew up to make us appreciate what we have. Even when we first moved here, late at night it was so quiet the only sounds you ever heard at night was a couple trains in the distance. That's all you heard. [And] there was still wildlife: squirrels, raccoons . . . you feel like you're in the countryside."[93] For Simon, suburbanization was the actualization of the American Dream. The cherry on top was having a country living address, which added prestige to his identity as a homeowner and as an Asian immigrant.

Simon and his cohort of settlers considered suburbs like Diamond Bar as prime examples of western frontier nostalgia. But critics questioned whether Diamond Bar could still claim an agrarian identity as the East Valley's population continued to soar as well as diversify. As the region's Asian population increased, residents worried that Diamond Bar was on its way to becoming the next Monterey Park—that is, a suburb with a hyper-visible Asian presence. In 1988, the year the Has moved to Diamond Bar, white residents were sowing the seeds for cityhood (also known as incorporation). Pro-incorporation activists claimed becoming a city would protect Diamond Bar's country living image because they would have greater local control. For cityhood supporters, East Valley rurality was under threat amid these demographic shifts and transformations in the built environment as seen in neighboring Hacienda Heights, Rowland Heights, and City of Industry.

Debates around incorporation occurred amid Slow Growth movements happening across the valley, signaling a strong connection between these respective political causes.[94]

On the whole, despite critics alleging that Asian immigrants lacked a respect for country living, homeowners like Simon, Ivy, Bella, and Joaquin appreciated the region's pastoral character and sought this lifestyle. This was partly why they deliberately avoided Asian ethnoburbs, which contained built landscapes characterized as déclassé and far from what they understood as American. Asian homeowners knew the East Valley prided itself as a place that cherished its rural western past. Though not considered typical suburbanites (i.e., middle-class, native-born, white), Asian immigrants did not want to disrupt the status quo. This was because of their reverence for the valley's agrarian heritage. It was also out of a desire to assimilate. Asian families in country living often abided by the unwritten rules of suburbia to ensure their presence was muted. As they saw it: Asian immigrants were new suburbanites, new citizens, and were not on the same plane as "true" Americans (i.e., white Americans). That is not to suggest Asian suburbanites were not American, were racially inferior, or were subservient to their white neighbors. Rather, instead of making a splash in the suburbs, Asian residents unconsciously and consciously assumed the role of "model minority." Over time, Chinese, Filipino, and Korean homeowners in wealthier suburbs used social control over their co-ethnics to prevent perceivably transgressive behavior (e.g., renovating a home's exterior to look "typically" Asian in design). Asian families disciplined each other as much as they were constrained by the influence of their white neighbors who watched to make sure they did not cross the line. Despite efforts to prove their boundless devotion to being upstanding Americans (evidenced in suburban homeownership), Asian immigrants remained outsiders and foreign in the eyes of their critics. By the mid-1990s, Asian homeowners used their power in numbers to shift these dynamics and assume greater control over the East Valley.

. . .

The East San Gabriel Valley attracted residents who wanted to experience a rural way of life. Despite differences in race, class, generation, or country of origin, three waves of East Valley suburbanites rallied around a set of ideals and interests. That is: to live in a romanticized, mythologized bygone era of the western frontier and to achieve the suburban American Dream. Set against the backdrop of the Cold War and an increasingly global L.A., the East Valley's boom was a product of anti-urbanism; a repudiation of liberalism; and a confirmation that the campaigns and media propaganda boasting sunny Southern California resonated beyond American borders.

Well into the twenty-first century, country living shaped how East Valley homeowners conducted their lives, engaged in civic activity, and built relationships with their neighbors. The region's increasing heterogeneity resulted in tensions and growing pains between the three waves of postwar settlers, inhibiting possibilities for community building. As Asian immigrants emerged as the primary cohort of new residents by the late 1980s and 1990s, the lifestyle and rhetoric of country living evolved into a political tool. It set the boundaries of who and what belonged in these towns. Amid social pressures to embrace multiculturalism and broad notions of racial liberalism (e.g., "tolerance") in the closing decades of the late twentieth century, residents widely utilized country living to dictate the terms of inclusion, thus demonstrating residents' weak commitments to suburban diversity from the start. At the same time, as illustrated in the remaining chapters, the politics and cultures of country living ironically served as a class-based source of unity for residents across racial lines. Ultimately, the intrigue of country living brought together disparate populations who, despite their differences, otherwise lived in equanimity or worked toward achieving it.

THREE

Asian Families Making a Home in the Suburbs

THROUGHOUT THE 1980S AND 1990S, newspapers across the United States wrote about an unusual phenomenon happening in Los Angeles: the suburbanization of Asian immigrants in the San Gabriel Valley. From the *New York Times* to *Wall Street Journal*, journalists, think tanks, and social scientists wanted to understand what brought Asian families—particularly diasporic Chinese—to Southern California. Stories suggested they exoticized lily-white towns, lacked the desire or wherewithal to assimilate, and disrupted suburbia's equilibrium. But what was often left out of these write-ups was how Asians attempted to integrate into the suburbs. They did so in ways less obvious to the naked eye. In actuality, Asian immigrants demonstrated a willingness to comply or integrate albeit in a manner that did not always appease all skeptics.

Asians' processes of suburbanization were dissimilar to the post–World War II settlement of ethnic Europeans, whose whiteness gave them access not afforded to immigrants from the so-called Pacific Rim. Ideas of the Asian "other"—sentiments developed well before they settled in the United States—made it harder for them to "blend in" the way Irish, Italian, or Polish immigrants were able. Beyond physical characteristics, the diversity of Asian languages, religions, and social practices accentuated cultural differences, concretizing their peripheral position in suburbia—a place popularly understood as reserved for white families. Asians' stranger status complicated their attempts to assimilate or—at the very least—adapt to a mainstream lifestyle dictated by a Euro-American middle class. Wealth granted Asian families some latitude and advantages, but it did not translate into full acceptance.

This chapter explores the ways in which Asian immigrants fashioned spaces of belonging in the East San Gabriel Valley through the incorporation of ethnic-based religious and retail spaces. Rather than being seen as acts or sites of cultural retaliation, I argue that these landscapes were gestures toward assimilation. Immigrants believed houses of worship and businesses catering to their needs eased their transition to their new host country. In numerous ways, these sites gave them a sense of place as new suburbanites and as new Americans. While critics lambasted or read these landscapes as "for Asians only," these were otherwise everyday fixtures of postwar suburbia—that is, churches, temples, and shopping centers.[1]

The influx of spaces tailored for immigrants were seldom welcomed, especially in the early years of mass Asian settlement. By not wholly "blending in," white residents believed Asian families engaged in misconduct, breaking the rules of suburbanization and concurrently, assimilation. Because immigrant landscapes were not aimed at a white clientele, critics targeted them. They articulated their concerns through coded language or positioned Asian residents as the figures of exclusion, not white residents. Despite these criticisms, on the whole, Asian immigrants abided by the "all-American" ideals of heteronormative suburban conformity. They were doing what non-Asian suburbanites were doing: worshipping and buying stuff. And though they were berated for introducing divergent or deviant forms of homemaking, Asian families generally followed social cues because embracing the local cultures of "country living" afforded them degrees of privilege or a proximity to the privileges of whiteness Asians in less affluent suburbs did not experience. Chinese, Filipino, and Korean immigrants and their children practiced the mores expected of them as American suburbanites. They, however, selected what parts of their heritage to celebrate and what parts of mainstream Euro-American culture to accept. This give-and-take was a crucial strategy in how Asians navigated suburbia during a time of major transformation and racial anxieties across Southern California.

. . .

During the 1980s and 1990s, residents asked if country living was coming to an end as Asian families settled in the region. Critics, particularly white homeowners, held contradictory views on having Asian neighbors, resulting in a torrent of mixed messages. The sharpest critics perceived Asians as a grave threat to suburbia and attempted to exclude them by any means necessary. On the whole, however, Asian suburbanites found earnest or tepid support from white allies and other people of color who were invested in helping them integrate or assimilate. However, that support came with conditions. That is, while practicing Asian culture was permissible in the private domain, Asians were expected to keep public displays of ethnic expression to a minimum. For those who crossed the line, critics alleged Asian residents disrespected suburban tradition. Asian immigrants were subject to a type of criticism that not only questioned their legitimacy as suburbanites but as Americans too. In perceived moments of transgression, local leaders responded by enacting building ordinances, design measures, and zoning laws intended to conceal or halt displays of Asian language and aesthetics. These actions—often passed under the guise of safety and visual continuity—veiled the prejudiced motivations of those who created or backed these policies. In numerous cases, municipalities covertly enacted these codes before Asians reached a critical mass. Essentially, these forms of social control allowed critics to pass certain political agendas while not looking racist or xenophobic. In effect, muting Asian culture—by, for example, enforcing use of the English language—protected the force of whiteness and maintained the status quo of postwar suburbia. No matter how diverse these suburbs became, the cultures and landscapes of the East Valley would suggest that white families remained the racial majority and in power.

Outsiders interpreted these acts as solely stemming from white NIMBY discontent.[2] But criticism of "too much" Asian culture on display came from Asian homeowners as well. Those in wealthier communities actively or tacitly supported design or spatial regulations because they too believed the ambiance of suburbia should embody Euro-American standards. Some of these attitudes stemmed from cultural beliefs in Asia. In Hong Kong, the Philippines, Vietnam, and India, European or Euro-American cultural imperialism through US, British, French, and Spanish rule situated whiteness as most desirable and dignified. For Asian families, maintaining the pastiche of country living protected prestige and thus encouraged them to comply with white homeowners' recommendations or pressures. By downplaying ethnicity in social settings and in the built environment, Asian residents endorsed the idea that suburbs perceived to be white (at least externally) held greater economic or social clout. Local officials and residents pressed Asian residents and property owners to subscribe to "design assimilation"—that is, limiting ethnic expression in architecture as a gesture of conformity to Euro-American suburban customs.[3] Asian suburbanites generally abided, particularly wealthier families. By taking this approach, the growing Asian population did not mar the landscape with perceptible "foreign" or "exotic" touches. Asians' compliance with these design norms perpetuated ideas of the "model minority"—which families generally understood as a positive stereotype—particularly when compared to the mostly negative stereotypes of Blacks and Latinos.

Asians' attachment to suburban mores and the "model minority" image ensured them a level of protection as people of color in "country living." That is, by not ruffling feathers, they would be left alone as the "exotic," racial "other." But those protections only went so far. Residents—including those who sought interethnic harmony and promoted inclusion—remained nonetheless critical of Asian suburbanites' moves and motivations. They held Asian families to higher standards and alleged they were not doing enough in proving their commitment to "country living." Even if their actions, rhetoric, or rumors suggested otherwise, Asian immigrants willingly made important concessions and forged key alliances so they too could feel at home in suburbia.

NOT ABOUT RACE OR RELIGION BUT FIT: THE CASE STUDIES OF HSI LAI AND ST. LORENZO

Though media and residents recognized the growing presence of Chinese, Filipino, and Korean immigrants across the East Valley, this demographic shift was not always apparent in the built environment, particularly in residential neighborhoods. The near-invisibility of Asian culture was especially evident in wealthier country living communities like Walnut, Diamond Bar, and Chino Hills, where their largely master-planned infrastructure and design correlated with ideas of Euro-American refinement or status. Along with residential and commercial spaces, religious sites were scrutinized if they did not conform to the ideals of "country living." Homeowners widely panned two particular projects: Hsi Lai Buddhist Temple in Hacienda Heights and St. Lorenzo Ruiz Catholic Church in Walnut. Critics rejected these immigrant-friendly religious sites citing concerns with aesthetics, land use, and the need to protect frontier nostalgia. Their usage of broad, coded language were mechanisms for veiling religious or racial apprehensions about the populations these spaces served.

To critics, Hsi Lai and St. Lorenzo did not attempt to conform to "country living." Opponents claimed they were not prejudiced or held nativist views; they were simply enforcing the formal and unspoken rules of local design.

It just so happens, they argued, that these sites catered to Asian families and those in support of these projects were politicizing white criticism. But many Hsi Lai and St. Lorenzo opponents knew the language they deployed mattered in fighting unwanted development. In the age of promoting multiculturalism and diversity, critics used seemingly innocuous, color-blind terms to avoid accusations of intolerance. These rhetorical strategies worked in delaying the projects from moving forward, but they were not successful in halting construction or stopping Asian suburbanization.

In Hacienda Heights, critics admonished Hsi Lai Temple's design, scale, and its potential to draw so-called "outsiders" into the community. Indeed, like any major religious complex, Hsi Lai attracted people from beyond Hacienda Heights. In this case, it was predominantly Chinese immigrants. The temple opened its doors in 1988, but its journey to the grand opening took nearly a decade. In 1979, members of Taiwan-based Fo Guan Shan (International Buddhist Progress Society [IBPS]) visited the United States to minister to L.A.'s growing Buddhist population. They initially established a makeshift temple in Gardena, a suburb located in the South Bay. A couple years later, temple leaders proposed construction of a twelve-acre worship grounds in the hills of Hacienda Heights. To the IBPS, the East Valley's ethereal setting and lush, open environment was an ideal spiritual site. Moreover, since four hundred of its worshipers lived in the valley, they felt it was apt to move closer to their homes.[4] In February 1981, the County of Los Angeles issued the IBPS a conditional use permit to allow construction of a temple complete with a main hall, offices, and living quarters for nuns and monks. Since the proposed temple followed zoning rules, IBPS leaders anticipated minimal challenges.[5]

Named Hsi Lai (translated "Coming West" in Chinese), the temple was estimated to cost five million dollars and was slated to be the largest Buddhist temple in the Western Hemisphere.[6] Regional planning authorities quietly approved the temple's plans, and the project was on its way toward groundbreaking until Hacienda Heights homeowners learned about its details. After Hsi Lai's application was introduced before the Los Angeles County Zoning Board, plans were immediately stalled when hundreds of letters opposing the project flooded county offices. In fall 1981, the Hacienda Heights Improvement Association (HHIA)—a homeowners association that liaised with county leadership and governed the unincorporated community—met with IBPS attorney Michael Hannon and Hsi Lai spokesman Tony Yang. They discussed the temple's plans before a standing room audience of two

FIGURE 11. Hsi Lai temple entrance, Hacienda Heights, CA, December 2011. Photo taken by James Zarsadiaz.

hundred attendees, most of whom came to express their disapproval.[7] Critics and supporters engaged in three hours of heated debate with Hannon, Yang, and zoning officials.[8]

Leading the charge against Hsi Lai was homeowner Sharon Pluth. She and a cadre of residents alleged the proposed temple violated zoning laws. They argued the temple's design was inappropriate and out of scale for a traditional bedroom community. Wilfred Briesmeister, president of the HHIA, agreed: "The (Hacienda Heights) general plan provides the hillsides be preserved. This is something more than a church in a residential area because of its size."[9] HHIA board member Glenda Smith believed Hsi Lai was not a religious space but more like a convention center. Opponents also compared the proposed temple to theme parks like Disneyland or Busch Gardens. Pluth claimed, "It's not just a community church. As residents, it's not fair to have something that big in our backyard."[10]

But Hannon, Yang, and Hsi Lai supporters believed residents' anger was not about the temple's size or design, nor was this a simple case of NIMBYism. Rather, supporters alleged that opponents' concerns were rooted in xenophobia and religious intolerance. County leaders said church proposals often received pushback, typically in regard to traffic. However,

Hsi Lai elicited stronger community reactions tinged with racism. These included disparagement of the temple's design and questions of Buddhism's legitimacy as a non-Western religion. Anna Fuller, a Hacienda Heights homeowner since 1977, said "it was terrible to build this thing in a residential area and bring all these kinds of people here that we're not used to."[11] Mark Volmert, an aide to L.A. County Supervisor Pete Schabarum—whose district included Hacienda Heights and most of the East Valley—believed the county and Hsi Lai leaders willingly negotiated with critics. Temple opponents, however, refused to cooperate or back down: "The truth of the matter was that the opposition . . . had less to do with the size of the project than with racial overtones. They were concerned it wouldn't be a Baptist church or something more familiar" as predominantly white, Christian homeowners.[12] Homeowners like Roy Taylor refuted those claims: "I don't care if they are Catholics or Buddhists or atheists. It just doesn't belong here." Longtime resident Miriam Jones similarly expressed that this was not about race or religion; this was about Hsi Lai unwilling to "conform to the community."

Critics further alleged the temple would be used for unusual ceremonies like animal sacrifices. Some homeowners believed Hsi Lai would ring loud gongs and emit noxious odors and incense throughout the day. Others confused Buddhists with Hare Krishnas or religious cults, all of whom did not belong in the suburbs.[13] Around the same years, thirty-seven miles away in the San Fernando Valley community of North Hollywood, white residents near the Wat Thai Buddhist temple expressed analogous concerns about Buddhism's foreignness and their impositions on the suburban status quo (i.e., Euro-American, Christian).[14] As Mark Padoongpatt argues, opposition to temples like Wat Thai reflected how homeowners were "constructing and articulating a suburban ideal in relation to their own perceptions of urban culture."[15] Critics associated ethnic landscapes with density, traffic, noise, and cultural heterogeneity—all of which were urban characteristics and defeated the purpose of suburban living. These concerns were only heightened in the East Valley's master-planned communities where conformity and rural innocence were pivotal to homeowners' identities.

To alleviate opponents' concerns, Hsi Lai temple leaders and architects quickly rescinded plans to build a twelve-story pagoda with "Chinese red" roofs and a seven-story Buddha statue. Critics said these symbols were far from the norms found on Christian churches. Instead of a traditional Buddhist temple color scheme of red, black, and gold, temple leaders agreed to use earth tones and "California-style tan and stucco colors" to minimize Hsi

Lai's exoticism.[16] Architects also agreed to a two-story height restriction. Vastly different from the original vision, temple leaders proposed these alterations as olive branches to wary residents. During the next five years, residents, Hsi Lai leaders, and county officials litigated the terms of the temple's construction. Critics knew the temple's construction was inevitable, but they found ways to delay the process by regularly proposing modifications to the project. Opponents hoped their suggestions to the temple's façade would further mute its presence even though Hsi Lai leaders consistently agreed to pare down its size and traditional Buddhist design.

In 1986, the Hsi Lai plan was approved thanks to a group of active temple worshippers and Buddhist residents who worked with county officials, HHIA, and critics. This was also due in part to oppositionists' fatigue from the ongoing battle. In addition, Hsi Lai leaders were able to convince enough residents that the temple would serve as a unique community venue.[17] Temple worshippers, along with nuns and monks who lived on a horse ranch across the street from the proposed site, reached out to neighbors and critics while the project was in limbo. As Hsi Lai neared completion, worshippers promoted a message of inclusion throughout Hacienda Heights. The congregation said the temple would welcome everyone. But their message was not fully received by all. Encounters with racism and religious discrimination remained common occurrences. In light of the harassment, Hsi Lai's monastic community had to keep a careful eye on the property until the temple was fully built and secure.[18]

Two years later, Hsi Lai opened its doors to the public. Temple leaders and worshippers continued their campaign to demystify Buddhism and change residents' perceptions. However, within months of opening, the temple was desecrated. Hsi Lai worshippers and community leaders fell victim to threats, theft, or direct acts of violence. On several occasions, vandals shattered priests' car windows and released open-air gunshots to frighten worshippers. In one instance, a jeep parked near the temple was set on fire.[19] In July 1989, an assailant hurled three Molotov cocktails at the home of Hsi Lai priest Pachri (Pat) Phongpharnich. Suspected as a hate crime, Phongpharnich urged "people to not be upset, [but] to be happy" and not let critics scare them away from Hacienda Heights.[20] In the spirit of pacifism, Phongpharnich encouraged the community to meditate, chant for peace, and projected—once again—the passivity expected of "model minorities." Hsi Lai leaders and worshippers were determined to not be seen as menaces nor react with anger, fearing further retribution.

FIGURE 12. Hsi Lai temple grounds, Hacienda Heights, CA, December 2011. Photo taken by James Zarsadiaz.

Over time, Hsi Lai was able to gain a foothold in Hacienda Heights. By forging partnerships with schools, nonprofit organizations, and businesses, they persuaded residents that their presence was not a threat to the suburban idyll, nor were they progenitors of an Asian-led movement to "take over" the valley, per critics' theories. Rather, Hsi Lai was just like other religious communities who wanted a place to practice. Nuns and monks proactively sought neighborhood acceptance by hosting open houses, making charitable contributions to civic groups, and extending personal invitations to non-Buddhists to their annual Chinese New Year celebrations. For example, the local Kiwanis Club emerged as a vital ally, particularly as Hacienda Heights' Chinese population climbed during the 1990s. Kiwanis president Bud Welch said his stance on Hsi Lai changed after getting to know its worshippers. He called the temple a "very attractive structure" and "an enhancement" to Hacienda Heights.[21]

Some residents changed positions after interacting with the monastic community or by educating themselves about Buddhism. This included homeowner and early Hsi Lai critic Sandy Johnson: "I have no problems with the Buddhists being there. Sometimes things like that can enrich a community."[22] John Healy, a homeowner since 1978, considered Hsi Lai a "good neighbor." Healy, once adamantly against the temple, told the *Los Angeles Times*, "We see them [nuns and priests] on the street, and wave and say hello."[23] Donna Wedell—another Hacienda Heights resident—admitted, "I probably wasn't as accepting 10 years ago as I am now. [Demographic changes] bothered me before, and I had to relearn some things [about acceptance]."[24] Wedell, a part-time teacher and president of the local Parent Teacher Association (PTA), said spending time with Asian parents and their children helped her "understand the differences better" while encouraging her to adapt to a diversifying suburb.[25]

After a period of growing pains, Hsi Lai Buddhists passed muster as suburbanites who shared similar values of social conservatism palatable to their white neighbors. This diplomatic work of changing the public's perception was due in part to Hsi Lai leaders presenting themselves as "good" Asians. They appealed to the community by accentuating their devout spirituality and by promoting a culture of hospitality. As their spokesperson throughout the 1980s, Yang felt it was the temple's duty to clarify whites' misunderstandings about Buddhism and why Hsi Lai chose Hacienda Heights. Yang suggested temple leaders sought a harmonious, calm setting evocative of the worshipers' demeanor: "We're very conservative. We don't bother anybody. [And we] wish to maintain a lower profile." Temple leaders believed they were not disrupting the suburb's traditionalist milieu.[26] In essence, by positioning themselves as compliant, amicable "model minorities," they could also claim to be model neighbors.

The Hsi Lai controversy revealed the complex ways white suburbanites resisted ethnic change by deploying veiled language and tactics. Critics alleged their opposition to the temple was not about race or religion. This was really about how "fit" a space of this sort was in "country living." Their actions and reactions reflected what Eduardo Bonilla-Silva termed "racism without racists" whereby whites and some people of color used race-blind discourse and euphemisms to shield themselves from accusations of bigotry.[27] Throughout the temple controversy, Pluth maintained innocence, insisting her opposition was about keeping away outsiders and poorly planned buildings. This was, for her, not race-related: "It's in the wrong location. . . . I would have fought just the same if they wanted to put Disneyland in my community."[28] For liked-minded critics, this was about preserving the sanctity of "country living." It just so happened, Pluth argued, that the outsiders were mostly Chinese and not Christian: "The sad thing is that some of us are being called racial antagonists. We're just concerned about what's happening to our community. We've put a lot of time into this community. We have fought fires and mud slides together. People don't realize the community feeling among residents here."[29]

With this logic, Buddhists were agitators undermining Hacienda Heights' tight-knit neighborhoods. Opponents continued to dismiss claims that they harbored prejudiced views. Yet critics believed "the Buddhists," as Pluth referred to Hsi Lai worshippers, manipulated the system in order to build in Hacienda Heights. Pluth alleged the county gave IBPS favorable treatment even though IBPS acted within their rights as landowners. Pluth intimated that the inherently cunning nature of the Chinese won over county leaders: "The Buddhists may not know English themselves but they certainly hired people who did. They seemed to know how to do things better than most of us who were born here."[30] Contradictorily, Pluth—who claimed no prejudices throughout the project's deliberations—expressed after Hsi Lai's opening that Buddhists "don't want to mix, they don't want to become Americans. As an American, I feel a little strange in my own country." Pluth's criticisms highlighted her assumptions of Asians' illegality. Critics like Pluth also conflated Buddhists with foreigners, not citizens; they were unfit for the suburbs and unfit for America. The veiled rhetoric of contemporary white racism provided a means to express outrage in less explicit forms. This resulted in inconsistent positions when critics were confronted with their biases.

Despite Hsi Lai's concessions and community outreach, a vocal faction of Hacienda Heights residents remained unmoved. Years after opening, longtime critics claimed the temple destroyed the East Valley's bucolic feel. To them, Hsi Lai wreaked havoc on the suburb and encouraged a greater influx of Asian immigrants. Anna Fuller, originally from Texas, said she settled in Hacienda Heights because "it was kind of like country." But because of Hsi Lai, "a lot of foreigners . . . bought homes up in the hills [near the temple]. . . . There's so many of them that they've begun to call it 'Slant hill.'"[31] The entrance of global capital and Asian immigration made the valley feel less American, and accordingly, less "country."

Throughout the controversy, Chinese immigrants felt obligated to go the extra mile in making their visions for a Buddhist temple a reality. Had Hsi Lai been a Protestant church, they believed there would not have been as many hurdles. White residents had double standards on what was deemed proper use of suburban space. The debate over Hsi Lai is one of numerous examples in which Asians ceded to critics' demands as a means of creating a sense of place in the suburbs. They acquiesced to try to keep the peace.

While their concessions or compromises could be read as defeatist or over-accommodating, their commitment to making these suburbs their home demonstrated an ability to engage with local politics. They used different tools and tactics of outreach to their advantage. Moreover, immigrants' desires to integrate spiritual life into their new lives as American suburbanites were degrees of assimilationist behavior even when critics denounced their actions as rejections of it.

. . .

Ten miles away from Hsi Lai, residents in Walnut resisted a proposal for St. Lorenzo Ruiz Catholic Church. In the early 1990s, organizers were well on their way to building the parish until a powerful contingent of city officials and homeowners spoke out in opposition. Named after a Filipino saint, critics alleged the church was too ethnic-specific and thus exclusionary to non-Filipinos. They further claimed its design did not align with the aesthetics or cultures of "country living." Those in support of St. Lorenzo could not figure out if critics resisted because they were genuinely concerned about protecting western rurality, or if they feared the parish would attract more Filipino immigrants to the well-to-do hamlet.

Founded in 1987, St. Lorenzo was established by a group of young families patronizing St. Martha Catholic Church in nearby Valinda, a working-class unincorporated area. They lobbied archdiocese officials to open a parish in Walnut, where most of the founders lived. To measure demand, the Archdiocese of Los Angeles urged organizers to conduct a survey of Catholic families residing in Walnut. Having outgrown St. Martha's capacity, in 1989, families convened as a satellite parish in a leased warehouse at Lemon Avenue and Valley Boulevard, an intersection where walnut trees, lemon groves, and strawberry patches once stood. Recognizing Walnut's burgeoning Catholic population, in September 1991, the archdiocese assigned Dennis Vellucci as permanent pastor of the newly formed parish. St. Lorenzo was intended to serve Walnut's Catholic community indiscriminate of race or ethnicity. At the same time, church leaders wanted to minister to the area's rapidly growing Filipino population, most of whom identified as Catholic.[32] Between 1980 and 1990, the Filipino population rose 151 percent in West Covina, 250 percent in Rowland Heights, and 577 percent in Walnut, among the largest Filipino population increases in the United States during the 1980s.[33] Despite these demographic shifts, critics considered the

FIGURE 13. St. Lorenzo Ruiz Catholic Church, Walnut, CA, April 2012. Photo taken by James Zarsadiaz.

parish too Filipino-centric since it was to be formally named in honor of the Philippines' protomartyr. As news spread of a new parish named after a Filipino saint, St. Lorenzo became a religious and cultural hub for the East Valley's Filipino immigrant community. St. Lorenzo's registration swelled to over three hundred families. During Sunday services, the warehouse-turned-church frequently reached capacity. To accommodate overflow, parish staff provided worshippers folding chairs and set up outdoor movie screens and speakers to project live mass on the parking lot. St. Lorenzo leaders once again lobbied the archdiocese for support, but this time, in the hopes of convincing them to build a freestanding church.

In 1991, the newly installed Cardinal of Los Angeles, Roger Mahony, purchased an eighteen-acre plot of land in Walnut's Meadowpass neighborhood. Nestled between Brookside Equestrian Center and a row of custom-built, multimillion-dollar mansions, the archdiocese believed the site would be a quiet, upscale place for services. Archdiocese leaders did not anticipate resistance in Walnut since it was regarded as a church-friendly suburb. In 1992, parish leaders and the architect tapped to build the parish approached Walnut's Planning Commission with their plans. Commissioners consisted of longtime residents, some of whom were part of the Old Guard. This was a group of mostly white homeowners known to oppose commercial and industrial development. But they generally approved proposals for single-family homes, small-scale tract housing, and churches since they fit Walnut's

FIGURE 14. Custom-built homes in Meadowpass (Walnut, CA), March 2012. Photo taken by James Zarsadiaz.

bedroom community image. St. Lorenzo leaders were surprised to learn the Planning Commission took issue with numerous aspects of the church plan. Designed by Newport Beach-based architect James Darling, the original drawings for its exterior featured swooped curves and prominent right angles. The site itself included a ninety-six-thousand-square-foot assembly hall with a two-tiered sanctuary that could accommodate about twelve hundred people. Along with the Planning Commission, city councilmembers and residents critiqued the St. Lorenzo proposal. They claimed the façade was futuristic and incongruous with Walnut's country living identity. Some likened the silhouette to a rocket or spaceship. Councilmember June Wentworth chided the design as "too ultramodern for Walnut."[34] A resident since 1966, Wentworth was in the Old Guard and was known as a persistent advocate for upholding "country living." She believed the project was inappropriate for Walnut's "rural or rustic" architectural style as suggested in the city's General Plan. Ironically, though Walnut leaders claimed this community standard, the Meadowpass neighborhood featured a mélange of custom-built mansions in styles ranging from English Tudor and New Classical to Art Deco and Postmodern.

When Darling learned of the community's reactions, he lambasted Walnut residents alleging their ignorance of broader architectural trends. Darling dismissed city leaders' claims that Walnut had a special aesthetic: "There's not one building in Walnut that I even consider architecture. If they build this church in Walnut, people from around the nation would come to look at it."[35] Vellucci weighed in too, criticizing the Planning Commission for what he considered illogical reasoning: "We got crucified. . . . We're not trying to deface the city; we're trying to build a church."[36] He believed nonresidential spaces were not rural in design and demanded the city provided a clear definition of "rural." Vellucci argued homes in Walnut, especially in Meadowpass, were far from modest or provincial. City leaders like Councilmember Drexel Smith remained unyielding. Smith was concerned that "this particular design for this particular neighborhood" was unsuitable.[37] Deploying a message of "following the rules of 'country living'" disguised individual or collective apprehensions that could be read as prejudiced. Critics used color-blind language or the logic of sound planning and design to express their discomfort of a church primarily catering to Filipino immigrants.

One of the city's newest leaders, William Choctaw, was conflicted. When he ran for city council, he vowed to protect country living and won on that promise. But as Walnut's first Black councilmember, he empathized with St. Lorenzo because its congregation was more diverse than other churches. "It's the ultimate arrogance when a governmental body tries to dictate to a church . . . [of] what it should look like," said Choctaw. "Just because someone doesn't like the way it looks doesn't mean it should be changed."[38] Choctaw recalled one city council meeting where tensions ran high. He believed issues beyond St. Lorenzo's design triggered white resistance:

> A lot of people didn't want [the church]. There was a lot of yelling, screaming, name-calling. . . . The [Planning Commission] chair was part of the Old Guard and was absolutely against it. I was disgusted at what I saw. . . . [One of their issues with the project] was the height of the cross. And that was what they decided to get them on. "No! The cross is too high!" [or)] "It interferes with the ambiance of the city." What does that mean? That doesn't mean anything. . . The [Planning Commission] chair said that [the] cross will not be x number of feet tall because "Catholics are no taller than anybody else." When I said I wouldn't let this happen under my watch [as councilmember] they said they will defeat it [anyway] because "we run this city."[39]

Critics conflated Catholics with Filipinos. Rather than addressing racial apprehensions, they used Catholicism and design as less-polarizing mechanisms to halt construction. The Old Guard's threats worried Choctaw, a racial optimist who wanted to peacefully integrate the "new" Walnut with the suburb's established white population. Choctaw and others who supported racial and religious pluralism continued to seek a middle ground with critics. In May 1992, Choctaw was appointed to a city-sponsored subcommittee on the St. Lorenzo plan. The subcommittee included Darling, Vellucci, and two Walnut planning commissioners who were tasked to address underlying issues of discrimination and bring resolution to the entire matter.

However, deliberations about the fate of St. Lorenzo continued into the fall and emerged as a hot topic in the November city council election. Three white men, a Black woman, a Chinese woman, and a Filipino man vied for a vacant seat left by a white councilmember who died in office.[40] The election deepened divisions between Walnut's older white residents and the city's multiethnic newcomers. All candidates said they wanted to maintain Walnut's "rural" charms. But Old Guard candidates emphasized that besides prioritizing the protection of "country living," they also knew how to curtail the suburb's swift pace of development and population growth, alluding to the town's demographic turn. At the same time, Old Guard candidates did not address how they would achieve this goal or what they meant by harboring discomforts with Walnut's changes. The implicit meaning spoke volumes to Asian residents. One candidate, Ernest Aguilar, made the St. Lorenzo impasse a central part of his campaign. Born in the Philippines, Aguilar wanted to represent Walnut's growing Filipino population. If elected, supporters hoped he would move St. Lorenzo's construction forward. Aguilar believed "the city should stay away from telling people how to build their religious buildings" and felt it was time for "fresh blood" in Walnut's historically white leadership.[41] "We, the newer residents, have a different view of what the city should evolve into," said Aguilar, alluding to Asians' cultural differences with the Old Guard.[42] Like some of his nonwhite counterparts running for office, Aguilar believed that though he was not white, he too valued Walnut's rural qualities. The church, he argued, did not threaten the prestige and allure of "country living." Jack Isett, a planning commissioner and member of Walnut's Old Guard, also ran for the seat and was a frontrunner. Unlike Aguilar, Isett focused on the fiscal health of the city since the St. Lorenzo impasse upset supporters and opponents alike. With the diverse field of candidates, Walnut voters decided they were not ready for new blood. Isett handily won. Aguilar came in at second place, illustrating Walnut's sharpening racial and generational divides as well as residents' competing ideas of what was permissible for "country living." Asian residents embraced this ideal, but for some critics, Filipinos' attempts to permanently weave ethnic customs into the everyday landscapes of suburbia overstepped the boundaries of proper behavior.

After numerous church subcommittee meetings, revised blueprints, and legal deliberations, a construction crew broke ground on March 27, 1994. The $2.3 million complex was scaled back from its original plans as a compromise between St. Lorenzo and city officials. St. Lorenzo's influential Filipino Association along with the support of white parishioners and a coalition of religious leaders and politicians brought the two-year battle to an end. Church supporters claimed St. Lorenzo was within their rights to construct a parish despite claims of it not aligning with Walnut's design standards. They also successfully argued that accusations of racial and religious discrimination contributed to diminishing community morale, evinced in the city council election. Residents agreed the standoff needed to conclude so all parties could move forward. On March 17, 1996, St. Lorenzo Ruiz Catholic Church opened its doors. While critics still chastised parish leaders for transgressing the aesthetics of "country living," supporters believed St. Lorenzo was not all that different from other neighborhood churches. The difference was that the church was named after a Filipino saint and that the facility catered to a booming Filipino population. For opponents, St. Lorenzo was not just a Catholic church. It was a foreboding symbol—if not another catalyst—of how the region was developing into an Asian immigrant hub.

The St. Lorenzo controversy illustrated the ubiquity of using country living as a political tool against change and unwanted development. Rhetoric of protecting and preserving country living sounded innocuous, but critics' intentions were—at their core—motivated by racial apprehensions. As Laura Barraclough notes, similar actions occurred in the San Fernando Valley where white "rural dwellers" promoted exclusionary politics through the prism of "favoring color-blindness." They "often appealed to a rhetoric of 'common interests' that appeared to be based on demonstrated commitments to a rural landscape and lifestyle but elided the ways in which access to that lifestyle has been and continues to be structured by patterns of economic inequality and social practices of exclusion."[43] By positioning Asian immigrant-targeted spaces as transgressive or disruptive to suburban norms despite their non-Asian façades, opponents effectively made it harder for Asians to integrate. These criticisms came from those who vocally rejected Asian families and even those who claimed to support diversity. Over time, country living was not only a term to describe a specific way of life. It was a rhetorical mechanism for curbing "change" in the East Valley.

"WE DON'T WANT IT!": 99 RANCH, CLASS, AND THE SYMBOLISM OF ASIAN STORES

The implied permanence of religious landmarks like Hsi Lai and St. Lorenzo heightened critics' concerns about the valley's demographic transformation. Similarly, the rise of Asian commercial and retail sites emboldened wary homeowners and nativists to stop change. Ethnic-specific shopping centers exemplified how race was inscribed into yet another typical suburban landscape. Critics censured full-service Chinese supermarkets and Asian strip malls for not complying with the aesthetic or cultural status quo, in some cases even before projects were proposed. The scale and perceived exoticism of Asian wares and the prevalence of non-English signage were sources of white critics' anxieties. But disapproval came from fellow Asian residents as well. They too subscribed to Euro-American understandings of how suburbia should look or feel, particularly those in wealthier country living communities.

In the early 2000s, 99 Ranch Market—a Chinese grocery chain—set their eyes on Chino Hills. By this time, 99 Ranch operated multiple stores in the East Valley including two in Rowland Heights.[44] The first of the two stores opened in 1989, which sat next to what remained of John A. Rowland III's ranch. He was the grandson of John A. Rowland, the namesake of Rowland Heights. The Rowland ranch's proximity to 99 Ranch served as a visual reminder and symbol of the valley's older settlers standing in contrast to its immigrant newcomers. Officials of 99 Ranch anticipated Chino Hills would join an expanding group of Asian-majority towns across the San Gabriel Valley. Company leaders saw opportunities for profit, particularly because of the area's upper-income consumers.[45] In 1997, 99 Ranch purchased the space of a former Ralphs, a Southern California supermarket chain. Sitting at a major intersection of Rolling Ridge village—a large subdivision within the master-planned suburb—meant its prime location ensured store visibility.

Upon word of 99 Ranch's plans, city leaders received a barrage of complaints. Opponents considered the supermarket inappropriate for Chino Hills and worried about 99 Ranch's impact on the look, feel, and demographics of the agrarian-themed suburb. Critics argued 99 Ranch would accelerate Asian settlement and immigrant-driven development, which previously occurred in older West Valley suburbs like Monterey Park, San Gabriel, Rosemead, and Alhambra. They cited these suburbs as examples of communities plagued with traffic or aesthetic disorganization thanks to its Asian residents. For them, the 99 Ranch proposal was a telltale sign that country living was coming to an end; its opening, the death knell. At the time, Chino Hills' Asian population was climbing. It quadrupled between 1990 and 2000.[46] Along with new Asian residents came Asian-owned businesses. Racial apprehensions existed well before 99 Ranch's plans. Several years prior, residents circulated yellow buttons with the words, "Chino Hills, Not Chino's Hills" around the community.[47] (*Chino* is "Chinese" in Spanish.) Across the East Valley, whites' disassociations of Asian culture with Western rurality raised the question of Asians' place in the pastiche of "country living." It was easier for white residents to link Asian bodies to urban spaces like Chinatown or the bustling metropolises of Shanghai and Seoul rather than Southern California's pastoral hinterlands and suburban tracts.

Resistance to 99 Ranch in Chino Hills was not the first time East Valley homeowners objected to the supermarket. A decade before, rumors of a 99 Ranch opening in Walnut circulated the community. Shortly after his election to the city council in 1995, Joaquin Lim, a Chinese immigrant from Hong Kong, asked constituents for their thoughts on having a 99 Ranch in town. Joaquin recalled strong opposition from white residents, particularly from the Old Guard. Much to his surprise, stronger protests came from Asian homeowners including Chinese immigrants. They feared 99 Ranch would increase local traffic, attract outsiders, and threaten property values. Like white critics, Asian opponents internalized orientalist stereotypes of Chinese businesses. Critics associated the presumed unsanitariness of Asian stores to the inherent character of Asian people. These cultural imaginations of disruptive, downtrodden, and "dirty" Chinese were indelibly tied to nineteenth-century notions of an urban, menacing "yellow peril," or more contemporaneously, akin to ethnoburbs where Asian culture was on full display and resulted in a low-rent ambiance. Lim said,

> The reason [residents opposed 99 Ranch] was loud and clear: "We choose to live in Walnut because we wanted a quiet environment. We don't need 99 Ranch because there's a 99 Ranch Market [in the ethnoburbs of Rowland Heights and Hacienda Heights]. We can travel no more than ten minutes and go into a neighborhood to go shopping. But we want to return to a

pastoral environment." You know, [they said] "We want quiet, we don't want traffic." [Plus] Asian markets carry a lot of live stuff: live fish, live crabs, live lobsters, and those products . . . there's an issue with the smell. . . . I think that's what happens when you walk into a Chinese market. . . . So, the people in Walnut, Diamond Bar said, "Look, we don't mind driving. . . ." I was really surprised. When I ran it by my people [Chinese friends or constituents], [I thought] they would say, "Oh great!" But no, it was almost totally in unison: "We don't want it!"[48]

Judy Chen Haggerty, a Rowland Heights homeowner and community college board trustee, had similar observations about her Chinese neighbors' reactions to Asian-owned properties or higher density projects, which some understood as synonymous: 'I think for Chinese [residents], if [they] feel [their] interests are threatened, then they come out [in opposition]. There's a common interest [with white residents]" to stop projects understood as detrimental to "country living."[49] From Haggerty's perspective, a shared belief across ethnic or racial lines was "anti-growth, anti-developer, and all that."[50] For Diamond Bar homeowner Helen Wei, the East Valley is "a very conservative area. [Residents and community leaders] don't allow certain businesses . . . coming into town," which included Asian stores deemed incongruous with upscale country living towns.[51] Asian residents in Walnut, Diamond Bar, and Chino Hills considered themselves more refined and assimilated than immigrants living in L.A., ethnoburbs like Monterey Park, or even fellow country living suburbs with ethnoburb-like commercial zones such as Rowland Heights or Hacienda Heights. Homeownership, wealth, and a well-to-do suburban address in a less "Asian-looking" community separated the "good" Asians from the "bad." For Asian residents in "design assimilation" suburbs like Chino Hills, the near-invisibility of Asian culture on display protected the indestructability and standards of "country living." For many Asian homeowners, this was ideal because it kept commercial and residential spaces uniform and mainstream.[52]

Ironically, despite white critiques of immigrants' inabilities to appreciate "country living," many were actually attuned to the trendiness of these suburbs. They acquired Western standards of taste while living abroad. Wealthier Asian immigrants adopted the lingua franca and cultures of postwar American modernity before moving to California. This was partly because their education or economic privilege afforded them exposure to middle- or high-brow Western culture across the Pacific.[53] Even immigrants from modest backgrounds were still exposed to American culture on a regular basis. Through their travels or consumption of American media and goods, middle-class and affluent immigrants established lives in country living with advantages over their working-class counterparts in the city or in the ethnoburbs. They did not just have financial capital; they had cultural capital as well, which they used to distinguish themselves from their poorer co-ethnics.[54] These markers of class difference and signifiers of finesse boiled down to things like how close one lived to Asian shopping centers. For richer Asian suburbanites—while convenient in terms of distance—the closer you lived to a store like 99 Ranch, the less sophisticated the neighborhood and its people.

Diamond Bar homeowner Jenny Chang said Asians residing in the city or in ethnoburbs did not change their "bad habits" and were un-assimilated unlike those in wealthier country living communities, particularly master-planned ones because they evoked order and elegance. Though Rowland Heights, for example, had upscale tracts, Chang and her co-ethnics from Hong Kong and Taiwan believed a town's reputation was measured by the aesthetics of its public spaces and the class of its overall population. Accordingly, Asian families in tonier country living suburbs were "more polite [and] follow[ed] the rules." They distanced themselves from their less affluent counterparts because they felt they were better integrated. Finally, Jenny believed living in close proximity to Asian strip malls, such as those in Monterey Park or in parts of Rowland Heights, Hacienda Heights, and nearby City of Industry kept immigrants in a bubble. For her, families shielded from "typical" Americans (i.e., whites) and "respectable" American landscapes (e.g., master-planned suburbs, mainstream shops) meant that they preferred to live as if they were still in Asia, thus reinforcing ideas of the self-segregating immigrant.[55] Some residents disagreed with Jenny's observations. Rowland Heights homeowner Cary Chen, for example, claimed the perceived déclassé milieu of these spaces were relatively contained: "Rowland Heights' businesses and residents are very separate, with the businesses separated from the peaceful residential areas. Therefore, [the] Chinese American population have really enjoyed the seclusion [from Asian business districts)]."[56] Cary's views, however, were not in alignment with many of his co-ethnics, especially those who lived in tonier suburbs like Diamond Bar.

Similar to how homeowners reacted to the 99 Ranch rumor in Walnut, a contingent of Chinese residents joined their white neighbors in opposition to the 99 Ranch project in Chino Hills, making the battle to open more difficult. Chinese residents opposed to the market believed immigrants' allegiance to the homeland through things like ethnic retail discouraged assimilation, a process that is supposed to occur concomitantly with suburbanization. Reverend Andy Wu, a Chinese Lutheran minister, feared 99 Ranch would undermine whites' respect for assimilated or integrated Asians: "We've tried very hard to build up ourselves and build up our image to Caucasian people here. I hope 99 Ranch will hold up to that high standard."[57] Status-conscious Asian residents further worried that 99 Ranch would invite a lower class of consumers thus cementing stereotypes of the tacky Asian business. They preferred to discreetly shop at Asian stores outside of town to stave off white accusations that they refused to support mainstream businesses or join the proverbial "melting pot."

Asian supporters said as long as 99 Ranch was executed correctly for suburbia, it would be welcomed—obliquely affirming criticism that Asian stores lacked refinement or a place in "country living." They wanted to show that establishments like 99 Ranch could be tasteful and not akin to the cryptic, unsanitary, or disorderly shops of Chinatown.[58] In their eyes, a well-designed, American-style store would showcase diasporic Asian cultures in a way that was palatable for those who doubted immigrants' suitability as suburbanites.[59] Chino Hills resident Cindy Wu thought the plans provided "a good opportunity" for Asians "to earn a good reputation" among white families. Moreover, 99 Ranch supporters believed a Chinese supermarket in a country living suburb would undoubtedly be classier because of its wealthier clientele. These "assimilated" immigrants, supporters claimed, would ensure this and similar businesses were appropriate for the master-planned town. Roger Chen, 99 Ranch's CEO, alluded to sharing similar views. Aware of the hesitancy among some white consumers, Chen said 99 Ranch leaders "were trying to upgrade and improve the image of Chinese grocery stores by using Western skills to sell Asian products"—something they took especially seriously in upper-income suburbs like Chino Hills.[60]

With increasing pressure from Chino Hills residents, 99 Ranch officials approached the store plans with caution. Signage was a critical factor in quelling fears of an Asian "takeover." The store's owners tried to assure residents that bilingual signage would primarily remain indoors. Opponents, however, worried other businesses would take their cues from 99 Ranch and forego English signage altogether. Critics claimed non-English signage and window posters mirrored the ethnoburban-like retail landscapes of Colima Road, a main thoroughfare stretching across Rowland Heights, Hacienda Heights, and Industry. As one homeowner put it, Colima Road "looks like

Hong Kong (or) the Ginza (District) in Tokyo."[61] The conspicuously Asian built environment rendered sections of Rowland Heights and similar towns "un-suburban" in form. Critics went as far as to claim that these spaces facilitated acts of "reverse racism"—that is, stores like 99 Ranch were designed to keep white consumers out.

Chino Hills leaders told residents there were limits to what the city could do without violating the property and civil rights of Asian business owners. Mayor Gwenn Norton-Perry said the city was not allowed to require English signage. Federal civil rights statutes banned municipalities from creating codes that articulated such guidelines. Instead, as Councilmember Peter Rogers noted, officials could "strongly encourage" Asian-owned businesses to use English signage, minimize aesthetic exoticism, and be more mainstream friendly. Chino Hills leaders used the encouragement method as a less invasive, racially charged way of shaping and policing space. In describing the desired parameters for the store, leaders deployed color-blind rhetoric or couched criticisms with verbalized support of multiculturalism and diversity to avoid accusations of bigotry. Rather than explicitly expressing their discomforts with change, residents opted for a message of promoting national unity via the English language and nondescript, Euro-American design. This strategy relayed ideas that following these rules demonstrated respect and good citizenship and allowed critics to publicly protest while concealing racist and/or classist views. It also permitted residents open to diversity but resistant toward displays of Asian culture to speak up.

Though 99 Ranch executives agreed early on to retain the site's existing pseudo-Mediterranean façade and traditional American supermarket layout, as criticism mounted, 99 Ranch officials felt additional pressures to "blend in" per the city's recommendation. By acquiescing, store leaders hoped these compromises would make 99 Ranch appealing to non-Asian residents as well. Similar to how Asian business owners operated in Diamond Bar and Walnut, stores like 99 Ranch in Chino Hills complied with these design standards and took their cues from white residents. At the same time, Asian residents who did not take a side or stayed silent spoke volumes in terms of how important it was to have a visible cultural presence in "country living."

Meanwhile, on and off the record, white opponents claimed no animosity toward their Asian neighbors, yet they deployed orientalist stereotypes or nativist rhetoric to make a case against Asian businesses. One of the most vocal critics was homeowner Larry Blugrind. He said he enjoyed Chino Hills' diversity and noted his daughter-in-law was Japanese. He feared

Chino Hills would transform into an ethnoburb if chains or white-owned shops continued to change hands to Asian ones: "My worry is that 99 Ranch could be a steppingstone for it to become all Asian. I don't want another Hacienda Heights."[62] In another forum, Blugrind wrote, "We have diversity in Chino Hills and I am HAPPY with the degree of diversity we now have in Chino Hills. In Rowland Heights, THERE IS NO DIVERSITY—IT'S ALL ASIAN!!!"[63] A fellow 99 Ranch opponent said he did not want to see "little Chinatowns all over the Hills filled with Asian signs (he) can't read."[64] Resident Carolyn Matta agreed and claimed 99 Ranch would "turn [Chino Hills] into another Rowland Heights. We're not going to be welcomed in our neighborhood." [65] In a letter he addressed to the city council, Blugrind claimed a strip mall anchor like 99 Ranch would "result in a run-down center that is the equivalent of a Chinese Pic 'N' Save [discount store] less than a mile from the high-quality shops" already in the community.[66] Even with 99 Ranch's design concessions, opponents believed 99 Ranch was déclassé and unworthy of a Chino Hills address.

Ultimately, for Blugrind and likeminded critics, a Chinese supermarket did not fit within the aesthetic parameters of country living and the white, rural imaginary of the American West. In municipal politics, homeowners across the region made claims of potential Asian "takeovers," arguing that electing Asian officials would result in more Asian stores, temples, and people. In nearby La Habra Heights, voters in the affluent equestrian-themed hamlet opposed a Chinese candidate to the city council because they feared the community would turn into a crowded ethnoburb upon his election. According to Rowland Heights resident Albert Chang, "People were all like, 'Oh no. We can't elect this guy or we're gonna have three-story commercial buildings built to the sidewalk in our beautiful community.' They use the example of Rowland Heights [to make a case against voting for Asian leaders or Asian-owned spaces]."[67]

After much debate and multiethnic opposition, 99 Ranch opened its doors in 2007. Despite earlier resistance, a number of homeowners and city leaders like Norton-Perry embraced the economic benefits and consumer perks provided by Asian establishments. She believed 99 Ranch was "a reflection of changing demographics" and that she planned to shop at the new store.[68] Others welcomed Chino Hills' diversifying landscape in the spirit of racial liberalism. Michael Newton, a resident in neighboring Chino said, "Let us put our bigotry aside and welcome the Indians, Hindus, Asian, and other ethnicities into our neighborhoods,"[69] embracing diversity for the sake

FIGURE 15. 99 Ranch Market, Chino Hills, CA, January 2022. Unlike other 99 Ranch stores in the region, this location has "fresh" included in the signage. Photo courtesy of Phil Ige.

of having peace. Once open, 99 Ranch—initially feared as the beginning of the end for country living—melded into the Chino Hills landscape thanks to the concessions store leaders and advocates made. Its opening was also possible because incorporated suburbs like Chino Hills had greater control over the space. City leaders were thus successful in deterring atypical modifications in the built environment. Unincorporated areas like Rowland Heights and Hacienda Heights, however, lacked the governmental authority necessary to enforce and police formal or informal community standards. This made it easier for property owners to overlook, transgress, or disavow rules encouraging design assimilation. Finally, unlike homeowners' reactions in Walnut (where there was a significant presence of Chinese civic leaders), in Chino Hills, 99 Ranch opened with a predominantly white city council and bureaucracy. This quelled fears of an Asian "takeover" from the strip mall to city hall because Asian residents were not yet in senior positions within Chino Hills' leadership.

The 99 Ranch controversy was one in a pattern of public condemnations of the East Valley's shifting built and cultural landscapes. Though the Chinese supermarket chain elicited strong reactions about its fit for the suburbs, this boiled down to residents' discomfort with change. Anti-Asian sentiments fueled some of these reactions. But this did not necessarily trigger or motivate all opposition especially since critics included Asian homeowners. Rather, this and similar controversies revealed suburbanites' complicated and oftentimes paradoxical feelings with diversity and multiculturalism. On one hand, residents across ethnic lines said they welcomed pluralism. Popular culture and changes in social attitudes suggested broad support of racial liberalism. On the other hand, there were limits to how far one could express ethnic traditions or practices. Beyond racial anxieties, residents were responding to collective fears that western rurality was on the verge of extinction. Residents, particularly older homeowners, worried about an end to simpler times and old-fashioned values—all of this occurring in the shadow of a globalizing L.A.

"ENGLISH ONLY" AND THE "VISUAL CLUTTER" OF ASIAN SPACES

Reactions to Asian businesses and store signage illuminated residents' varying degrees of acceptance of Asian immigrants into the community. Chinese, Filipino, and Korean retail and consumer dollars generated profit for suburbs, which was welcomed for bolstering funds to local schools and infrastructure. However, leaders and everyday residents across racial lines worried about the scale and impact of Asian immigrants' presence in the East Valley, especially physical displays of East Asian languages or aesthetics, which critics preferred to be invisible. Even those who advocated for diversity feared that by fully bringing Asian immigrants into the fold, inclusion came with the potential to destroy the cultures and aesthetics of "country living." Thus, support from their neighbors was not wholesale. It came with conditions.

Throughout the region, city and county leaders proposed "English Only" (or "English Also") language ordinances for official government business. Signage, however, became a greater area of interest. English Only advocates called for English to be the sole or primary language on privately owned property signage. Codes required Roman letters and Arabic numbers. Business owners, particularly those with stores primarily serving Chinese or Korean clients and patrons, felt targeted since residents overlooked businesses with French, Italian, or Spanish names. Concomitantly, these local debates occurred amid a wider English Only movement in the 1980s and 1990s and growing Asian settlement in the valley.[70] (English was made the official state language in 1986 through Proposition 63.) Those who backed English signage ordinances claimed these laws were not racially motivated. Rather, this was a matter of public safety for first responders.[71] Supporters worried police officers and firefighters would not be able to locate businesses despite their numbered addresses. Moreover, proponents said this was simply a good business practice since English signage implied non-Asians were also welcomed in these establishments. Critics claimed Asian signage was akin to "reverse discrimination" and disrupted the look and feel of "country living." Therefore, this trend needed to be stopped for the sake of aesthetic continuity. Some even claimed English signage promoted racial harmony. Particularly in master-planned suburbs like Diamond Bar, residents who lobbied for language codes believed English signage as well as design uniformity unified a diverse community. In the spirit of assimilation, they claimed these measures ensured spatial and cultural homogeneity, and by extension, thus celebrated a color-blind society removed from liberal identity politics.[72] Other signage proponents argued, contradictorily, that supporting English Only laws actually reinforced suburbanites' twin commitments to inclusion and diversity because it demonstrated a willingness to see everyone as the same or as their equals. More importantly, signage proponents believed language codes protected the western idyll native- and foreign-born residents sought as East Valley residents. In Walnut, for example, officials claimed English signage promoted "an uncluttered, aesthetically pleasing streetscape consistent with the rural environment of the city as encouraged by the General Plan."[73] Transgressions in the landscape made country living susceptible to the types of spatial and visual disorganization residents associated with places like L.A.'s Koreatown or working- and middle-class (and oftentimes, multi-racial) suburbs like Monterey Park and Cerritos in L.A. County or Westminster and Garden Grove in Orange County.

Ordinance supporters, particularly those afraid of offending Asian residents or fearful of being accused of racism used these "neutral" reasons to explain why they backed English signage.[74] Walnut homeowner Sandra Thompson said, "A place with a sign in a foreign language, it says to you: 'If you don't speak this, we don't want your business. . . .' Whether you live here or drive through [Walnut] it should welcome everybody."[75] Sandra believed English was unifying and that color-blind approaches to landscaping and governance would help suburbs achieve racial harmony. Harsher critics claimed non-English signs were symbols of hostility toward white Americans. They argued these signs demonstrated immigrants' mass disinterest in assimilation. Linda

Ruggio, also a Walnut resident, thought non-English signage on what she categorized as "foreign businesses" promoted "native[-born] American exclusion" (i.e., white): "You see, foreign businesses . . . do not advertise in both ENGLISH and their own language. This tells me . . . that they only wish their own nationality to patronize these businesses. How are we supposed to keep the economy going, and enforce racial equality and blending when we can't understand the signs on the walls? . . . After all, this is America, and the primary language, not to mention the universal language, is still ENGLISH."[76]

Their sentiments resonated with white residents threatened by the influx of Asian newcomers. To critics, this was not the East Valley they moved into nor signed up for. Chinese entrepreneurs questioned the validity of their arguments and read the subtext. Sheila Ma established her Rowland Heights accountancy business in 1987, not far from her home. Her agency had English and Chinese signage since day one: "I've been here [over] twenty years [and] I've only had one customer that's Caucasian walk in."[77] She too believed in conforming to a traditional suburban landscape. But Sheila also felt that signage laws and other expectations of immigrant-owned businesses "need[ed] to be realistic."[78] Asian entrepreneurs claimed white consumers held double standards. Asian residents patronized white-owned businesses and American chain stores, but white residents did not reciprocate or seem interested in exposing themselves to non-European cultures. White critics countered by arguing that Asians who chose to live in the suburbs consented to an unspoken agreement of Euro-American conformity. By being visually conspicuous as Asians, they were breaking this social contract.

On July 22, 1985, Monterey Park was among the first cities in the valley to propose or adopt an English-signage ordinance, following a surge of Asian settlement occurring since the late 1970s.[79] Critics rushed to make English the city's official language and wanted to require English on all commercial signage. Monterey Park's liberal Chinese and Nisei Japanese population opposed, positioning signage and design restrictions as civil rights issues. They claimed these rules curtailed citizens' rights to ethnic expression. Unsatisfied with the pace of regulating signage, critics of Monterey Park's racial and spatial transformations ran for city council on English Only platforms hoping to cement their demands.[80] When Councilmembers Lily Lee Chen, David Almada, and Rudy Peralta opposed efforts to make English the suburb's official language, they were voted out.[81]

While English Only and English-signage supporters throughout the valley proposed these measures as a response to rapid demographic change, cities and unincorporated communities took up signage laws as prevention. After what occurred in Monterey Park, English-signage advocates elsewhere feared their towns were next, as Asian settlement continued to extend into the East Valley, the Inland Empire, and Orange County—areas with abundant, new housing stock and growing pockets of Asian immigrant communities. In West Covina, city leaders drafted the East Valley's first English-signage law days after Monterey Park's proposal. Likening these issues to disease, Mayor Forest Tennant considered English signage necessary: "Let's get this ordinance on the books before signs in Korean or Arabic become a problem. . . . Prevention is a lot better than [a] cure."[82] Both Monterey Park and West Covina's move to regulate signage had a cascading effect. Following their lead, Baldwin Park, Diamond Bar, and Walnut joined the West Valley cities of Arcadia and San Marino in proposing or creating English signage codes.

However, unlike the contentious debates that occurred in Monterey Park, incorporated country living suburbs implemented codes with relative ease. Diamond Bar and Walnut, for example, quietly enacted and revised signage ordinances throughout the 1980s and 1990s when the rate of new Asian settlement was at their highest.[83] Most residents were likely unaware of these ordinances because both towns were largely master-planned; language and design codes were assumed to be par for the course. Walnut's code stated: signs "written in a language other than the English language shall also contain an English-language translation of the words written in the foreign language." Walnut leaders claimed they passed this and other codes "to protect the public health, safety, and welfare" of customers and residents.[84] Diamond Bar also acted swiftly as the suburb moved toward an Asian majority at the turn of the century. Diamond Bar homeowner Janice Stewart claimed that Rowland Heights, unlike Diamond Bar, was unsightly because of the "foreign" character of its shopping centers: "It's like Hong Kong coming down Colima (Road). (It's a) neon city. We don't want that (in Diamond Bar). (The way it looks is) probably (because of) different income levels."[85] Stewart equated Rowland Heights' busy Asian commercial areas to crowded, unmanageable urban centers. She suggested Rowland Heights' class diversity—measured by the wider variety of housing stock (e.g., apartments, townhomes, mobile homes)—was why the community was visually offensive compared to other heavily Asian albeit affluent suburbs like Diamond Bar, Walnut, and Chino Hills.

Though vocal supporters of English Only and signage codes were often white residents, these measures would not have been possible without vocal or tacit support from Asian residents. Across the San Gabriel Valley's richer suburbs, Asian residents were among the staunchest backers of English signage laws and Euro-American design standards. This was particularly apparent in historically prosperous suburbs or in master-planned communities, which were oftentimes newer, wealthier, and had more right-leaning residents. For instance, in 1991, the Asian Pacific American Legal Center of Los Angeles (APALC) sought to challenge Arcadia's signage ordinance which required 66 percent of letters to be in English. APALC called the ordinance discriminatory, putting an unwelcomed spotlight on the otherwise low-profile, well-to-do West Valley suburb. To the surprise of civil liberties organizations, APALC was quickly rebuffed by Chinese leaders who backed the ordinance because they preferred a muted ethnic presence in Arcadia.[86] Meanwhile, in Diamond Bar, city leaders urged commercial signage rules limiting "foreign" characters. Asian constituents backed these recommendations.[87] Diamond Bar councilmember Wen Chang—a Taiwanese immigrant and the city's first Chinese resident elected to the council—sided with white critics and thought Asian business signage was a form of "reverse discrimination." Chang encouraged architectural uniformity and believed non-English signage was divisive. He also argued it was a poor business strategy: "You want to be in business to serve all, not just a fraction of the total population."[88] Diamond Bar homeowner, Helen Wei, said immigrants must comply with the norms of American life even if that meant making concessions: "When you are in the US, you have to have the US culture and get involved."[89] For her, Asian immigrants must adapt to Euro-American mores and embrace its standards for suburbia. She considered assimilation a social expectation as well as a moral obligation. As foreign-born citizens, rather than standing out, Helen believed immigrants should blend in. Joven Gahon, a Filipino resident in nearby West Covina, believed that a command of English and an appreciation for mainstream customs was critical to survival. He expected fellow immigrants to embrace East Valley suburban traditions and American pastimes. In other words, "When in Rome, do as the Romans do," he joked.[90] Asian immigrants' support for these measures not only illustrated their commitment to protecting "country living." It also demonstrated a willingness to assimilate or conform to the status quo despite being told by white allies that diversity and practicing ethnic customs were welcomed.

Country living residents across racial lines thought explicitly ethnic landscapes were inappropriate. Even though Asian immigrants patronized businesses owned by their co-ethnics, having the Asian strip malls of Hacienda Heights, Rowland Heights, and City of Industry nearby—examples of déclassé spaces—constantly reminded country living residents to prevent these forms of development from happening in their backyard. For immigrants in particular, transgressing mainstream customs—no matter how big or small—gave their neighbors the impression that they chose to live unlike white and native-born Americans. Moreover, Asian critics of less assimilated immigrants feared their co-ethnics reinforced stereotypes of clannishness, undermining the efforts of those who have tried to prove their American-ness via assimilation or compliance with the cultures of suburbia and western rurality. Asian suburbanites did not expect full white approval, nor did they prioritize that, but they nonetheless sought acceptance since their behavior was under surveillance and because they constantly walked a shaky line between insider and outsider.

Incorporation was another important factor in shaping how Asian a community looked. Incorporated, master-planned suburbs like Diamond Bar, Walnut, and Chino Hills had tighter restrictions and greater control over land use. Strict zoning laws and design guidelines were created prior to or amid telltale signs of an Asian population boom. Nonwhite property owners minimized ethnicity inside and out because of municipal rules as well as class-based pressures to maintain the country living aesthetic norm. Rather than install a café sign in Chinese, for example, owners in wealthier suburbs opted for an English translation and left out Asian characters aside from printing them on menus. By maintaining nondescript façades, these suburbs looked untouched by an otherwise globalizing L.A. Asian residents hardly spoke out against these ordinances because master plans and city governments had them set in stone before anyone could challenge the informal rules of "country living." In contrast, unincorporated areas had a looser regulatory environment. County supervisors overseeing populous jurisdictions were unable to enforce business and structural codes from disparate parts of the region. This included the East Valley's longtime supervisors Pete Schabarum, Deane Dana, and Don Knabe, all of whom were Republican officials presiding over vast, diverse districts sometimes stretching as much as forty contiguous miles. Moreover, unincorporated areas comprised a larger cross-section of lower-middle- or working-class Asians with a greater number of apartment dwellers. Renters were less invested in community image or property values compared to homeowners.

In the "ethnic" commercial districts of Hacienda Heights and Rowland Heights, Asian culture was on display. Critics claimed such spaces lacked refinement, restraint, and a respect for order. They perceived of immigrants

FIGURE 16. Neon Chinese and English language signs on European cas-
tle-/country-inspired shopping center, Pacific Plaza, Rowland Heights, CA,
October 2012. Photo taken by James Zarsadiaz.

in these unincorporated areas as having less reverence for country living tradition. This is partly because of a higher concentration of apartments and
working- or lower-middle-class residents. Accordingly, they were not as as-
sertive in civic matters because they lacked time and commitment or faced
difficulties navigating county government. Compared to their wealthier counterparts in incorporated suburbs like Walnut, Asians in towns like Rowland
Heights were not as concerned about prestige and were therefore less vocal or
demanding. Rows of Asian shops and offices suggested to critics—including
fellow Asian suburbanites—that unincorporated areas contained immigrants
who were not as well-traveled or did not consume American and/or European culture across the Pacific. Indeed, less affluent Asian residents were not
as primed for life in the United States and were therefore likelier to overstep
the boundaries of "respectable" suburban behavior.

Since the late 1980s, shopping centers such as Hong Kong Plaza and
Pacific Plaza in Rowland Heights donned neon signs in Asian languages,
challenging the conventional image of the subdued suburban mall. Critics
in unincorporated areas responded by encouraging cityhood. Becoming a
city, proponents claimed, would guarantee residents autonomy over their
communities. This meant they could curb or reverse the Asianization of
the built environment through direct policy.[91] Compared to nearby incorporated suburbs like Walnut, critics in unincorporated areas believed their

FIGURE 17. Like many popular strip malls in Rowland Heights, CA, East Asian characters (particularly Chinese) dominate the main signage of this retail hub, October 2012. Photo taken by James Zarsadiaz.

suburbs looked disorderly and less "country" (and less American) than they once did. Frustrated with growing displays of Asian signage and accusations of suburban blight, a group of Rowland Heights residents revived the Rowland Heights Coordinating Council (RHCC) in the 1990s. Some of the motivation to resurrect RHCC was fueled by pro-incorporation forces. Comprised of volunteers, RHCC liaised with the County of Los Angeles Board of Supervisors to implement the Rowland Heights Community Standards District (RHCSD). Beyond signage, their concerns included traffic congestion and density, particularly along Colima Road, which residents considered the East Valley's main corridor of Asian commerce. Rowland

Heights' adjacent neighbor, City of Industry—an incorporated suburb zoned 92 percent for industrial purposes and 8 percent for commercial space—also elicited community outcry about its traffic and lenient policies on multilingual signage.[92] Industry's high concentration of transnational Chinese import-export firms, factories, restaurants, and shops deepened fears of a regional Asian "takeover." The city's proximate location blended into Rowland Heights' landscape heightening critics' anxieties about the decline of "country living."

Rather than propose an English Only ordinance that could have resulted in civil rights litigation and accusations of discrimination, Rowland Heights leaders compromised with business owners to allow storefront names in different languages so long as it was accompanied with an English translation. White residents who held more moderate or liberal political views lobbied for bilingual signage as a middle ground and gesture of goodwill for racial accord.[93] Approved in November 2001, county and community leaders hoped this would curtail the visual disorder activists considered unsightly. While a number of East Valley cities and unincorporated areas proposed various signage laws on language, they seldom followed through, particularly after the 1989 *Asian American Business Group v. City of Pomona* ruling.[94] Local leaders did not concretize signage and other design codes, largely out of fear that such policies would be infringements of civil and property rights. When governments enacted codes, they were often written in a manner that was vague enough to not be flagged as prejudiced. Furthermore, leaders placed their trust on social control. They expected proprietors to use reason in how they designed their space and to conform to the aesthetic status quo as a means of protecting property values. In other words, residents would be responsible for policing space. It was up to them to address problems if and when they occurred. Ultimately, whether these were unincorporated communities like Rowland Heights or incorporated towns like Walnut, homeowners across racial lines sought to preserve some semblance of a Euro-American flavor even as the population did not reflect those cultural or ethnic sensibilities. For class-conscious suburbanites, the minimization or erasure of an Asian presence was how it was supposed to be.

• • •

Across the San Gabriel Valley, design and signage emboldened critics' frustrations with change. By altering the norms of suburban space rather than wholly "blending in," they felt Asians repeatedly crossed the line of acceptable behavior. Even residents who claimed to not harbor prejudiced views believed there needed to be controls on the influence of Asian culture in the public sphere. These sentiments were strongest in country living communities where homogeneity was an essential part of their appeal. Critics nonetheless insisted their demands came from good intentions and that their desires for aesthetic or cultural uniformity fostered a spirit of unity. But their calls and demands were rooted in the hope that by curbing an Asian presence, these tactics and rules would sustain Euro-American fictions of a rural, exclusively white, American West—something that was under assault in a rapidly changing L.A.

At times, Asian families were told their rights to ethnic expression and suburban homeownership were welcomed. Once they wished to integrate culture into religious or commercial landscapes, however, challenges followed. In the cases of Hsi Lai, St. Lorenzo, 99 Ranch, and the battle over English signage, Asian residents learned inclusion had its limits. Their acceptance and abilities to live in country living rested on the standards of Euro-American suburban respectability. Critics suggested Chinese, Filipino, and Korean immigrants were not acting as dutiful neighbors and dutiful Americans, disavowing the process of assimilation expected of them. By situating local issues like architecture as measures of assimilation and good citizenship, critics were able to position Asian immigrants—rather than the white residents—as propagators of exclusion and division. Popular thinking about Asians as "forever foreigners" or members of a "yellow peril" facilitated an environment in which immigrants were seen as unable or unwilling to blend in. However, contrary to critics' arguments, Asian immigrants' choice to suburbanize and their accommodations to land use, design codes, and other local norms demonstrated an openness to assimilate and abide by the formal and informal rules of "country living." If that was not enough, Asian suburbanites embraced the concept of being the "model minority" to reach deals or achieve some semblance of racial harmony. Asian families recognized and denounced their experiences with discrimination, but ultimately, they consciously complied for the sake of keeping the peace and to protect the ideals and cachet of "country living."

FOUR

Asian Suburbanites in the "In-Between"

IN 1992, voters in California's Forty-First Congressional District elected the first Korean American to the US House of Representatives: Chang Joon Kim, also known as Jay Kim. His victory illuminated the undeniable force of Asian immigrants in Southern California and signaled a new era of San Gabriel Valley politics. Kim served three terms and was a rising star in the Republican Party. The district—which spanned parts of Los Angeles, Orange, and San Bernardino counties—encompassed large swaths of the East San Gabriel Valley's "country living" suburbs.[1] Upon winning, Kim suggested his ascension from working man to white-collar suburbanite to a member of the American political elite symbolized the possibilities of achieving the American Dream: "This is a heavily white district and they selected me. Nobody can know how emotional I feel right now. I said to myself, my God, this could only happen in America."[2]

Kim's unprecedented win was the result of growing multiethnic right-wing alliances across the region in the 1990s and 2000s, namely between white and Asian homeowners. Kim simultaneously embodied the profile of the East Valley's older generation as well as the characteristics of its newer settlers: conservative, educated, and propertied, but also an immigrant. Kim was not unlike his Asian counterparts in that he was open about practicing ethnic customs in the spirit of multiculturalism—an attitude Kim's white contemporaries said they supported. Yet he still championed assimilation and accentuated his American qualities over his Korean heritage knowing this was a right-leaning community. In doing so, immigrants including Kim found opportunities to forge relationships and alliances with white suburbanites who otherwise questioned Asians' suitability as neighbors.

To make a home for themselves in country living, Asian immigrants like Kim neither fully embraced nor fully resisted assimilation. Rather, they took a middle lane of doing both. Asian homeowners led transnational lives: Taiwanese entrepreneurs did business with Taipei firms from their suburban tracts and Filipino residents regularly traveled to and from the homeland. Yet these families practiced elements of mainstream American culture. They most demonstrated that by supporting cultural, political, or aesthetic norms that preserved postwar suburbia's Euro-American character and backed conservative policies protecting their privileges as a propertied class.

As a result, Asian families were simultaneously seen by others as friends and foes. They were "model minorities." At the same time, they had the potential to ruin country living. This constantly kept them in an "in-between" space between desired and unwanted. Asian residents, however, used this position to their advantage. They harnessed authority through their numbers and, accordingly, their financial and social capital. By the 1990s, white residents slowly shifted their opinions of Asian families. Whites and Asians fostered cross-racial partnerships because white residents were forced to engage with the growing population of Asian immigrants. Nevertheless, there were still limits to whites' receptiveness to diversity and to building community with Asian suburbanites despite overlapping economic or political interests.

For Chinese, Filipino, and Korean immigrants, there was always a tipping point or line not to be crossed. They were aware of that fragility. Asian residents could have challenged the East Valley's white conservative apparatus, but most chose not to. Asian immigrants believed there was value in keeping suburbia an exclusive, perceivably white domain. From schools to taxes, Asians proved they were not passive actors in neighborhood issues. Contrary to critics' assumptions of Asian apathy, many were civically informed and activated. By the mid-1990s, Asian residents were able to exercise their influence to affect policy, run for office, and become leaders representing entire communities, not just their co-ethnics. Asian conservatives—who either had volatile or apprentice-like relationships with the Old Guard—gained power, carrying the torch of their predecessors by committing themselves to keeping country living alive in the new century.

ASIAN "WHIZ KIDS" AND THE RACIAL POLITICS OF PUBLIC SCHOOLS

Like elsewhere in suburban America, public schools played a key role in the East Valley's growth.[3] Numerous school districts were prestigious, fueling a new housing boom between the 1970s and 1990s. While residents might have shared the same zip code, their kids did not always attend the same schools, nor were they afforded the same privileges. Developers, builders, and especially realtors established which areas were of highest value. However, homeowners, parents, and even their children also worked to deepen inequality and exacerbate stereotypes based on school district.

Since the 1960s, white homeowners distanced themselves from Black and Latino residents in the East Valley's working-class sections of Pomona, La Puente, West Covina, and Azusa. In the 1970s and 1980s, as white families continued to flee L.A. and its older suburbs, developers, builders, and real estate agents emphasized the quality of San Gabriel Valley school districts to sell new homes. They used schools as a marketing tool, hoping to lure middle-class and affluent buyers away from competitive suburban housing markets like those in Orange County. By the late 1980s, as wealthy Chinese immigrants from Hong Kong and Taiwan reached critical mass, they joined white residents in hierarchizing local schools and exacerbated existing educational or class divisions through real estate. Along with white agents, Asian realtors promoted specific suburbs in the San Gabriel Valley. They stressed the strength of area schools in the transnational market of Southern California real estate. Chinese agents, in particular, touted the exclusivity of select school districts in advertisements in both L.A. and in Asia, while badmouthing poorer ones. Influenced by stereotypes of Blacks, Latinos, and working-class Asians, realtors kept white-collar immigrants away from school districts serving those populations. Chinese realtors intentionally steered homebuyers to neighborhoods based on the academic reputation and demographics of its schools.[4] By advertising the valley's higher-performing schools in Hong Kong and Taiwan, and later, Mainland China, US- and Asia-based realtors created transnational buzz and hierarchies from thousands of miles away. While Monterey Park was widely known as America's "first suburban Chinatown," San Marino, Arcadia, and South Pasadena on the valley's west side were considered classier towns with better schools.[5] On the valley's east side, Walnut and Diamond Bar were held in similar esteem, with Chino Hills subsequently joining this trans-Pacific "hot list" in later years. Rounding out the group of acceptable suburbs were Alhambra, San Gabriel, Rowland Heights, and Hacienda Heights; housing in these communities were less aspirational but passed muster because of their well-regarded or satisfactory school districts.

For Asian immigrants shopping for houses in America, school districts were a deal-breaker. As Willow Lung-Amam notes, immigrants in Northern

California's Silicon Valley placed a premium on education because they came from countries with strong testing cultures. In Taiwan, China, and India, exams often determined one's career and pathway to financial success.[6] There was pressure to succeed on both the parents' and children's part because immigrants made sacrifices leaving the homeland to build new lives in America. Immigrants believed suburban schools opened doors to top US universities, thus increasing their children's chances for upward mobility. Sending their kids to US institutions was also a matter of practicality since the top universities in Hong Kong, Taiwan, Mainland China, South Korea, and Singapore were extremely selective, and in some cases, more selective than elite US schools.[7]

Throughout the 1980s and well into the 2000s, property values surged in country living communities. In multiple towns, however, price differences were stark depending on the school district. Housing values varied by neighborhood because school district boundaries rarely corresponded with city and Census-designated place (CDP) borders. These lines were drawn before towns like Diamond Bar, Walnut, or Chino Hills incorporated.[8] For example, west Walnut homes (served by Rowland Unified School District) were generally less expensive than east Walnut homes (served by Walnut Valley Unified School District). In Diamond Bar, houses in the southern part of the community (served by Walnut Valley Unified School District) were costlier than those in the north (served by Pomona Unified School District). Highly coveted school districts such as Walnut Valley Unified or individual schools like Wilson High in Hacienda Heights consistently ranked among the state's best, thus centralizing pockets of wealth contingent upon school prestige. By the mid-1990s, the influx of rich Asian families enticed longtime residents to leave, particularly those uncomfortable with the demographic shifts. White homeowners sold their houses at inflated prices, handsomely profiting from eager buyers willing to pay.[9] The demand was so high that Chinese buyers oftentimes bypassed realtors altogether. They cold-called homeowners or knocked on their doors pressuring them to sell. Some immigrants even stood on homeowners' porches with cash stuffed in nondescript briefcases or designer luggage.[10]

While a handful of school districts were acclaimed before mass Asian settlement, residents across racial lines believed US- and foreign-born Asian students raised the bar and international profile of East Valley schools. In historically mid-performing schools in Rowland Heights, Hacienda Heights, and Chino Hills, residents claimed housing prices and school reputations soared as more Asian students enrolled in the 1990s and 2000s. Asian children were "model minorities" whose academic success came from a culture of discipline and studiousness.[11] As one prominent local activist noted, she and her white neighbors understood Asians to be "very into education."[12] These widespread assumptions resulted in ideas of the overly competitive—if not cunning and ruthless—"whiz kid." A presumed inherent brilliance positioned Asian kids as cherished commodities, directly impacting the value and cachet of country living suburbs. Over time, the public school became a social laboratory and site of class formation. They were important sites of racialization and cultural exchange. Interactions or ideas learned on campus informed dynamics between whites, Asians, and other suburbanites of color. Teachers, administrators, realtors, and parents who praised Asian "geniuses" did so at the expense of positioning Black and Latino youth as morally suspect or lacking intellectual prowess. They also joked that Asian students inspired "lazy" white students to stay on par.

Stereotypes were particularly pervasive among the youth. In higher-performing schools in Walnut and Diamond Bar, for example, white students and Asian students tried to make sense of each other's worlds albeit by perpetuating race-based myths. Asian youth viewed their white peers as pleasure-seeking, laid-back kids who preferred recreation over academics. White students, on the other hand, saw their Asian classmates as foreign, overachieving, and lacking social or athletic skills. Outside of the classroom, Asians were chastised for self-segregating behavior (e.g., ethnic cliques), making them prone to accusations of "reverse discrimination" or—especially for first-generation children—refusing to assimilate.[13] From the town library to the baseball diamond, parents and their children shaped ideas about race and made clear-cut geographic and class distinctions between families living in the "good" parts of town versus the "bad," with school districts determining hierarchies of place and privilege.

Despite white residents' praise of Asians' intrinsic academic talent, Asian families were simultaneously accused of creating a cutthroat environment. Critics denigrated Asian parents for robbing K–12 education of innocence and "fun" through helicopter parenting or purposefully stifling the popularity of sports programs and extracurricular courses like woodworking. Meanwhile, if they were not accused of being domineering parents, others alleged Asian parents were physically or emotionally distant from their kids because they overlooked obligations like attending back-to-school nights or PTA meetings.[14] With the popularity of "parachute children"—that is, kids dropped off in America to attend school while their parents entirely or partly lived in Asia—critics believed Asian parents were irresponsible and therefore unfit as suburbanites.[15] These forms of transnational families left their children with large sums of money and then forced them to raise themselves in a new country. Criticisms of the phenomenon also came from Asian parents who believed parachute children—particularly from extremely wealthy Chinese families—were entitled and materialistic. Rowland Heights homeowner Chen-Li Hsia bemoaned the trend:

> I see a lot of Chinese people coming in here [to the East San Gabriel Valley] ... really rich.... Their kids are very spoiled. [They] drive [a] good car, [and are)] very irresponsible. They can have $10,000 allowance a month! They see something, they want it, they buy it. They [and their parents] can afford it.... I know one friend's son.... They play computer ... don't study ... don't get up in the morning... but he got accepted into USC because of [his parent's] donation [to the school].[16]

Notwithstanding these criticisms, local actors used the "model minority" trope to their advantage. Realtors and politicians marketed schools with larger Asian populations as hubs of academic stimulation, which in turn resulted in greater housing demand and higher property values. These ideas did not apply to schools with substantial Black or Latino populations. Racially triangulated vis-à-vis whites and Blacks or whites and Latinos, Asians stood in between as the preferred racial group. In the East Valley, Asians maintained—if not embraced—what Claire Jean Kim calls their "valorized position" above other people of color because they materially benefited from occupying this zone. On its surface, the politicization of Asian kids had minimal effect on residents' lived experiences. On the contrary, the ways in which Asian students were commodified, celebrated, and criticized influenced the social, political, and economic landscape of wealthier country living suburbs. Measuring neighborhood prestige contingent on how many Asian kids lived there played a role in making certain areas more exclusive and thus more desirable. This was notable considering the scrutiny Asians received in other arenas of suburban life. Unlike religious or retail spaces, when it came to education, the more Asian a school district was perceived to be, the better it was. These ideas about race, class, intellect, and safety were made markedly clear in regional battles over school district boundaries during the 1980s and 1990s.

Homeownership within the boundaries of Walnut Valley Unified was so desirable that Diamond Bar and Walnut homeowners not residing in the district consistently went to court to change the boundaries. Class interests and racial anxieties generally motivated residents' attempts to redraw district lines. However, homeowners—who were worried about being called elitist or racist—deployed class- and color-blind language in redistricting campaigns to avoid accusations of prejudice. They argued that redistricting was about the protection and safety of their children, the quality of education, and for having a cohesive civic identity, particularly in master-planned country living communities where most of the resistance occurred.

The most organized redistricting movements occurred at the height of regional development. In the late 1980s, stay-at-home mother Susan Kelley believed west Walnut children were denied the right to attend Walnut Valley Unified schools, the district that shared the name of their suburb. Kelley, whose tract house was located in Walnut's new Creekside neighborhood, lived within the boundaries of Rowland Unified. Like her neighbors, Kelley was not concerned about their assigned elementary school which enjoyed a prestigious reputation.[17] White parents, in particular, were worried about the district's intermediate and high schools—Rincon and Nogales—which served west Walnut children as well as kids from nearby West Covina and La Puente. Rincon and Nogales were located in older, unplanned suburbs with larger working-class and lower-middle-class Latino and Asian populations. Both schools had lower California Academic Performance Index (API) test scores compared to their wealthier counterparts in south Rowland Heights, east Walnut, and south Diamond Bar.[18] Nogales, especially, held a disreputable image. On-campus bomb explosions, ethnic gangs, drive-by shootings, and neighborhood violence associated with Nogales students marred the school's credibility.[19]

Hundreds of west Walnut homeowners called upon city and district leaders from Rowland Unified and Walnut Valley Unified to redraw the existing boundaries. Kelley led the grassroots battle of predominantly white and Asian homeowners. On March 8, 1989, Walnut mayor Drexel L. Smith advised Rowland Unified and Walnut Valley Unified superintendents and administrators to "evaluate the feasibility of transferring territory so that residents of the City of Walnut attend the Walnut Valley Unified School

District."[20] Walnut Valley Unified leaders were supportive of this potential acquisition plan since public school districts received additional state funding and higher revenue limits per student. Officials also understood the Rowland Unified students they would take in lived in Walnut, not West Covina or La Puente. However, the district worried they were unable to accommodate these students since Walnut was in the middle of a new housing boom. In June, Kelley and fellow Walnut homeowner Marsha Bracco sent a letter to the Rowland Unified school board and community leaders urging a boundary change: "Walnut is divided by being part of two districts."[21] Kelley and Bracco added, "By attending Rowland schools, we are left out of things in Walnut—we have been ignored." They alleged, "People won't buy (Walnut) homes that are in the Rowland district," even though they knew their homes were located within boundaries prior to sale.[22] Residents claimed realtors did not disclose this information or downplayed the district's reputation. They felt cheated as property owners and as parents. Redistricting supporters believed Walnut politicians and bureaucrats—most of whom lived on the town's east side—intentionally overlooked Creekside residents because of its Rowland Unified affiliation.[23]

In May 1990, redistricting advocates collected over one thousand signatures supporting the transfer of eighteen hundred west Walnut students to Walnut Valley Unified schools. Activists organized as United Neighbors Involved for Youth (UNIFY).[24] The name suggested a desire to bring together Walnut children separated by two school districts. Moreover, UNIFY's name publicly reminded residents of Walnut's master-planned suburban identity, reinforcing their argument for the need of a singular school district. UNIFY's petition was immediately met with resistance from Rowland Unified board members, administrators, and personnel. Redistricting opponents suspected classism and bigotry motivated UNIFY activists, not just the academic reputation of Rowland Unified schools.[25] At the time of UNIFY's mobilization efforts, Walnut Valley Unified's two largest student populations were white (46.4%) and Asian (24.3%). In contrast, Rowland Unified's two largest student populations were Latino (46.1%) and white (24.3%).[26]

White and Asian parents in Walnut and in wealthier parts of Rowland Heights worried about the influence of students from predominantly working- and lower-middle-class suburbs like La Puente or poorer sections of Rowland Heights. Rowland Unified administrators and teachers noticed hesitation from Chinese and Korean parents in sending their children to schools with sizable Latino populations, alluding to a prevalence of gangs, drugs, and violence.[27] Asian parents cited cultural dissimilarities and degrees of studiousness as reasons to place their kids in schools with mostly white and Asian students. Fears of the "other" were cloaked under the guise of protecting their kids' interests so young people did not have to constantly reconcile cultural differences during their formative years. One of UNIFY's strongest nonwhite supporters included Councilmember William Choctaw, Walnut's first Black elected official. While he and others in UNIFY hailed Walnut's increasing diversity, they felt Rowland Unified's demographics were radically different from the makeup of their neighborhoods. Choctaw said, "I don't think it should be the parents' primary responsibility to bring a school district up to any level. That is the professionals' responsibility, the responsibility of those people employed by the district. If you're a parent, your first responsibility is to those children." Choctaw believed parents should have full say where their kids attended school.[28] He and his UNIFY counterparts argued that all of Walnut needed to be within Walnut Valley Unified boundaries to enhance the suburb's identity and morale and because parents were within their rights to provide children with the best quality of education possible—even if that meant seceding from their legally assigned district.

Among the harshest critics of UNIFY was former Rowland Unified school board member Rolland Boceta, a Filipino homeowner in West Covina. He alleged racism fueled UNIFY's activism. Boceta said their plans made his "blood boil" and speculated, "If Nogales High School wasn't 45% Hispanic, I don't think we'd have these problems" over district boundaries.[29] Former Rowland Unified school board member Albert Chang, a US-born Chinese resident in Rowland Heights, also believed racism played a role: "You could never say that in public because you'd be deemed racist. You know, there was that 'concern about gangs' in Walnut High School [too]." Because Walnut Valley Unified's richer and predominantly white and Asian student body suggested a safer, more innocent environment, UNIFY either overlooked or were unaware that Asian gangs lived in upscale parts of Walnut and Diamond Bar. Nevertheless, they were deemed less threatening compared to Latino gangs whose turf included areas covered by Rowland Unified.[30]

Beyond class or racial anxieties, redistricting opponents alleged Asian residents in Creekside allied with their white neighbors because they thought redistricting would raise property values. For Boceta, UNIFY members were driven by the economic interests of homeowners: "To say real estate is not an issue would almost be the same thing as saying Saddam Hussein is a saint."[31] A Filipino resident claimed, "[Their rationale was] 'If my home is in Walnut [Valley] Unified, it will be a better value for my home.' Asians are looking at it as an economic issue. . . . [What will] bring more value to their homes? Because when a prospective buyer says, 'Where will my kids go?' [They will look at] Rowland's test scores and look at Walnut's . . . [and they will choose Walnut Valley Unified]."[32] Indeed, realtors—particularly Chinese agents—typically inflated home prices located within the boundaries of Walnut Valley Unified knowing rich immigrants were willing to spend more.[33] Money was no object among the Asian diasporic elite purchasing properties in the valley. One UNIFY activist estimated home values between the districts differed as much as 15–30 percent because of the influence of Chinese realtors and their clients.[34] For immigrants, their homes were global investments. School districts served as a barometer of prestige, desirability, and the potential for high resale values. These were houses for their families, but ultimately, these were important commodities in the international orbit of Asia-to-California real estate. Once the owners' kids finished their K–12 education, they would then sell their home to a younger Asian family, thus repeating the cycle of wealthy transnational families seeking suburban homeownership in prestigious school districts.

UNIFY petition signatories insisted their desires to redraw the boundaries was so their children attended school in the suburb they called home. Kelley said the request was not motivated by racism or class separation but one of community cohesion: "Our children . . . are separated from their natural neighborhood peers. Important aspects of their development such as after-school day-care services, youth sports programs, recreation programs . . . are coordinated through the Walnut Valley Unified School District."[35] Kelley further claimed Walnut's public cable television station, Channel 56, presented favorable news of Walnut Valley Unified schools while excluding Rowland Unified from their coverage. West Walnut homeowners also believed they were shut out of scholarship opportunities from civic groups (e.g., Kiwanis, Lions, and Rotary clubs) even though they lived within city boundaries.[36] District unification, as far as Kelley was concerned, would end these divisions. Moreover, for UNIFY organizers at least, this was a class- and color-blind issue affecting homeowners interested in protecting Walnut's well-to-do reputation. Critics of UNIFY said UNIFY's feelings of exclusion from the rest of Walnut was selective ignorance and that assertions of victimhood were bogus. Critics further alleged that their claims of wanting suburban unity were meant to distract residents from the underlying motivation: finding a way for west Walnut residents to disassociate from Rowland Unified's diverse, less affluent student body. Redistricting opponents thought UNIFY went out of their way to distance themselves from West Covina and La Puente residents because their communities did not embody country living.

To address one of UNIFY's concerns, Rowland Unified administrators negotiated with the Walnut Recreation Department to allow west Walnut residents to use their facilities. In addition, they urged city leaders to keep west Walnut homeowners abreast of youth programming regardless of school district. But that was not enough to please petitioners who still felt marginalized. Kelley responded, "I don't think there's anything short of a transfer that will absolutely cure the problem that we have. We have to constantly remind people that we are part of this city."[37] Critics of UNIFY remained unmoved. One resident noted in a local newspaper, "I feel sorry for the affluent, well educated Walnut residents who don't take the time to read the *Highlander* along with all the many signs and posters advertising Walnut's programs, events and calendars. . . . As far not wanting to buy in Rowland District, all these red flag waving, petition thinking residents did with eyes wide open. Rowland had and still has a terrific record—what's changed?"[38] To be sure, UNIFY's claims were not off base. Sympathetic Walnut Valley officials agreed with Kelley, including its deputy superintendent.[39] Walnut Valley Unified and the City of Walnut worked closely together in a variety of festivals and initiatives that gave west Walnut residents the impression of favoritism, partly because east Walnut homeowners understood they lived in a wealthier area thanks to its school district. By claiming a country living address, Walnut parents on both sides of town felt entitled to a set of privileges, which included access to whiter, richer schools.

After garnering the signatures required to explore the feasibility of redrawing school boundaries, in fall 1990, the Los Angeles County Committee on School District Reorganization held two public meetings on what redistricting entailed.[40] In November, the county denied UNIFY's request citing school districts statewide serviced multiple communities. Walnut's situation was not exceptional. Disappointed with the county's decision, UNIFY leaders appealed to the State Board of Education. The board argued that because district lines were drawn a century before and prior to the creation of cities such as Walnut, there were insufficient reasons to redraw the boundaries. They also cited the costliness in student transfers and staff redistribution as additional problems with the plan. State officials further agreed with county leaders by arguing that few school districts in California lined up with municipal boundaries.

Following a series of legal defeats, UNIFY halted attempts to redraw district lines. Dissatisfied parents enrolled their children in private school hoping to protect them from the perceived vices and negative influences of Rincon and Nogales students. Some families moved away. Others stayed in Creekside but found ways to send their kids to Walnut Valley Unified schools. Kelley, for example, joined personnel at Walnut Valley Unified. As a staff member, she was permitted to enroll her children.[41] Years after the UNIFY battle of the late 1980s and early 1990s, redistricting advocates stayed committed to the cause. By the end of the 1990s, Creekside's Asian homeowners—not its white residents—remained steadfast advocates of joining Walnut Valley Unified. But their efforts were often derailed by local leaders, school administrators, and county officials who continued to cite legal precedent as reasons to keep the lines in place.[42] Homeowners' attempts to use the argument of suburban planning (i.e., country living) and class- or color-blind notions of "unifying" Walnut failed. For those who fought, this was not the suburban American Dream they envisioned and were sold.

Similar efforts to redraw school district lines occurred in neighboring suburbs as well. In Diamond Bar—a country living suburb serviced by two school districts—white activists and a cadre of Asian homeowners sought to redraw boundaries throughout the 1980s and 1990s. Children in north Diamond Bar attended Pomona Unified schools, which drew in students from largely Black and Latino sections of neighboring Pomona. Residents sometimes referred to these areas as "Sin Town," a nickname created by the Crips, a local gang.[43] Like families in west Walnut, homeowners in north Diamond Bar sought annexation from Walnut Valley Unified for decades. White parents grew increasingly frustrated, particularly after the US Department of Justice implemented a mandatory integration plan for Pomona Unified's Ganesha High school in 1979. Residents vehemently resisted, claiming integration plans and "forced busing" were forms of communist social engineering.[44] One mother, Carol Herrera (who would later become Diamond Bar mayor), said she was against busing because suburbanites had the right to "take advantage of the schools" and that Pomona's schools were too "urban" for her family.[45] North Diamond Bar homeowner Janice Stewart quickly pulled her daughter Elizabeth out of Ganesha, fearing Elizabeth would succumb to immoral behavior: "It was too big a jump [from her time in private middle school]. I should've kept her in private school. . . . Way too big a jump . . . [and a] backwards [one] unfortunately!"[46] Determined to protect Elizabeth from the influence of Pomona kids, Janice's friends pulled strings to get Elizabeth into Walnut High, a school with more white and Asian students. Janice recalled the area near Ganesha was "all Black . . . and not the atmosphere she was used to [in Diamond Bar]. It would've not been a good match. That was ghetto up in that corner" of Pomona.[47]

For white homeowners like Janice, a lack of exposure to people of color informed her attitudes about what type of "atmosphere" she wanted her children to experience. Much of this had to do with the fact that many of the East Valley's white residents originally came from less diverse rural areas or small towns of the Midwest and South. Newcomers to the area—many of whom were Asian immigrants originating from racially or ethnically homogenous nations—would also become stalwart critics of Pomona Unified schools in the 1990s. Like their white neighbors, they absorbed Black or Latino stereotypes recycled through globally disseminated US media. Moreover, histories of European colonialism in their native lands like Hong Kong, the Philippines, and India cemented ideas around whiteness and colorism. Mass culture's derision of Blacks, Latinos, and darker-skinned immigrants informed white and Asian parents' decisions on whether to allow their children to socialize with them.

Some residents, however, were unfazed by Pomona Unified's demographics. Shawn Dunn, a north Diamond Bar resident of mixed white and Korean heritage, attended Ganesha High in the early 1990s. Growing up in Oregon, he admitted Ganesha was a "culture shock." But he believed realtors, homeowners, and critics across ethnic lines distorted Ganesha's image based on the school's diversity. Shawn thought rumors about Ganesha's racial tensions and gang violence were unsubstantiated: "People were very friendly to me [and] I wasn't ever bullied [despite being white and Korean]."[48] Residents' criticism encouraged Ganesha students to write op-eds, think pieces, or letters to area newspapers attempting to assure north Diamond Bar parents that Blacks and Latinos did not threaten the quality of its school nor the safety of their kids. Mechelle Taylor, a Black student, wrote, "The people at Ganesha are . . . a complete mixture. The teachers are there to teach, not babysit," suggesting that instructors and staff did not coddle students unlike their peers at whiter or wealthier schools.[49] Taylor's white classmate, Derek Engdahl agreed, "Unlike many other high schools, Ganesha exists in the 'real world,'" arguing its diversity was reflective of a changing California.[50]

But their praises were ignored. North Diamond Bar homeowners continued to pull kids out of Pomona Unified schools. If they did not send their children to private schools, they asked friends on the south side to use their home addresses. Other parents created fraudulent addresses to register their kids.[51] In 1997, after years of lobbying leaders and thanks to voter-approved bonds, Pomona Unified opened Diamond Ranch High School on the hills of Phillips Ranch. The new school, which served north Diamond Bar and Phillips Ranch, was created to meet the needs of a booming population in these country living communities and to appease frustrated homeowners. This included Asian immigrants who actively found ways to send their children to different schools. District and city leaders recognized the growing political and cultural capital of affluent immigrants, especially of diasporic Chinese from Hong Kong, Taiwan, and later, Mainland China. Rather than dealing with redistricting fights and losing revenue from under-enrollment, Pomona Unified yielded to their demands. Residents believed Diamond Ranch's creation was due in part to homeowners' doggedness, especially Asian immigrants whose money swayed local officials to act. As one Chinese resident claimed, "They built that high school because a lot of [north] Diamond Bar kids . . . were fleeing [for Walnut Valley Unified or private schools]. If you're living in a million-dollar home in Diamond Bar, why would you let your kid go to Ganesha in Pomona? It doesn't make sense. So that's why they built Diamond Ranch—to basically stop the exodus of all the students [particularly Asian children]."[52]

In north Diamond Bar, west Walnut, and other sections of East Valley country living, white residents stood at the forefront of redistricting battles with the vocal or tacit support of Asian homeowners. Parents hoped to shield their children from suburbanites who they believed exhibited values of "city people." At the same time, their high expectations as investors in country living colored what caliber of education their kids received. To them, socioeconomically diverse schools and proximity to "urban" problems did not align with the neatly packaged image of a master-planned western lifestyle. For Asian immigrants especially, there was more to lose than their white neighbors. Homeownership and how well their children performed in school were important measures of their success and abilities to survive in America. If their children fared well during their K–12 years, this foreshadowed a prosperous future. It also allowed them to save face among relatives or friends who doubted their abilities to make it in a new country. How one thrived in the United States depended on early decisions like where families lived and the schools their children attended. Besides achieving economic success, this was a matter of demonstrating social citizenship.[53] Avoiding risks allowed them to reach these benchmarks of "American-ness" faster.

Access to a quality education in the suburbs was a universal draw for postwar families across demographic lines. In the East Valley, however, education was commodified in ways that impacted Asians' degrees of inclusion. Despite criticisms of unbalanced parenting or extreme studiousness, Asian families and their children were used to illuminate the academic rigor of area schools. They were lauded for bringing a layer of distinction to classrooms and, concomitantly, real estate. Moreover, their activism in redistricting efforts as a means of concentrating resources or consolidating white and Asian students to particular schools positioned them as both "model minorities" and good neighbors. They were, along with their white counterparts, acting in accordance for the sake of country living. In doing so, they reified ideas of the "good immigrant," Asians who—thanks to US immigration policies prioritizing intellectuals, students, and businesspeople—were part of an elite class devoted to academic and material ambitions.[54] Asian families embraced these "positive" stereotypes, while affirming their privilege as a wealthier, transnational immigrant cohort thus making them less threatening to their white neighbors.

Interestingly, while some aligned with the "model minority" image, they also challenged these notions through their political activism and defiance in fully adopting American models of learning or parenting. East Valley schools proved to be a crucial site of racialization because they illustrated how Asian families were perennially caught in a space between. To their neighbors, Asian residents were friends and enemies whose presence elevated suburbia yet had the potential to mar its reputation. On the whole, when it came to schools, Asian families exercised their "model minority" status for leverage, gaining social clout and a reputation as respectable suburbanites despite neighbors' apprehensions.

POLITICIZING WASTE AND THE CLASS-BLIND OPTICS OF DEFENDING COUNTRY LIVING

In the 1990s, critics remained wary over the influx of Asian settlers. Yet many residents simultaneously applauded them for joining forces with neighbors in fighting unwanted development. Gradually, Asian homeowners became NIMBY (Not In My Back Yard) allies, thus alleviating critics' anxieties of being threats to country living.[55] Class-based issues thrust immigrants into the political sphere, which some used as a platform to climb the ranks of government. Well into the new century, Asian homeowners vacillated between foe and friend; foes when they transgressed norms, and friends when they backed policies popular among the right. Over time, Asian immigrants with political or social influence used their voices to challenge white control, becoming the new faces of suburban conservativism and NIMBYism. From landfills to public housing, successful opposition to controversial projects illustrated the force of these interracial coalitions.

In fall 1993, City of Industry proposed construction of a landfill known as the Material Recovery Facility (MRF). Almost entirely zoned for industrial, commercial, or retail purposes, the city had been a controversial neighbor to country living suburbs for decades, largely because of its prioritization of business above residential matters. Industry's MRF plan was immediately met with objections across the East Valley, particularly from homeowners who lived in towns bordering the proposed facility. MRF was intended to serve as a separation plant where recyclables were divided into types and then sent to different recycling plants. Like other regional landfills, MRF would have been a part of a profitable global business of waste management. The forty-five-acre refuse complex was proposed to sit along Industry's most-eastern end—adjacent to Diamond Bar; within miles of Chino Hills, Phillips Ranch, and a tonier neighborhood of West Covina known as South Hills; and directly across from Snow Creek, one of Walnut's higher-end master-planned tracts.

Residents were incensed, especially Asian homeowners. Though MRF leaders and proponents claimed residents would not be exposed to hazardous or toxic chemicals, homeowners nonetheless believed MRF would cause health or environmental problems. They also feared MRF would generate more traffic and welcome "outsiders" into their communities. Residents further argued that dumps had no place in country living because these facilities were antithetical to the sylvan idyll they paid a premium for. The politics surrounding MRF brought Asian immigrants from their living rooms and into city hall. Pressured by their constituents—including a number of influential conservative activists and wealthy Asian leaders—Walnut and Diamond Bar councilmembers pressed MRF and City of Industry officials to address residents' concerns. To quell criticism, Industry leaders proposed to move the site farther away from Snow Creek. But the distance was still unsatisfactory to opponents. On June 11, 1994, hundreds of Walnut and Diamond Bar residents met outside Walnut City Hall to march against the landfill. Organized by the MRF Task Force—a multiethnic community-based organization who opposed the project—homeowners across racial lines chanted and picketed. News crews from L.A. filmed the spectacle putting a spotlight on the quiet bedroom community. Protestors accused Industry officials of valuing profit over residents' safety and quality of life.

Heading the MRF Task Force was Joaquin Lim, a Walnut homeowner and leader in the valley's Chinese community. He, along with a core group of Asian homeowners, were among MRF's earliest and fiercest critics. At city council or commission meetings in Diamond Bar, Walnut, and City of Industry, Asian residents publicly challenged leaders to stop MRF from moving forward. Industry council meetings attracted so many residents that dozens were turned away from the chambers. At one meeting, chamber seats were at capacity while another two hundred people stood outside waiting to address the council during public testimony. This included Asian protestors with limited English proficiency. Lim urged his contemporaries to insist on talking, even if the city did not have Chinese, Korean, or other language translators on site so their names and views were on record. Lim believed Industry officials "tried their very best to make life difficult" for Asian residents. He claimed racial bias because they restricted speaking time and discouraged Asian protestors from having the mic. For future meetings, MRF Task Force leaders demanded translators for both the council and the public: "Some people came up to me and told me they wanted to testify, but couldn't because of a language barrier."[56] While banned inside, Asian MRF opponents joined their non-Asian counterparts outside chanting "No MRF" throughout the hearings, generating more frustration from MRF and Industry leaders distracted by the din.

To homeowners like Elaine Chan, having MRF nearby undermined the country living ideal beyond property values. This would bring an end to a model suburban lifestyle they dreamed about while living in Asia. This was also the potential loss of their status as homeowners in an affluent master-planned community—something that set Asian families in towns like Walnut, Diamond Bar, and Chino Hills apart from their counterparts in ethnoburbs like Monterey Park. Chan believed, "The openness, cleanliness, and serenity I sought when I chose to live in Walnut are being threatened by the MRF and the value of the investment will plunge precipitously with the first shovelful of dirt removed to build this abomination."[57] She commended Asian anti-MRF activists like Joaquin Lim for "an outstanding job of leading" the cause on behalf of all homeowners.[58] By coordinating public protests and through building a multiethnic coalition of homeowners across the valley,

Asian immigrants emerged as key faces of the opposition. The prominence of their activism dispelled assumptions of Asians' political apathy and assuaged tensions between foreign-born and native-born residents.

Asian residents against MRF mobilized the community by engaging ethnic-based organizations like Chinese associations and Asian church groups. MRF opponents helped transform these transnationally tied cultural clubs into informal grassroots political action committees. Traditionally, Chinese associations concentrated on cultural programming or initiatives. This included funding scholarships for students to study in Asia or hosting events for diplomats from "sister cities" in Taiwan.[59] Despite their suburban base, Chinese organizations were more globally focused than locally minded. Neighborhood issues like MRF encouraged ethnic clubs to engage at home in the valley rather than directing their efforts to the homeland. With the robust financial resources of a transnational class, the Diamond Bar Chinese Association (DBCA) and the Chinese Association of Walnut (CAAW), for example, allocated funds to participate in anti-MRF activism. DBCA and CAAW purchased poster boards and supplies for picketing. They printed five thousand flyers and form letters in Chinese and in English "to educate the public at large."[60] They encouraged Chinese associations in Chino Hills and Rowland Heights to engage because of their large memberships and geographic proximity to City of Industry. William Pao, president of CAAW, even enlisted elementary school students to make anti-MRF posters. Along with Chinese groups, church-based clubs including St. Lorenzo Church's Filipino Association participated in anti-MRF activism. These nonpolitical, ethnic-based associations—which were initially less integrated into the mainstream—started working with traditionally white-led homeowners associations.[61] MRF and other growth- or land-use-related issues served as critical sites of interethnic coalition building. Cultural differences aside, white residents and homeowners of color had more in common than what was perceived on either end. White suburbanites—particularly those of the Old Guard—started to change their views on having Asian families as neighbors. Witnessing their grassroots investment in the country living ideal positioned Asian immigrants as political allies rather than threats to the valley.

After years of back-and-forth negotiations and legal challenges, City of Industry and MRF leaders withdrew their plans. This was due to a broad coalition of city councilmembers, state legislators, residents, homeowners associations, and Asian organizations.[62] These disparate populations found common ground and a shared class-based interest in stopping the dump from marring country living. The seemingly mundane case of a landfill served as a cautionary tale of what could happen if homeowners did not police their neighborhoods and stay attuned to civic affairs, particularly as the region of new tract homes continued to grow by the thousands. Moreover, the visibility of Asian activism throughout MRF's controversies disrupted whites' assumptions of their Asian counterparts. Until this point, critics generally saw Asian immigrants as apolitical, if not menacing in matters of the built environment because of the rise of ethnoburban landscapes. Crucially, Asians' active involvement throughout the MRF fight showed suburbanites how "model minorities" were not only reliable conservative allies. By the end of the 1990s, Asians had the wherewithal to be ideal leaders and defenders of country living.

At the same time, there were limits to how far Asians could go in terms of using their power and newfound cultural capital. Even as white residents descended into a racial minority at the turn of the century, they—particularly the Old Guard—continued to exercise their authority over the East Valley. To keep their political influence and agenda in preserving country living alive, white homeowners needed to work with Asian residents so their legacies were felt for decades to come. Ultimately, this multiethnic alliance sought to uphold an image of the area rooted in white settler colonialism as a means of keeping these towns exclusive. Euro-American country living design and standards of the postwar suburban lifestyle inscribed and protected the force of whiteness in the East Valley well into the twenty-first century—ideas kept alive by residents who believed suburbia was supposed to look and feel "mainstream" no matter the year or ethnic makeup of the peoples residing in these communities.

TRANSFERS OF POWER: OLD GUARD OUT, ASIAN CONSERVATIVES IN

Judy Chen Haggerty entered local politics after years of witnessing a lack of proper representation from the Old Guard, which she considered "very Republican" and believed was uncomfortable with the influx of Asian immigrants. A Rowland Heights homeowner since the early 1980s, Judy—like many of her Asian neighbors—was highly educated, held a professional background as a practicing attorney, and—like the Old Guard—held right-leaning views. However, she disapproved of the Old Guard's brand of conservatism, how they governed, and how they dealt with change. She believed older whites felt threatened by Asian immigrants because of their perceived exoticism and wealth. A native of Taiwan, Judy's father "always said [to] 'just mind your own business'" and focus on making money as Americans. But she had enough. She regularly experienced discrimination in everyday settings, alluding to attitudes of the Old Guard mirrored in the actions of various people she encountered in the community, particularly in the years after settling: "When you go to [a mainstream] supermarket . . . people ask about you. They're very resistant [to me]. I don't feel right. . . . I remember one time at Vons market, the cashier is very friendly [to the white customers in front]. . . . And so, come to me, it's just like [they] shut down. Maybe he [thought] I don't speak English so when I take out the credit card [to pay] and then [sign] the slip, he just threw the pen at me. And I go, 'Wait a minute. You were so friendly with him!'"[63]

In another instance, when Judy and her husband (who is white) were registering for their wedding at Robinsons-May, the department store sales assistant (an older white woman) refused to acknowledge Judy and only spoke to her spouse. Even Judy's US-born daughter was subject to stereotyping, including the time school officials encouraged her to enroll in English as a Second Language (ESL) classes because they thought she did not speak English and because she preferred playing piano over athletics. Together, these triggering encounters with what Judy called "very subtle" acts of Old Guard bigotry compelled her to address anti-Asianism while encouraging her to "Americanize" through politics.[64] In 2001, Judy was elected to the Board of Trustees of Mt. San Antonio College (Mt. SAC), a community college serving Walnut, Diamond Bar, Rowland Heights, and surrounding suburbs. Some members of the Old Guard initially doubted her electability (a seat she has held for two decades): "[I] sort of [ran for] a racial reason. I'm sorta rebelling [by serving in office]. If (someone is doubting me) because of my race, I'm not gonna take it. I fight harder." With broad support, particularly from Asian voters in her first run, Judy came into office at a time when Asian residents increasingly exerted their influence in the public sphere, a realm the Old Guard dominated for decades.

From school redistricting to land use issues, Asian immigrants like Judy demonstrated they were more invested in local politics than their critics assumed. White residents who were otherwise skeptical or wary of their Asian neighbors found allies. This union became stronger during the mid-1990s in concert with growing right-wing activism across the suburban and rural

Sunbelt. The East Valley's tradition of electing Republicans (and "Reagan Democrats") for local, state, and federal office informed the voting habits of Asian residents throughout the region. Its agrarian character and tracts of comfortable suburban families—coupled with its physical proximity to "red" territories like the Inland Empire and the "Orange Curtain" (i.e., Orange County)—kept the East Valley safely in GOP hands for decades.[65]

White conservatives and pro-business activists—including the Old Guard—found formidable partners in Asian suburbanites because of their wealth and the specter of the Cold War. In the 1980s and 1990s, Asian voters generally leaned on the right, especially among the diaspora's richer classes who owned businesses or worked in white-collar fields.[66] Neoliberal economic policies and relaxed trade barriers passed through conservative congresses and during the Ronald Reagan, George H. W. Bush, and Bill Clinton presidencies strengthened the influx and influence of Pacific Rim capital in Southern California. Pro-business policies, coupled with the GOP's hawkish stance against communism made the Republican Party appealing to immigrants and refugees displaced by the ideology. Like the valley's core group of white Republicans, Asian residents held strong anti-communist views. They escaped violent or unstable political regimes (e.g., Mainland China, South Korea, Taiwan, Vietnam, Cambodia). Others lived under colonial or neocolonial rule (e.g., Hong Kong, the Philippines, India) where subjects and subsequent generations were taught to embrace Western ideals rooted in benevolent assimilation. In turn, as American suburbanites, immigrants, and refugees regularly backed right-wing, libertarian, or moderate policies at what Tom Sugrue dubbed the "crabgrass-roots" level.[67] Under the banner of economic freedom, Asian suburbanites supported low-taxation and anti-union legislation, particularly if they were entrepreneurs.[68] Furthermore, Asian voters aligned with conservative positions on social issues like abortion and same-sex marriage since these were also shunned across the Pacific. From Vietnamese enclaves in Orange County to Chinese ethnoburbs in the San Gabriel Valley, the first waves of post-1965 Asian immigrants or refugees did not stand with the left like Black and Latino voters, with class and Cold War geopolitics informing their views. From 1980 to 1996, a majority of Asians supported Republican presidential candidates.[69] In California, Asian voters backed numerous Republican-endorsed propositions including Proposition 187, the controversial "Save Our State (S.O.S.)" initiative denying "illegal aliens" access to health care, education, and other public services. 57 percent of the Asian electorate voted in favor of Proposition 187, with many of those voters living in the suburbs.[70] Emotionally, culturally, and financially, immigrants held onto their ties to Asia. But their lives as California homeowners encouraged them to assimilate into the mainstream. This included endorsing policies benefiting their economic interests or those that gave them clout as people of color in suburbia.

Strengths of Asian conservatism in the valley varied by community and class. With the exception of Chinese homeowners in well-to-do suburbs like San Marino or Arcadia, the West Valley's Asian electorate leaned left. The West Valley's proximity to L.A. and heavily working-class or Latino communities like East L.A., Boyle Heights, and the "Gateway Cities" of Pico Rivera and Bell informed regional politics. These were sites of liberal or radical activism and Brown Power mobilization in the 1960s and 1970s.[71] In Monterey Park, for instance, first- and second-generation Chinese residents forged coalitions with Latino suburbanites during the 1980s amid a groundswell of nativism. Chinese activists found further support from Japanese residents, some of whom had deep ties to Monterey Park, El Monte, and Montebello as descendants of agricultural workers or survivors of internment during World War II.[72]

Asian residents on the valley's east side, especially homeowners living in country living communities, typically stood on the right. This is partly because a number of California's most influential Republican leaders and conservative firebrands represented the region. This included state senators Frank Hill and Dick Mountjoy—the latter best known for introducing Proposition 187 in the Assembly.[73] During the 1980s and 1990s, the valley boasted Republican delegations at state and national party conventions that were among the largest after its neighbor Orange County.[74] This network included a robust cohort of Asian Republicans admired by party leaders for helping diversify the GOP. Though many Asian voters independently joined the party, much of their support was the result of targeted outreach from local Republican machines. As the Asian population soared in the 1990s, a savvy collective of white activists reached out to Chinese, Filipino, and Korean residents, particularly those with deeper pockets. Conservative leaders knew Asian immigrants owned or worked at profitable transnational companies and were vehemently anti-communist. Republicans capitalized on their suspicions of the left, while working-class suburbanites claimed Asians disregarded blue-collar concerns. For example, during a regional strike of multiple American grocery chains in Diamond Bar, Chino Hills, Pomona, Hacienda Heights, Rowland Heights, and Glendora, white union workers claimed Asian consumers who crossed picket lines would "pretend they don't speak English so they don't have to support unions."[75] One worker alleged Asian suburbanites "don't care about us. Half of 'em drive past our picket line in their brand new BMWs. They got it made here in the US."[76] Finally, Republicans appealed to Asian voters by emphasizing their commitments to friendly trans-Pacific relations or by increasing funding for law enforcement as the purported party of law and order, an idea that regional leaders exploited following the 1992 L.A. riots and media-driven narratives of the so-called Black-Korean conflict.[77]

Over time, politicians across rank and ideological spectrum sought support from Asian voters because their influence in trade and business were critical to California's postindustrial, globalizing economy. In November 1988, newly elected President George H. W. Bush visited the East Valley during Covina's "International Festival." He touted the region's diversity as a model of suburban multiculturalism. Bush posed for photos with a Korean folk-dance troupe and acknowledged the crowd, many of whom wore traditional Chinese, Filipino, Japanese, and Korean attire as part of the festival's novelty.[78] In 1996, Vice President Al Gore attended a Democratic National Committee fundraising event at Hsi Lai Temple in which temple funds were illegally used to finance the Clinton-Gore reelection campaign.[79] In 2002, Republican gubernatorial candidate Bill Simon hosted an elaborate fundraiser with US Secretary of Labor Elaine Chao in L.A.'s Chinatown, wooing Asian Republican donors based in Walnut, Diamond Bar, Hacienda Heights, and Rowland Heights.[80] Simon's wife, Cindy, held a fundraiser with First Lady Laura Bush, targeting valley-based Asian voters.[81] Beyond businessmen, white GOP activists directed their outreach to women and young voters. In the 1990s and 2000s, Republican women's clubs courted Taiwanese and Korean immigrants because they were—as one local GOP operative said—"an extremely patriotic people . . . [who] love this country and conservatives."[82] Activists recruited high schoolers well before they reached voting age. They encouraged teenagers to start or revive Republican clubs. This included Tea Party chapters in later years, some of them founded by Asian students.[83]

Locally, the Republican Party expanded its base because they spoke a type of political language post-1965 Asian immigrant and refugee voters appreciated. This often revolved around one's personal connections to Asia or Asian culture even if only through a spouse or business relationships. In 1990, for example, eight Republicans—almost all of whom identified as businessmen—ran for a State Assembly seat representing the East Valley. Candidates appealed to voters by discussing their personal and economic ties to Asia.[84] Veteran politicians like Paul Horcher boasted his wife's background as an ardent anti-communist refugee. Horcher suggested it was because of his Vietnamese spouse, Van Le, that he had strong affinities for the Asian community. Horcher further suggested that because many of his neighbors in Diamond Bar were Chinese, Indian, and Korean, he had expanded his knowledge of Asian traditions. Horcher's involvement as a Slow Growth activist also resonated with Asian homeowners who wished to protect country living during a pivotal moment of East Valley development. Horcher won the seat and held that post until fellow Diamond Bar Republican, Gary Miller, took over several years later.[85] Other prominent state and federal leaders from the East Valley rose in the ranks of the GOP as suburban warriors and for their ties to Asian residents. Recognizing the growing force of Asian conservatives, in 1996, presidential nominee Bob Dole put Matt Fong—a former state treasurer and Hacienda Heights and Pasadena resident—on his shortlist of potential running mates.[86] Riding on the years-long wave of the 1994 "Republican Revolution," Fong challenged incumbent Barbara Boxer for her US Senate seat in 1998 with the vocal support of Senate Majority Leader Trent Lott (Miss.) and House Speaker Newt Gingrich (Ga.). Fong relied on Asian leaders to support his bid. He hosted bipartisan fundraisers in the valley's Asian strongholds, banking on voters' disposable income.[87] Though Fong generated robust Asian support and the backing of prominent Sunbelt Republicans, he lost the election.

The growing Republican network of Asian immigrant leaders encouraged more Asians to run for office. But because of their "otherness" as immigrants and people of color in suburbia, Asians appealed to voters across racial lines by emphasizing their traits as "model minorities" since their platforms alone did not get them votes.[88] They had to earn confidence from non-Asian voters, especially conservatives. One particular figure used the playbook of emphasizing the "model minority" suburbanite: Jay Kim. He built a reputation as a "good Asian" who—according to a former Diamond Bar mayor—was "very nice and never ruffled any feathers" despite the cutthroat nature of small-town politics.[89] His record of fighting against higher taxes, promoting assimilation, and defending country living during his tenure propelled him to Congress. When he ran for the House of Representatives, Kim claimed consultants said he made a mistake sending mailers about his rise from a "poor immigrant to head of a prosperous engineering company" and that he was the ultimate "rags-to-riches" story. At the same time, Kim claimed he wanted voters to judge him "on the merits of his political ideas, not his race" or his background as a foreign-born American. After winning his congressional seat in 1992, Kim said he was not voted in to advocate for Asians. Instead, Kim candidly declared his loyalty was mainly reserved for "conservative, white, rich people" because they elected him, not solely Asian immigrants.[90] He remained a reliable, outspoken, rank-and-file Republican until leaving office in 1999 (due to ethics violations).[91] While in Congress, he pleased conservatives for taking firm positions on trade, foreign policy, and illegal immigration.[92]

During Kim's tenure on the city council and in Congress, he and longtime Chinese activist Norman Hsu built a strong coalition of Asian conservatives across country living suburbia. They encouraged civic engagement among first- and second-generation Asian residents, some of whom served as state legislators, mayors, councilmembers, and school board officials. Those who ran for office painted themselves as "model minorities" on the campaign trail: hardworking, educated, loyal, family focused, and proudly suburban. This appeased voters who were suspicious of Asians' political intentions and thus generated broader support including the valley's white conservative voting bloc.[93] Whether vying for city hall or Capitol Hill, candidates who ran in the East Valley used those tactics well into the twenty-first century. Playing up the image of "model minority" suburbanite translated into electoral success.[94]

But getting to a place of mutual cooperation between the white political establishment and Asian residents took years. Despite overlapping views on social and economic issues, racial distrust complicated what could have otherwise been natural, stronger ideological alliances from the start. After a series of growing pains, white and Asian suburbanites in country living learned to work together for common class-based goals. By the mid-1990s, in towns like Walnut and Rowland Heights, earlier apprehensions turned into tepid support as whites realized the demographic tide was turning such that whites were becoming a racial minority. White homeowners, particularly those in public office, had to make friends with their Asian neighbors or lose their grip on power. As the Old Guard retired or moved away, white residents—including former critics of Asian settlers—took on mentorship roles to younger immigrant candidates who wished to preserve country living. Under their tutelage, Chinese, Filipino, and Korean immigrants were elected or appointed to city councils, commissions, and school boards carrying out the agenda of previous generations. This included oppositions to development, conservative approaches to city expenditures, and a reliance on private agencies in handling public utilities or goods.

In some cases, white leaders and the Old Guard turned to Asian leaders or Chinese associations to carry local traditions of country living culture into the next generation. For instance, numerous Chinese organizations including the Hacienda Heights Chinese Association helped plan and finance the Hacienda Heights July 4th Parade.[95] In the late 2000s and early 2010s, organizers of Rowland Heights' annual Buckboard Days—an equestrian-themed community-wide festival that began in 1970—needed the financial and physical support of Chinese organizations to proceed.[96] Similar cooperation between Chinese associations, Asian religious clubs, Asian youth groups, and Asian donors occurred in other regional festivals like the rodeo-themed Diamond Bar Ranch Festival (began in 1985) and Walnut Family Festival (began in 1975).[97] Events that were otherwise largely led by white volunteers and paid for through donations, sponsorships, or chapters of mainstream civic organizations (e.g., Kiwanis, Lions, and Rotary clubs) for decades needed Asian support as the white population declined and as area businesses changed. Moreover, generational attitudes toward civic engagement and institutions shifted, with Generation X residents and some baby boomers less likely to attend community events or engage in civic affairs as much as older whites born before World War II.[98] These cross-cultural and civic partnerships facilitated relationships between Asian residents and non-Asian residents—dynamics that were rare or not publicly visible in the 1980s.

At the same time, there were limits to whites' commitments to suburban diversity and their trust in the Asian community. Despite political inroads made with conservative Asian residents, alliances were demonstrably volatile. Throughout the 1990s, tensions between the Old Guard and Chinese community ran high amid gossip about racial manipulation or gaslighting in Walnut's city council elections. When Mei Mei Ho-Hilger ran for council in 1992, she had the support of Chinese activists. Though she knew it was an uphill battle to run in a suburb governed by white conservatives, Ho-Hilger believed it was important to show face and disprove critics' assumptions of immigrant apathy or inability to govern: "[To] win or lose is not important, but we must gain respect from the mainstream community."[99] Ho-Hilger, a Republican, narrowly lost the election, but she remained involved in East Valley politics. Over time, Ho-Hilger deduced that the Old Guard was neither ambivalent nor supportive of Asian residents. She believed they were hostile toward most Asians. A few years after her first run, Ho-Hilger tried once more, energized by what she called the hypocrisy of "racist conservatives."[100] She promoted herself as a modern, pro-diversity immigrant conservative. Ho-Hilger lost. She told the Chinese-language paper, *Chinese Daily News*, "Racial discrimination is basically a choice without common sense. You try to reason with them [Old Guard], request them not to discriminate. . . . That won't work unless you utilize political power. . . . In this society, if you are not involved in politics, you would not know the acuteness of the problem. Donating money—that will not make everything go your way. You don't have a seat. You don't have the right to speak. That's the reality of [American and East Valley] politics."[101]

In 1995, Joaquin Lim announced he was running for a seat on the Walnut City Council. His leadership of the MRF Task Force resulted in key endorsements from white conservatives who attributed his activism as proof that he could defend country living. Voters across racial lines rallied behind Lim because of his willingness to work with non-Asians. Along with Lim's political bona fides, his public displays of patriotism and immigrant gratitude toward America positioned him as a palatable Asian suburbanite running for office: "I still speak English with an accent, but I believe I'm all-American in my heart."[102] Lim found widespread support because he stood by the hallmarks of right-wing Sunbelt populism emblematic of the times. He promised to create a friendlier environment for business, refrain from proposing new or additional taxes, and "preserve [Walnut's] environment" and "General Plan to Protect [its] neighborhoods." He also vowed to kill the controversial MRF landfill project, something residents considered an example of how development was moving in the wrong direction.[103] Furthermore, he emphasized his commitments to conservative values and country living, which were inextricably aligned with his image as a "good Asian" and "model minority." Lim's amicable relationship with the Old Guard deterred Ho-Hilger and fellow Asian Republicans from running. Numerous Chinese leaders and empathetic white conservatives who saw a need for Asian representation feared multiple Asian candidates would split the vote.

Despite Ho-Hilger's ideological conservatism, she did not downplay her Chinese heritage in the ways Lim did, making him more agreeable to non-Chinese voters. Observers suspected the interracial agreement to only rally behind Lim was the Old Guard's strategy in limiting an Asian presence in government. Rather than Asian residents' splitting the vote on multiple Asian candidates, nativists feared the opposite: an Asian plurality or majority on the council. Critics worried Asian immigrants lacked leadership skills or abilities to govern, while some believed Walnut's prestige would decline despite Asian candidates running on similar policy platforms to their white counterparts.[104] Prior to the election, Ho-Hilger said, "The [white] conservatives endorsing Lim ... are just using Lim to reach their propaganda goal: to split us. They recognized when Lim comes out, I then will not come out. They have already reached their goal." In other words, though Walnut's Asian population hovered around 38 percent at the time, white residents thought only one Asian on the five-person council was enough. By encouraging intra-Asian division, critics or those lukewarm to the idea of Asian councilmembers believed their growing influence would taper off if factions formed within the Asian community.

Indeed, the election created fissures, particularly within the Chinese community. Some were upset at Asians who acquiesced to white pressure and the Old Guard. Others were frustrated at Chinese voters who did not understand the strategies and nuances involved with small town politics. The city council race also soured relations between conservatives who were open to diversity on the council versus conservatives who remained adamantly against Walnut's immigrant newcomers. On several occasions, city council candidates accused competitors of stealing campaign signs off homeowners' lawns, spreading anti-Asian-laced rumors, and pitting nonwhite conservatives against each other. (Along with Lim, Bob Pacheco—a Latino Republican—ran for council.)[105] Ultimately, this and similar elections across country living in the 1990s revealed whites' openness to racial diversity so long as it was on their terms.

Beyond MRF, a series of unpopular land-use proposals throughout the 1990s and 2000s—including the construction of a Target-anchored twenty-six-acre shopping center in Walnut (1993) and a seventy-five-thousand-seat NFL stadium in City of Industry (2008)—strengthened Asian activism and pushed them to the center of civic life. Asian homeowners and politicians became the face of NIMBYism and suburban opposition to growth.[106] By embracing the "positive" stereotype of the "model minority," figures like Lim and Kim were able to carve spaces in predominately white institutions (i.e., city councils, Congress). This strategy helped Asian leaders harness white support. As Lim told the *Los Angeles Times*, "People used to say an Asian couldn't get elected in Walnut. Well, I smashed that glass ceiling."[107] Asian homeowners showed their white neighbors that they too shared an interest in right-wing governance and preserving the valley's rural ideal. As the Asian population reached critical mass in country living toward the new century, reliance on white support became less important to Asian public officials and activists. Nevertheless, Asian immigrants continued to uphold the East Valley's longstanding conservatism and political objectives for restrained development. By the twenty-first century, it was no longer the Old Guard who dominated the local establishment. Asian immigrants, especially Chinese homeowners, emerged as important leaders—and the new gatekeepers—of East Valley suburbia.

. . .

Asian immigrants regularly found themselves in the crosshairs of debates over the East San Gabriel Valley's changing landscape. White residents praised their Asian neighbors for supposed innate values and traits that made them "model minorities." Asians leveraged this image to gain trust and, in some ways, power over white residents who often doubted their credentials as acceptable neighbors. As homeowners, Asian immigrants frequently aligned with the right for the sake of preserving country living. While these interracial alliances improved dynamics between residents, at its core, these were unions based on exclusionary politics. In their attempts to experience and protect the American Dream, Asian homeowners joined their white neighbors in trying to keep their suburbs walled off from the outside. This included limiting access to "others" (i.e., working-class Asians, Blacks, Latinos) and curbing disreputable forms of development (e.g., landfills, discount stores, professional sports stadiums).

At the same time, Asian residents were neither immune to discrimination nor blind to it. Some spoke out, only to find there were social or political repercussions if they did. In the spirit of late twentieth-century multiculturalism, Asian immigrants openly practiced ethnic traditions. Despite an openness to racial liberalism, many white residents nonetheless exercised methods of social control to make sure Asians did not go "too far." Critics policed how "ethnic" Asians could be in country living. Asian families were criticized for altering commercial spaces, introducing "exotic" religions, and not fully abiding by Euro-American standards of proper suburban behavior. Because Asians' perceived foreignness marked them as outside the norms, notwithstanding their affluence or efforts to blend in, they did not (or could not) identify with whiteness nor attain its privileges.

On the whole, Asian families tried to assimilate or integrate to appease their neighbors and to feel a part of the wider citizenry. This was partly because Chinese, Filipino, and Korean suburbanites saw themselves as the visitor who needed to adapt, acquiesce, and abide. Immigrants only pushed the boundaries so far because this was not their homeland. Their vocal or tacit support of exclusionary, class-based policies were informed by their allegiances to meritocracy and the "model minority" myth—ideas rooted in the Cold War and baked into the Asian American experience of the late twentieth century. In other words, if they played by the rules, worked hard, and followed the pack, Asian suburbanites could enjoy the amenities easily afforded to their white neighbors. In the process, by embracing an image that they—like their white counterparts—were modern settlers of the L.A. frontier, immigrants demonstrated that they too could happily live in country living without disturbing the cultural myths that brought them and their neighbors there. By taking a middle lane of both accepting and rejecting elements of assimilation, Asians were perennially caught "in between." Even so, this widened opportunities to make a home for themselves and to assume political power from people who did not think they had it in them to govern.

FIVE

Growth and the Imminent Death
of "Country Living"

ON A WARM AUGUST EVENING IN 1989, longtime Walnut homeowner Maurice Cofer stood in front of the four-hundred-member Gartel-Fuerte Homeowners Association and declared, "There are too many damn people here already."[1] Cofer was responding to a proposal of a new rural-themed luxury development on a site eventually known as Walnut Hills. The plan by William Lyon Homes included 695 single-family homes, each priced around $700,000. The blueprints also featured a hotel, golf course, retail shops, and equestrian trails.[2] While Cofer's neighbors bristled at his frank delivery, they agreed with his point of view. That is, this project did not belong in a suburb that prided itself as a model of East San Gabriel Valley "country living." As communities across the region reached buildout toward the end of the twentieth century, residents wondered if they could still claim residence in the country. Swift development since the 1960s turned horse ranches and citrus groves into full-fledged suburbs. By the end of the 1980s, homeowners were fed up seeing bulldozers around town. Suburbanites lobbied for policies and initiatives intended to slow the pace of development and population growth even though residents themselves contributed to the boom. Because of their remote location, buyers wanted larger houses, bigger lots, and more retail and recreational options. These demands resulted in busier communities. All the while, residents habitually challenged tax increases, transportation policies, or physical and political infrastructure reforms aimed at improving the issues agitating them most.

Two grassroots movements encouraged residents to flex their political muscle under the guise of curbing sprawl, improving their quality of life, and protecting country living. The first was known as the "Slow Growth" movement, which is the focus of this chapter.[3] A second and related movement—the focus of the next chapter—was municipal incorporation (also known as cityhood). I argue that both movements were reactions and responses to various forms of "change," a word that residents deployed as a catch-all term to express dissatisfaction. Their anxieties about transformations in suburbia's everyday rhythms and landscapes (e.g., density, traffic) stood at the heart of Slow Growth and cityhood activism. But there were other reasons as well. First, residents' trepidations about change were tied to feelings of disempowerment among the propertied class. Homeowners alleged they lacked political influence in government, especially those who lived in unincorporated areas. Second, residents believed country living was coming to an end and with that, the loss of innocence and traditionalism rooted in Western agrarianism. Third, and most crucially, homeowners bemoaning change connected issues around development with demographic shifts. A rising multiethnic Asian presence worried homeowners across racial lines, particularly older residents and conservatives unaccustomed to living in heterogeneous communities. By the late 1980s, Slow Growth and cityhood politics became synonymous with anti-Asianism even if activists did not (or claimed to not) hold racist views. Ultimately, these movements showcased how homeowners coped with a purported demise of the myths shaping their identities as modern settlers of L.A.—those of suburbia, the American West, and the American Dream. Rather than adapt to change, they railed against it.

SLOW GROWTH SAN GABRIEL VALLEY

Since the 1950s, prescient East Valley residents understood growth was on the horizon. By the late 1960s and 1970s, civic and business leaders claimed significant development was inevitable and, for some, was a necessary marker of progress and civilization.[4] Longtime ranchers and farmers, whose livelihood depended on raising cattle and crops, worried about the effects of mass suburbanization. At the same time, they acknowledged its potential benefits including a diversifying regional economy beyond agriculture. In 1961, the *Los Angeles Times* declared the East Valley as the next frontier, with Walnut and surrounding suburbs leading the way as the "center of . . . new growth, destined to become one of the hottest homebuilding areas in the Southland."[5] Anticipating swift changes, civic leaders attempted to regulate growth by introducing tighter zoning measures. Before "Slow Growth" entered everyday vocabulary, valley residents articulated a language of so-called "quality growth" in the 1960s and 1970s to encourage restrained and limited development.[6] Walnut officials claimed taking preventative actions meant homeowners could set the rhythm and style of future development as a means of avoiding "bad" suburbanism.

Homeowners in East Valley towns established a culture and developed the language of Slow Growth before it became an official movement in the mid-1980s.[7] Slow Growth movements were able to thrive in greater Los Angeles because of its political fragmentation. As Robert Fogelson and Jon Teaford have argued, residents' calls for autonomy and self-determination as well as Southern California's physical disjointedness was what made L.A. unique relative to other cities emerging in the late nineteenth and early twentieth centuries.[8] Sunbelt communities generally embraced decentralized, localized forms of government. This increased civic participation through the person-alization of politics, but it also placed additional pressures on municipalities and those holding office. As Mark Baldassare notes, "It may be fairly easy for citizens to threaten small, relatively powerless local governments" like those in the East Valley because officials constantly worried about ramifications otherwise insignificant in bigger jurisdictions where retail politics mattered less. These conditions accelerated homeowners' revolts.

As demand for housing increased, longtime agrarians and property owners felt pressured to sell. Farmers took advantage of financial incentives to make room for development. Some gave up their land only if the new owners promised to build in the name of "quality growth." Bill Vogel, for example, owned a parcel growing corn. He sold his harvests from the back of a pick-up truck. In the 1970s, Vogel converted the land into an industrial park limited to small companies, firms, and banks. He rejected offers from fast-food or liquor stores because he believed those would "cheapen" and undermine the integrity of Walnut's country living identity. In his eyes, a business complex was suitable. To pay homage to the region's Western past, Vogel assigned Spanish surnames for the streets within the office park. Street designations like Paseo Tesoro (Treasurer Trail) or Paseo Del Prado (A Walk through the Meadow) evoked the romance of old California so those memories re-mained after the land's corporatization.[9]

Other property owners resisted change, particularly members of Walnut's Old Guard. They worked for decades to preserve the town's rural heritage and were particularly active in the 1980s as development moved at a swifter pace. Influential Old Guard residents included Walnut mayor, William

Wentworth—husband of future Walnut mayor and Slow Growth activist June Wentworth. He claimed the "people [of Walnut] are more interested in the city becoming a bedroom community than having high-density development" and stayed committed to upholding those ideals in office. For the Wentworths' generation, they believed it was their responsibility to protect the East Valley's agrarian roots before newer families moved in. In 1978, Walnut residents approved a General Plan articulating their desires in remaining a suburb of single-family homes. The main city rule for housing developers: the higher the elevation, the lesser its density.[10] The General Plan set a legal foundation ensuring Walnut stayed a low-density town. Nearby country living communities followed suit as media and word-of-mouth continued to highlight the East Valley's potential for growth. The same year Walnut enacted new codes in the General Plan, the Southern California Association of Governments (SCAG) publicly announced their predictions for rapid long-term growth in Walnut and across the region thus heightening residents' concerns. "The greatest amount of urban expansion [in Los Angeles County]," according to SCAG, "is shown to occur in the East San Gabriel Valley. The growth is due to the relatively large amounts of available land and its access to employment."[11] Indeed, families priced out of L.A.'s inner-ring suburbs flocked to the up-and-coming East Valley for more space, better value, and country living. New buyers moved in with the promise of a bucolic ambiance only to find the countryside was filling up, along with resentment from residents who planted roots before them.

The Slow Growth movement gained momentum in the 1980s, picking up steam toward the end of the decade as large-scale development in eastern Los Angeles County spilled into San Bernardino, Orange, and Riverside counties. In the San Gabriel Valley, pockets of Slow Growth activism started in the west, emerging in Monterey Park, San Gabriel, and Alhambra. Longtime residents complained about increased density and traffic. But Slow Growth politics quickly took a racial turn. Numerous activists spoke about their discomforts with Asian settlement; most were subtle critiques, while some were blatantly xenophobic. Collectively, they were dissatisfied with immigrants from Asia, namely from Hong Kong and Taiwan. Many settlers arrived with substantial global capital and integrated Chinese or pan-Asian stores into these suburbs.[12] Working-class Chinese immigrants and Vietnamese refugees were also shifting the retail and residential landscapes of West Valley suburbs like Rosemead and Temple City, resulting in a cascade of anti-Asian attitudes in historically white communities.

Slow Growth politics moved eastward. Critics in Hacienda Heights, Row-land Heights, Diamond Bar, Walnut, and surrounding suburbs shared the sentiments of their counterparts on the other side of the valley. However, whereas West Valley residents worried about protecting its modest postwar suburban character, in the East Valley, homeowners claimed adopting Slow Growth measures safeguarded country living. In towns like Diamond Bar, Slow Growth activists deployed mythologies of Western Americana to stress the need to curb development as well as push for local autonomy via incorpo-ration. Like the planners, developers, builders, and realtors who sold residents on country living, activists invoked language and imagery of a romanticized white frontier—complete with cowboys and horses—in political pamphlets and at fundraisers.[13] This resonated with residents even though Blacks and Asians have called California home since the 1800s and indigenous Americans and Latinos occupied the West well before European contact.[14] By champion-ing the protection and preservation of country living as a unifying objective for both movements, activists positioned themselves as guardians of a revered way of life. This included the protection of whiteness and the East Valley's Euro-American suburban form. For local homeowners, the "American-ness" of their communities were inextricably tied to these cultural tropes.

Diamond Bar and Chino Hills incorporated in 1989 and 1991, respec-tively, partly out of fears that both suburbs were expanding and transform-ing too quickly. Residents in Hacienda Heights and Rowland Heights also attempted to incorporate under this logic, though that backfired when crit-ics suggested cityhood would only give Asian immigrants greater influence. Slow Growth and cityhood activists fought unwanted change because they feared a loss of status and the end of cultural ideals predicated on white set-tler colonialism. If country living lost its cachet, their identities as middle-class or wealthy suburban homeowners—baked into the fabric of what defined a proper American—would cease to exist. In essence, it was up to them to protect country living so the myths sustaining this lifestyle and their power stayed alive.

COUNTRY LIVING UNDER THREAT
AND THE BETRAYAL OF PROMISES

As metro L.A.'s population soared, consumer demand remained steady well in the 1980s and 1990s. More and more, the East Valley and the county's outer edges became attractive to buyers. Country living neighborhoods grew denser while builders pushed further inland. Despite homeowners' complaints of increased traffic and density, critics still believed (or wanted to believe) they resided in the country. They fought to protect this ideal even when their surroundings suggested otherwise. Thus, amid the panic and fears of change, the region became a hot spot of Slow Growth activism. On New Year's Eve 1989, the *Los Angeles Times* declared the Slow Growth movement the San Gabriel Valley's biggest news story of the year. Rounding out the top ten were issues adjacent to the movement's talking points: crime (#2), incorporation (#6), and English signage ordinances (#8).[15]

Nearly two-thirds of the valley's 200,000 new residents settled in the east side during the 1980s. Between 1980 and 1989, Walnut's population doubled to 24,113. Diamond Bar's jumped 60.2 percent to 45,000 residents. Homeowners, particularly those who settled during the 1960s and 1970s, felt the promise of country living was on the decline. As one L.A. County analyst said at the height of development, "[Diamond Bar and Walnut are] sort of the last remaining area[s] of open land in the east end of the county. And they're filling up," suggesting L.A.'s hinterland was reaching capacity.[16] Observers and residents alike claimed growth welcomed urbanization and that city life was finding its way to the fringe. Newspapers, including the *Los Angeles Times*, alleged "marauders from [the] inner city"—in this case, Black and Latino urbanites—targeted suburbs and posed a threat to newer communities.[17] These "small bands [of] young men desperate for money . . . prey upon the suburban middle and upper classes, sometimes with senseless savagery. . . . [They ride] the freeways like magic carpets to hit homes and businesses."[18] Journalists and pundits suggested the groundswell of affluent families living in these up-and-coming suburbs was why "marauders" set their eyes out east.

Local media were just as likely to insinuate that "city life" was coming to "country life." In a community newspaper survey conducted in 1983, "Mrs. Swanson," a Diamond Bar resident since 1962 said, "[As] one of the original [settlers] . . . I feel Diamond Bar has been ruined by putting in apartments and condominiums." Jannee Sprague, a resident since 1974 concurred: "[Diamond Bar] has fallen short of country living because of all the condos and high density. It's very different from the community which we first moved into." Janet, a resident since 1976 expressed her disappointment in Diamond Bar's growth: "I expected Diamond Bar to be more of Country Living; it is becoming too much like a big city. I'd rather drive a few miles to get to the grocery store" rather than having shops within reach. Lois Campbell, a Diamond Bar resident since 1978, articulated similar feelings: "Everything is getting congested and things are the same here now as it is in Los Angeles; especially the traffic."[19] Ingrid Brunner, a resident since 1972, and Ev Howard, a resident since 1974, challenged those critiques and the grievances of their neighbors. They believed Diamond Bar was "as country as you can get in the L.A. area" and that the "picturesque part of 'country living' is still here more so than in other communities."[20] They did not deny Diamond Bar's suburban form or believe it was authentically country from the start, but for them, it provided the best version of rurality possible in metro L.A.

East Valley homeowners who sought an agrarian lifestyle felt local leaders disregarded residents' interests. Along with the first wave of postwar settlers, families who lived in newer country living subdivisions believed a coterie of planners, developers, builders, and realtors who sold them this packaged lifestyle betrayed their trust. Residents accused them of prioritizing profit and were disinterested in the needs of the communities they created. They were not shielded from the urban vice or disorder alluded to in brochures, mailers, and ads that glossily showcased the virtues and benefits of country living. Critics berated politicians for failing to deliver on promises that they would maintain a sylvan setting or—at the very least—low-density suburbs. They claimed developers, builders, and realtors, in particular, were elitist and acted against the values of western agrarianism.[21] Indeed, these actors seldom kept residents' interests at heart. Amid the fervor for new single-family houses in the 1980s, money undoubtedly swayed developers' and builders' interests. Rather than addressing the concerns of those who already bought into country living, they instead turned their attention to newer waves of wealthier families who wanted their slice of country living. As one Diamond Bar homeowner noted, she and her husband moved to the East Valley in the mid-1980s because the relaxed environment felt as though they were constantly on holiday. She and her neighbors saw the area as a reprieve from the perceived disorder and grimness of L.A.[22] However, after years of growth, they saw their piece of the countryside as less and less desirable.

As more families settled toward the end of the decade and into the 1990s, this group of newcomers joined the chorus of older, longtime residents who had been vocalizing their opposition to development for years. Families who lived on sprawling farms since the 1960s teamed up with residents who purchased master-planned homes built in the 1980s. Despite generational differences, homeowners agreed excessive growth marred their visions of western agrarianism. The continuous construction of large-scale tracts or industrial and commercial spaces, the rise of Asian settlement, and sensationalized rumors of "city life" infiltrating suburbia triggered residents' fears of impending, unwelcomed transformations. For them, property values and investments were at stake in the shadow of an internationalizing L.A.[23] Rather than promote policies benefitting a cross-section of East Valley communities, country living homeowners pushed agendas that further cemented their privileges as a propertied class.

. . .

In Walnut, Maurice Cofer emerged as a key figure of the cause. He built a reputation as an agrarian who vocally railed against development. His neighbors in the Gartel-Fuerte area were older, white, and middle- or lower-middle-class residents. They prided themselves in their modest, "authentic" rural lifestyle: unpaved roads; limited or no sidewalks; informal, non-uniform fencing; and sparse to no street lighting. Compared to their counterparts in planned tracts, Gartel-Fuerte was raw and unmanicured. They preferred it that way. Cofer and his neighbors were always skeptical of Walnut's boom. Developing Walnut Hills pushed them to a breaking point.

The original 1989 drawings for the proposed site consisted of 1,200 homes. City leaders immediately refused these plans citing its size as out of scale for a bedroom community. Earlier that August during a city council meeting, over fifty residents representing numerous homeowners associations vowed to kill the plan. When William Lyon consultants revealed the Environmental Impact Report (EIR) in the council chambers, attendees scoffed at their claims that developing Walnut Hills would enhance—not undermine—the community's natural beauty and rural charms. Walnut's Old Guard—many of whom lived in self-built ranch-style houses or modest housing tracts—joined younger, wealthier families to collectively oppose these plans. Homeowners associations (HOAs) in Creekside, Hunters Hill, Marlborough, and Snow Creek—master-planned, agrarian-themed subdivisions built in the 1980s—were especially vocal because they lived closest to Walnut Hills. Echoing the Old Guard's sentiments, Snow Creek HOA president Kyen Jenkins asked why the town needed another rural-themed tract, especially on a location paradigmatic of Walnut's heritage. "They've been cutting up hills all over the city," Jenkins exclaimed. "What is the rush to develop it all now?"[24] This multigenerational coalition of homeowners

FIGURE 18. Older, modest homes next to a newer tract home, Walnut, CA, June 2016. Photo taken by James Zarsadiaz.

was the backbone of regional Slow Growth and cityhood movements in the 1980s and 1990s.[25] Regardless of the year of settlement, country living residents subscribed to the beliefs and practices of their predecessors. That is: come in, shut the door behind you, and keep urbanism away from the valley.

Pressuring elected officials was not enough for Slow Growth warriors. Homeowners thrust city bureaucrats to the center of controversy. Politics got so personal, it tarnished the careers of city staff deemed ineffective to handle these issues. This included smear campaigns against public servants who—in the eyes of local activists—did not take hard-enough positions on development. In Walnut, activists dragged its city manager, Linda Holmes, into these debates. Holmes stated amid the bruhaha that local officials empathized with residents' trepidations, and they were aware of Walnut's celebrated country character. This was something she wished to protect as well: "We are trying to maintain the rural atmosphere. That's one reason it's desirable for people from Los Angeles to move this way."[26] But activists continued to press her for not meeting Slow Growth leaders' demands in a quicker manner. All the while, Holmes and other officials were simultaneously burdened with quelling tensions between homeowners of color and white residents, many of whom attributed Walnut's development problems with its newfound diversity. It did not help that Holmes—amid the Slow Growth movement—called out nativists and intimated that the same people lamenting racial changes were also championing Slow Growth policies.[27] George Shindo, Walnut's planning director, was unsurprised by the community's reactions and sympathized with their frustrations: "It's the same old story of people saying, 'I'm here, I'm looking at these beautiful hills and I want to keep looking at the beautiful hills.'"[28] Yet Holmes, Shindo, and the city council wanted to appease multinational developers anxious to build in a suburb well regarded for its affluence and concentration of homeowners with Pacific Rim capital. Furthermore, civic leaders supported modest development to generate city income for its twenty-nine thousand residents. The expensive homes and posh businesses planned for the Walnut Hills project were expected to provide sizable property and sales tax bases for services in a suburb whose General Plan limited commercial space. The city needed more money to meet homeowners' demands in sustaining a manicured country environment as well as wanting better infrastructure and recreational amenities.[29]

Developers and a handful of pro-growth advocates tried to persuade residents to support Walnut Hills. Nadine Brown, a Diamond Bar resident and a close ally of Walnut's Old Guard, repeatedly spoke out against the plan. Brown was a prominent figure known for her eccentric brand of conservative activism and racial politics. She often garnered attention for her views on the valley's growing Asian population, suggesting they were welcomed only if they assimilated. (In 1993, Brown proposed to the Walnut city council that they establish an Anglo American Club to counter the suburb's growing number of identity-based organizations [e.g., Chinese American Association of Walnut, Black Parent Teacher Association chapter]).[30] She was mostly known for the widely circulated periodical, *Walnut Times Magazine*, which she owned and published. Attuned to Brown's influence, Walnut Hills Development Company—which oversaw the project—convinced her that the Walnut Hills project would strengthen Walnut's reputation as a prestigious country living suburb. Brown used her platform to try to shift public opinion: "[Walnut residents] take pride in the rural atmosphere that balances residential living with greenbelts, open areas, equestrian trails, parks, and an abundance of recreational facilities. As our city reaches 'build-out,' much of the community emphasis shifts from planning and building to maintaining, protecting and enhancing our rural setting."[31] Continuing, Brown suggested that developing the hills would not undo Walnut's pastoral aesthetic because the city had codes and cultures in place to safeguard threats of urbanization. But activists and HOA leaders were unmoved by Brown's call. They continued to lobby against the project. Their efforts paid off. Because of homeowners' activism, developers agreed to scale down the number of houses and delayed construction. Despite the compromises, William Lyon withdrew their plans out of frustration from dealing with Walnut residents. Opponents claimed victory. Their win protected what many considered one of the East Valley's last bastions of untamed open space.

A few miles south, Diamond Bar residents also garnered attention for their coordinated oppositions to development. Diamond Bar boasted a strong Slow Growth network because its HOAs and the Diamond Bar Municipal Advisory Committee (DBMAC) were the sole community leaders until incorporation in 1989. These ad hoc forms of governance—mostly run by homeowners—established a foundation where the propertied class held the most civic influence. Diamond Bar's anti-growth reputation traces to the 1960s and 1970s, when the town warmed up to new housing construction.[32] One of Diamond Bar's first tests as a community occurred in 1977 when a developer sought to build a Swiss-Austrian-themed ski resort and village. Hoping to mimic life in the Alps, the project plan included a ski slope (with artificial snow) and chairlift, a water slide, and a toboggan slide. The project included a 188-room hotel, restaurants, shops, a movie theater, a parking garage, and various recreational spaces. Developers wished to capitalize on the trendiness of winter sports and alpine culture, particularly among yuppies and wealthier suburbanites. Residents vehemently opposed the project citing issues over traffic, noise, crime, and density. The project was nixed.[33] By the late 1970s, amid countless proposals to build in Diamond Bar, homeowners realized this packaged rural lifestyle was going to be available for purchase for thousands of other families. The eastward spurt of development incited panic, encouraging homeowners to take preventative measures. Homeowners like DBMAC chairman Ron Foerstel bemoaned the scale of growth across the valley: "There is a tendency in the development of the community away from the country living we all moved here for."[34] If residents did not act, Foerstel claimed, Diamond Bar would acquire the characteristics and flaws associated with city life. Besides halting new development through grassroots political action, Foerstel claimed incorporation was necessary as another layer of protection against urbanization: "If we don't stop [growth] now [through incorporation], it may be to[o] late."[35] Thus, cityhood and Slow Growth activism were intimately tied as necessary political strategies in curbing development.

Beyond their immediate neighborhoods, Slow Growth leaders understood unwanted development in any community was detrimental to the entire valley. In the spirit of preserving country living, activists believed it was a neighborly obligation to partner with homeowners in other suburbs. For example, in spring 1987, Diamond Bar leaders learned of a new Shea Homes tract planned for Rowland Heights. Fearing congestion and an erasure of open space, as a gesture of homeowner solidarity, DBMAC members joined their Rowland Heights neighbors in warning Shea and county officials that both unincorporated communities were watching their moves. DBMAC chairman Paul Horcher pleaded residents to protest all large-scale projects in the pipeline for Diamond Bar, Rowland Heights, and nearby suburbs. He cited the need to severely limit growth if the East Valley wanted to remain a rural place: "Diamond Bar already has more than its share of high-density housing, and we don't need anymore."[36] If Shea Homes made any more advances closer to the Diamond Bar community line, Horcher threatened to have DBMAC request a full Environmental Impact Report (EIR) and a comprehensive traffic study, thus delaying developers' plans. But Diamond Bar leaders were not only worried about the size of the new tract. They feared Shea's encroachment could affect boundary changes in Diamond Bar and Rowland Heights should any of these communities incorporate. Ultimately, residents in both suburbs saw the Shea project as an example of corporate greed and an abuse of power. Homeowners claimed innocence; they were victimized by the interests of big business. Residents alleged this was another example of the county's coziness with multinational corporations who profited from selling Western frontier nostalgia, yet developers and public leaders failed to preserve this ideal. For homeowners, county leaders had long been out of touch with the needs of their constituents.[37] Critics' frustrations continued to mount as new residential and retail development requests bombarded Diamond Bar leadership in the mid- and late 1980s, thus emboldening both Slow Growth and cityhood activists.[38] On nearly every occasion, housing plans—especially ones for apartments or condominiums—were met with residents' disapproval because they were incongruent with the country living ideal.[39]

Motivated by anti-development sentiments across the San Gabriel Valley, residents in Walnut, Diamond Bar, and Chino Hills appealed to their neighbors through the language of environmental assault. Environmentalists, conservationists, and landscape architects popularized these rhetorical strategies in the 1960s as a response to postwar suburbanization.[40] Conservative and liberal critics alike claimed industrial and commercial growth—exacerbated by the forces of a globalizing marketplace—contributed to suburbia's demise. While environmentalists were particularly keen on using these talking points, the right deployed the rhetoric of ecological danger and capitalist greed too, which revved up support against development, often deployed through gendered language and analogies of bodily or sexual violence. Slow Growth activists embraced a populist approach, alleging multinational corporate builders bullied small towns. In Walnut, growth critics and Old Guard leaders like Maurice Cofer claimed development was an attack on the land as well as the values of rural dwellers: "We are opposed to the raping of the hills simply for profits."[41] Another East Valley resident, Orlene Cook, asked, "What is being done to prevent the further raping of the mountains? It's a tragic sight from our freeways!"[42] Hillary Winston, a longtime homeowner, expressed comparable rhetoric in pressuring the urgency for Slow Growth policies: "I've lived in the San Gabriel Valley all of my life and have witnessed the raping of this area—all in the name of community redevelopment. . . . We live here because of its relaxed, rural atmosphere and want to keep it that way."[43]

As open space grew scarcer, land was increasingly feminized when mentioned in public debates. The East Valley's landscape—once described by local boosters as a place primed for the individualist, rugged, masculine pioneer—was now characterized as weak, passive, and helpless. The valley's feminized country living communities were unable to prevent growth because of powerful, aggressive developers. Feminist geographers argue that these gendered tropes about rurality, conquest, and the production of land are not uncommon in Western nations like the United States.[44] These ideas are rooted in nineteenth-century myths about the frontier and the expanses of the West's "virgin land."[45] Backlashes to suburbanization and sprawl coincided with social campaigns to protect the Earth.[46] International concerns over the environment occurred as social movements including second-wave feminism drew attention to the need for reform. Yet right-leaning suburban homeowners adopted the environmental movement's talking points for their own economic interests. Slow Growth activists deployed a moralistic language of ecological destruction to build support. By coopting the left's language, they were able to move forward with purportedly class- and

color-blind politics like Slow Growth. This way, activists did not look prejudiced and were thus able to achieve policy wins that ultimately favored the
propertied. This included the problem of traffic and limiting access to "outsiders" in country living.

GRIDLOCK IN THE COUNTRY:
THE GRAND AVENUE EXTENSION

Beyond activists' macro fears of ecological destruction, Slow Growth advocates most complained about day-to-day issues brought on by mass suburbanization. Traffic, in particular, stirred emotions, since many white-collar
professionals commuted daily to the major industrial and business corridors
of Los Angeles and Orange County.[47] Because of traffic, "Diamond Bar, the
'Land of Country Living,' will be dead soon," declared homeowner Gary
Lawson. In his *Los Angeles Times* op-ed, Lawson joked, "Soon the 'Land
of Country Living' will be replaced by the 'Land of Eternal Gridlock.'"[48]
Lawson and his neighbors mourned the death of their imagined frontier and
blamed unregulated development for their woes. Ironically, though growth
critics wanted to minimize the presence of automobiles to keep the valley's
rural feel, residents nonetheless relied on private transportation and prioritized improvements for drivers. Voters repeatedly shot down proposals to
strengthen public transit, claiming non-commuter buses and trains encouraged urbanization, density, and welcomed transients into the community.[49]
Despite county and local governments' attempts to alleviate traffic by extending roads and freeways, homeowners—with the support of conservative leaders—refused to pay additional taxes. Getting residents to open their
wallets and purses or to cosign on public transit or other infrastructure plans
proved to be a challenge even though these would have lessened gridlock and
helped sustain the country living imaginary activists sought to safeguard.[50]

At the height of the regional building boom, one particular transit
project outraged residents. The extension of Grand Avenue was a turning
point, encouraging them to push harder for Slow Growth policies as well as
cityhood. To address constituents' concerns about traffic, San Bernardino
County leaders approved plans to extend the thoroughfare that ended at the
Los Angeles and San Bernardino County lines separating Diamond Bar and
Chino Hills. Supporters claimed the extension would redistribute neighborhood and regional traffic, which was necessary since Chino Hills neared its

expected capacity of thirty-five thousand homes.[51] San Bernardino County planners and supervisors underestimated the volume of vehicles on local roads and admitted they could not meet the needs for sound infrastructure. Thoroughfares like Carbon Canyon Road—which linked Chino Hills, Diamond Bar, and Phillips Ranch residents to Orange County—could handle a maximum of fifteen thousand vehicles per day. By 1988, over seventeen thousand cars sped daily along the corridor resulting in constant traffic and road maintenance issues. County officials claimed conditions would worsen since large-scale housing development was anticipated to grow in the adjacent suburbs of Chino, Corona, and Mira Loma.[52] This was on top of new subdivisions under construction in Rowland Heights, Walnut, and Phillips Ranch. With this in mind, supporters thought extending Grand Avenue would be a viable, uncontroversial option.[53] Residents disagreed. They claimed the proposed extension would destroy an iconic greenbelt and cow pastures illustrative of East Valley agrarianism. Opponents further speculated the extension would actually invite more development and traffic because the roads would connect the two booming suburbs divided by hills and government fencing. The seemingly innocuous transportation project irritated homeowners who believed politicians and bureaucrats continued to misuse their power and implement poor policies.

While most local leaders rejected the plan, Diamond Bar officials were particularly frustrated. They argued that Chino Hills residents would use Diamond Bar's surface streets to get on and off the 57 (Orange) and 60 (Pomona) freeways, which were critical linkages to Orange County and Downtown L.A., respectively. This would most benefit Chino Hills commuters during morning and evening rush hour. Especially worrisome, for homeowners at least, was the potential decline of Diamond Bar's prestige. Slow Growth activist Gary Lawson said the extension was "going to ruin Diamond Bar" and that "property values throughout south Diamond Bar"—a tonier part of the master-planned suburb—"will be jeopardized."[54] In other words, increased traffic would urbanize Diamond Bar and undermine its country living façade. Gary Miller, who would later represent Diamond Bar and Chino Hills in Congress, "anticipated it would be bad" for both towns and encouraged neighbors to vocalize their disapproval.[55] Chino Hills residents agreed and refuted proponents' claims.

Energized by rumor and mounting tensions between county officials and constituents, Diamond Bar and Chino Hills residents banded together in the name of protecting country living. They received support from Walnut and Phillips Ranch residents as well because they feared spillover; the extension had the potential to bring "outsiders" into their respective communities. In 1988, Lawson and Diamond Bar residents founded the Stop Grand Avenue Expressway Committee (SGAEC), a group known for what some called "aggressive activism."[56] Chino Hills residents created Chino Hills in Traffic, Chino Hills Against Traffic (CHITCHAT). Both citizens groups urged county leaders, developers, and planners to decrease commuter gridlock, minimize new housing construction, and modernize existing infrastructure. Within months of organizing, SGAEC and CHITCHAT forged a Slow Growth alliance.[57] Another watchdog group, Concerned Citizens for Diamond Bar Traffic Control (CCDBTC), formed under the leadership of Gary Miller.[58] These grassroots groups, along with HOAs, built critical Slow Growth coalitions and helped strengthen the force of anti-development politics across the region.

In January 1989, San Bernardino County officials confirmed residents' fears about the extension. Kunzman Associates, a traffic engineering firm, concluded that 38,100 vehicles would use Grand Avenue everyday thus increasing congestion.[59] Without the extension, about 26,000 vehicles used the road on a daily basis. Lawson said the study was the wakeup call residents needed to hear. The study emboldened critics to oppose the plan, with some doubling down on the need to forge alliances with other anti-development organizations in the area. Feeling beholden to county authority, the study further encouraged Diamond Bar residents to push for cityhood as a means of protecting their quality of life. According to Lawson, "The county of San Bernardino is not complying with the Chino Hills Specific Plan, and the county of Los Angeles is sitting idly by. Two county governments are playing God and the people of Diamond Bar don't have a say in anything."[60] Following Diamond Bar's lead, CHITCHAT and Slow Growth advocates urged Chino Hills residents to incorporate. Otherwise, they claimed, residents were letting bureaucrats and elites take full ownership of Chino Hills' destiny. The next month, after a flurry of complaints, L.A. County Supervisor Pete Schabarum ordered the installation of a fence and wooden barricade on Grand Avenue. It was a defiant symbol of Diamond Bar's desire to keep Chino Hills at a distance.[61] Schabarum claimed the move was meant to protect the safety of Diamond Bar residents.[62] It mainly served to appease angry constituents opposed to cutting into the hills.[63] San Bernardino County officials including Supervisor Larry Walker—who represented Chino Hills— sued L.A. County in April claiming the fence was an illegal obstruction of a public right-of-way. They sought a court order to remove what some folks joked as a chain-link version of the Berlin Wall separating two wealthy suburbs at war over who benefited from the extension.[64]

The Grand Avenue extension was planned to open by late March, around the time Diamond Bar voters were to vote for or against incorporation. Tensions grew when CCDBTC alleged SGAEC leadership used the extension controversy as a platform to push for Diamond Bar cityhood and its concurrent city council election on March 7, 1989. SGAEC activists including Lawson, Donna Rhode, and Benjamin Quan (among Diamond Bar's first Asian residents to run for office in the community) were running for the proposed city council. Miller, also a city council candidate, believed the lawsuit was meant to draw attention to candidates associated with SGAEC, thus giving them favorable publicity among Grand Avenue extension critics and Slow Growth warriors. In other words, candidates running on platforms vowing to preserve country living used the extension controversy as leverage.

When Diamond Bar incorporated on April 18, 1989, voters expected its inaugural city council to enact immediate controls on development. Because they were elected on Slow Growth platforms, Phyllis Papen, Paul Horcher, Gary Werner, John Forbing, and Gary Miller were tasked with not only building a new government; they were also tasked with preserving country living for the near and foreseeable future. Additionally, the new city inherited the legal woes and debts from the Grand Avenue extension fight, which conservative activists claimed was worth the money even though they frequently promoted restrained spending and balanced budgets. In September, the new City of Diamond Bar and San Bernardino County reached a deal. Along with opening up Grand Avenue, county officials agreed to extend major thoroughfares like Chino Hills Parkway and local roads to siphon traffic from Grand Avenue. In addition, San Bernardino County vowed to decrease its development cap in Chino Hills from 35,000 to 25,810 housing units. Additionally, Diamond Bar said they would build street improvements and extensions as a gesture of goodwill between San Bernardino County and the newly incorporated suburb. Lawson and SGAEC dropped the lawsuit against San Bernardino County in light of the agreement. After months of debate, construction delays, and litigation, the Grand Avenue extension opened on September 1, 1990.[65] These compromises not only assuaged critics' worries about traffic. The deals calmed residents' fears that urbanism and "city life" were en route to ruining the East Valley's frontier quality.[66] Slow Growth activists and conservative residents did what they came to do, successfully utilizing the rhetoric of country living and homeowners' rights to sustain their privilege and to keep this lifestyle an exclusive one.

. . .

Residents complained local governments could not keep up with the pace of growth. Indeed, they did not.[67] In the East Valley, over-development, traffic, and a host of growth-related issues disrupted country living—even though, ironically, residents were the main causes of the problems they protested.[68] The Walnut Hills plan and Grand Avenue extension were seemingly mundane neighborhood issues. But they were turning points in homeowners' perennial wars to protect frontier nostalgia. In these episodes of suburban politics, a primary fear among residents was that the romance of the American West they sought to experience, maintain, and paid a premium for was under attack. What made projects like Walnut Hills and the Grand Avenue extension particularly worrisome was the allusion that country living was going away. For families, transformations in the built environment endangered the lifestyle that brought them to the East Valley in the first place. How these controversies played out was a testament to the political clout of homeowners. As these young suburbs matured, residents exercised their influence in a range of everyday issues like land use, taxation, and infrastructure. Country living homeowners believed they were entitled to certain protections and privileges as a propertied class. At the same time, there were limits to their influence. Homeowners realized they needed to reform their governments in order to initiate and enforce their classist desires (i.e., emancipating from county control).

Homeowners rode the populist wave of Slow Growth politics well into the 1990s. During those years, residents' discomforts with growth increasingly aligned with fears about change, prompting louder calls for incorporation. What were broadly understood at the time as mere movements for governmental autonomy were actually strategies to stop the Asianization of the East San Gabriel Valley. A collective class-based interest in protecting and preserving country living cut across demographic lines, creating unexpected and oftentimes complicated or tenuous coalitions between white and Asian suburbanites, which is the focus of the next chapter.

SIX

To Remain Country, Become a City

IN THE 1980S AND 1990S, suburbanites across greater L.A. protested in droves to stop mass development. They rallied behind the phrase "Slow Growth," a movement that pulled them from their living rooms and into city hall. From the San Fernando Valley to Orange County, residents were fed up with growth, claiming city and county governments were not doing enough to stop what they broadly referred to as "change." At the height of the Slow Growth movement, numerous East San Gabriel Valley towns were simultaneously drumming up support for incorporation (also known as cityhood). Though not discernable or explicit to outside observers, these were interconnected movements with overlapping political interests. Both movements stoked residents' fears about change in "country living," or rather, concerns about density, over-development, and safety. Cityhood and Slow Growth activists worried their communities were moving away from the norms of mainstream suburbia. By not having an independent government, residents of unincorporated areas felt they lacked autonomy or—as activists put it—control over their destiny. Thus, residents in Diamond Bar, Chino Hills, Rowland Heights, and Hacienda Heights felt a need to incorporate.[1] While these concerns fueled their activism, I argue that class and racial anxieties most energized residents to engage in cityhood politics. In some towns, residents claimed cityhood was the best route for curbing unwanted neighborhood transformations, which included the "Asianization" of suburbia. In other communities, remaining unincorporated was the most logical solution. In either case, residents' discomforts with demographic shifts informed debates over cityhood. Whether in favor or in opposition, activists were committed to maintaining an East Valley that embodied a mythical California. That is, a place devoid of diversity and the perils of modernity—social phenomena critics associated with the failures of urbanism and liberalism in late twentieth-century America.

The cultures of postwar America cemented middle-class white families as the faces of suburbia. For years, this was the case in the East Valley, until the mass entrance of Asian immigrants in the 1980s and 1990s. Their wealth, cosmopolitanism, and growing influence complicated those notions. Affluent and civically engaged Asian families in elegant subdivisions did not fit the conventional stereotypes of the lowly, poor immigrant living in the city. Because these Asian families challenged residents' assumptions, white critics and the Old Guard were empowered to strengthen the paradigms that maintained their authority in suburbia. The coded rhetoric of protecting country living—manifested in cityhood politics—provided them a language to articulate apprehensions pertaining to class, race, and neighborhood change. Ironically, white cityhood activists found support from Asian immigrants— the communities some activists blamed as the reasons for these unwanted changes—because they too appreciated country living. For homeowners, including Asian families, the swift pace of development coupled with transformations in the built environment undermined the sanctity of East Valley rurality. In the eyes of residents, incorporating (or not) ensured country living stayed intact.

PREVENTING AN "ASPHALT JUNGLE" VIA INCORPORATION

For much of the nineteenth and early twentieth centuries, unincorporated communities across the United States trusted the services provided by their county or township. As cities and urbanized suburbs in Southern California became greedier for land or economic control, unincorporated areas threatened by nearby spheres of influence emancipated from county rule. As Jon Teaford notes, between 1954 and 1960, twenty-six communities became independent cities in Los Angeles County. This was largely due to the popularity of the Lakewood Plan, which contracted well-established county services to incorporated suburbs.[2] While cityhood provided autonomy, municipal fragmentation in the county often stalled regional political action. Towns had their respective interests when it came to issues like infrastructure, transportation, and environmental regulation. Nevertheless, the ubiquity of cityhood politics continued to inspire disgruntled residents of unincorporated areas for the rest of the century. When residents did not like the direction their community was going, cityhood seemed to outweigh the benefits of staying unincorporated. In the East Valley, typical suburban concerns (e.g., taxation, development, infrastructure) fueled cityhood movements. In numerous towns, however, what residents broadly referred to as "change" (i.e., spatial, aesthetic, or demographic changes) influenced how residents understood those issues.

After three major attempts to incorporate, Diamond Bar became a city on April 19, 1989, the eighty-sixth of eighty-eight cities in L.A. County.[3] For supporters, cityhood ensured residents had control over their community and that they now had the abilities to keep Diamond Bar rural as greater L.A. continued to grow. Activists did not anticipate the journey taking as long as it did. One of the earliest attempts to break from county control was in 1973. The Diamond Bar Homeowners Association (DBHOA) expected significant growth in accordance with the Master Plan. Members wanted development to remain "orderly" and "low density" in order to protect "Diamond Bar's 'country-living atmosphere.'"[4] Despite interest in the community, a vote for cityhood never reached the ballot box. Six years later, a group of young homeowners sought incorporation. They feared Transamerica's impending ownership release of Diamond Bar Ranch in 1984 would result in decreased property values.[5] Though criticized as poor managers of the master-planned country living ideal they promoted, Transamerica footed upkeep expenses approximating $200,000 per year. Upon Transamerica's exit, financial authority and landscaping would be released to the County of Los Angeles. Homeowners argued county leaders—most of whom did not live in or near Diamond Bar—lacked knowledge or sensitivities for understanding the region's appreciation for Western pastoralism. DBHOA president and pro-cityhood leader John Forbing pressed his neighbors to back incorporation to keep Diamond Bar closer to its heritage. Forbing claimed, "The County of Los Angeles will pave . . . not mow." Activists alleged if left in the county's hands, leaders in L.A. would urbanize the countryside. In the *Diamond Bar Windmill* (an HOA newsletter), Forbing asked, "Do we want Diamond Bar to become an Asphalt Jungle?"[6] He urged residents invested in the "Country Living we all paid so dearly for . . . to keep the power in the hands of the people instead of abdicating to downtown [L.A.]."[7] For cityhood supporters, a city of Diamond Bar—with officials who live in the community, not urban Angelenos—would be better equipped in protecting its agrarian profile.

Cityhood advocates turned to DBHOA to get the ball rolling with incorporation. Like other HOAs, DBHOA was an ad hoc form of government comprised of propertied residents. Neighborhood or community-wide HOAs encouraged homeowners to sort out issues of landscaping, maintenance, and safety; acted as a liaison between residents and local or county officials; organized events and initiatives for the community; and helped shape the culture, design, and politics of its tracts, subdivisions, and villages.[8] In postwar suburbs, particularly newer and master-planned ones like Diamond Bar, HOAs (also called improvement associations) served as productive sites of political activism.[9] As Sunbelt suburbanites became increasingly private and inward with the rise of new technologies (e.g., television, personal computers), larger houses (and thus less intimacy among inhabitants), a distrust of civic institutions, and a decline in club memberships, homeowners mainly engaged in the public sphere when it came to issues threatening their class privilege.[10] HOAs provided a third space for civic engagement beyond grassroots organizations and the official halls of governance.

Throughout the East Valley and across America, homeowners association memberships rose as the nation suburbanized. In 1962, only 500 HOAs existed nationwide. Thirty years later, there were 150,000 HOAs, with a total membership surpassing thirty-two million Americans.[11] Philip Langdon argues HOAs provided "a distinct identity on a small scale, a haven against impersonal mass society," a sentiment felt among East Valley residents who worried that the speed of growth, advances in technology, and shifts in American culture at large undermined intimacy between neighbors.[12] HOAs also thrived because of rising environmental concerns brought on by sprawl. As homeowners railed against taxation, financially strapped city and county governments were unable or unwilling to provide the parks, recreational facilities, and amenities suburbanites and exurbanites demanded. (Anti-government rhetoric and conservative-backed tax revolts in California during the 1970s and 1980s—led by Howard Jarvis and Grover Norquist—contributed to a lack of public funds and voter support for basic infrastructure.)[13] When officials refused, HOAs lobbied on homeowners' behalf or facilitated payment through private funds to grant requests.[14] In turn, in the last third of the twentieth century, HOAs emerged as powerful voices in policy and planning. They inadvertently weakened and decentralized governmental authority, which was welcomed by the right during the Cold War. In the East Valley, HOAs accrued greater influence between the 1970s and 1990s, at the height of the building boom. A space of participatory democracy,

HOAs grew in strength as deregulation and neoliberal approaches to governance encouraged civilians to find solutions to everyday problems. Issues that what were previously handled by municipalities became the responsibility of homeowners or the private sector. This encouraged residents in unincorporated areas to back cityhood so the propertied controlled the levers.[15]

In January 1980, the Diamond Bar Municipal Advisory Council (DBMAC), an official community liaison to the County of Los Angeles, formed the Self-Determination Committee.[16] This was a collaborative organization supported by DBHOA. The Self-Determination Committee's responsibilities included studying the Los Angeles County Local Agency Formation Commission (LAFCO) guidelines for cityhood, compiling persuasive data, and organizing support for incorporation. DBHOA, DBMAC, and the Self-Determination Committee raised money to explore incorporation's feasibility, which advocates believed was doable and in the community's best interest. Others were cautious, if not skeptical. DBMAC Councilmember Ronald Foerstel, who served as the Self-Determination Committee's co-chair, argued that if the study concluded Diamond Bar would be "best served by (DB)MAC and remain unincorporated," then residents should instead build a strong relationship with the county rather than fight its leaders. He suggested incorporation was unnecessary if residents were civically engaged, constantly held county officials accountable, and kept their eyes on the community. Like his contemporaries, he did not think local control was achievable by centralizing power with the county. Foerstel believed, "All Diamond Bar residents wish to preserve and enhance the natural scenic and rustic beauty we all moved here for," so it was important he and his neighbors explored the possibilities of emancipation.

Pro-cityhood activists talked about the need for self-governance and expressed concern of what the future of country living could look like as L.A. shifted from an imperial city to a global metropolis.[17] Amid these fears, pro-incorporation leaders used a language of "loss" to rouse support. One homeowner wrote in an HOA newsletter that the town's pastoral environment was under threat because of development and because homeowners demanded too many modern conveniences in a landscape intended to be rural. They wrote, "[Diamond Bar's] magnificent hills, tranquil valleys, and walnut trees have been replaced by homes. . . . Parks were carved into the landscape for recreation, commercial entities filled open spaces to bring modernization and convenience. . . . Churches and schools now stand where cattle once lazily grazed . . . while corroding the rural atmosphere." The author warned readers that the Diamond Bar they now enjoyed was at risk unless residents had total control.[18] Cityhood advocates deepened residents' anxieties by suggesting "city life" was inevitable, alluding to Diamond Bar's proximity to Pomona—an urbanized community with sizable Latino and Black populations—as reasons to take preventative action. Beyond the loss of land, cityhood proponents warned of a depreciation in cultural capital, believing property values would decline if country living was no longer Diamond Bar's signature style.

In May 1981, the Self-Determination Committee presented its report to the community and devised a plan of action.[19] A year later, activists started their campaign for Diamond Bar cityhood and formed the Incorporation Petition Committee (IPC). Beginning in summer 1982 and into fall 1983, pro-cityhood activists fundraised and circulated petitions. They distributed campaign literature claiming a City of Diamond Bar was necessary to protect country living, a linguistically contradictory message but one that resonated with homeowners against urbanization.[20] Some activists argued that becoming a city paid homage to Diamond Bar's founders because incorporation would safeguard the suburb's master-planned identity, which was understood as an unusual, forward-thinking concept at its genesis. Finally, cityhood advocates suggested it was their destiny to incorporate in order to protect the integrity of a wild West frontier threatened by the triple specters of urbanization, globalization, and modernity.[21]

Beyond pamphlets and public testimonials, incorporation advocates promoted the preservation of country living in their fundraising efforts. At a "Diamond Bar Country Day" fundraising event, organizers set up equestrian demonstrations, country fair activities, and a "western barbeque," visually reinforcing the valley's agrarian past. Event profits went to Diamond Bar Citizens for Cityhood (DBCC).[22] Beyond knocking on doors and holding festivals, for maximum visibility, activists turned to the everyday sites of suburbia to make their case that cityhood protected country living. Advocates electioneered outside the post office and department stores like K-Mart.[23] The DBCC's campaign headquarters sat in the center of a Safeway supermarket strip mall hoping to solicit voters between grocery trips.[24] Incorporation proponents raised over $28,000 in the summer and fall of 1982. The cityhood movement gained additional momentum when well-known conservative figures like US Senator Pete Wilson (CA) and anti-taxation leader Howard Jarvis endorsed incorporation, recognizing its importance to sustaining Diamond Bar's rural profile.[25]

Pro-cityhood activists' main argument was protecting country living. But they did not have a monopoly on this idea. Opponents used this point as a strategy too. As support for cityhood picked up steam, a different faction of conservative residents believed incorporation led to higher taxes, bigger government, and would thus be a heavier burden on property owners.[26] DBMAC Councilmember Donald Stokes refuted those claims noting 1978's Proposition 13—which dramatically froze and lowered California property taxes and energized a state-wide tax revolt in the late 1970s and 1980s—protected homeowners.[27] Stokes and cityhood activists suggested residents were "sending more tax dollars out of this community" than what was returned. Residents against incorporation argued a city of Diamond Bar would actually encourage urbanization rather than preserve country living since independent municipalities needed a robust tax base to function. This was typically achieved by having significant industrial and retail options within city limits.

Among cityhood's stalwart critics was Diamond Bar homeowner Lavinia Rowland, wife of John A. Rowland IV, descendant of Rowland Heights' namesake.[28] Lavinia headed the Anti-Incorporation Committee, a group of longtime homeowners and libertarians who worried that cityhood would undermine their political and physical freedom as rural dwellers. The Anti-Incorporation Committee opposed cityhood on the grounds that incorporation would fiscally overburden the community and attract unwanted development. Fellow anti-incorporation activists further argued Diamond Bar's public works, first respondents, and utilities were better managed through the County of Los Angeles because they had the financial resources and infrastructure already in place. Anti-cityhood activists claimed an isolated hamlet whose collective identity revolved around an agrarian lifestyle did not need their own government because it was oppressive. Others feared incorporation would lead to Diamond Bar's financial collapse, which would economically impact tax-paying homeowners in the long run. The question of incorporating became a matter of whose brand of country living conservatism was more convincing: Forbing's or Rowland's?

Lavinia Rowland and her small but enthusiastic brigade successfully swayed public opinion. In November 1983, 46 percent of Diamond Bar's 14,600 registered voters went to the polls and narrowly defeated incorporation by 230 votes.[29] Pro-cityhood activists blamed the Anti-Incorporation Committee for scaring the electorate into believing Diamond Bar was not ready to become a city and claimed anti-cityhood activists were

narrowminded. But for cityhood critics, leaving Diamond Bar unincorporated kept it a small western town. For Rowland and her supporters, "real"
agrarians and populist country folk resisted the lures and false protections
of institutional formality—even if it were to be run by fellow conservatives.
Cityhood, in other words, invited more regulation and was, in effect, a system where residents lost autonomy if they succumbed to the structures and
forces of modernity. Despite the pro-cityhood movement's endorsements
from right-wing firebrands, Diamond Bar voters were convinced incorporation would destroy residents' freedom—in all its definitions. While residents
shared a belief in needing to protect Diamond Bar's pastoralism, the election
revealed ideological disagreements about suburban governance and what was
considered proper, authentic country living.

IF NOT NOW, WHEN?

In July 1987, incorporation advocates introduced the proposed boundaries
for the City of Diamond Bar before the County of Los Angeles.[30] Learning from their mistakes in the 1983 campaign, activists aggressively educated
and mobilized voters to ensure a vote in November 1988.[31] For supporters,
if they did not incorporate, then Diamond Bar would surely urbanize. The
proposed city included the existing boundaries from the 1983 Diamond
Bar General Plan as well as eight hundred acres of Tres Hermanos Ranch.[32]
These newly drawn borders included the ranch's scenic greenbelts, rolling
hills, and manufactured trails to reinforce Diamond Bar's sylvan origins.
Pro-cityhood activists hoped the modified boundaries would sustain the
town's rural identity for the future and thus protect property values; this
would encourage voters to back incorporation.

Comprised of volunteers, the Incorporation '88 Committee stressed
that cityhood was essential for maintaining country living. They claimed
that since Diamond Bar's failure to incorporate in 1983, "L.A. County has
1) ignored local opposition to the rezoning of properties for proposed apartment projects; 2) refused to update the Diamond Bar Community Plan;
3) ignored neighborhood/developer commitments to address local neighborhood traffic and noise concerns; 4) approved freeway signs in violation
of local community policy; [and] 5) advocated the development of Grand
Avenue into Chino Hills," all of which worked to devastate Diamond Bar's
quality of life.[33] Among the loudest voices in the cityhood debate was Paul

Horcher, a businessman and Republican activist who would later represent the East Valley's country living communities in the state Assembly. A resident since 1968, Horcher believed cityhood would help reverse the course of Diamond Bar's rapid growth. He claimed developers lied and continued a "series of broken promises" that undermined a lifestyle he cherished since childhood.[34] According to Horcher, "Diamond Bar was conceived as a master-planned community intended for country living, with open spaces and lots of parks. . . . That's how Diamond Bar was originally promoted, but it was a false dream." Beyond emphasizing the demise of country living, cityhood supporters appealed to voters through notions of civic obligation and patriotism. They suggested supporting cityhood was an act of good citizenship, demonstrating one's loyalties to the American tenets of liberty, autonomy, and self-responsibility.

During previous attempts to incorporate, pro-cityhood activists noticed generational divides in opinion. With this in mind, activists for this campaign emphasized cityhood as a "quality of life" issue that transcended age, ideology, and party lines. When it came to development, incorporation leaders and even some anti-cityhood activists claimed the county wielded power carte blanche. For cityhood supporters, it was time for residents to take the reins for the good of the community. One particular talking point resonated more in 1988 than in past years: politicians and county bureaucrats in Downtown L.A. did not understand country living, nor did they care to protect their interests. Mirroring the broader anti-establishment politics of the late 1980s, homeowners railed against the status quo, or what conservatives bemoaned as "liberal big government." In a March 1988 mailer, homeowner Diana Garrett wrote, "We feel that the County Supervisors sitting at the county seat some 40 miles away are not in touch with our needs. We need local representation that we can hold responsible for Diamond Bar's interests alone."[35] Residents chastised county officials who overlooked the East Valley, citing a lack of trust between leaders and their constituents. The vote for cityhood was, as Garrett believed, a chance for residents to grab control from metropolitan elites and dysfunctional bureaucracies.[36] Cityhood thus emerged as a values issue between "selfish," urban leftists and "pragmatic," suburban or rural conservatives.

Pro-cityhood activists held a number of advantages going into the 1988 election. They found themselves amid a state-wide and national political climate favorable toward limited, decentralized government. (Ironically, "local control" via cityhood meant another layer of government.) This mood allowed them to ride the decade's right-wing populist wave. Second, many of Diamond Bar's postwar settlers of the 1950s and 1960s moved out of the area or passed away, some of whom vocally opposed earlier cityhood campaigns because they feared regulation and higher taxes. Lastly, pro-cityhood movement leaders were typically active with DBMAC and DBHOA (renamed Diamond Bar Improvement Association [DBIA] in 1986), the main governing bodies of the community. They had the tools and knew strategies to sway public opinion on local issues, especially incorporation. One advantage was their access to the community newspaper, the *Diamond Bar Windmill*, published by DBHOA. Cityhood advocates used the print space to run favorable news or op-eds backing incorporation.[37] By having significant editorial say, they had greater opportunities to control the narrative. On occasion, to stir emotions and drum up support, the *Diamond Bar Windmill* ran letters from residents fleeing or thinking about leaving Diamond Bar because the community was losing its rural charms. One letter to the editor expressed disappointment in the town's changing landscape, attributing it to past failures to incorporate:

> Dear Editor:
> The Honers spent a very happy and active 26 years in Diamond Bar and were active in community affairs much of that time. We have both believed in incorporation and have worked for it and voted for it over the years. However, we decided to retire to a smog-free, traffic-free, less congested area and are now enjoying the clear blue skies of St. George Utah. We regret that we will not be there to cast our 2 votes for incorporation. We thank the Incorporation '88 Committee for all its hard work and hope the community responds this time around.
> Sincerely,
> Elizabeth G. Honer (Mrs. Stanley M. Honer)[38]

Honer suggested that she and her husband left Diamond Bar because it became too crowded. Instead, the Honers—like their contemporaries who fled the East Valley in the 1980s and 1990s—resettled in a less diverse, more rural part of the American West.[39] The Honers' new home in St. George, Utah, is what Rich Benjamin dubs a "whitopia," an overwhelmingly white suburb or exurb popular among former Californians disenchanted with the state's diversification and density.[40] Settlers who retreated to whitopias in Colorado, Iowa, Montana, Oregon, and Utah claimed the slow-paced, sparsely populated, old-fashioned small towns of Southern California (i.e., rural, whiter, blue-collar or middle-class) were no longer there. Ex-Californians like the Honers vocalized their support for city-hood because they believed autonomy was a logical solution for stopping unwanted change. The growth and transformations were too fast to keep them there, and thus they absconded to a whitopia to find a lifestyle of yesteryear elsewhere.[41]

Enthusiasm for cityhood was particularly high in The Country, Diamond Bar's marquee gated community of high-end ranch-style homes and custom-built mansions.[42] Citing the need for rural autonomy, in June 1987, homeowners claimed if Diamond Bar did not become a city, they would incorporate as the City of The Country. One of The Country's homeowners, Jim Magner—a former Palmdale city manager—claimed there was a sufficient tax base despite plans to only annex one shopping center for its two thousand residents.[43] Diamond Bar cityhood advocates dismissed Magner's claims, including The Country's HOA president who said these calls distracted from the main movement.[44] Theatrics aside, The Country's forceful plea and the publicity it generated encouraged Diamond Bar residents to move swiftly with incorporation.

As public pressure mounted, Diamond Bar cityhood activists kicked off a series of petition drives and information campaigns. Activists conducted so-called "neighborhood blitzes."[45] Organizers and canvassers went door to door "armed with petitions, information brochures, and voter registration lists."[46] Tasked with getting over three-fourths of Diamond Bar voters to sign for a vote for incorporation, supporters gathered enough signatures—approximately 6,500—by the January 1988 deadline.[47] The vote to incorporate Diamond Bar was now placed on the November ballot. Energized by supporters' enthusiasm, in February 1988, the Incorporation '88 Committee held monthly meetings to discuss fundraising strategies and how to engage voters. But in July, incorporation advocates were thrown a curveball. Six residents wrote a letter to LAFCO claiming incorporation would financially ruin the master-planned community. Phyllis Papen, one of the Incorporation '88 Committee leaders, chastised the letter's signatories: "Their 25-cent postage stamp . . . cost the community over $1 million in lost surplus revenue." Cityhood supporters alleged this was deliberately timed to stall a vote before the community, which was now pushed to March 1989. The pro-cityhood movement believed the eleventh-hour LAFCO request to delay the election actually energized their base: "What they have done is outraged people, where we will see a good voter turnout in March. People are in a state of shock. They can't believe that, for no cause, they won't be able to vote on it in November."[48]

In January 1989, a handful of homeowners organized a formal anti-cityhood group.[49] These residents considered themselves "true" country folk, typically living in self-built houses or in modest homes set on agricultural lots. Chaired by Al Rumpilla, the Vote No on Diamond Bar Incorporation in '89 Committee opposed cityhood on the idea that incorporation added unnecessary rules. Building off Lavinia Rowland's previous efforts in 1983, the "Vote No" faction argued cityhood would increase taxes and curtail their liberties as rural dwellers. Their definition of a country lifestyle, which they ideologically grounded in libertarianism, did not align with pro-cityhood residents whose shared antipathy for regulation was not necessarily about less government. Rather, it was about having a strong local government that protected the interest of homeowners. The anti-incorporation movement's talking points resonated with older residents, a group that Diamond Bar's newcomers (many of whom were pro-cityhood) hoped would change positions since incorporation was expected to protect Diamond Bar's agrarian heritage via stricter land use measures implemented by a council.

From the perspective of the anti-cityhood faction, newer settlers purchased a sanitized, saccharine version of country living; those in tract houses bought simulations—not real versions—of Western pastoralism.[50] They suggested younger families were therefore accustomed to formality and rigidity, something a city government provided. For older critics against cityhood, their pioneering spirit and quest for an authentic country lifestyle meant they were self-sustaining, independent people removed from the constrictions of authority. This was ironic considering anti-cityhood activists preferred to be managed by supervisors of America's most populous county, not to mention one of the nation's most fragmented and bureaucratic agencies.[51] Recalling the 1988 campaign, one city councilmember joked anti-incorporation activists were not principled libertarian warriors. Rather, they were "natural anarchists" who fought "government . . . [and] any change. [They wanted] to be left alone, yet they won't leave anybody else alone. . . . Some of them were real obnoxious asses."[52]

In the weeks heading into the March 1989 election, Diamond Bar's pro- and anti-cityhood activists wrote passionate appeals in community newspapers hoping to sway voters, each side claiming their position was the most logical for protecting country living. One resident supporting incorporation wrote,

> In 1983, Diamond Bar was STILL a quiet, residential community with a strong sense of rural living. Freeway congestion in OUR area was unheard

of commercial incinerators and waste disposal was not even an issue. Chino Hills was still somewhere you could find a herd of deer on a quiet morning walk. . . . NOW, our community is heavily impacted by what were thought to be "regional" issues. Freeway congestion has become "Diamond Bar" congestion. We NEED quality, effective, LOCALLY responsive representatives who can address OUR needs at County and State hearings, who can join other CITIES to voice concerns over issues which DIRECTLY affect OUR standard of living.—Michael Lowe, resident, businessman and voter FOR the City of Diamond Bar[53]

Another resident, Jayne Staley—who settled in the mid-1980s—was convinced to vote for incorporation after attending a series of meetings. In a letter to the *Highlander,* Staley wrote, "The county could have far more pressing issues to wrestle with than the traffic jams and the consequences of poorly planned real estate development that will be crippling the powerless citizens of an unincorporated Diamond Bar in the early 1990s." In other words, Diamond Bar needed local control because county supervisors had too much on their plate to care about their town. Staley claimed longtime opponents of cityhood—like Rowland and Rumpilla—lacked common sense, particularly when Rowland suggested Diamond Bar did not have capable residents to govern: "I'd like to know on what study Lavinia Rowland has based her conclusion that 'Diamond Bar lacks qualified residents interested in running for city council'? This is a rapidly growing community with a fairly upscale, educated profile. If 'running a city is like running a business,' I'd venture to guess that Diamond Bar has more qualified residents than most neighboring communities can boast."[54]

Staley, Lowe, and other cityhood supporters argued incorporation would remedy the problems caused by liberal, out-of-touch county leaders. The electorate agreed. After a decade of attempts and a four-month election delay, on March 7, 1989, 76 percent of voters favored the creation of a City of Diamond Bar. Among the challenges for its inaugural council: to protect, preserve, and defend country living, a promise that voters wanted their new leaders to keep as L.A. approached a new decade and century.

RACE, CLASS, AND CITYHOOD

> I really think the main difference [why Diamond Bar, Walnut, and Chino Hills look and feel "less Asian" compared to Rowland Heights and Hacienda Heights] is that Rowland Heights and

Hacienda Heights are unincorporated. When you're a city, let's
say Diamond Bar or Walnut for example, the residents elect their
leaders. If [you're a builder and] your development . . . follows
the rules of the development code [it's fine for residents]. [But]
let's say: it's gross, goes up to the curb, it's outlandish, has neon
signs [in an Asian language.] . . . [Then] why does the (county
supervisor) from Lancaster give a shit about how it looks? . . .
[And] why would a county supervisor from Santa Monica care
about a commercial building in Rowland Heights? [With a city
council voted in by residents], there's local accountability for
the leaders of that community [if they approve a controversial
project or design].

—ALBERT CHANG, Rowland Heights resident and former
Rowland Unified School District board member[55]

Race and class informed pro- and anti-cityhood campaigns across the East
Valley. Activists' trepidations with change directly correlated with increased
Asian and Latino settlement. In country living communities, though, Asian
immigrants were positioned as a bigger threat than Latinos because critics
generalized Asian languages, cultures, and religions as collectively foreign,
exotic, and far from the norms of the Euro-American mainstream. Com-
plicating this was the affluence of Asian immigrant homeowners whose
resources and cosmopolitanism had the potential to change the suburbs
en masse. The economic privilege of diasporic Chinese from Hong Kong,
Taiwan, or Singapore—compared to, for example, working-class Mexican
immigrants—afforded them greater opportunities to purchase property in
exclusive subdivisions, influence political campaigns, and therefore widened
the possibilities for transgressing the local cultures of East Valley country living. East Asian immigrants were especially singled out for altering neighborhoods in towns like Rowland Heights and Hacienda Heights, where most of
the alleged misconduct and "ethnoburb"-like development took place. This
was because both suburbs had higher concentrations of Asian businesses
and were adjacent to City of Industry, which contained a significant number of Asian-owned establishments and transnational import-export firms.
Whether in well-to-do Diamond Bar or middle-class Hacienda Heights,
residents' concerns about the influx of Asian settlers influenced their decisions on whether or not to incorporate.

The relationship between race and the politics of cityhood in country living goes back to the 1970s when the City of Pomona threatened to annex
unincorporated Diamond Bar. Pomona officials argued annexation would

bring additional revenue to the city, since Diamond Bar was a predominantly white, middle-class community. Pomona leaders believed acquiring Diamond Bar would soften Pomona's reputation as a working-class Black and Latino enclave plagued with crime and gang activity. In neighborhood issues where race and class were divisive and decisive factors, activists deployed veiled, color- and class-blind rhetoric to dodge potential accusations of discrimination. In the decades following the civil rights movement, "smiling face" discrimination became a preferred mechanism for upholding racism and classism in a liberalizing society.[56] These rhetorical devices allowed Americans to voice discomfort or animosity without looking prejudiced. Across the San Gabriel Valley, white homeowners were able to enact policies marginalizing working-class communities and people of color because they seldom articulated their disapproval in explicit language. This included a range of zoning, residential, or design codes meant to suppress and deter cultural practices (e.g., multigenerational households [common among Asian or Latino families]) and various forms of ethnic expression in the built environment.

Since the 1960s, white suburbanites have used discreet, color-blind rhetoric to galvanize neighbors in populist campaigns against school integration, busing, and public services.[57] Homeowners, particularly in the Sunbelt, embraced what Matt Lassiter calls the "politics of middle-class consciousness based in subdivision associations, shopping malls, church congregations, PTA branches, and voting booths."[58] "Crabgrassroots activists" who called for stricter regulatory behavior and municipal policies harbored discriminatory views of working-class peoples and racial or religious minorities even if they publicly said otherwise. By subscribing to color-blindness, homeowners were allowed to situate residential segregation and other forms of disenfranchisement as not the product of intentional discrimination. Rather, one's status or access was the result of their respective work ethic, thus evading America's long arc of systemic racism and white supremacy.[59] Conservatives claimed meritocracy and hard work was the formula to achieving the American Dream. These arguments and rhetorical strategies helped bring former New Dealers and moderate Democrats into the tent of Richard Nixon and Ronald Reagan's Republican Party, which received a lot of its newfound strength in places like the East Valley. In country living suburbia, young families stood at the helm of class-driven revolts including the Slow Growth movement and concomitantly, incorporation politics.

In relation to race, what also remained overlooked in the noise of cityhood and Slow Growth politics was the role of globalization vis-à-vis conservative-backed neoliberal economic policies. Moves to dismantle the welfare state, citizens' protections, and workers' rights began as early as the 1940s and escalated in the 1970s and 1980s.[60] From laissez-faire trade laws to favorable tax codes for the rich, from business incentives for immigrant entrepreneurs to the rise of automation, the forces of globalization and the Pacific Rim economy—fueled by America's thirst for economic domination in the international consumer marketplace—changed the look, feel, and people of the San Gabriel Valley. Structurally, the right's proclivities for deregulating business and cutting government programs resulted in the fragmented political, social, and built landscapes suburbanites came to detest. Residents' frustrations, such as their lack of civic autonomy, was the result of their distrust in authority and resistance toward centralized governments whose agencies attempted to address their needs. Ironically, by the 1980s— amid a fierce anti-establishment, limited government political climate in the United States—East Valley residents believed another layer of government to police communities was the answer to the problems they helped create. The politics of incorporation illustrated residents' contradictory beliefs in government as both good cop and bad cop. For conservative homeowners, government was intrusive and bureaucratic yet useful in protecting class interests. Stronger local control through a city council and formal commissions were necessary for keeping out the "unwanted" (e.g., "non-assimilating" immigrants, the working class, renters).

In Diamond Bar, residents' urgency for cityhood was seen all the more necessary as Pomona exercised their sphere of influence. Pro-cityhood activists like Phyllis Papen perennially distanced themselves from their largely blue-collar neighbors in Pomona. Keeping Diamond Bar independent was a logical reason for incorporation: "Diamond Bar has a strong community identity that would not blend well with Pomona," Papen said, alluding to demographic differences between the two towns.[61] Incorporation supporters like DBMAC councilmember Dan Buffington believed Diamond Bar's "quality of life" would decline should the suburb merge with Pomona and all its "urban problems." Buffington expressed his hesitation through subtle, coded language: "I wouldn't say they [Diamond Bar residents] look down their noses at Pomona, but they hear about the gangs and the other problems Pomona has and they say, 'We don't want [to be] part of that.'"[62] Similarly, in Hacienda Heights, residents attempted to stave off potential annexation from nearby Whittier and City of Industry. Residents especially feared Industry, an almost completely commercial and industrial suburb. The city often wielded authority over neighboring towns through economic force. Hacienda Heights residents cited Industry's sphere of influence as reasons to incorporate, particularly when city leaders announced plans to open a trash incinerator and landfill.[63] Hacienda Heights residents feared the landfill would harm the environment and bring in strangers to the intimate community. Opponents of annexation cited Industry's residential demographics (i.e., Latino, working class) and built environment (i.e., office parks, strip malls, Asian-owned factories or shops) as reasons for their incompatibility.

Various efforts to incorporate Rowland Heights and Hacienda Heights repeatedly failed since the 1970s. In the mid-1980s—amid booming Chinese settlement—a confluence of xenophobia and weak campaign coordination undermined these attempts. Cityhood advocates in both communities did not stress the need to protect country living as forcefully as activists did in Diamond Bar, even though Rowland Heights' and Hacienda Heights' older residents considered themselves among the valley's pioneers and original guardians of rurality. Like their younger neighbors, they too were disappointed in the changing style and scale of regional development.

Opponents of Hacienda Heights' 1992 incorporation campaign claimed the East Valley's spirit of Western frontierism meant residents were averse to being told what to do. Charlie Gray, a longtime cityhood critic, declared a widely held view when asked about efforts to incorporate: "We don't want another layer of government."[64] Darlene Williams, another Hacienda Heights resident, concurred in her letter to the *Los Angeles Times*. Williams claimed her neighbors were not the type of people who enjoyed being "bound by added rules, regulations, etc. like those imposed by neighboring cities."[65] They prided themselves in their individualism and cherished their freedoms from impositions of order and government control. In other words, Hacienda Heights residents lived in unincorporated L.A. County partly because they rebuffed regulation or bureaucratic oversight. At the same time, they expressed their concerns about change, citing spatial, aesthetic, or cultural transgressions that went against the valley's rural heritage. Particularly for older settlers, witnessing large-scale suburban development in the 1980s coupled with a burgeoning Asian population heightened their fears, and ultimately ruined their ideas of the region's real and imagined past—that is, pastoral, white, modest, conservative, and suspended in time.

Despite energetic support in its initial stages, pro-cityhood advocates struggled to stay on message when influential anti-cityhood activists challenged their campaign. The spreading of nativist-driven gossip about

Chinese residents' plans to "takeover" Hacienda Heights further derailed their efforts. As Asian immigrants continued to move into the region, space was increasingly discussed on a racialized plane and thus informed the tenor of the movement. In 1991, for instance, residents complained about the possible expansion of Puente Hills Landfill (once the largest landfill in the United States) in City of Industry.[66] The site was a global attraction, with Chinese tourists curious about its elaborate waste-treatment system.[67] Cityhood proponents hoped to prevent the proposed expansion via incorporation, particularly since Hacienda Heights housed the Western Hemisphere's largest Buddhist temple, Hsi Lai. Critics feared the combination Hsi Lai and the proposed landfill expansion would result in additional Asian tourism, or worse, permanent settlement. From their perspective, foreign visitors and trans-Pacific exposure only reinforced the valley's reputation as a global Asian destination. These concerns were on top of mounting disapproval of Chinese and Korean businesses. Rather than pique curiosity, the perceived exoticism of Asian wares or attractions made white and older Latino critics uncomfortable.[68]

Year after year, campaign materials, meetings, and debates were aimed at the non-Asian electorate. The exclusivity of cityhood politics left little room for Asian residents to participate because some residents lacked English proficiency or were unfamiliar with American civic practices. In turn, Asian immigrants had their own conversations. A series of misunderstandings coupled with intentional racial separatism resulted in heated debates on who Hacienda Heights belonged to. In the 2003 cityhood movement, critics speculated once again that Hacienda Heights' new city council would be dominated by Asian immigrants. They suggested that the prospect of a majority- or all-Asian city leadership would make the country living suburb feel less American (i.e., white).[69] During the campaign for both cityhood and the future city council, Chinese community leaders organized a town hall featuring Chinese candidates running for the proposed five-member governing body. At first, organizers only invited candidates of Chinese descent. Eventually, organizers opened up the forum to all candidates. White residents negatively received the optics of the event. They accused the Chinese community of cryptic behavior and suggested the forum was an intentional act of self-segregation or "reverse racism." Chinese leaders organized independently, mainly on the grounds of feeling comfortable among their co-ethnics. But they also organized on their own because white activists either did not know how to or did not care to include the Chinese.

Often concentrated within ethnic- or religious-based organizations, Asian residents' levels of community engagement differed from their white neighbors who were accustomed to occupying all realms of mainstream politics and suburban civic life—that is, from city hall to national clubs like Rotary or Lions. These were spaces less inclined to attract Asian residents and historically drew in white residents. Lastly, bitterness lingered among Chinese leaders who recalled the 1991 campaign. Deep-seated racism and exclusion were as present in 2003 as it was in 1991, thus keeping whites and Asians in their respective corners. Tensions rose again when Norman Hsu, a well-known Chinese community leader in Hacienda Heights, advocated for a Chinese-majority council in a Chinese language newsletter. White critics saw the publication as another devious act expected of the Chinese.

While Asian homeowners fostered alliances with white pro-cityhood activists, the Old Guard remained wary of incorporation and were especially suspicious of Chinese supporters' intentions.[70] White support for Hacienda Heights cityhood dwindled as more residents felt the campaign was for the purpose of electing Chinese candidates. David Fang, who was in favor of cityhood and ran for the proposed city council, believed "some voters had the feeling that they were going to be excluded by the Chinese candidates or Chinese community" upon incorporation.[71] Opponents believed they were victims of a hostile takeover or a political "yellow peril" threatening to undermine Hacienda Heights' rural lifestyle. In their efforts against cityhood, residents like anti-incorporation movement leader Jim Crabtree were not explicitly discriminatory toward Asian residents, knowing criticism could be read as racist or xenophobic. Critics harboring prejudiced views of Asians typically expressed their discomforts through veiled, color-blind language. In an interview with the Los Angeles Times, Crabtree claimed if Hacienda Heights incorporated, "inexperienced, amateur politicians will get involved with corruption and display general incompetence that we've seen in other cities like Compton," alluding to the leadership of the predominantly Black suburb in L.A.'s South Bay.[72] Chinese residents like Tom Chang said the anti-cityhood movement enjoyed "pushing racial buttons" instead of focusing on taxation, infrastructure, and the need for local control—day-to-day concerns that transcended race and ethnicity. Chinese residents, including those who ran for the new city council, alleged white residents feared Hacienda Heights would become the next Monterey Park, a cautionary tale of an "all-American" suburb turned epicenter of L.A.'s new Chinese diaspora.[73] As Hung Yu-Ju notes, for critics, the "'Chinatownized' commercial strips and

Asian shopping . . . degraded the status of their town and deterred investors" from the East Valley, especially whites and mainstream American companies.[74] Critics believed the region was attracting the wrong type of people and establishments. Rather than having settlers from the Plains, Rockies, or across the Atlantic, their new neighbors arrived from the Pacific Rim and thus disturbed the rhythms or mores of suburbia.

Along with incorporation, voters had to decide between seventeen candidates (six whites, five Latinos, five Chinese, one African American) running for the proposed five-person city council. On election day, voters rejected cityhood 62.67 percent to 37.33 percent. While voters' trepidations about regulation or higher taxes informed their decisions, ultimately, the idea that country living would die in the hands of a potential Asian-majority governing body caused greater concern.[75] Most of the candidates were not Chinese, but critics feared their worst-case scenario of high Asian voter turnout and support for Asian candidates, thus resulting in an inaugural council with few to zero non-Asians. Judy Chen Haggerty—a Chinese immigrant and East Valley resident since the early 1980s—was not surprised. She claimed racism stifled efforts to incorporate: "Hacienda [Heights] tried [multiple] times. [It] didn't work [and it's] a shame. [I'll] tell you why . . . [The] problem was how many candidates are Chinese . . . That scared [whites] off and the tactic was '[the] Chinese is coming.' That's a very clear cut of [the] Old Guard saying, 'No way' [to cityhood because of xenophobia]. [That was] not that long ago. [Those feelings among the Old Guard are] still there . . . They feel there is a threat."[76]

Until the end, anti-cityhood activists like Dennis Mathewson insisted their concerns were not about race: "[The Chinese were] trying to pull 'the race card.' . . . Five Asians are not going to control the community. . . . We are getting sick and tired of this race thing they keep pulling."[77] Even people who supported diversity claimed Asian residents were going too far, forcing their way into power. Old and young critics suggested Hacienda Heights' Asian community were not assimilated enough to govern. While overt and covert modes of racism marred multiple cityhood campaigns, the political efficacy and importance of Asian suburbanites during these battles moved them from the fringe to the center. By mobilizing their friends and co-ethnics, they were not passive subjects in debates over community sovereignty. Rather, they exercised their rights as voters and entitlements as property owners to help shape local issues.

Next door in Rowland Heights, similar concerns over a declining "quality of life" and unchecked commercial growth encouraged residents to incorporate. Proponents cited the need for local control, particularly on matters of planning, development, and land use.[78] Supporters argued incorporation would help deal with—as one homeowner called it—the town's aesthetic "messiness."[79] Albert Chang, a US-born Chinese resident, believed many critiques of visual clutter were warranted, while others—particularly those coming from non-Asian residents—were simply xenophobic: "What does 'look more Asian' mean? Does it mean just new development or does that just mean there's a new Chinese restaurant that you're not comfortable going into? I think 'looks more Asian' means more like, 'Hey there's a Chinese restaurant. I walk in. Everyone is Chinese. They speak Chinese to you.' Or like, 'There's a Chinese supermarket and it smelled bad and they sell weird fish.'"[80] Critics insinuated that Rowland Heights would feel more like an urban Chinatown and less like country living if the electorate voted in a majority-Asian council. Residents' racial fears increased when organizations like the Rowland Heights Chinese Association started to partner with the Rowland Heights Coordinating Council on cityhood-related matters. For some, the coziness between the two groups—an ethnic organization and the town's legislative liaison to the county—suggested collusive behavior between private and public interests.

After several attempts, in 2009, Rowland Heights residents tried to incorporate once more. Cityhood advocates sought local control and, if incorporated, hoped to prevent Diamond Bar from annexing a patch of land in Rowland Heights known as Crestline.[81] Robert Lewis, a member of Rowland Heights Advocates for Cityhood (RHAC), believed incorporation provided residents the authority to block annexation, especially amid plans to build a 3,600-unit master-planned community on the site.[82] Chinese leaders like Henry Woo, a member of the Rowland Heights Coordinating Council, opposed annexation and pushed for cityhood hoping to curtail this and other development.[83] Similar to what occurred in Hacienda Heights, incorporation became a divisive racial matter, pitting Asian residents against the rest of the community. Rather than emphasizing concerns over taxation or civic freedom, anti-cityhood forces made analogous claims of a Chinese takeover. Nativist-laced innuendo eventually dominated public debates about cityhood. One critic, "Rudeee," said incorporation would not help Rowland Heights because it was already a place with "shoulder to shoulder Asian restaurants."[84] Rudeee suggested cityhood would not "whiten" the community nor make it country like it once was. Other critics like "Donna" claimed Rowland Heights "looks like a town straight out of China." She said, it was "a shame Rowland Heights was allowed to become so densely populated," alluding to past failures to incorporate, which could have prevented Rowland Heights' "Asianization."[85]

Leaders of neighboring suburbs thought Rowland Heights did not organize swiftly enough to protect their slice of country living. Former Diamond Bar councilmember John Forbing thought the 2009 pro-cityhood campaign was set up to fail because Rowland Heights activists lacked coordination and a clear message: "In Rowland Heights, your basic group of people had their HOAs doing what they wanted and said their [proposed new] city government was going to change Colima [Road]," a major commercial thoroughfare of Chinese and Korean eateries, boutiques, and grocery stores. Forbing claimed cityhood opponents "didn't see any point in incorporation" because a new City of Rowland Heights would not be able to transform what already developed. In other words, it was too late to use cityhood as a means of restricting the aesthetic and cultural "Asianization" of the community. Decades of lax regulation could not rehabilitate Rowland Heights to its former rural state. Asian community leaders like Judy Chen Haggerty agreed. Though she chided the nativism behind the criticism, she understood their point of view: "For me, I think it's a little too late."[86] Because it is not incorporated, Rowland Heights is "like 'anything goes.' It sorta brings down the class."[87] In contrast, she believed incorporated suburbs like Diamond Bar or Chino Hills were "cleaner, more organized" because they were either fully planned or implemented strict zoning laws prior to mass Asian settlement.[88] Haggerty joked, "[Everyone has the] same house, same color, same dog, same car. Rowland [Heights] . . . is like you're in Hong Kong."[89] Along with the loss of mainstream American businesses—including, as she cited, Chuck E. Cheese (a children's arcade and restaurant chain)—Rowland Heights lost land to neighboring Diamond Bar when they became a city.[90] Despite revived interest, the push for cityhood fell short again.

Rowland Heights' efforts failed because of the timing and residents' lack of political will. In contrast, anticipating significant Asian settlement, Diamond Bar incorporated in 1989, well before the suburb neared an Asian majority at the turn of the century. Once a city, Diamond Bar's leadership staved off possibilities of an Asian "takeover" by quickly building an elite group of white leadership, many of whom were influential before incorporation. Later, this group would include conservative Asian residents who supported the preservation of Diamond Bar's aesthetic and political status quo. Throughout the 1990s and well into the 2000s, elected and appointed officials—white and nonwhite alike—discreetly implemented policies protecting country living. This included strict land use and English signage laws and limitations to the types of commerce in accordance with the General Plan.[91] Residents in Chino Hills deployed similar tactics in the years leading to its incorporation in 1991. In a region increasingly defined by its high Asian population and despite the trans-Pacific ties of its residents, Chino Hills' incorporation squashed the possibilities of having a built environment akin to its ethnoburban counterparts. For most folks, this was ideal.

• • •

Beyond the East Valley, cityhood attempts occurred elsewhere in greater L.A. During the 1980s and 1990s, a confluence of annexation threats and anti-development sentiments resulted in the incorporation of West Hollywood, Santa Clarita, and Malibu.[92] Similar issues motivated residents in Diamond Bar, Chino Hills, Hacienda Heights, and Rowland Heights. But in these four communities, race and class proved to be more important factors in shaping the debate over incorporation and Slow Growth. Crucially, activists' tactics included strategies that prevented people from looking prejudiced in a post–civil rights movement, pro-multiculturalism, pro-diversity era. From signage laws to church design, citing country living as a reason to support or oppose various projects or policies made it possible for homeowners to discriminate without looking prejudiced. Class- and color-blind approaches allowed suburbanites to act on their discomfort, enforce Euro-American social norms, and enact exclusionary measures. By cloaking and shrouding their feelings in careful rhetoric and behavior, suburbanites—including people of color—exerted power in strategic ways that outright honesty or bigotry no longer allowed. Ultimately, slowing or stopping change motivated most residents who engaged in cityhood and Slow Growth politics. To those who resisted change, having a multiethnic landscape disrupted the mythologies of suburbia, the West, and the American Dream—tropes residents hoped to maintain for generations to come. As populations transformed before their eyes, it made sense to residents that the preservation of these Western frontier imaginaries was only possible through grassroots activism and by encouraging homeowners' revolts. Despite the multidecade effort of activists, by the end of the aughts (and with a valley population approaching 1.5 million residents), more people came to acknowledge that country living was undoubtedly in name only.[93] Perhaps it always was.

Epilogue

On our way to see the largest Buddhist temple in the Western
Hemisphere, we stopped for gas in the eastern reaches of China
Valley, where all the Spanish-style houses in the quintessential
southern-California subdivisions look alike. . . . Much of the
population has attained the standard trappings of the American
good life—the shiny car, the new house, the well-tended lawn,
maybe even the pool. But the San Gabriel Valley['s] . . . charm
is how it juxtaposes this superficial homogeneity—what some
might even call sterility—with the vibrant and the strange.

—SCHWARZ AND SCHWARZ,
"Going All Out for Chinese"[1]

IN 1999, Benjamin and Christina Schwarz documented their exploration of
L.A.'s San Gabriel Valley, which they cheekily referred to as "China Valley."[2]
From Hong Kong–style cafes to Shanghainese dumpling shops, they wanted
to try "the best Chinese food in America" in a part of the county generally unknown to Angelenos west of the 405 freeway.[3] In between meals, the
two writers visited various sites of "Los Angeles' newest Sino-suburbs" to
absorb local culture.[4] Their stops included Hsi Lai temple, a once-polarizing
landmark and harbinger of what was to come in the Asianization of the
valley's east side. In their quasi-ethnographic accounts, the Schwarzes said
these suburbs were not like traditional urban Chinatowns with working-
class denizens, tight sidewalks, and boisterous street life. Rather, these ethnic
enclaves contained families with very comfortable backgrounds basking in
the luxuries of suburbia. They noticed parking lots were "stuffed with the
Mercedes, Infinitis, and BMWs of customers who can afford to pay $40 for
braised goose webs with spiny sea cucumbers and $90 for bird's-nest soup."[5]
After a sumptuous supper and retail therapy at one of the various Asian strip
malls modeled after Spanish villas or Medieval castles, families returned to
their faux-Mediterranean homes like any Southern California suburbanite.

Sitting in an unassuming Rowland Heights food court that unapologetically catered to Asian patrons, the Schwarzes realized they were—for once—in a space that did not "belong" to them. They acknowledged that unlike most suburbs, when it came to the San Gabriel Valley, whites were the outsiders and not the other way around. "Yes, we were a spectacle," they joked, "In this case two Caucasians eating in a mall in the middle of suburbia made a very weird sight indeed." It was a moment of discomfort and delight. What they witnessed and felt was unusual to them, but for hundreds of Asian families, this was another day in "the SGV." The Schwarzes relished knowing these places existed twenty miles from L.A. To folks who have long lived in the area, however, the region's transformation into "China Valley" was not welcomed and not how they envisioned it was to be. Critics, particularly white families, thus fled "country living" in the aughts and 2010s. Their exodus opened doors for more Chinese, Filipino, Korean, and other Asian families to stake their claim in the suburban American Dream, East Valley style.[6]

The Schwarzes published their piece the year CNN hailed Walnut as a suburban "model of diversity." Months before that, the *Los Angeles Times* reported kids in Walnut regarded multiculturalism at school "commonplace, comfortable—and cool." Titled "Learning to Look Past Race," the article claimed the East Valley was a successful social experiment in what suburban diversity looked like going into the new century. As these features suggested, ethnically or racially heterogenous communities did not always descend into conflict or translate into a poor quality of life. Simply put: subscribing to color-blindness plus multiculturalism was the paradoxical formula to finding peace in a multiracial California—something country living residents executed (or attempted to execute) during four decades of growth and diversification. As the *Times* journalist earnestly wrote: this was simply life "way out in the San Gabriel Valley." And despite their distance from L.A. and the "cookie cutter" character of these towns, these were cosmopolitan suburbs that supposedly figured out how to live in harmony.

CNN and the *Times* celebrated the region's diverse composition, as did the Schwarzes. But the Schwarzes alluded to something other media did not catch: that the suburbs of the East San Gabriel Valley were neither novelties nor truly racially diverse. By the 2000s, suburbs with large Asian populations existed across the country—from Edison, New Jersey to Daly City, California. Moreover, country living suburbs or subdivisions grew increasingly racially homogenous, with Asian immigrants—especially diasporic Chinese from Hong Kong, Taiwan, and later, Mainland China—constituting the racial majority of suburbs like Walnut, Diamond Bar, and Rowland Heights.[7] That is not to say other racial groups did not call the East Valley home. Overall, though, Asians were now the everyday faces of country living. It was no longer the white homeowner with Midwestern or Southern roots who embodied the typical local.

Over time, the currency of East Valley suburbia and its reputation as the heart of L.A. country living made way for a different form of cultural capital. In the last decade and a half, "the 626" and "the 909" have emerged as sources of pan-Asian American pride. Suburbs like Monterey Park and Arcadia in the West Valley or Diamond Bar and Rowland Heights in the east are places intrinsically tied to the experience of being Asian in Southern California. For 1.5- or second-generation Asians who grew up in these towns, their sense of identity and perceptions of suburbia were informed by their unique up-bringings. That is, the trans-Pacific ties of valley residents and local industries and politics shaped the region's look, feel, and flavor. For the valley's Asian community, their unusual experiences fostered a sense of belonging or fraternity in a society that otherwise kept them at the margins. They did not find it strange that plenty of their neighbors had Asian surnames, that Korean Bible school was mandatory for children, that elderly Chinese women took over the park for morning *tai chi*, and that high schoolers preferred grabbing boba over milkshakes after class.

Today, so common is it to be Asian from the San Gabriel Valley that even if you did not grow up in the region, you knew about these suburbs—knowledge that has penetrated the internet, consumer, and youth cultures. For Asian American millennials and Zoomers, to be from "the SGV"—dare they say—has cachet. The valley's relevance as a hub of Asian America is no longer relegated to people "in the know." This is illustrated in the popularity of events like the 626 Night Market (modeled after the outdoor food stalls of Asia) or through viral videos of YouTube celebrities like the Fung Brothers.[8] It is exemplified through the prevalence of popular Asia- or US-based Asian brands that established headquarters or opened some of their first US or suburban locations in the valley: 85 Degrees Bakery-Cafe (Chinese/Taiwanese), Cathay Bank (Chinese), Din Tai Fung (Chinese/Taiwanese), East West Bank (Chinese), Hung Fong Foods/Sriracha (Chinese-Vietnamese), Jollibee (Filipino), Panda Express (Chinese), Red Ribbon Bakery (Filipino), and Seafood City Market (Filipino).[9] Television shows like *Crazy Ex-Girlfriend* or culinary experts like Jonathan Gold and Padma Lakshmi (who was raised

FIGURE 19. Campaign signs of local Asian American Republican candidates at an intersection, Diamond Bar, CA, May 2014. Photo taken by James Zarsadiaz.

in the East Valley) praised the region for its cultural novelties and gastronomic contributions. As noted in Anthony Bourdain's *Parts Unknown*, the valley is befuddling, for its landscape is quintessentially suburban and pays homage to old California. Yet hidden behind these façades are communities totaling half a million Asian Americans: "The San Gabriel Valley has the sleepy, sepia tones of a cowboy Western—a lot of buildings look, from afar, like they just might be a country-style honky-tonk joint. A closer look will reveal the Chinese-language signage, and you'll realize you're in one of the hidden treasures of cosmopolitan Los Angeles."[10]

The demographics of country living have changed, but on the whole, the East Valley has sustained its conservative influence in state and local politics. In 2018, Republican gubernatorial candidate John Cox spoke at a packed City of Industry conference hall of mostly Chinese voters and entrepreneurs—an event hosted by Asian GOP operatives and business leaders including Mei Mei Huff (longtime East Valley Republican activist and wife of former California Senate minority leader, Bob Huff) and former Monterey Park mayor and one of the founders of East West Bank, Betty Tom Chu.[11] In November

2020, while the world's eyes were laser-focused on the presidential race between Donald Trump and Joe Biden, there were hotly contested House seats in the region. This included the race for the Thirty-Ninth Congressional District, which covered Diamond Bar, Chino Hills, Hacienda Heights, and Rowland Heights.[12] Republican Young Kim, a Korean immigrant, beat one-term incumbent Gil Cisneros (D) making Kim among the first Korean American women to serve in Congress.[13] Cisneros rode the "blue wave" into office in 2018. But voters brought back a Republican, which was not altogether surprising given country living suburbia's reputation as a conservative stronghold. (Kim took over a seat once held by fellow Republican and the House's first Korean American member, Jay Kim.)

While the GOP's national grip on suburbia has weakened in recent times, their influence and the politics of the East Valley Old Guard lives on thanks to younger Asian suburbanites like Young Kim.[14] Generations later, Asian residents have sustained the relationships their elder co-ethnics built with white homeowners in the 1990s, when it was evident Chinese, Filipino, and Korean families and voters were here to stay. Many of the valley's older white settlers left years ago. However, class-based alliances, NIMBYism, and collective interests in preserving the image and exclusivity of country living suburbia remained. In 2008, East Valley residents fumed at the idea of an NFL stadium in City of Industry. The complex was planned to sit near tracts in Walnut, Diamond Bar, and Phillips Ranch. Once again, residents of Asian descent including homeowners' rights warrior Joaquin Lim led the battle.[15] At one Walnut city council meeting attended by two hundred people, homeowner Shiuh-Ming Ellis exclaimed, "If this stadium is not stopped, our quality of life will be completely destroyed. Walnut will become a suburban slum."[16] After years of litigation, including involvement from Governor Arnold Schwarzenegger, local citizens groups killed the plan.[17] In 2007, residents scoffed at a proposal to build a 775-unit apartment complex in Rowland Heights, citing its density and design as the guaranteed death knell of country living. After a series of regional planning meetings—one of which attracted two to three thousand people—residents successfully defeated the plan.[18] As Judy Chen Haggerty observed, "Why [was the apartment complex] drawing all the protests? Because Chinese residents are among those [who did not like it, not just the Old Guard]."[19] In 2007, proposals to expand a Zen center in Walnut, and in 2011, plans to erect a Buddhist temple in Rowland Heights generated similar reactions, including opposition from Asian homeowners who feared these sites would undermine the area's "rural atmosphere."[20] Most recently, the East Valley's notoriety as a hub of "maternity tourism"—that is, foreign women (mostly Chinese) who pay maternity tourism business owners to help them give birth in America (thus allowing their children to receive citizenship)—once again pushed critics over the edge, claiming the region was being overrun by distrustful, scheming immigrants.[21] From apartments in Rowland Heights to palatial compounds in Chino Hills, "maternity hotels" outraged country living suburbanites embarrassed by the phenomenon and the daily scenes of pregnant Chinese women walking between parks, horse trails, and strip malls without husbands in tow. In all cases, residents across demographic lines claimed to not harbor prejudice or malintent in their criticisms related to development, land use, or local culture. Just like their white predecessors, Asian suburbanites said their criticisms were never about race, religion, or class; they were only looking out for everyone's "quality of life."

In the 2020s, among the rows of red-tiled Venetian-inspired tracts and sprawling ranch homes are communities continuing to evolve. Families cycle in and out, yet residents' anti-urbanist spirit and devotion to protecting the myths of suburbia, Western rurality, and the American Dream remain a common thread in uniting East Valley residents. Planners, developers, builders, and realtors laid the foundations and gave life to country living. Ultimately, residents themselves gave it meaning and worked to protect its legacies, predicated on a combination of real and imagined histories. Despite people's differing views on how country living should look or feel, homeowners collectively fought to preserve this lifestyle by any means necessary. Whether it was developing a local culture rooted in settler colonialism or implementing laws regulating growth and aesthetics, the people of country living actively or tacitly resisted difference and transgression. Looking at how these suburbs developed in relation to greater L.A. since the 1960s, it is evident why places committed to staying the same have, for the most part, done just that. By defending the East Valley, residents—in effect—upheld the myths that brought them there in the first place. Particularly for post-1965 Asian immigrants, they pursued and experienced a lifestyle historically not made available to them. In the East Valley, Chinese, Filipino, and Korean families created a home for themselves in the suburbs, making concessions as well as building tenuous political alliances with their white neighbors so everyone could coexist in the frontier. On the whole, suburbanites came to understand that their Asian neighbors were not just defined by their racial or class background. Their worthiness as suburbanites was also measured by their political loyalties to country living.

This story was about a collection of Southern California suburbs and how the power of American myths shaped suburbanites' experiences as the world changed around them. For years, seeing an Asian family residing in suburbia was an anomaly. Until recently, the suburbs of "the SGV" were among those exceptions. Today, whether it is Northern Virginia, Buford Highway outside Atlanta, or the pastoral communities of Diamond Bar and Chino Hills, it is safe to say that the contemporary Asian experience in the United States is not an urban one. It is a suburban one.

. . .

It was late February 2020, a few weeks before places shut down in response to coronavirus. As I traveled to L.A. for a weekend visit to see family, I read about the growing dangers of COVID-19. Like many of us, I was not sure of what this all meant. A couple days prior, a California-born Chinese friend called me saying a stranger on the street accused them of "giving the world another illness." Meanwhile, Donald Trump began his geopolitical strategy of blaming China and Chinese people's habits for what would be declared a global pandemic.[22] Amid the noise and unknowns, I found myself driving around the East Valley to remember why I wanted to tell this story.

It was a still, balmy morning. I stopped by a Filipino bakery for *pan de sal*. As I ate at a park near my childhood home in Walnut's Creekside neighborhood, I randomly came across a set of Chinese YouTube videos extolling the virtues of the East Valley. The narrator praised the area's natural surroundings, peaceful landscapes, and humorously, the "economical meals and healthy offerings of soup and salad" at the Puente Hills Mall Souplantation, a now-defunct restaurant chain that had a cult-like immigrant following until its liquidation in May 2020 (another business casualty of the pandemic).[23] This particular Souplantation had cultural significance. It was on the parking lot of the fictional Twin Pines/Lone Pine Mall featured in the 1985 blockbuster, *Back to the Future*.[24] Evidently, in the eyes of film location scouts, the East Valley's backdrop conveyed the quaintness of Marty McFly's made-up California town.

It was now late afternoon. I was on my way home. At a long red light in Diamond Bar, I zoned out with the windows down, staring at the hills, letting the breeze envelop my mother's sedan. In front of me was an older white woman in a Chevy pickup blasting an unidentifiable country song, followed by "Half-Breed"—a tune, with racially insensitive undertones, that defined Cher's 1970s western persona. To her left was a middle-aged Chinese male in a Tesla, also with the windows down, playing Mandarin pop at an audible volume. Disinterested in the high-impact rhythms of the disco-era classic, he swiftly rolled up the passenger window and nodded at the woman. She chuckled and waved her hand suggesting she was unbothered. This brief moment, to me, embodied everyday life in country living for the last thirty years. The East Valley is ordinary and extraordinary. It is a place where residents—in spite of their differences and individual biases—find common ground so all can experience the suburban good life. It is a complicated balance and relationship still tested today. The signal turned green and I continued my journey home.

NOTES

INTRODUCTION

1. Carl Schoner, Amazon.com book description of *Suburban Samurai: The Asian Invasion of the San Gabriel Valley* (self-published, 2006), https://www.amazon.com /gp/product/1411698878?pf_rd_r=WKGW14TGSTX2AQN1XM9P&pf_rd_p= 9d9090dd-8b99-4ac3-b4a9-90a1db2ef53b, accessed December 24, 2020. The book description is as follows: In the author's words, "'A friendly invasion is an invasion nonetheless.' This is a humorous, outrageous perspective of how the new wave of Asian immigrants pouring into the San Gabriel Valley has transformed life there. As seen through the eyes of the Artist/Author (who has lived in the area for 45 years) this book paints a picturesque exposé of the changing demographics of the Valley that is as serious as it is funny. This is a wild ride of essays and cartoons that touch upon such flash points of interest as Samurai Image and Wealth, Politics, Samurai Restaurants and Dining Experiences, Music and Entertainment, Feng Shui, the Dating Disparity Issue, the Asian Intellectual Superiority Myth, Karaoke Clubs, Suburban Samurai Supermarket Adventures, and much more! This perspective is essential reading for anyone interested in Asian American studies!"

2. Carl Schoner, Amazon.com book description of *When We Were Cowboys* (self-published, 2009), https://www.amazon.com/When-Were-Cowboys-Carl-Schoner /dp/B005881PKS, accessed December 24, 2020. The book description is as follows: "'When We Were Cowboys' is a collection of stories about my personal adventures growing up in Southern California after moving here from New York in 1961. While this book is intended primarily as a memoir for family and friends, there are many stories within it that will stir the fondest memories of all young people who were lucky enough to have grown up in the more open expanses of Southern California's San Gabriel Valley back in the good old days of the 1960's and 1970's."

3. Carl Schoner, oral history interview conducted by James Zarsadiaz, Diamond Bar, CA, June 22, 2018.

4. Schoner, oral history interview.

5. The Hart-Celler Act of 1965 abolished racial quotas, allowed for family reunification, and set up a preference system based on occupational need. On the whole, the act prioritized Asian immigrants with a college education and professional/white-collar background.

6. Yu-Ju Hung, "Transnational and Local-Focus Ethnic Networks: The Development of Two Types of Chinese Social Organizations in the San Gabriel Valley," *Southern California Quarterly* 98.2 (Summer 2016), 222; Judy Chen Haggerty, oral history interview conducted by James Zarsadiaz, Walnut, CA, June 23, 2016.

7. Hung, "Transnational and Local-Focus Ethnic Networks," 202–203.

8. Hung, 202–203.

9. Judy Chen Haggerty, oral history interview conducted by James Zarsadiaz, Walnut, CA, June 23, 2016.

10. Eduardo Bonilla-Silva, *Racism without Racists: Color-Blind Racism and the Persistence of Racial Inequality in America* (Lanham, MD: Rowman & Littlefield, 2003).

11. Mike Davis, *City of Quartz: Excavating the Future in Los Angeles* (New York: Verso, 1990); Robert M. Fogelson, *Fragmented Metropolis: Los Angeles, 1850–1930* (Berkeley: University of California Press, 1967); Greg Hise, *Magnetic Los Angeles: Planning the Twentieth-Century Metropolis* (Baltimore: Johns Hopkins University Press, 1997); Michael J. Dear (ed.), *From Chicago to L.A.: Making Sense of Urban Theory* (Thousand Oaks: Sage, 2002); Joel Garreau, *Edge City: Life on the New Frontier* (New York: Anchor, 1991); Edward Soja, *Third Space: Journeys to Los Angeles and Other Real-and-Imagined Places* (Malden: Blackwell, 1996); Edward Soja, "Los Angeles: City of the Future?," BBC/Open University (1991), https://www.youtube.com/watch?time_continue=16&v=pkYIwlcjCOI, accessed April 23, 2018.

12. Soja, "Los Angeles: City of the Future?."

13. John Chase, Margaret Crawford, and John Kaliski (eds.), *Everyday Urbanism* (New York: The Monacelli Press, 1999).

14. Karen Tongson, *Relocations: Queer Suburban Imaginaries* (New York: New York University Press, 2011), 3.

15. Laura Barraclough, *Making the San Fernando Valley: Rural Landscapes, Urban Development, and White Privilege* (Athens: University of Georgia Press, 2011); Matt Garcia, *A World of Its Own: Race, Labor, and Citrus in the Making of Greater Los Angeles, 1900–1970* (Chapel Hill: University of North Carolina Press, 2002); Genevieve Carpio, *Collisions at the Crossroads: How Place and Mobility Make Race* (Oakland: University of California Press, 2019); Tongson, *Relocations*; Paul J. P. Sandul, *California Dreaming: Boosterism, Memory, and Rural Suburbs in the Golden State* (Morgantown: West Virginia University Press, 2014).

16. Elson Trinidad, "L.A. County Is the Capital of Asian America," KCET, September 27, 2013, https://www.kcet.org/socal-focus/la-county-is-the-capital-of-asian-america; Asian Americans Advancing Justice, *A Community of Contrasts: Asian Americans, Native Hawaiians and Pacific Islanders in Los Angeles*

County (Los Angeles: AAJA, 2013), https://advancingjustice-la.org/our-reports-and-research/los-angeles-county/.

17. For studies regarding Chinese settlement in Monterey Park and the West San Gabriel Valley during the 1980s, see Timothy Fong, *The First Suburban Chinatown: The Remaking of Monterey Park, California* (Philadelphia: Temple University Press, 1994); John Horton, *The Politics of Diversity: Immigration, Resistance, and Change in Monterey Park, California* (Philadelphia: Temple University Press, 1995); Leland Saito, *Race and Politics: Asian Americans, Latinos, and Whites in a Los Angeles Suburb* (Urbana: University of Illinois Press, 1998).

18. Wei Li, *Ethnoburb: The New Ethnic Community in Urban America* (Honolulu: University of Hawaii Press, 2008).

19. Wei Li, "Spatial Transformation of an Urban Ethnic Community: From Chinatown to Ethnoburb in Los Angeles," in *From Urban Enclave to Ethnic Suburb*, ed. Wei Li (Honolulu: University of Hawaii Press, 2006), 74–94; Min Zhou, *Contemporary Chinese America: Immigration, Ethnicity, and Community Transformation* (Philadelphia: Temple University Press, 2009).

20. Wendy Cheng, *The Changs Next Door to the Diazes: Remapping Race in Suburban California* (Minneapolis: University of Minnesota Press, 2013).

21. Henry Nash Smith, *Virgin Land: The American West as Symbol and Myth* (Cambridge, MA: Harvard University Press, 1970).

22. Neil Smith, "New City, New Frontier: The Lower East Side as Wild, Wild West" in *Variations on a Theme Park: The New American City and the End of Public Space,* ed. Michael Sorkin (New York: Hill and Wang, 1992), 69.

23. Roland Barthes, *Mythologies* (New York: Hill and Wang, 1972), 129.

24. On scholarship about post-WWII suburbia and the "American Dream," see Elaine Tyler May, *Homeward Bound: American Families in the Cold War Era* (New York: Basic Books, 1988); Lizabeth Cohen, *A Consumers' Republic: The Politics of Mass Consumption in Postwar America* (New York: Vintage, 2008); Greg Castillo, *Cold War on the Home Front: The Soft Power of Midcentury Design* (Minneapolis: University of Minnesota Press, 2010).

25. "The 626" is a nickname of the San Gabriel Valley. This refers to the primary area code for the region. Diamond Bar, Chino Hills, Phillips Ranch, and parts of Walnut are in the "909" area code.

26. Willow Lung-Amam, *Trespassers? Asian Americans and the Battle for Suburbia* (Oakland: University of California Press, 2017); Willow Lung-Amam, "That 'Monster House' Is My Home: The Social and Cultural Politics of Design Reviews and Regulations," *Journal of Urban Design* 18.2 (April 2013), 220–241.

27. Jesse Katz, oral history interview conducted by James Zarsadiaz via telephone, March 22, 2018.

28. Along with Chinese immigrants, concerns about the influx of Japanese capital across greater L.A. informed discussions about real estate and rights to property ownership, especially if they did not live there full time. See Soja, "Los Angeles: City of the Future?"; Davis, *City of Quartz.*

29. Ronald Takaki, *Strangers from a Different Shore: A History of Asian Americans* (Boston: Little, Brown and Company, 1989).

30. Helen Hunt Jackson, *Ramona* (New York: Little Brown, 1884); Dydia DeLyser, *Ramona Memories: Tourism and the Shaping of Southern California* (Minneapolis: University of Minnesota Press, 2005). Studies by Genevieve Carpio, Matt Garcia, Jerry Gonzalez, and Gilda Ochoa provide rich, thick descriptions on Latinx and Chicanx suburbanization in the San Gabriel Valley and Inland Empire. See Carpio: *Collisions at the Crossroads*; Garcia, *A World of Its Own*; Jerry Gonzalez, *In Search of the Mexican Beverly Hills: Latino Suburbanization in Postwar Los Angeles* (New Brunswick, NJ: Rutgers University Press, 2017); Gilda Ochoa, *Becoming Neighbors in a Mexican American Community: Power, Conflict, and Solidarity* (Austin: University of Texas Press, 2004).

31. Asian Americans Advancing Justice, *A Community of Contrasts: Asian Americans, Native Hawaiians, and Pacific Islanders in the San Gabriel Valley* (Los Angeles: AAJA, February 2018), https://sgv2018.herokuapp.com/, accessed February 11, 2019.

32. In the context of the San Gabriel Valley, geographers, historians, and sociologists have recently used "ethnoburb" to describe suburbs with direct ties to Asia and/or suburbs where Asians (particularly Chinese immigrants) constitute a racial majority or plurality. It has also been used to describe suburbs with visible displays of Asian culture in the built environment. See Li, *Ethnoburb*; Hung, "Transnational and Local-Focus Ethnic Networks"; Becky Nicolaides and James Zarsadiaz, "Design Assimilation in Suburbia: Asian Americans, Built Landscapes, and Suburban Advantage in Los Angeles's San Gabriel Valley since 1970," *Journal of Urban History* 43.2 (March 2017), 332–371.

33. By "communities," this includes unincorporated areas like Hacienda Heights, country living communities within cities such as Phillips Ranch in the city of Pomona, or individual subdivisions and tracts.

CHAPTER 1. CONSTRUCTING "COUNTRY LIVING"

1. Shawn Dunn, oral history interview conducted by James Zarsadiaz, Walnut, CA, July 14, 2016.

2. "Quiet, Small-Town Ambiance Found at Snow Creek," *Los Angeles Times*, December 6, 1987, OC-E9.

3. "Quiet, Small-Town Ambiance."

4. "Quiet, Small-Town Ambiance."

5. "Tribal History," Gabrielino-Tongva Tribe website, http://www.gabrielino tribe.org/historical-sites-1/, date unknown, accessed September 1, 2020.

6. Wendy Cheng, "A Brief History (and Geography) of the San Gabriel Valley," KCET, August 4, 2014, https://www.kcet.org/history-society/a-brief-history-and -geography-of-the-san-gabriel-valley, accessed June 8, 2020; City of Diamond Bar and Diamond Bar Historical Society, *Images of America: Diamond Bar* (Charleston:

Arcadia Publishing, 2014), 7; City of Walnut and the Walnut Historical Society, *Images of America: Walnut* (Charleston: Arcadia Publishing, 2012), 7.

7. Paul J. P. Sandul, *California Dreaming: Boosterism, Memory, and Rural Suburbs in the Golden State* (Morgantown: West Virginia University Press, 2014); Matt Garcia, *A World of Its Own: Race, Labor, and Citrus in the Making of Greater Los Angeles, 1900–1970* (Chapel Hill: University of North Carolina Press, 2002); Lawrence Culver, *The Frontier of Leisure: Southern California and the Shaping of Modern America* (Oxford: Oxford University Press, 2010). The Pasadena Subdivision of the former Atchison, Topeka & Santa Fe Railway (AT&SF) passed through the East San Gabriel Valley cities of Azusa, Claremont, Glendora, La Verne, Pomona, and San Dimas (formerly Mud Springs).

8. Garcia, *A World of Its Own.*

9. Similarly, white migrants from the Midwest, South, and Plains region who settled in California's Central Valley between the 1930s and 1980s maintained their agrarian traditions despite the urbanization of places like Fresno, Bakersfield, and the San Joaquin Valley. See James N. Gregory, "The Okie Impact on California, 1939–1989," *California History* (Fall 1989), 74–85.

10. Los Angeles Almanac, "Historical General Population, City and County of Los Angeles, 1850 to 2010," http://www.laalmanac.com/population/po02.php, accessed December 16, 2020.

11. Jeff Clabaugh, "Loudoun 'Agri-hood,' Willowsford, among Top in the Nation," WTOP, January 12, 2018, https://wtop.com/business-finance/2018/01/loudon-agri-hood-willsford-among-top-in-the-nation/slide/1/, accessed March 21, 2018.

12. The term "old California" typically came up in new home advertisements to describe tracts or master-planned communities. For example, in one Hacienda Heights subdivision, the developer said the homes were designed "in the 'old California' architectural style of stucco walls and red tile roofs." See "Single-Family Homes in Hacienda Heights Open," *Los Angeles Times*, October 16, 1983, G23.

13. Kenneth Jackson, *Crabgrass Frontier: The Suburbanization of the United States* (New York: Oxford University Press, 1985), 68–70.

14. Henry Binford, *The First Suburbs: Residential Communities on the Boston Periphery, 1815–1860* (Chicago: University of Chicago Press, 1985); Robert F. Fishman, *Bourgeois Utopias: The Rise and Fall of Suburbia* (New York: Basic, 1989); John R. Stilgoe, *Borderland: Origins of the American Suburb* (New Haven, CT: Yale University Press, 2012 [1988]), 28, 32.

15. Robert F. Fishman, "American Suburbs/English Suburbs: A Transatlantic Comparison," *Journal of Urban History* 13.3 (May 1987), 238.

16. Catharine Beecher, "How to Redeem Woman's Profession from Dishonor," *Harper's New Monthly Magazine* 31 (November 1865); Andrew Jackson Downing, *The Architecture of Country Houses* (New York: D. Appleton & Co., 1850); Alex Krieger, *City on a Hill: Urban Idealism in America from the Puritans to the Present* (Cambridge, MA: The Belknap Press of Harvard University Press, 2019); Rebecca Messner (dir.), *Olmsted and America's Urban Parks*, film, PBS (2011).

17. Laura Barraclough, *Making the San Fernando Valley: Rural Landscapes, Urban Development, and White Privilege* (Athens: University of Georgia Press, 2011), 2, 29.

18. Suburban scholars and planning historians regard Irvine in Orange County as the model master-planned Sunbelt suburb of the late twentieth century. Irvine inspired similar patterns of suburbanization in the West, Southwest, and South in metropolises like San Diego, Orlando, Phoenix, Atlanta, and Houston. As Stephanie Kolberg notes, Sunbelt suburbs like Irvine (incorporated in 1971) were planned as cities with clusters of "Edenic villages." Cultural critics and urbanists like Joel Garreau, John Findlay, and Edward Soja bemoaned places like Irvine as "edge cities" modeled through the prism of Disneyland-like urbanism. Irvine was an urbanized setting with a manufactured rural-suburban identity. For more, see Stephanie Kolberg, "Crafting the Good Life in Irvine" in *City Dreams, Country Schemes: Community and Identity in the American West,* ed. Kathleen A. Brosnan and Amy L. Scott (Reno: University of Nevada Press, 2013); John M. Findlay, *Magic Lands: Western Cityscapes and American Culture after 1940* (Berkeley: University of California Press, 1992); Joel Garreau, *Edge City: Life on the New Frontier* (New York: Anchor, 1991); Edward Soja, "Los Angeles: City of the Future?," BBC/Open University (1991), https://www.youtube.com/watch?time_continue=16&v=pkYIwlcjCOI, accessed April 23, 2018; Michael Sorkin (ed.), *Variations on a Theme Park: The New American City and the End of Public Space* (New York: Hill and Wang, 1992); Mike Davis, *City of Quartz: Excavating the Future in Los Angeles* (New York: Vintage, 1992).

19. Philip Langdon, *A Better Place to Live: Reshaping the American Suburb* (New York: Harper Perennial, 1994), 32–33.

20. Kolberg, "Crafting the Good Life in Irvine, California," 40.

21. Irvine, in many ways, was not unlike Diamond Bar, Walnut, Chino Hills, and Phillips Ranch in that it presented itself as an upscale, forward-thinking community conscious of its humble, agrarian heritage. Irvine and its "New Town" counterparts like Reston, Virginia, and Columbia, Maryland, saw themselves as model suburbs of the future. Planners wanted to blend the conveniences of a city with the quaintness of small-town USA "New Towns" grappled with the unrealistic call of being simultaneously pro-development yet strict on growth.

22. Diamond Bar Homeowners Association ad, *Diamond Bar Windmill,* ca. 1980. Like other HOAs, Diamond Bar's HOA was created to "serve as a 'watchdog'" over issues like traffic, safety, land use, CC&Rs, and inter-neighbor relations. (CC&Rs means covenants, conditions, and restrictions. These are the rights, expectations, and obligations of homeowners in an HOA.)

23. Garreau, *Edge City.*

24. Findlay, *Magic Lands*; Garreau, *Edge City*; Soja, "Los Angeles: City of the Future?,"; Sorkin, *Variations on a Theme Park*; Davis, *City of Quartz.*

25. "Diamond Bar Ends Century-Old Isolation," *Southern California New Homes: Map Guide to New Housing,* April/May/June 1970, 11.

26. "A Guide to the Country Villages of Diamond Bar" brochure, ca. 1970.

27. "Country Living Comes Naturally: With a Heritage of Haciendas and Hospitality," *Highlander Community Newspaper,* July 31, 1974, 1.

28. "The Villages at Diamond Bar" brochure, McCombs Corporation, ca. 1980.

29. "Diamond Bar Country" brochure. The Diamond Bar Development Corporation, ca. 1980, 15.

30. City of Diamond Bar and Diamond Bar Historical Society, *Images of America: Diamond Bar* (Charleston: Arcadia Publishing, 2014), 7, 25.

31. New York millionaire Frederick E. Lewis II purchased his first ten horses for his California ranch from a farm in Massachusetts, whose bloodlines were traced to the original importation of Arabian horses to America in 1906. See City of Diamond Bar and Diamond Bar Historical Society, *Images of America: Diamond Bar* (Charleston, SC: Arcadia Publishing, 2014), 41.

32. The County of Los Angeles approved the Diamond Bar Master Plan in 1960.

33. "Presenting Diamond Bar: A Planned City," Quinton Engineers, Ltd., ca. early 1960s.

34. For more on Diamond Bar Ranch's history, see Lydia Plunk, "'A Meadow I Used to Know Every Inch Of,'" *Diamond Bar Patch*, May 31, 2011, https://patch.com/california/diamondbar-walnut/a-meadow-i-used-to-know-every-inch-of, accessed April 4, 2018; City of Diamond Bar and Diamond Bar Historical Society, *Images of America*, 49.

35. Ginger Lai, "Diamond Bar Making History . . ." *Highlander Community News,* November 2, 1983, 2.

36. Bill Boyarsky and Nancy Boyarsky, *Backroom Politics: How Your Local Politicians Work, Why Your Government Doesn't, and What You Can Do about It* (Los Angeles: J.P. Tarcher, Inc., 1974), 62.

37. "Diamond Bar," promotional brochure, Transamerica Corporation, ca. 1970.

38. "Concept 80" brochure, Boise Cascade Residential Community, ca. 1979.

39. Quinton, "Presenting Diamond Bar."

40. "Country Living Comes Naturally," 1.

41. "Country Living Comes Naturally," 1.

42. Quinton, "Presenting Diamond Bar."

43. "Presenting Diamond Bar."

44. Boise Cascade "Concept 80."

45. Boise Cascade "Concept 80."

46. Boise Cascade "Concept 80." The first home sold in Diamond Bar was in 1960. See "Diamond Bar . . . A Unique City in the Making" brochure, ca. 1966.

47. "Overview of an 8,000-Acre Planned Community: Diamond Bar," Transamerica Corporation, ca. 1975.

48. Critics assumed if governance was left in the hands of Los Angeles County, residents would be forced to fight urbanization on their own. Residents believed the county paid less attention to Diamond Bar after its inaugural years of development.

49. "Diamond Bar Country Estates" brochure, Diamond Bar Country Estates, ca. 1970, 3.

50. "The Country: Comforts of Costly Homes Amid Rugged Terrain," *Los Angeles Times*, June 26, 1980, SG1.

51. Ibid.

52. Transamerica operated and controlled The Diamond Bar Country Estates Association from 1969 until 1977, when it transferred ownership of the grounds to The Country's homeowners. The renamed Country Estates Homeowners Association (CEHA) assumed control over architecture, landscaping, and the enforcement of deed restrictions and association bylaws. In 1979, CEHA sued Transamerica for not carrying out various promises including thirty-five miles of horse paths, inadequately maintaining its riding arena, and a host of complaints ranging from infrastructure problems to corporate transparency. Nevertheless, homeowners in The Country believed the transfer of ownership from the San Francisco–based company helped ensure greater aesthetic harmony and local control. Even though this added another layer of governance, its conservative leadership believed this helped protect the country living ideal.

See "The Country: Comforts of Costly Homes Amid Rugged Terrain," *Los Angeles Times*, June 26, 1980, SG1; Mark Landsbaum, "Residents Sue Developer of 'The Country,'" *Los Angeles Times*, August 2, 1979, SG1.

53. Setha Low, *Behind the Gates: Life, Security, and the Pursuit of Happiness in Fortress America* (New York: Routledge, 2003), 75.

54. "Diamond Bar Country Estates" brochure. Diamond Bar Country Estates, ca. 1970, 4.

55. "Diamond Bar Country Estates" brochure, 4.

56. "Diamond Bar Country Estates" brochure, 4.

57. "Diamond Bar Country Estates" brochure, 4.

58. "Diamond Bar Country Estates" brochure, 4.

59. "Diamond Bar Country Estates" brochure, 6.

60. Boyarsky and Boyarsky, *Backroom Politics*, 61.

61. Barraclough, *Making the San Fernando Valley*, 119, 206.

62. Local architecture and open spaces visually reminded residents of Hacienda Heights' and Rowland Heights' agrarian past, which was why people still considered these non-master-planned suburbs as part of the East Valley country living landscape.

63. City of Walnut and the Walnut Historical Society, *Images of America*. The nut was the inspiration for Walnut's city name. Its town seal features a walnut tree, mountains, and a pioneer stagecoach to evoke its western past.

64. City of Walnut and the Walnut Historical Society, *Images of America*, 108.

65. Walnut's General Plan was approved in 1979, which included language that homes east of Grand Avenue were to be built on smaller lots with abundant open space. Along with the open space requirement, developers were required to have a balance of parks and recreational areas. They also had to designate sites for schools. See City of Walnut and the Walnut Historical Society, *Images of America*, 110.

66. City of Walnut and the Walnut Historical Society, *Images of America*, 99.

67. Michael Dear defines NIMBYism as "the protectionist attitudes of and oppositional tactics adopted by community groups facing an unwelcome development in the neighborhood." See Michael Dear, "Understanding and Overcoming the NIMBY Syndrome," *Journal of American Planning Association* 58.3 (1992), 288–300. Also see Gregory M. Maney and Margaret Abraham, "Whose Backyard? Boundary Making in NIMBY Opposition to Immigrant Services," *Social Justice* 35.4 (2008–2009), 66–82.

68. Dear, "Understanding and Overcoming the NIMBY Syndrome"; Maney and Abraham, "Whose Backyard?"; Jeffrey Miller, "Little City of Walnut Breaks Out of Shell," *Los Angeles Times*, June 26, 1986, SG1.

69. Miller, "Little City of Walnut," 111.

70. Ginger Lai, "New Mayor Returns to City Hall Again and Again and Again," *Highlander Community News*, April 29, 1981, 1.

71. Becky Nicolaides and James Zarsadiaz, "Design Assimilation in Suburbia: Asian Americans, Built Landscapes, and Suburban Advantage in Los Angeles's San Gabriel Valley since 1970," *Journal of Urban History* 43.2 (March 2017), 332–371; Yu-Ju Hung, "Transnational and Local-Focus Ethnic Networks: The Development of Two Types of Chinese Social Organizations in the San Gabriel Valley," *Southern California Quarterly* 98.2 (Summer 2016), 203.

72. Nicolaides and Zarsadiaz, "Design Assimilation in Suburbia"; "First 27 Lyon Co. Timberline Homes in Walnut Sell Out in 3 Hours," *Los Angeles Times*, February 7, 1988, DOC11; "The Palm Plan at Family Tree Homes Has Two Spacious Levels," *Los Angeles Times*, September 29, 1985, I20; "Large Crowds of Homeseekers Flock to Family Tree in Walnut," *Los Angeles Times*, March 24, 1985, J18; "Citation Opens Phase 10 at Country Hills," *Los Angeles Times*, December 15, 1985, L3. Beyond Walnut, neighboring country living suburbs contained their share of "executive homes." For example, in Rowland Heights, Shea Homes' Hidden Crest tract offered homes ranging from 1,882 to 3,432 square feet, priced from $150,995 to $289,995. Homes featured high-end appliances, crystal chandeliers, wood flooring, wet bars, three-car garages, and large backyards. See "Homes Located on Quarter-Acre Lots," *Los Angeles Times*, March 14, 1981, SG-A30. In Chino Hills, the Butterfield Ranch development featured homes with "Roman-style tubs" and two fireplaces in their "English-style" homes. See "Butterfield Ranch Making Debut at Chino Hills Site: Brock Homes Now Constructing Models," *Los Angeles Times*, September 12, 1987, SG-B1.

73. Barbara M. Kelly, *Expanding the American Dream: Building and Rebuilding Levittown* (Albany: State University of New York Press, 1993). For more on post-WWII suburban culture and domesticity, see Jackson, *Crabgrass Frontier*; Elaine Tyler May, *Homeward Bound: American Families in the Cold War Era* (New York: Basic Books, 1988).

74. Shea Homes, "The Estates at Snow Creek," advertisement, *Los Angeles Times*, January 11, 1987, H5.

75. Display Ad 368, "Two Elegant Neighborhoods, One Exceptional Community," *Los Angeles Times*, June 27, 1987, SG-B17.

76. The City of Walnut is home to twenty-six miles of bridle trails located within city limits. The city made it mandatory for builders to construct bridle trails in front of most developments. See City of Walnut and the Walnut Historical Society, *Images of America*, 109.

77. Display Ad 250, "Bring the Family to Snow Creek: Discover the Lifestyle to Last a Lifetime," *Los Angeles Times*, September 22, 1985, H13.

78. Display Ad 335, "Five Things This Expert Looks for in a New Home," *Los Angeles Times*, December 7, 1985, S13.

79. Other planned tracts in Southern California, such as those in nearby Orange County, deployed similar marketing. Irvine advertisements sometimes showcased blonde children gallivanting in what Stephanie Kolberg called Irvine's "pollution-free, pastoral-tinged, purified environments." See Stephanie Kolberg, "Crafting the Good Life in Irvine, California," in *City Dreams, Country Schemes: Community and Identity in the American West,* ed. Kathleen A. Brosnan and Amy L. Scott (Reno: University of Nevada Press, 2013), 50.

80. Display Ad 273, "River Run by Shea Homes," *Los Angeles Times*, May 18, 1986, I18.

81. John Gregory, "Sleepy Chino Hills Stirring to Boom Talk," *Los Angeles Times*, July 20, 1973, OC1.

82. Chino correctional facility was built in 1941.

83. John Gregory, "Sleepy Chino Hills Stirring to Boom Talk," *Los Angeles Times*, July 20, 1973, OC1.

84. Orange and Los Angeles counties owned slivers of land, mainly along Carbon Canyon.

85. "Chino Hills Project Under Construction," *Los Angeles Times*, October 2, 1976, H4.

86. Laband Village advertisement, *San Gabriel Valley Tribune*, June 3, 1990; "Village Oaks Offers Affordability and a Rural Lifestyle," *Los Angeles Times*, November 1, 1986, P10.

87. Laband Village advertisement, *San Gabriel Valley Tribune*, June 3, 1990.

88. City of Chino Hills, CA, "Transcript: Celebrating 25 Years of Excellence: 2016 State of the City of Chino Hills, Mayor Art Bennett," June 9, 2016.

89. "American City Tours: California, Chino Hills, Part 1"; "American City Tours: California, Chino Hills, Part 2," TBWTV, April 7, 2012, https://www.youtube.com/watch?v=ql45vUoM1Do, https://www.youtube.com/watch?v=LwJez6EgI-w&t=2s, accessed February 2, 2021.

90. Pomona was incorporated in 1888. See County of Los Angeles, CA, "Incorporated Cities: Cities within the County of Los Angeles," 2010, http://file.lacounty.gov/SDSInter/lac/1043530_09-10CitiesAlpha.pdf, accessed January 24, 2021.

91. Garcia, *A World of Its Own*.

92. Some accounts note Louis Phillips purchased the land in 1864, not in 1862. See Ann Frank, "Phillips Ranch Project Nears," *Los Angeles Times*, September 6, 1964.

93. "Historic Ranch to Be Big Community," *Los Angeles Times*, November 15, 1964, O1.

94. City of Pomona, CA. *Report on Phillips Ranch*, ca. 1978, 6.

95. "Country Atmosphere Showcase The Ranch in Carbon Canyon," *Los Angeles Times*, May 18, 1985, O52.

96. City of Pomona, CA. *Report on Phillips Ranch*, ca. 1978, 5.

97. "Country Atmosphere Showcase," O52.

98. Phillips Ranch advertising supplement, *Los Angeles Times/Los Angeles Herald Examiner/San Gabriel Valley Tribune/Santa Ana Register*, ca. 1979.

99. Display Ad 107, *Los Angeles Times*, November 18, 1979, G9.

100. Display Ad 174, *Los Angeles Times*, November 1, 1979, K4; "Phillips Ranch: A Master Planned Community of Westmor Development Co.," Westmor Development Co., ca. early 1980s.

101. "Phillips Ranch: A Master Planned Community."

102. "Historic Ranch to Be Big Community," *Los Angeles Times*, November 15, 1964, O1.

103. "Pomona Comes of Age in Deadly Way," *Los Angeles Times*, October 29, 1989, SG-J1.

104. "Country Park Villas on Phillips Ranch site," *Los Angeles Times*, December 4, 1982, M2; "Meadow Ridge in Phillips Ranch Offers Best Neighborhoods," *Los Angeles Times*, May 21, 1983, J41; "Models Near Completion at Sun Country," *Los Angeles Times*, May 19, 1984, P22; "Phillips Ranch projects have many options," *Los Angeles Times*, July 14, 1984, J1; "Phillips Ranch: Rural Setting with Something for Everyone," *Los Angeles Times*, December 22, 1979, OC-D1.

105. "Phillips Ranch: Project Has Something for Everyone," *Los Angeles Times*, September 15, 1979, OC-B44.

106. City of Pomona, *Phillips Ranch Specific Area Plan and Environmental Impact Report*, November 10 and December 6, 1976.

107. City of Pomona, *Phillips Ranch Specific Area Plan*.

108. Craig Quintana, "Phillips Ranch Has Buyers Lining Up for Homes That Aren't Built Yet," *Los Angeles Times*, March 2, 1989, 10.

109. Becky Nicolaides, *My Blue Heaven: Life and Politics in the Working-Class Suburbs of Los Angeles, 1920–1965* (Chicago: University of Chicago Press, 2002); Becky Nicolaides and Andrew Wiese (eds.), *The Suburb Reader* (New York: Routledge, 2006).

110. Scott Garner, "Neighborhood Spotlight: Hacienda Heights' Suburban Living Sprouted Where Orchards Once Grew," *Los Angeles Times*, November 30, 2018.

111. Gentleman farmers settled in Hacienda Heights circa 1927. North Whittier Heights changed its name to Hacienda Heights in 1961 after a community petition and a preliminary master plan was drafted by the Hacienda Heights Improvement Association. See Marian Bond, "Houses Stand Where Orchards Grew: Hacienda Heights," *Los Angeles Times*, October 14, 1990. Similar communities of gentleman

farmers in the San Fernando Valley were comprised of settlers from the Midwest. See Barraclough, *Making the San Fernando Valley.*

112. George Ramos, "From 'Chicano Beverly Hills' to Street Vendor," *Los Angeles Times,* February 22, 1993; Eric Brightwell, "California Fool's Gold—Exploring Hacienda Heights," *Amoeblog: Amoeba Music Blog,* June 18, 2011, https://www .amoeba.com/blog/2011/06/eric-s-blog/california-fool-s-gold-exploring-hacienda -heights-.html, accessed August 4, 2018. Also see Jerry Gonzalez, *In Search of the Mexican Beverly Hills: Latino Suburbanization in Postwar Los Angeles* (New Brunswick, NJ: Rutgers University Press, 2017).

113. Bond, "Houses Stand Where Orchards Grew."

114. "Country Atmosphere Appeals to Residents at Countrywood," *Los Angeles Times,* April 12, 1975, OC40.

115. "Country Atmosphere Appeals," OC40. For a comprehensive look on the architectural and aesthetic inspirations of Frank Lloyd Wright, see Charles Aguar and Berdeana Aguar, *Wrightscapes: Frank Lloyd Wright's Landscape Designs* (New York: McGraw-Hill, 2002); William Allin Storrer, *The Frank Lloyd Wright Companion* (Chicago: University of Chicago Press, 1994).

116. The original Community General Plan was proposed in 1974. See County of Los Angeles, Hacienda Heights Community General Plan Part 1, County of Los Angeles Department of Regional Planning, July 1978; Yu-Ju Hung, "Chinese Americans and Cityhood Movement in Hacienda Heights in 2003," *Chinese Studies* 4 (2003), 95–109.

117. Frank Greenwalt, "Plan for Heights Wins Panel OK," *San Gabriel Valley Tribune,* July 7, 1978; County of Los Angeles, Hacienda Heights Community General Plan Part 1.

118. County of Los Angeles, Hacienda Heights Community General Plan Part 1.

119. Dave Johnson and Cathy Johnson (pseudonyms), oral history interview conducted by James Zarsadiaz, Rowland Heights, CA, February 26, 2012.

120. Scott Garner, "Neighborhood Spotlight: Rowland Heights, an Eastern Suburban Getaway," *Los Angeles Times,* January 20, 2017.

CHAPTER 2. THE PEOPLE OF "COUNTRY LIVING"

1. Urban riots in Watts and East Los Angeles, racial tensions in Koreatown, and other uprisings or cultural upheavals dominated media coverage of L.A. between the 1960s and 1990s. This includes Robert Reinhold, "In the Middle of L.A.'s Gang Wars," *New York Times Magazine,* May 22, 1988, https://www.nytimes.com/1988 /05/22/magazine/in-the-middle-of-la-s-gang-wars.html, accessed July 18, 2020; Jill Walker, "Surge of Hispanic Gangs Seen in Los Angeles," *Washington Post,* May 29, 1990, https://www.washingtonpost.com/archive/politics/1990/05/29/surge -of-hispanic-gangs-seen-in-los-angeles/29f64d05-b414-45ea-8969-d0d967ca198d/, accessed July 18, 2020.

2. Patricia Bowler, oral history interview conducted by James Zarsadiaz, Diamond Bar, CA, February 28, 2012.

3. Thomas J. Sugrue, *The Origins of the Urban Crisis: Race and Inequality in Postwar Detroit* (Princeton, NJ: Princeton University Press, 1996).

4. Laura Richardson (pseudonym), oral history interview conducted by James Zarsadiaz, Hacienda Heights, CA, October 13, 2011.

5. Bill Richardson (pseudonym), oral history interview conducted by James Zarsadiaz, Hacienda Heights, CA, October 13, 2011.

6. Bill Richardson, oral history interview.

7. Janice Stewart (pseudonym), oral history interview conducted by James Zarsadiaz, Diamond Bar, CA, March 7, 2012.

8. Stewart, oral history interview.

9. Stewart, oral history interview.

10. Stewart, oral history interview.

11. Stewart, oral history interview.

12. James Gregory, "Dust Bowl Legacies: The Okie Impact on California, 1939–1989," *California History* (Fall 1989), 74–85.

13. Dave and Cathy Johnson (pseudonyms), oral history interview conducted by James Zarsadiaz, Rowland Heights, CA, February 26, 2012.

14. Johnsons, oral history interview.

15. Ted Leibman and Bruce Cain, "Mapping California Voters," *Los Angeles Times*, October 19, 1986.

16. Leibman and Cain, "Mapping California Voters,".

17. Sandra Thompson (pseudonym), oral history interview conducted by James Zarsadiaz, Walnut, CA, March 7, 2012.

18. For more information on Midwestern migration to Southern California since the late nineteenth century, see Lisa McGirr, *Suburban Warriors: The Origins of the New American Right* (Princeton, NJ: Princeton University Press, 2001); Rob King, Spencer Olin, and Mark Poster (eds.), *Postsuburban California: The Transformation of Orange County since World War II* (Berkeley: University of California Press, 1991); Paul J. P. Sandul, *California Dreaming: Boosterism, Memory, and Rural Suburbs in the Golden State* (Morgantown: West Virginia University Press, 2014); Fred W. Viehe, "Black Gold Suburbs: The Influence of the Extractive Industry on the Suburbanization of Los Angeles, 1890–1930," *Journal of Urban History* 8.1 (November 1981), 3–26.

19. Display Ad 97: "Your Best Home Value Is from a Quality Builder," *Los Angeles Times*, January 9, 1977, I3.

20. Thompson, oral history interview.

21. Thompson, oral history interview.

22. From Philadelphia to Los Angeles, residents of numerous post-WWII suburbs were diverse in terms of ethnicity, class or profession, and educational attainment. They were not, however, racially integrated or racially heterogeneous. See Herbert Gans, *The Levittowners: Ways of Life and Politics in a New Suburban Community* (New York: Columbia University Press, 1967); Becky Nicolaides, *My Blue*

Heaven: Life and Politics in the Working-Class Suburbs of Los Angeles, 1920–1965 (Chicago: University of Chicago Press, 2002); Kenneth Jackson, *Crabgrass Frontier: The Suburbanization of the United States* (New York: Oxford University Press, 1987).

23. Thompson, oral history interview.

24. Thompson, oral history interview.

25. Sharon Smith (pseudonym), oral history interview conducted by James Zarsadiaz, Diamond Bar, CA, March 15, 2012.

26. Smith, oral history interview.

27. Smith, oral history interview.

28. Smith, oral history interview.

29. Smith, oral history interview.

30. For more on "executive homes," see chapter 1. See also Becky Nicolaides and James Zarsadiaz, "Design Assimilation in Suburbia: Asian Americans, Built Landscapes, and Suburban Advantage in Los Angeles's San Gabriel Valley since 1970," *Journal of Urban History* 43.2 (March 2017), 332–371.

31. Irene Chang, "Walnut Rejects Plan for Gate at Housing Development," *Los Angeles Times*, December 17, 1989, SG1.

32. US Census Bureau, 2000 Census, https://www.census.gov/prod/cen2000/phc-1-6.pdf, accessed January 8, 2021. In 2000, in Rowland Heights, the ethnicity breakdown was as follows: 51.7 percent Asian, 27.4 percent Latino, 15.6 percent White, 3.1 percent Other, 2.3 percent Black, https://maps.latimes.com/neighborhoods/neighborhood/rowland-heights/, *Los Angeles Times*, accessed February 15, 2021. In 2000, the ethnicity breakdown was as follows: 42.5 percent Asian, 30.9 percent White, 18.6 percent Latino, 4.6 percent Black, 3.5 percent Other, https://maps.latimes.com/neighborhoods/neighborhood/diamond-bar/, *Los Angeles Times*, accessed February 15, 2021. In 2000, in Walnut, the ethnicity breakdown was as follows: 56.2 percent Asian, 19.1 percent Latino, 18.5 percent White, 3.8 percent Black, 2.4 percent Other, https://maps.latimes.com/neighborhoods/neighborhood/walnut/, *Los Angeles Times*, accessed February 15, 2021.

33. William Choctaw, oral history interview conducted by James Zarsadiaz, Covina, CA, March 14, 2012.

34. Choctaw, oral history interview.

35. Choctaw, oral history interview.

36. Choctaw, oral history interview.

37. Choctaw, oral history interview.

38. Choctaw, oral history interview.

39. Mark Arax, "San Gabriel Valley: Asian Influx Alters Life in Suburbia," *Los Angeles Times*, April 5, 1987; Irene Chang, "Modern Advice: Go East, Young Business Person," *Los Angeles Times*, October 5, 1989, 1; David Pierson, "Close to L.A. but Closer to Beijing," *Los Angeles Times*, June 19, 2008.

40. For literature on immigrants moving directly to the suburbs, see Audrey Singer, Susan W. Hardwick, and Caroline B. Brettell, *Twenty-First Century Gateways: Immigrant Incorporation in Suburban America* (Washington, DC: Brookings

Institution Press, 2008); Sam Roberts, "In Shift, 40% of Immigrants Move Directly to Suburbs," *New York Times*, October 17, 2007.

41. Frank Clifford and Anne C. Roark, "Racial Lines in County Blur but Could Return Population," *Los Angeles Times*, May 6, 1991, 1.

42. K. Connie Kang and David Pierson, "Asian Population Surges in County," *Los Angeles Times*, February 12, 2004.

43. John Horton, *The Politics of Diversity: Immigration, Resistance, and Change in Monterey Park* (Philadelphia: Temple University Press, 1995); Timothy Fong, *The First Suburban Chinatown: The Remaking of Monterey Park, California* (Philadelphia: Temple University Press, 1994); Leland Saito, *Race and Politics: Asian Americans: Latinos, and Whites in a Los Angeles Suburb* (Urbana: University of Illinois Press, 1998).

44. Display Ad 145, *Los Angeles Times*, February 5, 1983, J9.

45. "Filipino Family Has Timberline Home in Walnut, Fraternity Ties," *Los Angeles Times*, February 10, 1990, OCAA43.

46. "Filipino Family Has Timberline Home."

47. Denise Hamilton, "Chart Houses: Taking Steps to Design Homes with Harmony," *Los Angeles Times*, May 18, 1995, SG1.

48. Karen E. Klein, "Learning Art of Selling to Asian Buyers," *Los Angeles Times*, April 20, 1997.

49. "L.A.'s Newest City Grew Up in a Hurry: Diamond Bar," *Los Angeles Times*, March 18, 1990.

50. A number of scholars across disciplines like criminology, communication studies, and media studies have written about news coverage of US cities including David Kidd-Hewitt, "Crime and the Media: A Criminological Perspective," in *Criminology: A Reader*, ed. Yvonne Jewkes and Gayle Letherby (New York: Sage, 2002); Steven M. Chermak, "Body Count News: How Crime Is Presented in the News Media," *Justice Quarterly* 11.4 (December 1994), 561–582; Eli Avraham, "Cities and Their New Media Images," *Cities* 17.5 (October 2000), 363–370; Donna M. Hartman and Andrew Golub, "The Social Construction of the Crack Epidemic in the Print Media," *Journal of Psychoactive Drugs* 31.4 (October–December 1999), 423–433; Natalie Byfield, *Savage Portrayals: Race, Media and the Central Park Jogger Story* (Philadelphia: Temple University Press, 2014). Moreover, popular film genres such as Blaxploitation—which typically highlighted stereotypes of Black criminality and urban danger—reinforced negative ideas of city life.

51. Jennifer Y. Fang, "To Cultivate Our Children to Be of East and West: Contesting Ethnic Heritage Language in Suburban Chinese Schools," *Journal of American Ethnic History* 34.2 (Winter 2015), 54–82.

52. Charlotte Brooks, *Alien Neighbors, Foreign Friends: Asian Americans, Housing, and the Transformation of Urban California* (Chicago: University of Chicago Press, 2009).

53. Cindy I-Fen Cheng, "Out of Chinatown and into the Suburbs: Chinese Americans and the Politics of Cultural Citizenship in Early Cold War America," *American Quarterly* 58.4 (December 2006), 1067–1090.

54. Nancy Kwak, *A World of Homeowners: American Power and the Politics of Housing Aid* (Chicago: University of Chicago Press, 2015).

55. Kwak, 92.

56. Eric Pido, "The Performance of Property: Suburban Homeownership as a Claim to Citizenship for Filipinos in Daly City," *Journal of Asian American Studies* 15.1 (February 2012), 70.

57. Pido, 70.

58. Klein, "Learning Art of Selling to Asian Buyers."

59. Verne G. Kopytoff, "Homes Near Los Angeles Heed Asians' Preferences," *New York Times*, August 27, 1995, R7.

60. Klein, "Learning Art of Selling to Asian Buyers."

61. "Lewis Homes Offers 2 Projects in One Master-Planned Community," *Los Angeles Times*, February 11, 1989, SG12.

62. "Construction Can Suit Chinese Tradition, Lore," *San Gabriel Valley Tribune*, January 17, 1988, C8–C9.

63. Kirsten M. Lagatree, "The Power of Place: Ancient Chinese Art of *Feng Shui* Helps Believers Determine If Placement of Home Ensures Prosperity," *Los Angeles Times*, July 18, 1993, K1.

64. Denise Hamilton, "Developers Trying to Make Asian Buyers Feel at Home in Southland," *Los Angeles Times*, June 17, 1995, 1. Mark Beiswanger was the president of KB Homes' Coastal Valleys division.

65. Denise Hamilton, "Chart Houses: Taking Steps to Design Homes with Harmony," *Los Angeles Times*, May 18, 1995, SG1.

66. Hamilton, SG1.

67. David M. Kinchen, "Stock of Unsold Homes Drops Dramatically," *Los Angeles Times*, April 2, 1989, H2.

68. Hamilton, "Chart Houses," SG1.

69. Richard Winton, "Addressing Unlucky Street Numbers," *Los Angeles Times*, October 3, 1993, SGJ1.

70. Winton, SGJ1. In contrast, valley suburbs like Pomona cost $40, La Puente cost $49.80, Pasadena cost $80, and West Covina, Sierra Madre, Claremont, La Verne, and Monrovia had no fees.

71. Winton, SGJ1.

72. "American City Tours: California, Walnut, Parts 1/2" TBWTV, April 27, 2012, https://www.youtube.com/watch?v=wqrydSUfE5U, accessed February 2, 2021.

73. "American City Tours: California, Chino Hills, Part 2," TBWTV, April 7, 2012, https://www.youtube.com/watch?v=LwJez6EgI-w&t=2s, accessed February 2, 2021.

74. Joaquin Lim, oral history interview conducted via telephone by James Zarsadiaz, February 18, 2015.

75. Lim, oral history interview.

76. "American City Tours: California, Walnut."

77. John M. Findlay, *Magic Lands: Western Cityscapes and American Culture after 1940* (Berkeley: University of California Press, 1992), 57.

78. Findlay, 57.

79. Bella Cristobal, oral history interview conducted by James Zarsadiaz, Walnut, CA, March 16, 2015.

80. Cristobal, oral history interview.

81. Cristobal, oral history interview.

82. Cristobal, oral history interview.

83. Cristobal, oral history interview.

84. Ivy Kuan, oral history interview conducted by James Zarsadiaz, Walnut, CA, June 24, 2016.

85. Kuan, oral history interview.

86. Kuan, oral history interview.

87. Johnsons, oral history interview.

88. Simon Ha, oral history interview.

89. Ha, oral history interview.

90. Ha, oral history interview.

91. Ha, oral history interview. Paul S. George, "Passage to the New Eden: Tourism in Miami from Flagler through Everest G. Sewell," *The Florida Historical Quarterly* 59.4 (April 1981), 440–463. As noted by historians and cultural critics including Kevin Starr, Mike Davis, and Lawrence Culver, the so-called narrative binary of "sunshine" and "noir" has long dominated the historiography of California, particularly studies about greater Los Angeles. See Kevin Starr, *Americans and the California Dream, 1850–1915* (New York: Oxford University Press, 1973); Kevin Starr, *The Dream Endures: California Enters the 1940s* (New York: Oxford University Press, 1997); Mike Davis, *City of Quartz: Excavating the Future in Los Angeles* (New York: Verso, 1990); Lawrence B. Culver, *The Frontier of Leisure: Southern California and the Shaping of Modern California* (New York: Oxford University Press, 2010).

92. Ha, oral history interview.

93. Maggie Ha, oral history interview conducted by James Zarsadiaz, Diamond Bar, CA, August 11, 2017.

94. Mike Ward, "Development Is Year's Hottest Issue," *Los Angeles Times*, December 31, 1989, J1; Heidi Evans, "'Slow Growth' Emerges as Key Issue in Local Politics," *Los Angeles Times*, November 2, 1986; Edmund Newton, "After Years of Unchecked Growth Developers Encounter New Opposition," *Los Angeles Times*, March 19, 1987, 1; Mayerene Barker, "Cityhood, Annexation Votes Highlight County Elections," *Los Angeles Times*, November 1, 1987.

CHAPTER 3. ASIAN FAMILIES MAKING A HOME
IN THE SUBURBS

1. On literature about post-WWII suburban culture vis-à-vis religion and consumption, see Lizabeth Cohen, *A Consumers' Republic: The Politics of Mass Consumption in Postwar America* (New York: Vintage, 2003); Elaine Tyler May,

Homeward Bound: American Families in the Cold War Era (New York: Basic Books, 1988); Gretchen Buggeln, *The Suburban Church: Modernism and Community in Postwar America* (Minneapolis: University of Minnesota Press, 2015).

2. NIMBY stands for Not In My Back Yard, a term that broadly describes residents' opposition to developments in their communities that are considered threats to property values or neighborhood prestige (e.g., landfills, large-scale shopping centers, public housing, prisons). See Michael Dear, "Understanding and Overcoming the NIMBY Syndrome," *Journal of American Planning Association* 58.3 (1992), 288–300.

3. Becky Nicolaides and James Zarsadiaz, "Design Assimilation in Suburbia: Asian Americans, Built Landscapes, and Suburban Advantage in Los Angeles' San Gabriel Valley since 1970," *Journal of Urban History* 43.2 (2017), 332–371.

4. Mayerene Barker, "Buddhist Vision of Temple Complex Clashes with Real World: Some 'Just Don't Want It' Built in Hacienda Heights," *Los Angeles Times*, February 21, 1982, SG1.

5. Victor M. Valle, "Temple at 'Square One' on Its County Permit," *Los Angeles Times*, September 26, 1982, SG1.

6. Gary Libman, "A Question of Basic Rights? Zoning: Designers and Religious Leaders Are Asking If the City Council Went Too Far by Restricting the Size and Design of a Mosque in Granada Hills Neighborhood," *Los Angeles Times*, September 19, 1990, 1.

7. For information on the Hacienda Heights Improvement Association (HHIA), see Hung Yu-Ju, "Chinese Americans and Cityhood in Hacienda Heights in 2003," *Chinese Studies* 4 (2015), 97–98.

8. Barker, "Buddhist Vision," SG1; Sarah Bottorff, "Neighbors Probably Have No Choice but to Accept Temple," *The Highlander*, ca. 1983.

9. Barker, "Buddhist Vision," SG1.

10. Jon F. Thompson, "Religious Leader Appeals for Better Understanding of Buddhism, Temple," *San Gabriel Valley Tribune*, February 3, 1988, B1; Edmund Newton, "Buddhist Temple Emerges from a Suburb," *Los Angeles Times*, January 17, 1988, AOC19.

11. Mark Arax, "San Gabriel Valley: Asian Influx Alters Life in Suburbia," *Los Angeles Times*, April 5, 1987, A1.

12. Edmund Newton, "East Settling into West: Buddhists Near End of Battles over Temple," *Los Angeles Times*, January 10, 1988, B1.

13. Barker, "Buddhist Vision," SG1.

14. Tanachai Mark Padoongpatt, "'A Landmark for Sun Valley': Wat Thai of Los Angeles and Thai Suburban Culture in 1980s San Fernando Valley," *Journal of American Ethnic History* 34.2 (Winter 2015), 83–114.

15. Padoongpatt, 97.

16. Bottorff, "Neighbors Probably Have No Choice."

17. To the surprise of longtime Hacienda Heights residents, Hsi Lai received vocal support from the High Tor Homeowners Association, an exclusive tract adjacent to the proposed temple site. In a letter to L.A. County Supervisor Pete

Schabarum, the High Tor HOA said Hsi Lai "would be an asset for Hacienda Heights." See Barker, "Buddhist Vision," SG1.

18. To keep out agitators, Hsi Lai Temple groundskeepers installed a wrought iron gate. Residents claimed it hindered drivers' mobility around the neighborhood. L.A. County officials cited Hsi Lai for erecting an illegal barricade to a public access road and was forced to remove the gate.

19. Thompson, "Religious Leader Appeals," B1.

20. "Local Buddhist Priest Home Fire-Bombed," *Los Angeles Times*, July 3, 1989, 1.

21. Philip P. Pan, "Temple Finding Acceptance in Neighborhood," *Los Angeles Times*, July 29, 1993.

22. Newton, "East Settling into West," B1.

23. Pan, "Temple Finding Acceptance."

24. Pan.

25. Pan.

26. Barker, "Buddhist Vision," SG1.

27. Eduardo Bonilla-Silva, *Racism without Racists: Color-Blind Racism and the Persistence of Racial Inequality in America* (Lanham, MD: Rowman & Littlefield, 2003).

28. Irene Chang, "Temple Residents Serve as Ministers of Culture," *Los Angeles Times*, June 14, 1990, SEJ10.

29. Barker, "Buddhist Vision," SG1.

30. Newton, "East Settling into West," B1.

31. Arax, "San Gabriel Valley," A1.

32. The Philippines is a majority-Christian nation, with approximately 86 percent of Filipinos identifying as Roman Catholic. For more information, see Jack Miller, "Religion in the Philippines," Asia Society, https://asiasociety.org/education/religion-philippines, accessed January 17, 2019.

33. Randal C. Archibold, "Political Awakening: Filipino-Americans Start to Reach for Reins of Power," *Los Angeles Times*, August 20, 1993, 1.

34. Steve Hirano, "For Church Design, Future Is in Doubt," *Los Angeles Times*, May 28, 1992, 1.

35. Hirano, 1.

36. Hirano, 1.

37. Hirano, 1.

38. Hirano, 1.

39. William Choctaw, oral history interview conducted by James Zarsadiaz, Covina, CA, March 14, 2012.

40. Steve Hirano, "Fund-Raiser by City Council Candidate Draws Criticism," *Los Angeles Times*, September 24, 1992, 3; Steve Hirano, "7 Political Newcomers Seek Council Seat Elections," *Los Angeles Times*, August 13, 1992, 7.

41. Hirano, "7 Political Newcomers," 7.

42. Hirano, 7.

43. Laura Barraclough, *Making the San Fernando Valley: Rural Landscapes, Urban Development, and White Privilege* (Athens: University of Georgia Press, 2011), 236.

44. Randye Hoder, "A Passion for Asian Foods," *Los Angeles Times*, June 6, 1991, SEJ4; "Cooks' Walks: Rowland Heights, Far Eastern Frontier," *Los Angeles Times*, June 4, 1992, H1.

45. "Some in Chino Hills Nervous about Ethnic Shift Exemplified by Asian Supermarket," *Press-Enterprise*, February 7, 2007.

46. US Bureau of the Census, 1990 Census, https://www2.census.gov/library/publications/decennial/1990/cp-1/cp-1-6-1.pdf, accessed March 31, 2021; US Census Bureau, 2000 Chino Hills, CA Census, , https://data.census.gov/cedsci/all?q=2000%20Chino%20Hills,%20CA%20Census, accessed March 7, 2022.

47. A yellow button with the words "Chino Hills, Not Chino's Hills" was found in the personal collections of an anonymous Chino Hills resident. Based on this person's recollections, the button was likely made between 1992 and 1994.

48. Joaquin Lim, oral history interview conducted via telephone by James Zarsadiaz, February 18, 2015.

49. Judy Chen Haggerty, oral history interview conducted by James Zarsadiaz, Walnut, CA, June 23, 2016.

50. Haggerty, oral history interview.

51. Helen Wei (pseudonym), oral history interview conducted by James Zarsadiaz, April 6, 2012, Diamond Bar, CA.

52. Nicolaides and Zarsadiaz, "Design Assimilation in Suburbia."

53. For more on the impact of wealthy diasporic Chinese in America, see Aihwa Ong, *Flexible Citizenship: The Cultural Logics of Transnationality* (Durham, NC: Duke University Press, 1999).

54. Ong, 351.

55. Jenny Chang, oral history interview by James Zarsadiaz, April 6, 2012, Diamond Bar, CA.

56. "American City Tours: California, Rowland Heights, Part 1" TBWTV, July 23, 2012, https://www.youtube.com/watch?v=MI65DfwyXXY&t=3s, accessed February 2, 2021.

57. Sara Lin, "An Ethnic Shift Is In Store," *Los Angeles Times*, April 12, 2007.

58. A number of Asian American historians have written about white perceptions of the Chinese and Chinatown, particularly during the late nineteenth century amid strong anti-Chinese sentiments in the West and urban Northeast. See John Kuo Wei Tchen, *New York before Chinatown: Orientalism and the Shaping of American Culture, 1776–1882* (Baltimore: Johns Hopkins University Press, 2001); Mary Ting Yi Lui, *The Chinatown Trunk Mystery: Murder, Miscegenation, and Other Dangerous Encounters in Turn-of-the-Century New York City* (Princeton, NJ: Princeton University Press, 2007); Nayan Shah, *Contagious Divides: Epidemics and Race in San Francisco's Chinatown* (Berkeley: University of California Press, 2001).

59. Lin, "An Ethnic shift Is In Store."

60. Denise Hamilton, "99 and Counting: Roger Chen's Chain of Ranch Markets Is Growing by Leaps and Bounds," *Los Angeles Times*, April 27, 1997, 1.

61. Janice Stewart (pseudonym), oral history interview conducted by James Zarsadiaz, Diamond Bar, CA, March 7, 2012.

62. Lin, "An Ethnic Shift Is In Store."

63. "Some in Chino Hills Nervous."

64. Lin, "An Ethnic Shift Is In Store."

65. "Some in Chino Hills Nervous."

66. Lin, "An Ethnic Shift Is In Store." Pic 'N' Save was a discount retailer, which was bought out by Consolidated Store Corporation. Pic 'N' Save stores converted to the Big Lots brand.

67. Albert Chang, oral history interview conducted by James Zarsadiaz, Rowland Heights, CA, April 3, 2015.

68. "Some in Chino Hills Nervous."

69. "Some in Chino Hills Nervous."

70. Across California, the English Only movement picked up steam during the 1980s and remained a pivotal social issue through the 1990s. Numerous San Gabriel Valley communities (e.g., Monterey Park, Arcadia) proposed English as their city's official language. In later years, residents in other suburbs including Walnut proposed English as their city's official language or the official language of city business and/or governmental records. See John Horton, *The Politics of Diversity: Immigration, Resistance, and Change in Monterey Park* (Philadelphia: Temple University Press, 1995); Timothy Fong, *The First Suburban Chinatown: The Remaking of Monterey Park, California* (Philadelphia: Temple University Press, 1994); Daniel HoSang, *Racial Propositions: Ballot Initiatives and the Making of Postwar California* (Berkeley: University of California Press, 2010); Leland Saito, *Race and Politics: Asian Americans: Latinos, and Whites in a Los Angeles Suburb* (Urbana: University of Illinois Press, 1998); Caroline Tan, "Proposal for 'English Only' Council Meetings Leads to Civil Rights Questions," NBC News, July 14, 2012.

71. Mike Ward, "Rival to English Initiative Proposed," *Los Angeles Times*, November 10, 1985; Frank Shyong, "Monterey Park Sign Ordinance Debate Recalls '80s Ethnic Controversy," *Los Angeles Times*, August 3, 2013.

72. Rodney Tanaka, "Bilingual Store Signs a Challenge," *Whittier Daily News*, January 4, 2003; Rodney Tanaka, "Sign Regulation Urged," *San Gabriel Valley Tribune*, September 25, 2000, 1; Denise Hamilton, "A Patchwork of Ethnicity, Decade Sees Large Increase in Foreign-Born Population in Many Cities," *Los Angeles Times*, October 25, 1992, 1; Edmund Newton, "Anglo Enclave Becomes an Ethnic Patchwork," *Los Angeles Times*, March 3, 1991, 1; Sandra Thompson (pseudonym), oral history interview conducted by James Zarsadiaz, Walnut, CA, March 7, 2012; Nick Villanueva (pseudonym), oral history interview conducted by James Zarsadiaz, Riverside, CA, October 12, 2011; Trisha Bowler, oral history interview conducted by James Zarsadiaz, Diamond Bar, CA, February 28, 2012; Tom Boyd (pseudonym), oral history interview conducted by James Zarsadiaz, Rowland Heights, CA, March 6, 2012.

73. City of Walnut, CA, City of Walnut Municipal Code, 25-258: Purpose of article, accessed January 13, 2013.

74. Tanaka, "Bilingual Store Signs a Challenge," *Whittier Daily News*, January 4, 2003.

75. Thompson (pseudonym), oral history interview.

76. Linda Ruggio, "Letters to the Editor: Don't Shut English Speakers Out!," *Walnut Times Magazine*, June 15, 1994, 6.

77. Sheila Ma (pseudonym), oral history interview conducted by James Zarsadiaz, Rowland Heights, CA, October 7, 2011.

78. Ma, oral history interview.

79. Horton, *The Politics of Diversity*; Fong, *The First Suburban Chinatown*; Saito, *Race and Politics*.

80. City of Monterey Park, CA, City of Monterey Park Sample Ballot and Voter Information Pamphlet, April 8, 1986, https://www.montereypark.ca.gov /DocumentCenter/View/8187/19860408-April-8-1986-General-Municipal-Election ?bidId=, accessed February 11, 2019.

81. Asian Americans Advancing Justice, "A Community of Contrasts: Asian Americans, Native Hawaiians, and Pacific Islanders in the San Gabriel Valley," https://sgv2018.herokuapp.com/, Los Angeles: Asian Americans Advancing Justice, February 2018, accessed February 11, 2019.

82. Mark Arax, "'English-Also' Sign Sentiments Gaining Favor," *Los Angeles Times*, July 14, 1985, SG1.

83. City of Walnut, CA, Ordinance No. 437, Article XXV: Signs, Sec. 25-260, July 9, 1986; City of Diamond Bar, CA, City Council Minutes, June 16, 1998, 12; City of Diamond Bar, CA, Ordinance No. 2, November 3, 1998, February 15, 2005; City of Walnut, CA, Ordinance No. 561, Sec. 1, January 12, 1994.

84. City of Walnut, CA, Ordinance No. 561, Sec. 1, January 12, 1994.

85. Stewart, oral history interview.

86. Nicolaides and Zarsadiaz, "Design Assimilation in Suburbia," 348.

87. City of Diamond Bar, CA, Planning Commission Minutes, August 19, 1997; Becky Nicolaides and James Zarsadiaz, "Design Assimilation in Suburbia," 356.

88. Tanaka, "Bilingual Store Signs a Challenge," *Whittier Daily News*, January 4, 2003. Wen Chang was elected to the Diamond Bar city council in November 1997. Along with being Diamond Bar's first Chinese American city council member, Chang was also the city's first Chinese American mayor. See City of Diamond Bar, CA, "Council Member Wen Chang," City of Diamond Bar biography PDF, February 2008.

89. Jenny Chang, oral history interview conducted by James Zarsadiaz, Diamond Bar, CA, April 5, 2012.

90. Mark Arax, "Family Finds Affinity for American Life Series," *Los Angeles Times*, April 19, 1987, 5.

91. John Forbing, oral history interview conducted by James Zarsadiaz, Diamond Bar, CA, December 19, 2011; Stewart, oral history interview; Bill and Laura

Richardson (pseudonyms), oral history interview conducted by James Zarsadiaz, Hacienda Heights, CA, October 13, 2011; Tom Boyd (pseudonym), oral history interview conducted by James Zarsadiaz, Rowland Heights, CA, March 6, 2012.

92. City of Industry, CA, "Facts about the City," http://www.cityofindustry.org /about-industry/facts-about-the-city, accessed February 8, 2019.

93. Boyd, oral history interview.

94. Dennis Baron, "Are Laws Requiring English Signs Discriminatory?," Oxford University Press Blog, July 21, 2011, https://blog.oup.com/2011/07/english -signs/, accessed January 14, 2019; Carol Schmid, *The Politics of Language: Conflict, Identity, and Cultural Pluralism in Comparative Perspective* (New York: Oxford University Press, 2001), 62; *Asian American Business Group v. City of Pomona*, No. CV 89-0828-RMT(Sx), U.S. District Court, C.D. California, July 14, 1989, https://scholar.google.com/scholar_case?case=2705315218726752196&hl=en& as_sdt=2006, accessed January 14, 2019. Pomona's 1988 ordinance provided that "on-premises signs of commercial or manufacturing establishments which have advertising copy in foreign alphabetical characters shall devote at least one half of the sign area to advertising copy in English alphabetical letters." The following year, state courts declared Pomona's ordinance a form of national origin discrimination, claiming it violated the first and fourteenth amendments.

CHAPTER 4. ASIAN SUBURBANITES IN THE "IN-BETWEEN"

1. US Congress, "California Forty-First District," in *Official Congressional Directory, 1997–1998: 105th Congress* (Washington, DC: United States Government Printing Office), 54. Kim's district included Diamond Bar and Phillips Ranch, as well as sections of Rowland Heights and Walnut.

2. Denise Hamilton, "In from the Sidelines: Asian-American Community Begins to Flex Its Political Muscle," *Los Angeles Times*, November 8, 1992.

3. There is robust literature on education in relation to suburban history and politics. See Matthew Lassiter, *The Silent Majority: Suburban Politics in the Sunbelt South* (Princeton, NJ: Princeton University Press, 2006); Matthew Lassiter, "The Suburban Origins of 'Color-Blind' Conservatism: Middle-Class Consciousness in the Charlotte Busing Crisis," *Journal of Urban History* 30.4 (May 2004), 549–582; Kevin Kruse, *White Flight: Atlanta and the Making of Modern Conservatism* (Princeton, NJ: Princeton University Press, 2007); Ronald Formisano, *Boston against Busing: Race, Class, and Ethnicity in the 1960s and 1970s* (Chapel Hill: University of North Carolina Press, 2004).

4. Some of these advertisements include Martee Shabsin, "Martee Shabsin, Prudential California Realty Ad," *The Windmill*, April 1995, 11; "Red Carpet: Elegant Properties, Inc.," *The Windmill*, January 1993, 44; Susan Lee, "Susan Lee: Coldwell Banker," *The Windmill*, September 1998, back cover; Susan Lee, "Susan

Lee: Coldwell Banker," *The Windmill*, April 1999, back cover; Susan Lee, "Susan Lee: Prudential," *The Windmill*, October 1991, 55; Audrey Tsang, "Audrey Tsang: Re/Max," *The Windmill*, April 1999, 23. Some residents discussed the ways in which developers and realtors promoted the Walnut Valley Unified School District (WVUSD). Others discussed how WVUSD enticed them to buy within district boundaries. Sandra Thompson (pseudonym), oral history interview conducted by James Zarsadiaz, Walnut, CA, March 7, 2012; Jenny Chang, oral history interview conducted by James Zarsadiaz, Diamond Bar, CA, April 5, 2012; Chen-Li Hsia, oral history interview conducted by James Zarsadiaz, Rowland Heights, CA, April 3, 2012; Sarah Wong (pseudonym), oral history conducted by James Zarsadiaz, Walnut, CA, April 9, 2012.

5. John Horton, *The Politics of Diversity: Immigration, Resistance, and Change in Monterey Park* (Philadelphia: Temple University Press, 1995); Timothy Fong, *The First Suburban Chinatown: The Remaking of Monterey Park, California* (Philadelphia: Temple University Press, 1994); Leland Saito, *Race and Politics: Asian Americans: Latinos, and Whites in a Los Angeles Suburb* (Urbana: University of Illinois Press, 1998).

6. Willow Lung-Amam, *Trespassers? Asian Americans and the Battle for Suburbia* (Berkeley: University of California Press, 2017), 64–66.

7. Louise Moon, "Inside Asia's Pressure-Cooker Exam System: Which Region Has It the Worst?," *South China Morning Post*, June 9, 2018, https://www.scmp .com/news/china/society/article/2149978/inside-asias-pressure-cooker-exam-sytem -which-region-has-it-worst, accessed April 20, 2019.

8. Howard Blume, "Battle Lines Drawn over School Districts," *Los Angeles Times,* January 10, 1991.

9. Mark Arax, "San Gabriel Valley: Asian Influx Alters Life in Suburbia," *Los Angeles Times,* April 5, 1987, A1.

10. Numerous white oral history interviewees noted this happening to them during the 1990s to present.

11. For literature on the Asian American "model minority" myth, see Ellen Wu, *The Color of Success: Asian Americans and the Origins of the Model Minority* (Princeton, NJ: Princeton University Press, 2015); Madeline Y. Hsu, *The Good Immigrants: How the Yellow Peril Became the Model Minority* (Princeton, NJ: Princeton University Press, 2017); Robert G. Lee, *Orientals: Asian Americans in Popular Culture* (Philadelphia: Temple University Press, 1999); Gary Y. Okihiro, *Margins and Mainstreams: Asians in American History and Culture* (Seattle: University of Washington Press, 1994); Keith Osajima, "Asian Americans as the Model Minority: An Analysis of the Popular Press Image in the 1960s and 1980s," in *Reflections on Shattered Windows: Promises and Prospects for Asian American Studies*, ed. Gary Y. Okihiro, Shirley Hune, Arthur Hansen, and John Liu (Pullman: Washington State University Press, 1988); Ronald Takaki, *Strangers from a Different Shore* (Boston: Little, Brown & Company, 1989).

12. Patricia Bowler, oral history interview conducted by James Zarsadiaz, Diamond Bar, CA, February 28, 2012.

13. Willow Lung-Amam writes about similar dynamics between white and Asian students in Northern California's Silicon Valley. See Lung-Amam, *Trespassers?*

14. If Chinese parents attended PTA meetings, it was generally for Chinese PTA meetings—founded by Chinese parents—which served as a support group for immigrant parents unfamiliar with the public school system. These were also spaces for Chinese parents to learn about American-style education or childrearing as a collective. Some white parents, however, saw these groups as self-segregating from the "mainstream" PTA rather than understanding these spaces as sites helping immigrant parents understand or assimilate to the norms of American public education. See Yu-Ju Hung, "Transnational and Local-Focus Ethnic Networks: The Development of Two Types of Chinese Social Organizations in the San Gabriel Valley," *Southern California Quarterly* 98.2 (Summer 2016), 221.

15. In multiple interviews, residents spoke about this phenomenon. See Albert Chang, oral history interview conducted by James Zarsadiaz, Rowland Heights, CA, April 3, 2015; Bowler, oral history interview; Wong, oral history interview; Bert Ashley, oral history interview conducted by James Zarsadiaz, Pomona, CA, April 7, 2012; Hsia, oral history interview. For literature on "parachute children," see Min Zhou, "'Parachute Kids' in Southern California: The Educational Experience of Chinese Children in Transnational Families," *Educational Policy* 12.6 (November 1998), 682–704.

16. Hsia, oral history interview.

17. In the Creekside neighborhood, children attended Stanley G. Oswalt Elementary School (now Academy). Rowland Unified School District, Stanley G. Oswalt Academy School Accountability Report Card, http://www.rowlandschools .org/ourpages/auto/2014/1/21/52855677/2013%20SARC%20Stanley%20G_ %20Oswalt%20Academy.pdf, accessed July 12, 2018. Oswalt was built in 1983 as part of the city plan to accommodate students in Creekside's flourishing master-planned subdivisions, which comprised mostly middle- and upper-middle-class families.

18. In 1999, the California State Legislature passed the Public Schools Accountability Act, which created the state academic performance measurement known as the California Academic Performance Index (API).

19. Irene Chang, "CAP Scores, Pride Climb Together at Nogales High," *Los Angeles Times*, April 25, 1990; Denise Hamilton, "Gang Wars Bring Sorrow to School Turf," *Los Angeles Times*, October 25, 1990, SGJ1; Don Hofer, "Teacher Lauds Acts by 'Remarkable Students,'" *Los Angeles Times*, April 22, 1990; Jesse Katz, "Gangs Fail to Sideline Game 2nd Time Around," *Los Angeles Times*, September 29, 1990; Jesse Katz and Mitch Polin, "Nogales Football Set to Resume After Gang Fears Canceled Game," *Los Angeles Times*, September 28, 1990, B1; Vicki Torres, "Shooting Leads to Tighter School Security: Violence: Access to Nogales High School is restricted. Male victim, 17, is in fair condition," *Los Angeles Times*, February 18, 1993; "Rowland Heights: Teen Shot While Standing on High School Ball Field," *Los Angeles Times*, February 18, 1993; "3 Students Hurt in Pipe Bomb

Explosion at La Puente School," *Los Angeles Times,* October 31, 1995; "San Gabriel Valley: Reward Offered in Bombing at School," *Los Angeles Times*, November 7, 1995.

20. Rowland Unified School District, RUSD School Board minutes, item 432A, March 30, 1989.

21. Susan Kelley and Marsha Bracco, letter to Rowland Unified School District, June 1, 1989.

22. Kelley and Bracco.

23. Wong, oral history interview.

24. Redistricting supporters initially organized under the name of Walnut Area Residents for Change (WARF). When their efforts garnered media attention, WARF reorganized as United Neighbors Involved for Youth (UNIFY), succinctly renamed for campaigning, fundraising, and publicity purposes.

25. Nick Villanueva (pseudonym), oral history interview conducted by James Zarsadiaz, Riverside, CA, October 12, 2011.

26. Specifically, Walnut Valley Unified's student population was 46.4 percent white, 24.3 percent Asian, 18 percent Latino, 4.9 percent African American, and 6.4 percent other. Rowland Unified's student population (19,000) was 46.1 percent Latino, 24.3 percent white, 12.1 percent Asian, 9.5 percent Filipino, 7.4 percent African American, and 0.6 percent other. See Denise Hamilton, "Parents Seek School District Switch," *Los Angeles Times*, May 17, 1990, 1. In another *Los Angeles Times* article, the data changed slightly. Walnut Valley's student population was "43% Anglo, 27% Asian, 19% Latino, 6% Filipino and 5% black." Rowland's student population was "49% Latino, 20% Anglo, 14% Asian, 9% Filipino and 8% black." See Blume, "Battle Lines Drawn."

27. David Pierson, "Close to L.A. but Closer to Beijing," *Los Angeles Times,* June 19, 2008; Chang, oral history interview.

28. Blume, "Battle Lines Drawn."

29. Denise Hamilton, "Parents Seek School District Switch," *Los Angeles Times*, May 17, 1990.

30. Chang, oral history interview.

31. Blume, "Battle Lines Drawn."

32. Villanueva, oral history interview.

33. Chang, oral history interview.

34. Wong, oral history interview.

35. Hamilton, "Parents Seek School District Switch."

36. Blume, "Battle Lines Drawn."

37. Blume.

38. "Letter to the Editor," *The Highlander,* ca. May 31, 1989.

39. Blume, "Battle Lines Drawn."

40. Rowland Unified School District, RUSD School Board minutes, item 65A, September 6, 1990.

41. Sandra Thompson, oral history interview conducted by James Zarsadiaz, Walnut, CA, March 8, 2012.

42. Several community leaders and residents discussed the school boundaries issue (during the UNIFY and post-UNIFY years): Ashley, oral history interview; Villanueva, oral history interview; Wong, oral history interview.

43. Jason Porterfield, *Tattoos and Secret Societies* (New York: Rosen Publishing, 2009), 18; "Pomona Comes of Age in Deadly Way," *Los Angeles Times,* October 29, 1989, SG-J1.

44. Arthur Palmer, "Forced Busing," *Diamond Bar Windmill,* March 1979, 1.

45. "Metropolitan Plan Wins No Support in Valley Districts," *Los Angeles Times,* November 16, 1978, SG1.

46. Janice Stewart (pseudonym), oral history interview conducted by James Zarsadiaz, Diamond Bar, CA, March 7, 2012.

47. Stewart, oral history interview.

48. Shawn Dunn, oral history interview conducted by James Zarsadiaz, Walnut, CA, July 14, 2016.

49. Mechelle Taylor, "Another Ganeshan Speaks Out," *The Windmill* 9.1 (January 1983), 23.

50. Derek Engdahl, "Another Ganeshan Speaks Out," *The Windmill,* October 1982, 30.

51. Dunn, oral history interview.

52. Chang, oral history interview.

53. Lisa Sun-Hee Park, *Consuming Citizenship: Children of Asian Immigrant Entrepreneurs* (Stanford, CA: Stanford University Press, 2005).

54. Hsu, *The Good Immigrants.*

55. NIMBY is an acronym broadly describing residents' oppositions to new development, particularly those considered threats to property values or community prestige (e.g., landfills, large-scale malls, public housing, prisons). See Michael Dear, "Understanding and Overcoming the NIMBY Syndrome," *Journal of American Planning Association* 58.3 (1992), 288–300.

56. Michael A. Martinez, "Battle over MRF Escalates," *Walnut Valley Independent,* July 20, 1994, 4.

57. Elaine Chan, "Letter to the Editor: Three Cheers for the MRF Task Force," *Walnut Valley Independent,* July 20, 1994, 6.

58. Chan, 6.

59. Walnut's two "sister cities" are both in Asia: Calamba City, Philippines and Shilin, Taiwan. Diamond Bar's sole "sister city" is also in Asia: New Taipei City, Taiwan (formerly Sanxia). Sister Cities International, Sister City Membership Directory 2012, https://www.sistercities.org/sites/default/files/SCI%20MEMBER %20DIRECTORY%202012, accessed May 28, 2020; "A Visit to Diamond Bar's Long Lost Sister City," *Diamond Bar Patch,* July 15, 2011, https://patch.com/california /diamondbar-walnut/a-visit-to-diamond-bars-long-lost-sister-city, accessed May 28, 2020; Diamond Bar Sister City, Inc., Information website, August 8, 1997, http:// www.citivu.com/db/sistercity/, accessed May 28, 2020.

60. Pamela Marsh, "MRF One Year Later: The Fight Goes On," *Walnut Valley Independent,* June 15, 1995, 8.

61. Dave Reynolds, "MRF Update," *The Windmill*, August 1994, 20.

62. Material Recovery Facility (MRF) was eventually built, but not in City of Industry. MRF was built further west in the unincorporated area of Rowland Heights, where county supervisorial control—not local city council control—eased its construction.

63. Judy Chen Haggerty, oral history interview conducted by James Zarsadiaz, Walnut, CA, June 23, 2016.

64. Haggerty, oral history interview.

65. Compared to other parts of Los Angeles County, the San Gabriel Valley remained a solidly conservative-libertarian, Republican bastion through the 2000s. During the 1980s and 1990s, political strategists and commentators commented on the influence of older, white, middle-class suburban voters in the valley. However, a number of columnists, pundits, and strategists also noted the rise of nonwhite conservative activism especially among Asians and some Latinos. See Kenneth Reich, "Conservatives Fight It Out: Heavy Reagan Vote May Push Dreier Over Lloyd," *Los Angeles Times*, October 20, 1980, C1; Mike Ward, "Local Races a Lesson in Contradiction: Elections," *Los Angeles Times*, June 4, 1992, SGJ1; Bill Boyarsky, "Edging Away from Their Liberal Roots," *Los Angeles Times*, January 25, 1991, B2; Bill Boyarsky, "Conservatives Win Control of Supervisors," *Los Angeles Times*, November 5, 1980, 1; Mike Ward, "Incumbents Face Soft Opposition in Race for Congress," *Los Angeles Times*, October 23, 1986, SG1; Antonio Olivo, "Democrats Reflect a New Face of San Gabriel Valley," *Los Angeles Times*, March 4, 2000; Dennis McLellan, "Robert Gouty, 73; Political Advisor to GOP Candidates," *Los Angeles Times*, October 21, 2001; Mike Ward, "GOP Seen as Tough to Beat in New Assembly Districts," *Los Angeles Times*, August 30, 1992, SGJ1; "Mapping California Voters," *Los Angeles Times*, October 19, 1986, 28; Richard Simon, "Antonovich Faces Little Opposition: 5th District Usually Elects Conservative," *Los Angeles Times*, March 18, 1984, SG1; "Torres, Molina Woo Ballot Losers: Elections," *Los Angeles Times*, January 24, 1991, SBB1; Bill Boyarsky, "Will Sun Belt Warm Up to Buchanan Bid?," *Los Angeles Times*, March 1, 1992, B2; Steven Greenhut, "California GOP's Final Death Throes," *The American Spectator*, December 1, 2016, https://spectator.org/california-gops-final-death-throes/, accessed February 20, 2019; Joe Mozingo, "In Orange County, Land of Reinvention, Even Its Conservative Politics Is Changing," *Los Angeles Times*, November 5, 2018.

66. Asma Khalid and Michel Martin, "The Shifting Allegiances of Asian-American Voters," NPR, October 9, 2016; Aihwa Ong, *Flexible Citizenship: The Cultural Logics of Transnationality* (Durham, NC: Duke University Press, 1999), 99; S. Mitra Kalita, *Suburban Sahibs: Three Immigrant Families and Their Passage from India to America* (New Brunswick, NJ: Rutgers University Press, 2003).

67. Thomas J. Sugrue, "Crabgrass-Roots Politics: Race, Rights, and the Reaction against Liberalism in the Urban North, 1940–1964," *Journal of American History* 82.2 (September 1995), 551–578.

68. On whites' perceptions of Asian consumers and their views on unions, see Jake B. Wilson, "The Racialized Picket Line: White Workers and Racism in the

Southern California Supermarket Strike," *Critical Sociology* 34.3 (April 2008), 349–367.

69. In 2000, Asian American voters roughly split the vote between George W. Bush and Al Gore. In 2004, Asian American voters shifted their support to Democratic Party presidential candidates, which has continued since. See Khalid and Martin, "The Shifting Allegiances of Asian-American Voters"; Ong, *Flexible Citizenship*, 99; Kalita, *Suburban Sahibs*; Karthick Ramakrishnan, "How Asian Americans Became Democrats," *The American Prospect*, July 26, 2016.

70. For Asian American views regarding Proposition 187 and Proposition 209, see Daniel Martinez HoSang, *Racial Propositions: Ballot Initiatives and the Making of Postwar California* (Berkeley: University of California Press, 2010), 185, 193, 240; "Prop. 187 Approved in California," *Migration News at UC Davis*, December 1994, http://migration.ucdavis.edu/mn/more.php?id=492_0_2_0, accessed February 18, 2014. For information on Asian American voter habits, see Leon Hadar, "The GOP's Asian-American Fiasco: How Republicans Alienated a Once-Allied Bloc of Voters," *The American Conservative*, November 9, 2012, http://www.theamericanconservative.com/articles/the-gops-asian-american-fiasco/, accessed February, 18, 2014; Lexington, "Are White Americans Unusually Individualistic?," *Economist*, March 20, 2013, http://www.economist.com/blogs/lexington/2013/03/asian-american-vote, accessed February 18, 2014.

71. South El Monte Arts Posse, "¡La Lucha Continua! Gloria Arellanas and the Making of a Chicano Movement in El Monte and Beyond," Tropics of Meta, UCLA Chicano Studies Research Center, January 22, 2015, https://www.chicano.ucla.edu/files/news/TropicsofMeta_LaLuchaContinua_12215.pdf, accessed December 18, 2020; Laura Pulido, *Black, Brown, Yellow and Left: Radical Activism in Los Angeles* (Berkeley: University of California Press, 2006); Laura Pulido, Laura Barraclough, and Wendy Cheng (eds.), *A People's Guide to Los Angeles* (Berkeley: University of California Press, 2012); Louis Sahagún, "East L.A., 1968: 'Walkout!' The Day High School Students Helped Ignite the Chicano Power Movement," *Los Angeles Times,* March 1, 2018, https://www.latimes.com/nation/la-na-1968-east-la-walkouts-20180301-htmlstory.html, accessed December 18, 2020.

72. Andre Kobayashi Deckrow, "A Community Erased: Japanese Americans in El Monte and the San Gabriel Valley," KCET, September 29, 2014, https://www.kcet.org/history-society/a-community-erased-japanese-americans-in-el-monte-and-the-san-gabriel-valley, accessed February 20, 2019; Ryan Reft, "Redefining Asian America: Japanese Americans, Gardena, and the Making of a Transnational Suburb," KCET, August 22, 2014, https://www.kcet.org/history-society/redefining-asian-america-japanese-americans-gardena-and-the-making-of-a, accessed February 20, 2019.

73. California Fair Political Practices Commission, Frank Hill for Assembly, November 21, 1989, http://www.fppc.ca.gov/content/dam/fppc/documents/advice-letters/1984-1994/1989/fppc-advice/89-667.PDF, accessed June 2, 2020; "Great Divide Defines Race in 59th Assembly District," *Daily News,* February 19, 2006, https://www.dailynews.com/2006/02/19/great-divide-defines-race-in-59th-assembly

-district/, accessed June 2, 2020; John Howard, "Where Are They Now? Former State Senator Frank Hill," *Capitol Weekly,* March 9, 2006, https://capitolweekly.net /where-are-they-now-former-state-senator-frank-hill/, accessed June 2, 2020. Mountjoy later ran as the Republican nominee for US Senate against incumbent Dianne Feinstein in 2006.

74. Frank Girardot, "Local GOP Delegation to Outnumber Those of 8 States," *Diamond Bar Highlander,* July 18, 1996, 12.

75. Wilson, "The Racialized Picket Line."

76. Wilson.

77. Claire Jean Kim, "The Racial Triangulation of Asian Americans," *Politics and Society* 27.1 (March 1999), 105–138.

78. Grace Wai-Tse Siao, "Asians Join Bush In Victory," *Asian Week,* November 11, 1988, 1.

79. "Al Gore and the Temple of Cash," *New York Times,* February 22, 1998, https://www.nytimes.com/1998/02/22/opinion/al-gore-and-the-temple-of-cash .html, accessed April 5, 2019.

80. Bill Lo (pseudonym), email correspondence with James Zarsadiaz, September 15, 2002.

81. Bill Lo (pseudonym), email correspondence with James Zarsadiaz, May 26, 2002. The fundraiser's organizing team included Asian GOP activists such as Diamond Bar Mayor Wen Chang and prominent Republican booster and Walnut resident Joseph Kung.

82. Bowler, oral history interview; Stewart, oral history interview.

83. Bowler, oral history interview.

84. Lee Romney, "Chinese Americans Make Political Strides," *Los Angeles Times,* November 28, 1993.

85. Mike Ward, "Local Elections: 8 in GOP Seek Hill's Seat; 2 Vie to Oust Moorhead 52nd Assembly District," *Los Angeles Times,* May 24, 1990, 1.

86. Girardot, "Local GOP Delegation to Outnumber Those of 8 States," 12. One of Dole's other potential vice presidential running mates was sixteen-term US Congressman David Dreier, who hailed from the cowboy-themed East Valley suburb of San Dimas. A powerful Republican Party leader and longtime chair of the House Rules Committee, Dreier represented the East San Gabriel Valley from 1980 to 2013.

87. Tony Perry, "Outspent Fong Seeks Donations from Asian Americans," *Los Angeles Times,* April 15, 1998, VYA3.

88. Throughout the 1980s and 1990s, liberal and conservative politicians appealed to Asians by emphasizing the "positive" qualities of the "model minority." In a 1988 Monterey Park-based congressional district race, Democratic and Republican candidates celebrated Asians' traditionalism and "family values." Republican candidate Ralph Roy Ramierez believed the GOP was the "Great Opportunity Party" for minorities, suggesting this included Asian immigrants because of their interest in freedom, limited government, low taxes, and law and order. Ramierez ran against Democrat Lily Chen, a vocal critic of Monterey Park's English Only policies. Despite Chen's Chinese identity, Ramierez gained support from Asian Republicans

including US Senator S. I. Hayakawa, a Bay Area Japanese academic who in 1983 founded U.S. English, a political organization dedicated to making English the official language of the United States, and was known for his ardent pro-assimilationist views. See Karen Lew, "GOP San Gabriel Valley Candidate Hails Rising Asian Population," *Asian Week*, June 3, 1988, 18; James Zarsadiaz, "Elaine Chao Is Sticking by President Trump. That Shouldn't Be a Surprise," *Washington Post*, November 13, 2017; Daniel HoSang, *Racial Propositions*.

89. Claire Spiegel and K. Connie Kang, "The Fast, Rocky Rise of Jay Kim," *Los Angeles Times*, October 27, 1993.

90. Spiegel and Kang.

91. Grace Wai-Tse Siao, "Korean Council Candidate Offers Multilingual Hot Line: Jay Kim Vows to Pay for Phone Service and Translation," *Asian Week*, February 16, 1990, 13; Irene Chang, "Election '90: Diamond Bar: Anonymous Flyers Heat Up Council Race," *Los Angeles Times*, March 22, 1990; Richard Reyes Fruto, "Mr. Kim Goes to Washington," *Korea Times*, November 12, 1992, 1, 6; Mike Ward, "Diamond Bar Mayor Would Be First Korean-American Elected to Congress If He Defeats Democrat Bob Baker in November. Solidly GOP District Includes Parts of Fullerton and Yorba Linda," *Los Angeles Times*, June 21, 1992; Chris Fuchs, "There Hasn't Been a Korean American in Congress since 1999. Come November, There Could Be 4," NBC News, August 28, 2018; US Congress, "Jay C. Kim," US House of Representatives History, Art & Archives, https:// history.house.gov/People/Detail/16304, accessed May 30, 2020. Gary Miller—his former Diamond Bar city council colleague and fellow Slow Growth advocate— defeated him in the GOP primary after Kim pleaded guilty for accepting illegal campaign contributions

92. US Congress, "Jay C. Kim."

93. Prominent Asian Republican elected officials from the East San Gabriel Valley's country living communities included Tony Cartagena, Albert Chang, Ling-Ling Chang, Wen Chang, Phillip Chen, Judy Chen Haggerty, Mei Mei Ho-Hilger, Joaquin Lim, and Mary Su.

94. Denise Hamilton, "In from the Sidelines," 1.

95. Hung, "Transnational and Local-Focus Ethnic Networks," 223.

96. Hung, 223; Rowland Heights Buckboard Days, "History," https://buckboard daysparade.org/history/, accessed February 11, 2021.

97. Lydia Plunk, "Origins of the Ranch Festival," *Diamond Bar Patch*, August 10, 2011, https://patch.com/california/diamondbar-walnut/origins-of-the -ranch-festival, accessed February 11, 2021; Ashley Ludwig, "Family Fair Celebration Planned In Walnut," *Diamond Bar Patch*, https://patch.com/california/diamondbar -walnut/family-fair-celebration-planned-walnut, accessed February 11, 2021.

98. Public confidence in government fell in the 1960s and 1970s and rose again in the 1980s and early 2000s. Relatedly, Americans' personal trust in each other has also declined. However, in the late twentieth century, levels of volunteerism and civic engagement generally increased across generations, with the Silent Generation as an outlier. For extensive data, surveys, and quantitative or qualitative analysis,

see Lee Rainie, Scott Keeter, and Andrew Perrin, "Trust and Distrust in America," *Pew Research Center*, July 22, 2019, https://www.pewresearch.org/politics/2019/07/22/trust-and-distrust-in-america/, accessed May 7, 2021; Kristin A. Goss, "Volunteering and the Long Civic Generation," *Nonprofit and Voluntary Sector Quarterly* 28.4 (December 1999), 378–415; Robert D. Putnam, *Bowling Alone: The Collapse and Revival of American Community* (New York: Simon & Schuster, 2000).

99. County of Los Angeles Sheriff's Department, Office Correspondence from Eddie Leung (Deputy, Walnut/San Dimas Regional Station) to Larry L. Waldie (Captain, Walnut/San Dimas Regional Station), "Subject: Translation of News Articles from *Chinese Daily News*," August 20, 1995.

100. County of Los Angeles Sheriff's Department.

101. County of Los Angeles Sheriff's Department.

102. Teresa Watanabe, "Chinese Take to U.S. Politics," *Los Angeles Times*, April 8, 2003, VYB1.

103. Diane Brown, "Candidates vie for Walnut Council Seats," *San Gabriel Valley Tribune*, October 23, 1995.

104. Romney, "Chinese Americans Make Political Strides."

105. Bob Pacheco (R) served on the Walnut Planning Commission in the 1990s, sat on the Walnut City Council from 1996 to 1998, and then represented numerous East Valley country living suburbs in the state Assembly from 1998 to 2004. Pacheco took over Gary Miller's old Assembly seat when Miller (R) was elected to the US House of Representatives.

106. Lee Romney, "26-Acre Mall Approved Over Protest of Committee," *Los Angeles Times*, August 29, 1993; "Citizens Group Files Second Lawsuit over Proposed NFL Stadium," *Daily Breeze*, August 8, 2009, https://www.dailybreeze.com/2009/04/08/citizens-group-files-second-lawsuit-over-proposed-nfl-stadium/, accessed May 28, 2020.

107. Richard Winton, "Asian Americans Flex Growing Political Muscle," *Los Angeles Times*, September 12, 2001, VCB1.

CHAPTER 5. GROWTH AND THE IMMINENT
DEATH OF "COUNTRY LIVING"

1. Irene Chang, "Project in Walnut Hits Opposition: Homeowners Cool to Developer's Plan," *Los Angeles Times*, August 13, 1989.

2. Chang, "Project in Walnut." The site—which was eventually called the Walnut Hills project—was a heavily contested stretch of land for decades. It remained undeveloped until 2011 when the City of Walnut approved construction of Three Oaks, a tract of million-dollar Mediterranean-style villas.

3. In newspaper articles or in oral history interviews, the Slow Growth movement was also referred to as "Smart Growth" or "No Growth."

4. Mark Baldassare, *Trouble in Paradise: The Suburban Transformation in America* (New York: Columbia University Press, 1986), 18–19.

5. Al Johns, "Walnut Valley, Bypassed Many Times, at Threshold of Boom," *Los Angeles Times*, July 23, 1961, 11.

6. Mark Landsbaum, "Houses Sprout in E. Valley: Area Booms to Dismay of Some Already There," *Los Angeles Times*, November 26, 1978, SG1.

7. "Slowing of Growth in Walnut Pledge by New Councilmen," *Los Angeles Times*, April 16, 1972, SG-A1. In 1972, Walnut's newly elected city councilmembers William Cotten and Robert Lovemark—wary of development from the start—vowed to sustain Walnut's modest growth. Cotten, Lovemark, and their contemporaries established a culture of anti-development/limited development politics; this informed future land use policies well into the late 1990s.

8. Robert Fogelson, *Fragmented Metropolis: Los Angeles, 1850–1930* (Berkeley: University of California Press, 1993); Jon C. Teaford, *City and Suburb: The Political Fragmentation of Metropolitan America, 1850–1970* (Baltimore: Johns Hopkins University Press, 1979); Jon C. Teaford, *The Metropolitan Revolution: The Rise of Post-Urban America* (New York: Columbia University Press, 2006).

9. City of Walnut and the Walnut Historical Society, *Images of America: Walnut* (Charleston: Arcadia Publishing, 2012), 106.

10. City of Walnut and the Walnut Historical Society, 107.

11. Landsbaum, "Houses Sprout in E. Valley."

12. Edmund Newton, "No-Growth Rebellion Grips a Once-Quiet City," *Los Angeles Times*, June 21, 1987, SG1; John Horton, *The Politics of Diversity: Immigration, Resistance, and Change in Monterey Park* (Philadelphia: Temple University Press, 1995); Timothy Fong, *The First Suburban Chinatown: The Remaking of Monterey Park, California* (Philadelphia: Temple University Press, 1994); Leland Saito, *Race and Politics: Asian Americans: Latinos, and Whites in a Los Angeles Suburb* (Urbana: University of Illinois Press, 1998).

13. "Cityhood Proponents to Hold Country Rally," *Highlander*, September 14, 1983; "Come one! Come all! To Cityhood Rally!," *Diamond Bar Windmill*, July 1983, 7; Untitled promotional piece, *Diamond Bar Windmill*, October 1982, 37; Dal Cabell, "My View," *Diamond Bar Windmill*, July 1983, 45. The same rhetoric was used again in the 1988 and 1989 campaigns. See Dal Cabell, "Letters to the Editor: My View," *Diamond Bar Windmill*, February 1988, 34.

14. Patricia Limerick, *The Legacy of Conquest: The Unbroken Past of the American West* (New York: W.W. Norton & Company, 1987).

15. Mike Ward, "Development Is Year's Hottest Issue," Los Angeles Times, December 31, 1989, J1.

16. Daryl Kelley, "San Gabriel Valley Growth Roars On: 200,000 Residents Added Since 1980," *Los Angeles Times*, February 19, 1989, 1.

17. Richard E. Meyer and Mike Goodman, "Marauders from Inner City Prey on L.A.'s Suburbs," *Los Angeles Times*, July 12, 1981, A1; Eric Malnic, "Article on Inner-City Criminals Criticized; Times Accused of Maligning Blacks in Story on Raids in Suburbs," *Los Angeles Times*, July 20, 1981, OC-A1.

18. Richard E. Meyer and Mike Goodman, "Marauders From Inner City Prey on L.A.'s Suburbs," *Los Angeles Times*, July 12, 1981, A1.

19. "Country Living: Diamond Bar Residents Were Asked about Their Community. Has the Promise of Country Living Been Fulfilled?," *Highlander Community News*, November 2, 1983, A-26, A-37.

20. "Country Living: Diamond Bar Residents."

21. Joel Villanova, "High School Heads Horcher's MAC Goals," *Highlander*, February 4, 1987, A3.

22. Sharon Smith (pseudonym), oral history interview conducted by James Zarsadiaz, Diamond Bar, CA, March 15, 2012.

23. Anne-Marie O'Connor, "Learning to Look Past Race," *Los Angeles Times*, August 25, 1999, VCA1.

24. Chang, "Project in Walnut."

25. Lee Romney, "Recall, Slow Growth Highlight Local Races," *Los Angeles Times*, November 4, 1993, SGJ1.

26. Kelley, "San Gabriel Valley Growth Roars On," 1.

27. Steve Hirano, "Election: Long List of Candidates but Not Many Issues," *Los Angeles Times*, October 25, 1992; Deborah Sullivan, "Walnut: City Manager Retires, Prompts Uproar Over Ethnic Tensions," *Los Angeles Times*, February 23, 1995; Daniel Philip, "Letter to the Editor: Walnut: Retirement of City Manager Holmes," *Los Angeles Times*, March 23, 1995.

28. Chang, "Project in Walnut."

29. Cecilia Rasmussen, "Community Profile: Walnut," *Los Angeles Times*, November 22, 1996, 2.

30. O'Connor, "Learning to Look Past Race."

31. Nadine Brown, "Let's Set the Record Straight," *Walnut Times Magazine*, April 1995, 23; Nadine Brown, "Editorial Opinion," *Walnut Times Magazine*, July 1996, 46.

32. City of Diamond Bar and Diamond Bar Historical Society, *Images of America*; "Diamond Bar Ends Century-Old Isolation," *Southern California New Homes: Map Guide to New Housing*, April/May/June 1970, 11.

33. City of Diamond Bar and Diamond Bar Historical Society, *Images of America*, 97.

34. Ron Foerstel, "An Open Letter to Diamond Bar Residents," *Diamond Bar Windmill* 7.12 (December 1981), 4–5.

35. Foerstel.

36. Joel Villanova, "Diamond Bar Watching Nearby Development," *Diamond Bar-Phillips Ranch Highlander*, April 8, 1987.

37. Mike Lewis, oral history interview conducted by James Zarsadiaz, West Covina, CA, October 5, 2011; Edmund Newton, "Pete Schabarum: The veteran county supervisor may be the San Gabriel Valley's most powerful politician, and he's used to getting results," *Los Angeles Times*, July 19, 1987.

38. At times, however, Diamond Bar leaders permitted projects if developers offered community amenities to sweeten the deal. Amid the Emerald Pointe scandal, DBMAC approved a new 150-single-family-home tract on the condition its developer, Arciero & Sons, would widen local roads and provide an upscale senior citizen

housing option. While the county had final say, DBMAC leaders gave the green light since single-family homes were considered the "community norm." Moreover, compared to apartments, senior housing was palatable to homeowners who were suspicious of renters and transient tenants. Senior housing also allowed Diamond Bar and Los Angeles County officials to claim a percentage of low-income housing in compliance with mandatory affordable housing laws, a loophole that other country living suburbs like Walnut used to their advantage. See City of Walnut, CA, "City of Walnut, 2013–2021 Housing Element," February 2014, http://www.hcd.ca .gov/community-development/housing-element/docs/walnut_5th_adopted021114 .pdf, accessed April 1, 2019, 30.

39. One particular project, Emerald Pointe, drew widespread criticism and signaled to residents that they lacked political autonomy. It also encouraged homeowners to push for cityhood believing their unincorporated status made them extra vulnerable to growth. In 1987, Lincoln Properties Company proposed a 160-unit "condominium standard" apartment complex adjacent to The Country, an exclusive gated equestrian community. Residents objected and demanded Los Angeles County officials uphold the land's "commercial-recreational" designation per the guidelines of the Diamond Bar Community Plan. But Lincoln Properties received county approval to have the land rezoned for residential use citing its hillside location as unsuitable for retail. Homeowners disapproved of the county's green light to rezone the land. To appease critics like Ivan Nyal, Don Stokes, and Dan Buffington, Lincoln Properties insisted Emerald Pointe would not look like a typical urban apartment complex. Nevertheless, opponents did not back down. They argued Emerald Pointe did not fit the suburb's country living ambiance and attributed apartments to traffic and a lower grade of residents. The project carried on.

40. Adam Rome, *The Bulldozer in the Countryside: Suburban Sprawl and the Rise of American Environmentalism* (Cambridge: Cambridge University Press, 2001), 149–150.

41. Chang, "Project in Walnut."

42. Orlene Cook, "Letters to the Editor: Raping mountains," *San Gabriel Valley Tribune*, April 23, 1988, B5.

43. Hillary Winston, "Letters to the Editor: Rape of the Valley," *San Gabriel Valley Tribune*, April 16, 1988, B5.

44. Jo Little and Ruth Panelli, "Gender Research in Rural Geography," *Gender, Place and Culture: A Journal of Feminist Geography* 10.3 (September 2003), 281–289.

45. Henry Nash Smith, *Virgin Land: The American West as Symbol and Myth* (Cambridge, MA: Harvard University Press, 1971).

46. Rome, *The Bulldozer in the Countryside*.

47. A *Los Angeles Times* poll asked Los Angeles area residents on their thoughts of L.A.'s "quality of life." Seventy-two percent of L.A. city residents were satisfied; 68 percent of L.A. County residents were satisfied. The category of "Crime/Violence" polled the highest percentage of city residents' concerns as well as in the San Gabriel Valley. In the San Gabriel Valley, "Transportation/Streets" and "Pollution/

Environment" came in second and third, respectively. See Kevin Roderick, "The Times Poll: Most in L.A. Pleased but Fear Crime," *Los Angeles Times*, March 25, 1985, SD3.

48. Gary Lawson, "Opening of Street to Spell Gridlock in Diamond Bar," *Los Angeles Times*, August 26, 1990, 3.

49. Residents in other parts of Los Angeles County, such as those in the "rural landscapes" and "semirural suburbs" of the San Fernando Valley, politicized mainstream issues such as infrastructure, voter rights, and city council redistricting. "Rural" residents associated low-income and high-density housing and the people living in them as threats to property values and local culture. See Laura Barraclough, *Making the San Fernando Valley: Rural Landscapes, Urban Development, and White Privilege* (Athens: University of Georgia Press, 2011), 236–237.

50. Mike Ward, "Pomona Votes No on Plan to Boost Tax by Half a Cent," *Los Angeles Times*, October 5, 1989, SG1; Blair Armstrong, "County Is Getting What It's Paying for in Transportation—Very Little," *Los Angeles Times*, August 6, 1989, OC-A6.

51. This figure was approved in the *1982 Chino Hills Specific Plan*. See County of San Bernardino, CA, *1982 Chino Hills Specific Plan*.

52. Mira Loma, CA is present-day Eastvale, CA, which incorporated in 2010.

53. Jeffrey Miller, "Growth Foes in Chino Hills, Diamond Bar Forge Alliance," *Los Angeles Times*, December 18, 1988, SG1.

54. Jeffrey Miller, "Study Predicts Traffic Jam in Grand Avenue Extension," *Los Angeles Times*, January 15, 1989.

55. Miller, "Study Predicts."

56. Jeffrey Miller, "Plan to Extend Road Drives Diamond Bar into Uproar," *Los Angeles Times*, December 1, 1988, SG1.

57. Miller, "Growth Foes."

58. Jeffrey Miller, "Study Predicts." Though CCDBTC had overlapping concerns with SGAEC and CHITCHAT, CCDBTC mobilized their agenda independently of the other two organizations. CCDBTC at times sparred with SGAEC, which local activists considered a "more militant citizens group" compared to Miller's organization.

59. Miller, "Growth Foes."

60. Miller, "Growth Foes."

61. Jeffrey Miller, "Diamond Bar Ready to Settle Dispute over Traffic Impasse," *Los Angeles Times*, July 16, 1989; Irene Chang, "Diamond Bar Fence to Go, Roads to Come," *Los Angeles Times*, September 28, 1989, SG1.

62. Jeffrey Miller, "Schabarum Draws Line on Road Extension," *Los Angeles Times*, February 25, 1989.

63. Miller, "Schabarum."

64. Miller, "Schabarum"; Miller, "Diamond Bar Ready."

65. "Spotlight: L.A., San Bernardino County Officials to Open Grand Avenue, Chino Hills Parkway Sept. 1," *Los Angeles Times*, May 27, 1990.

66. Chang, "Diamond Bar Fence."

67. Miller, "Growth Foes."

68. Brian Healy, "Town and Country: New Urbanism," *CBS Sunday Morning*, May 20, 2007, https://www.youtube.com/watch?v=LRrl7LwNUtw, accessed June 1, 2018; Joel Garreau, *Edge City: Life on the New Frontier* (New York: Anchor, 1992); Rob King, Spencer Olin, and Mark Poster (eds.), *Postsuburban California: The Transformation of Orange County since World War II* (Berkeley: University of California Press, 1995).

CHAPTER 6. TO REMAIN COUNTRY, BECOME A CITY

1. Chino Hills Incorporation Committee (CHIC), "Preserving the Future of Chino Hills . . . through Incorporation," brochure, ca. 1990; Dan Garcia and Dan Shapiro, "Heed the 'Have-Nots' on the Slow-Growth Issue," *Los Angeles Times*, September 8, 1987.

2. Jon C. Teaford, "Dividing the Metropolis: The Political History of Suburban Incorporation in the United States," in *The Routledge Companion to the Suburbs*, ed. Bernadette Hanlon and Thomas J. Vicino (New York: Routledge, 2019).

3. County of Los Angeles, CA, "Incorporated Cities: Cities within the County of Los Angeles," 2010, http://file.lacounty.gov/SDSInter/lac/1043530_09 -10CitiesAlpha.pdf, accessed January 24, 2021.

4. Phyllis Cannon, "Study in the Works: D.B. Eyes Cityhood in '84," *Progress Bulletin*, ca. December 1973.

5. Transamerica Corporation purchased the land in 1956 through its acquisition arm, The Capital Company.

6. John Forbing, "President's Thoughts," *Diamond Bar Windmill*, January 1980, 6.

7. Forbing, 6.

8. "Homeowner Unit to Push Civic Affairs," *Los Angeles Times*, November 17, 1972, SG6.

9. Thomas J. Sugrue, "Race, Rights, and the Reaction against Liberalism," *Journal of American History* 82.2 (September 1995), 557.

10. Robert Putnam, *Bowling Alone: The Collapse and Revival of American Community* (New York: Simon & Shuster, 2001); Sonia A. Hirt, *Zoned in the USA: The Origins and Implications of American Land-Use Regulation* (Ithaca, NY: Cornell University Press, 2019); Barbara M. Kelly, *Expanding the American Dream: Building and Rebuilding Levittown* (Albany: State University of New York Press, 1993).

11. Setha Low, *Behind the Gates: Life, Security, and the Pursuit of Happiness in Fortress America* (New York: Routledge, 2003), 177.

12. Philip Langdon, *A Better Place to Live: Reshaping the American Suburb* (New York: Harper Perennial, 1994), 89.

13. Arthur O'Sullivan, Terri A. Sexton, and Steven M. Sheffrin, *Property Taxes and Tax Revolts: The Legacy of Proposition 13* (Cambridge: Cambridge University Press, 1995); Kevin Drum, "Happy 35th Birthday, Tax Revolt! Thanks for Destroying

California," *Mother Jones*, June 7, 2013; Clyde Haberman, "The California Ballot Measure That Inspired a Tax Revolt," *New York Times*, October 16, 2016.

14. Langdon, *A Better Place to Live*, 89.

15. Mike Ward, "Homeowners United to Counter Rise in Crime," *Los Angeles Times*, August 4, 1974, SG6.

16. In 1971, the California legislature created municipal advisory councils (MACs) for unincorporated communities in the state. MACs served as liaisons to county governments. Diamond Bar applied for MAC status through L.A. County Supervisor Pete Schabarum in June 1973. On November 2, 1976, Diamond Bar voters approved the creation of the Diamond Bar Municipal Advisory Council (DBMAC). It was the first municipal advisory council in Los Angeles County. They, along with the Diamond Bar Homeowners Association (DBHOA)—renamed the Diamond Bar Improvement Association (DBIA) in 1986—would be liaisons to the county until 1989, when Diamond Bar incorporated. After the March 1989 election for incorporation, MAC was dissolved that month. See City of Diamond Bar and Diamond Bar Historical Society, *Images of America: Diamond Bar* (Charleston: Arcadia Publishing, 2014), 107.

17. Jessica M. Kim, *Imperial Metropolis: Los Angeles, Mexico, and the Borderlands of American Empire, 1865–1941* (Chapel Hill: University of North Carolina Press, 2019).

18. Ron Foerstel, "New Year's Message: Our Past is Not Our Potential," *Diamond Bar Windmill* 7.1 (January 1981), 13.

19. Pam Kathol, "The Beginnings of Incorporation," *Diamond Bar Windmill* 7.6 (June 1981), 10.

20. "Cityhood proponents to hold country rally," *Highlander*, September 14, 1983; "Come One! Come All! to Cityhood Rally!," *Diamond Bar Windmill*, July 1983, 7; Untitled promotional piece, *Diamond Bar Windmill*, October 1982, 37; Dal Cabell, "My View," *Diamond Bar Windmill*, July 1983, 45. The same rhetoric was used again in the 1988 and 1989 campaigns. See Dal Cabell, "Letters to the Editor: My View," *Diamond Bar Windmill*, February 1988, 34.

21. "Come One! Come All!", 7; "Horcher Announces Candidacy," *Diamond Bar Windmill*, September 1983, 46; Untitled promotional piece, 37.

22. Diamond Bar Citizens for Cityhood (DBCC) was renamed from Incorporation Petition Committee (IPC).

23. Elissa Cottle, "Cityhood Is Issue in Diamond Bar," *Progress Bulletin: Pomona*, February 3, 1986, 11.

24. "Incorporation Petitions" (advertisement), *Diamond Bar Windmill* 8.7 (July 1982), 21.

25. Mark Landsbaum, "Diamond Bar Council Has Votes but No City," *Los Angeles Times*, November 10, 1983, SG1.

26. Across the East San Gabriel Valley, conservative residents made similar arguments about incorporation including in Hacienda Heights. See Yu-Ju Hung, "Chinese Americans and Cityhood Movement in Hacienda Heights in 2003," *Chinese Studies* 4 (2003), 95–109.

27. William Fulton, *The Reluctant Metropolis: The Politics of Urban Growth in Los Angeles* (Baltimore: Johns Hopkins University Press, 2001), 233. For more on Proposition 13 and its legacies, see Jack Citrin and Isaac William Martin (eds.), *After the Tax Revolt: California's Proposition 13 Turns 30* (Berkeley, CA: Institute of Governmental Studies Press, 2009); Isaac William Martin, *The Permanent Tax Revolt: How the Property Tax Transformed American Politics* (Stanford, CA: Stanford University Press, 2008); Arthur O'Sullivan, et al., *Property Taxes and Tax Revolts.*

28. Marian Bond, "Where East Meets West: Rowland Heights," *Los Angeles Times*, April 21, 1996. In 1842, John Albert Rowland acquired Rancho La Puente through a Mexican land grant. Most of that land encompasses large swaths of the East San Gabriel Valley including Rowland Heights, Hacienda Heights, Walnut, West Covina, Covina, San Dimas, Baldwin Park, and City of Industry.

29. City of Diamond Bar and Diamond Bar Historical Society, *Images of America*, 112.

30. City of Diamond Bar and Diamond Bar Historical Society, 113. In 1985, there were calls to push for cityhood again. But activists' efforts did not receive enough signatures to put it on the November 1986 ballot.

31. City of Diamond Bar and Diamond Bar Historical Society, 117.

32. The new City of Diamond Bar boundaries also included four acres between Pathfinder and Brea Canyon Cut-Off roads.

33. "This Is the Right Time for Cityhood," *Diamond Bar Windmill*, February 1989, 4. The "development of Grand Avenue into Chino Hills" refers to the extension discussed in chapter 5.

34. Joel Villanova, "High School Heads Horcher's MAC Goals," *Highlander*, February 4, 1987, A3.

35. Diana Garrett, Diamond Bar Incorporation '88 Committee mailer, March 1, 1988. Competing visions of "rurality" were also an issue in municipal politics in the San Fernando Valley. See Laura Barraclough, *Making the San Fernando Valley: Rural Landscapes, Urban Development, and White Privilege* (Athens: University of Georgia Press, 2011), 206.

36. Diana Garrett, Diamond Bar Incorporation '88 Committee mailer.

37. While the *Diamond Bar Windmill*'s content skewed in favor of cityhood, established, wide-reaching regional newspapers like the *San Gabriel Valley Tribune* and the *Progress Bulletin* were more likely to publish opposing views less represented in HOA newsletters and community periodicals. This included editorials arguing cityhood would result in higher taxes and bigger government; incorporation would urbanize Diamond Bar instead of preserve country living; and that activists used this issue for personal or political gain (i.e., exposure). See Maggi Stamm, "Who Let the Committee Define Issues?," *San Gabriel Valley Tribune*, September 5, 1987; Elissa Cottle, "Candidate Says No to Cityhood," *Progress Bulletin*, August 25, 1986, 11.

38. Elizabeth G. Honer, "Letters to the Editor: Written to the Incorporation '88 Committee," *Diamond Bar Windmill*, September 1988, 22.

39. At the conclusion of most oral history interviews I conducted with East San Gabriel Valley homeowners, I asked interviewees where their neighbors moved. More often than not, former white neighbors typically left Chino Hills, Diamond Bar, Hacienda Heights, Phillips Ranch, Rowland Heights, and Walnut for exurbs or small towns of the Inland Empire and Riverside County as well as suburbs, exurbs, resort towns, or retirement villages in Arizona, Colorado, Idaho, Oregon, Utah, and Wyoming—states with whiter or less racially diverse populations compared to urban parts of Southern California.

40. Rich Benjamin, *Searching for Whitopia: An Improbable Journey to the Heart of White America* (New York: Hachette Books, 2009).

41. Barraclough, *Making the San Fernando Valley*, 266–267.

42. "This Is the Right Time for Cityhood," 4.

43. Donna Johnson, "City May Be Moving into The Country," *San Gabriel Valley Tribune*, June 21, 1987; Lee Nelson, "Exclusive Neighborhood Adds New Wrinkle to Cityhood Controversy," *Diamond Bar-Phillips Ranch Highlander*, June 24, 1987.

44. Lee Nelson, "Red Herrings, Fish Tales Cloud Cityhood Issue," *Diamond Bar-Phillips Ranch Highlander*, September 16, 1987.

45. "Petition Drive—November 7, Blitz," Letter to Incorporation '88 Committee, October 26, 1987.

46. "Petition Drive."

47. Lee Nelson, "Drive Reaches Goal," *Highlander*, January 13, 1988.

48. Jeffrey Miller, "Protests Derail Cityhood Drive in Diamond Bar," *Los Angeles Times*, August 4, 1988.

49. Renee Wallace, "Anti-cityhood Group Forms in Diamond Bar," *Diamond Bar-Phillips Ranch Highlander*, January 18, 1989.

50. Builders' attention to community and in-home amenities have been a fundamental part of suburban development since the 1940s. For new single-family homes built in the East San Gabriel Valley during the 1970s and 1980s, amenities extended beyond new kitchen appliances or access to public parks. Consumer demands now included features like indoor balconies, open lofts or "bonus rooms" that doubled as in-home offices or entertainment spaces, or kitchens that extended into the backyard. For more literature on post-WWII suburban homes and design, see Diane Harris, *Little White Houses: How the Postwar Home Constructed Race in America* (Minneapolis: University of Minnesota Press, 2013); Dolores Hayden, *Building Suburbia: Green Fields and Urban Growth, 1820–2000* (New York: Vintage, 2003); Paul Knox, *Metroburbia, USA* (New Brunswick, NJ: Rutgers University Press, 2006); Barbara Miller Lane, *Houses for a New World: Builders and Buyers in American Suburbs, 1945–1965* (Princeton, NJ: Princeton University Press, 2015).

51. John Hull Mollenkopf, "School Is Out: The Case of New York City," in *The City, Revisited: Urban Theory from Chicago, Los Angeles, and New York*, ed. Dennis R. Judd and Dick Simpson (Minneapolis: University of Minnesota Press, 2011), 169–185; Fulton, *The Reluctant Metropolis*, 233.

52. John Forbing, oral history interview conducted by James Zarsadiaz, Diamond Bar, CA, December 19, 2011.

53. Michael Lowe, "Letter to the Editor," *Diamond Bar Windmill*, February 1989, 15–16.

54. Jayne Staley, "Letter to the Editor," *Highlander*, ca. 1989.

55. Albert Chang, oral history interview conducted by James Zarsadiaz, Rowland Heights, CA, April 3, 2015.

56. Eduardo Bonilla-Silva, Amanda Lewis, and David G. Embrick, "'I Did Not Get That Job Because of a Black Man ...': The Story Lines and Testimonies of Color-Blind Racism," *Sociological Forum* 19.4 (December 2004), 555–581; Eduardo Bonilla-Silva, *Racism without Racists: Color-Blind Racism and the Persistence of Racial Inequality in America* (Lanham, MD: Rowman & Littlefield, 2003).

57. A robust historiography of Sunbelt suburban politics focuses on the rise of post-WWII conservatism. Much of the literature examines a "white backlash" against the civil rights reforms and cultural liberalism of the 1960s. This body of literature includes Kevin Kruse, *White Flight: Atlanta and the Making of Modern Conservatism* (Princeton, NJ: Princeton University Press, 2005); Matthew Lassiter, *Silent Majority: Suburban Politics in the Sunbelt South* (Princeton, NJ: Princeton University Press, 2006); Lisa McGirr, *Suburban Warriors: The Origins of the New American Right* (Princeton, NJ: Princeton University Press, 2001).

58. Matthew Lassiter, "Suburban Strategies: The Volatile Center in Postwar American Politics," in *The Suburb Reader*, ed. Becky Nicolaides and Andy Wiese (New York: Routledge, 2006), 402.

59. Lassiter, 402.

60. David Harvey, *A Brief History of Neoliberalism* (New York: Oxford University Press, 2005); George Monboit, "Neoliberalism—the Ideology at the Root of All Our Problems," *The Guardian*, April 15, 2016; James Zarsadiaz, "Why Gentrification Is So Hard to Stop," *City Lab*, February 17, 2014.

61. Jeffrey Miller, "Pomona Mayor Hints at Annexation if Diamond Bar Fails to Incorporate," *Los Angeles Times*, September 27, 1987.

62. Miller.

63. Yu-Ju Hung, "Chinese Americans and Cityhood Movement in Hacienda Heights in 2003," *Chinese Studies* 4 (2003), 100–101. The landfill was Puente Hills Landfill.

64. Irene Chang, "Cityhood Proponents in Hacienda Heights Hope 3rd Time Is the Charm," *Los Angeles Times*, March 10, 1991; John Forbing, oral history interview conducted by James Zarsadiaz, Diamond Bar, CA, December 19, 2011.

65. Darlene Williams, "Hacienda Heights Cityhood Vote," *Los Angeles Times*, June 14, 1992.

66. David Pierson, "Cityhood Vote Divides Hacienda Heights," *Los Angeles Times*, June 1, 2003; Liyna Anwar, "Closing America's Largest Landfill, without Taking Out the Trash," NPR, February 22, 2014, https://www.npr.org/2014/02/22/280750148/closing-americas-largest-landfill-without-taking-out-the-trash, accessed May 24, 2018. The landfill closed in 2014.

67. Chang, "Cityhood Proponents in Hacienda Heights."

68. Chang.

69. Pierson, "Cityhood Vote."

70. Local Chinese activists fostered political relationships with cityhood proponents including Barbara Fish, Felicia Minardi, and Ken Manning, local leaders who enjoyed support from the wider community.

71. David Pierson, "Hacienda Heights Wonders: Now What?," *Los Angeles Times*, June 5, 2003.

72. Pierson, "Cityhood Vote."

73. Pierson; Becky Nicolaides and James Zarsadiaz, "Design Assimilation in Suburbia: Asian Americans, Built Landscapes, and Suburban Advantage in Los Angeles' San Gabriel Valley since 1970," *Journal of Urban History* 43.2 (2017), 332–371; John Horton, *The Politics of Diversity: Immigration, Resistance, and Change in Monterey Park* (Philadelphia: Temple University Press, 1995); Timothy Fong, *The First Suburban Chinatown: The Remaking of Monterey Park, California* (Philadelphia: Temple University Press, 1994); Leland Saito, *Race and Politics: Asian Americans: Latinos, and Whites in a Los Angeles Suburb* (Urbana: University of Illinois Press, 1998).

74. Hung, "Chinese Americans," 104.

75. Hung, 101–104.

76. Judy Chen Haggerty, oral history interview conducted by James Zarsadiaz, Walnut, CA, June 23, 2016.

77. Hung, "Chinese Americans," 104.

78. Tom Boyd (pseudonym), oral history interview conducted by James Zarsadiaz, Rowland Heights, CA, March 6, 2012.

79. Dave and Cathy Johnson (pseudonyms), oral history interview conducted by James Zarsadiaz, Rowland Heights, CA, February 26, 2012.

80. Albert Chang, oral history interview conducted by James Zarsadiaz, Rowland Heights, CA, April 3, 2015.

81. Catherine Ho, "Rowland Heights Tries Again for Cityhood," *Los Angeles Times*, January 8, 2009; Ching-Ching Ni, "Rowland Heights Fears Being Annexed Away," *Los Angeles Times*, October 12, 2009; Jennifer McLain, "Leftovers from City Hall: Rowland Heights and Cityhood," *San Gabriel Valley Tribune*, December 27, 2007.

82. Ni, "Rowland Heights Fears."

83. Ni.

84. "Rudeee," comments on online discussion board on "Rowland Heights' Cityhood Nears Reality," *San Gabriel Valley Tribune*, October 12, 2008.

85. "Donna," comments on online discussion board on "Rowland Heights' Cityhood Nears Reality," *San Gabriel Valley Tribune*, October 12, 2008.

86. Judy Chen Haggerty, oral history interview conducted by James Zarsadiaz, Walnut, CA, June 23, 2016.

87. Haggerty, oral history interview.

88. Haggerty, oral history interview.

89. Haggerty, oral history interview.

90. Haggerty, oral history interview.

91. Nicolaides and Zarsadiaz, "Design Assimilation in Suburbia."

92. L.A. County cities that incorporated around the time of active pro- and anti-cityhood campaigns in the East Valley: West Hollywood (1984), Santa Clarita (1987), Malibu (1991). Mayerene Barker, "Cityhood, Annexation Votes Highlight County Elections," *Los Angeles Times*, November 1, 1987; Nathan Masters, "How the Town of Sherman Became the City of West Hollywood," KCET, December 1, 2011, https://www.kcet.org/shows/lost-la/how-the-town-of-sherman-became-the -city-of-west-hollywood, accessed May 11, 2018.

93. San Gabriel Valley Economic Partnership and Cal Poly Pomona College of Business Administration, *2019 San Gabriel Valley Economic Forecast Summit*, Los Angeles County Economic Development Corporation, San Gabriel Valley Economic Partnership, April 2019, https://laedc.org/wp-content/uploads/2019/04 /2019_SGV_Econ_Summit_final_w_appendices.pdf.

EPILOGUE

1. Benjamin Schwarz and Christina Schwarz, "Going All Out for Chinese," *Atlantic*, January 1999, https://www.theatlantic.com/magazine/archive/1999/01 /going-all-out-for-chinese/305473/, accessed April 24, 2018.

2. Schwarz and Schwarz.

3. Schwarz and Schwarz.

4. Schwarz and Schwarz.

5. Schwarz and Schwarz.

6. Jennifer Medina, "New Suburban Dream Born of Asia and Southern California," *New York Times*, April 28, 2013; James Zarsadiaz, "What Really Drew Asian Immigrants to the Suburbs?," *City Lab*, October 12, 2012; Merlin Chowkwanyun and Jordan Segall, "The Rise of the Majority-Asian Suburb," *City Lab*, August 24, 2012; Asian Americans Advancing Justice, "A Community of Contrasts: Asian Americans, Native Hawaiians, and Pacific Islanders in the San Gabriel Valley," https://sgv2018.herokuapp.com/, , February 2018, accessed February 11, 2019; Christopher Yee, "More Asian-Americans live in San Gabriel Valley than in 42 states, report says," *San Gabriel Valley Tribune*, February 22, 2018.

7. Asian Americans Advancing Justice, "A Community of Contrasts"; Yee, "More Asian-Americans Live in San Gabriel Valley"; US Bureau of the Census 2000 Census, https://data.census.gov/cedsci/.

8. Medina, "New Suburban Dream"; Oliver Wang, "San Gabriel Valley Goes Viral: The Fung Bros Rep the 626," KCET, May 7, 2012, https://www.kcet.org /shows/artbound/san-gabriel-valley-goes-viral-the-fung-bros-rep-the-626, accessed January 2, 2021.

9. Randye Hoder, "A Passion for Asian Foods," *Los Angeles Times*, June 6, 1991, SEJ4; "Cooks' Walks: Rowland Heights, Far Eastern Frontier," *Los Angeles*

Times, June 4, 1992, H1; Red Ribbon, "About Us: Our Sweet Story," http://www .redribbonbakeshop.us/, accessed February 11, 2019; Farley Elliott, "Din Tai Fung's Original US Location in Arcadia to Close after 20 Years," *L.A. Eater*, June 10, 2020; *Asian Journal* staff, "Filipino Fast Food Giant Jollibee Opens North American Headquarters in West Covina," *Asian Journal*, November 23, 2019; Jim Thurman, "85c Bakery-Café Opens in Hacienda Heights," *L.A. Weekly*, August 15, 2011; Dunson Cheng, "Chinese Banks: An Economic Engine for Community Growth," in *L.A. Chinatown Souvenir Book*, (Los Angeles, ca. 1996); Kerry Hannon, "For Panda Express Owners, It's About Family," *New York Times*, March 22, 2018; Ed Leibowitz, "The Real Reason Sriracha Has to Stay in Southern California," *Los Angeles Magazine*, July 21, 2014; Foremost Foods Corporation, Information Page, http:// foremostfoods.com/pages/866365/index.htm, accessed April 12, 2019. Foremost Foods Corporation (which includes the Pamana food label) supplies Seafood City supermarkets, ChowKing restaurants, and Max's of Manila restaurants. Seafood City has locations in the United States and Canada. ChowKing operates restaurants across Asia, North America, and the Middle East including the Philippines, Indonesia, and Dubai. Max's of Manila has locations in the Philippines, United Arab Emirates, Kuwait, Canada, and Australia.

10. Massour Hayoun, "This Is America's Best Chinese Food," *Anthony Bourdain's Parts Unknown*, April 4, 2017, https://explorepartsunknown.com/koreatown -la/san-gabriel-valley-chinese-food/, accessed January 1, 2021; Asian Americans Advancing Justice, "A Community of Contrasts."

11. Kayiu Wong, "Republican Candidate John Cox courts Chinese American Business Leaders in San Gabriel Valley," *San Gabriel Valley Tribune*, July 20, 2018.

12. Redistricting occurred in 2021 following the 2020 US Census.

13. Jonathan Bastian, "OC Elects Conservative Korean Americans to US House, GOP Has Invested in Asian Candidates for Generations," KCRW, November 30, 2020; Libby Denkmann, "Four Lessons from the Southern California House Seats Republicans Reclaimed in 2020," *LAist*, December 3, 2020. Another Korean American woman from Southern California was elected to the US House of Representatives in November 2020. Michelle Park Steel, a longtime Republican politician representing central and southern Orange County, will represent California's 48th congressional district. Steel is married to Shawn Steel, a former chair of the California Republican Party, Republican National Executive Committee member, and cofounder of the recall campaign of Governor Gray Davis in 2003. Young Kim and Michelle Park Steel are the first two Korean American women from California to serve in the House.

14. For extensive data on the Asian American electorate and party support, see Karthick Ramakrishnan, Janelle Wong, Taeku Lee, and Jennifer Lee, "Asian American Voices in the 2016 Election," National Asian American Survey, http:// naasurvey.com/wp-content/uploads/2016/10/NAAS2016-Oct5-report.pdf, accessed April 18, 2021.

15. "Walnut Council, Residents Oppose Proposed NFL Stadium," *Daily Breeze*, September 25, 2008.

16. "Walnut Council, Residents."

17. Corina Knoll, "Feeling Bullied by Stadium Project," *Los Angeles Times*, October 24, 2009; David Zirin, "Football in L.A.," *Los Angeles Times*, October 29, 2009; Arash Markazi, "Holes in Industry NFL Stadium Plan," ESPN, October 11, 2011; Jason Henry, "Industry NFL Stadium Proposal Overshadowed by Inglewood, Carson," *Pasadena Star News*, February 26, 2015.

18. "Rowland Heights Housing Plan Denied," *Inland Valley Daily Tribune*, November 6, 2010.

19. Judy Chen Haggerty, oral history interview conducted by James Zarsadiaz, Walnut, CA, June 23, 2016.

20. Corina Knoll, "Zen Center Is Suing Walnut, Alleging Religious Discrimination," *Los Angeles Times*, September 25, 2011; "Construction of Controversial Rowland Heights Buddhist Temple Under Way," *Los Angeles Daily News*, February 6, 2011.

21. Shayna Rose Arnold, "Home Birth: Inside a Chino Hills 'Maternity Hotel,'" *L.A. Magazine*, December 23, 2013; Victoria Kim and Frank Shyong, "'Maternity Tourism' Raids Target California Operations Catering to Chinese," *Los Angeles Times*, March 3, 2015; Associated Press, "20 Charged with Running Chinese 'Birth Tourism' Schemes across SoCal," KTLA, January 31, 2019.

22. The World Health Organization (WHO) upgraded the status of the COVID-19 outbreak from epidemic to pandemic on March 11, 2020. See United Nations, "Five Things You Should Know Now about the COVID-19 Pandemic," March 16, 2020, https://news.un.org/en/story/2020/03/1059261, accessed May 22, 2021.

23. "American City Tours: California, Rowland Heights, Part 2" TBWTV, July 23, 2012, https://www.youtube.com/watch?v=6vfPzj554PE&t=2s, accessed February 2, 2021; Steven Blum, "The Cult of Souplantation: How a Salad Bar Became an Institution for Seniors, Immigrants, and Hipsters," *Los Angeles Magazine*, March 13, 2019; Sewell Chan, "As an L.A. Newcomer, I Adored Souplantation. I'm Grieving Its Closing," *Los Angeles Times*, May 7, 2020.

24. Elijah Chiland and *Curbed* Staff, "The Ultimate '*Back to the Future*' Filming Locations Map," *Curbed*, March 31, 2020, https://la.curbed.com/maps/back-to-the-future-filming-locations, accessed January 7, 2022.

BIBLIOGRAPHY

Aguar, Charles, and Berdeana Aguar. *Wrightscapes: Frank Lloyd Wright's Landscape Designs.* New York: McGraw-Hill, 2002.

"Al Gore and the Temple of Cash." *New York Times,* February 22, 1998.

"American City Tours: California, Chino Hills, Part 1." TBWTV, April 7, 2012. https://www.youtube.com/watch?v=ql45vUoM1Do.

"American City Tours: California, Chino Hills, Part 2." TBWTV, April 7, 2012. https://www.youtube.com/watch?v=LwJez6EgI-w&t=2s.

"American City Tours: California, Rowland Heights, Part 1." TBWTV, July 23, 2012. https://www.youtube.com/watch?v=MI65DfwyXXY&t=3s.

"American City Tours: California, Rowland Heights, Part 2." TBWTV, July 23, 2012. https://www.youtube.com/watch?v=6vfPzj554PE&t=2s.

"American City Tours: California, Walnut, Parts 1–2." TBWTV, April 27, 2012. https://www.youtube.com/watch?v=wqrydSUfE5U.

Anwar, Liyna. "Closing America's Largest Landfill, without Taking Out the Trash." NPR, February 22, 2014.

Arax, Mark. "'English-Also' Sign Sentiments Gaining Favor." *Los Angeles Times,* July 14, 1985, SG1.

———. "Family Finds Affinity for American Life Series." *Los Angeles Times,* April 19, 1987, 5.

———. "San Gabriel Valley: Asian Influx Alters Life in Suburbia." *Los Angeles Times,* April 5, 1987.

Archibold, Randal C. "Political Awakening: Filipino-Americans Start to Reach for Reins of Power." *Los Angeles Times,* August 20, 1993, 1.

Armstrong, Blair. "County Is Getting What It's Paying for in Transportation—Very Little." *Los Angeles Times,* August 6, 1989, OC-A6.

Arnold, Shayna Rose. "Home Birth: Inside a Chino Hills 'Maternity Hotel.'" *L.A. Magazine,* December 23, 2013.

Ashley, Bert. Oral history interview conducted by James Zarsadiaz, Pomona, CA, April 7, 2012.

Asian American Business Group v. City of Pomona, No. CV 89-0828-RMT(Sx), US District Court, C.D. California, July 14, 1989.

Asian Americans Advancing Justice. *A Community of Contrasts: Asian Americans, Native Hawaiians and Pacific Islanders in Los Angeles County*. Los Angeles: AAJA, 2013. https://advancingjustice-la.org/our-reports-and-research/los-angeles -county/.

———. *A Community of Contrasts: Asian Americans, Native Hawaiians, and Pacific Islanders in the San Gabriel Valley*. Los Angeles: AAJA, February 2018. https:// sgv2018.herokuapp.com/.

Asian Journal staff. "Filipino Fast Food Giant Jollibee Opens North American Head-quarters in West Covina." *Asian Journal*, November 23, 2019.

Associated Press. "20 Charged with Running Chinese 'Birth Tourism' Schemes across SoCal." KTLA, January 31, 2019.

Avraham, Eli. "Cities and Their New Media Images." *Cities* 17.5 (October 2000), 363–370.

Baldassare, Mark. *Trouble in Paradise: The Suburban Transformation in America*. New York: Columbia University Press, 1986.

Barker, Mayerene. "Buddhist Vision of Temple Complex Clashes with Real World: Some 'Just Don't Want It' Built in Hacienda Heights." *Los Angeles Times*, February 21, 1982, SG1.

———. "Cityhood, Annexation Votes Highlight County Elections." *Los Angeles Times*, November 1, 1987.

Baron, Dennis. "Are Laws Requiring English Signs Discriminatory?" Oxford University Press Blog, July 21, 2011. https://blog.oup.com/2011/07/english-signs/.

Barraclough, Laura. *Making the San Fernando Valley: Rural Landscapes, Urban Development, and White Privilege*. Athens: University of Georgia Press, 2011.

Barthes, Roland. *Mythologies*. New York: Hill and Wang, 1972.

Bastian, Jonathan. "OC Elects Conservative Korean Americans to US House, GOP Has Invested in Asian Candidates for Generations." KCRW, November 30, 2020.

Beecher, Catharine. "How to Redeem Woman's Profession from Dishonor." *Harper's New Monthly Magazine* 31 (November 1865).

Benjamin, Rich. *Searching for Whitopia: An Improbable Journey to the Heart of White America*. New York: Hachette Books, 2009.

Binford, Henry. *The First Suburbs: Residential Communities on the Boston Periphery, 1815–1860*. Chicago: University of Chicago Press, 1985.

Blum, Steven. "The Cult of Souplantation: How a Salad Bar Became an Institution for Seniors, Immigrants, and Hipsters." *Los Angeles Magazine*, March 13, 2019.

Blume, Howard. "Battle Lines Drawn over School Districts." *Los Angeles Times*, January 10, 1991.

Bond, Marian. "Houses Stand Where Orchards Grew: Hacienda Heights." *Los Angeles Times*, October 14, 1990.

———. "Where East Meets West: Rowland Heights." *Los Angeles Times*, April 21, 1996.

Bonilla-Silva, Eduardo, Amanda Lewis, and David G. Embrick. "'I Did Not Get That Job Because of a Black Man . . .': The Story Lines and Testimonies of Color-Blind Racism." *Sociological Forum* 19.4 (December 2004), 555–558.

———. *Racism without Racists: Color-Blind Racism and the Persistence of Racial Inequality in America.* Lanham, MD: Rowman & Littlefield, 2003.

Bottorff, Sarah. "Neighbors Probably Have No Choice but to Accept Temple," *The Highlander*, ca. 1983.

Bowler, Patricia. Oral history interview conducted by James Zarsadiaz, Diamond Bar, CA, February 28, 2012.

Boyarsky, Bill. "Conservatives Win Control of Supervisors." *Los Angeles Times*, November 5, 1980, 1.

———. "Edging Away from Their Liberal Roots." *Los Angeles Times*, January 25, 1991, B2.

Boyarsky, Bill, and Nancy Boyarsky. *Backroom Politics: How Your Local Politicians Work, Why Your Government Doesn't, and What You Can Do About It.* Los Angeles: J.P. Tarcher, 1974.

Boyd, Tom (pseudonym). Oral history interview conducted by James Zarsadiaz, Rowland Heights, CA, March 6, 2012.

Brightwell, Eric. "California Fool's Gold—Exploring Hacienda Heights." *Amoeblog*, June 18, 2011, https://www.amoeba.com/blog/2011/06/eric-s-blog/california -fool-s-gold-exploring-hacienda-heights-.html.

Brooks, Charlotte. *Alien Neighbors, Foreign Friends: Asian Americans, Housing, and the Transformation of Urban California.* Chicago: University of Chicago Press, 2009.

Brown, Diane. "Candidates vie for Walnut Council Seats." *San Gabriel Valley Tribune*, October 23, 1995.

Brown, Nadine. "Editorial Opinion." *Walnut Times Magazine*, July 1996, 46.

———. "Let's Set the Record Straight." *Walnut Times Magazine*, April 1995, 23.

Buggeln, Gretchen. *The Suburban Church: Modernism and Community in Postwar America.* Minneapolis: University of Minnesota Press, 2015.

"Butterfield Ranch Making Debut at Chino Hills Site: Brock Homes Now Constructing Models." *Los Angeles Times*, September 12, 1987, SG-B1.

Byfield, Natalie. *Savage Portrayals: Race, Media and the Central Park Jogger Story.* Philadelphia: Temple University Press, 2014.

Cabell, Dal. "Letters to the Editor: My View." *Diamond Bar Windmill*, February 1988, 34.

———. "My View." *Diamond Bar Windmill*, July 1983, 45.

California Fair Political Practices Commission. Frank Hill for Assembly, November 21, 1989, http://www.fppc.ca.gov/content/dam/fppc/documents/advice -letters/1984-1994/1989/fppc-advice/89-667.PDF.

Cannon, Phyllis. "Study in the Works: D.B. Eyes Cityhood in '84," *Progress Bulletin*, ca. December 1973.

Carpio, Genevieve. *Collisions at the Crossroads: How Place and Mobility Make Race.* Oakland: University of California Press, 2019.

Castillo, Greg. *Cold War on the Home Front: The Soft Power of Midcentury Design.* Minneapolis: University of Minnesota Press, 2010.

Chan, Elaine. "Letter to the Editor: Three Cheers for the MRF Task Force." *Walnut Valley Independent*, July 20, 1994, 6.

Chan, Sewell. "As an L.A. Newcomer, I Adored Souplantation. I'm Grieving Its Closing." *Los Angeles Times*, May 7, 2020.

Chang, Albert. Oral history interview conducted by James Zarsadiaz, Rowland Heights, CA, April 3, 2015.

Chang, Irene. "CAP Scores, Pride Climb Together at Nogales High." *Los Angeles Times*, April 25, 1990.

———. "Cityhood Proponents in Hacienda Heights Hope 3rd Time Is the Charm." *Los Angeles Times*, March 10, 1991.

———. "Diamond Bar Fence to Go, Roads to Come." *Los Angeles Times*, September 28, 1989, SG1.

———. "Election '90: Diamond Bar: Anonymous Flyers Heat Up Council Race." *Los Angeles Times*, March 22, 1990.

———. "L.A.'s Newest City Grew Up in a Hurry: Diamond Bar." *Los Angeles Times*, March 18, 1990.

———. "Modern Advice: Go East, Young Business Person." *Los Angeles Times*, October 5, 1989, 1.

———. "Project in Walnut Hits Opposition: Homeowners Cool to Developer's Plan." *Los Angeles Times*, August 13, 1989.

———. "Temple Residents Serve as Ministers of Culture." *Los Angeles Times*, June 14, 1990, SEJ10.

———. "Walnut Rejects Plan for Gate at Housing Development." *Los Angeles Times*, December 17, 1989, SG1.

Chase, John, Margaret Crawford, and John Kaliski (eds.). *Everyday Urbanism.* New York: The Monacelli Press, 1999.

Cheng, Cindy I-Fen. "Out of Chinatown and into the Suburbs: Chinese Americans and the Politics of Cultural Citizenship in Early Cold War America." *American Quarterly* 58.4 (December 2006), 1067–1090.

Cheng, Dunson. "Chinese Banks: An Economic Engine for Community Growth." In *L.A. Chinatown Souvenir Book.* Los Angeles, ca. 1996.

Cheng, Wendy. "A Brief History (and Geography) of the San Gabriel Valley." KCET, August 4, 2014. https://www.kcet.org/history-society/a-brief-history-and-geography-of-the-san-gabriel-valley.

———. *The Changs Next Door to the Diazes: Remapping Race in Suburban California.* Minneapolis: University of Minnesota Press, 2013.

Chermak, Steven M. "Body Count News: How Crime Is Presented in the News Media." *Justice Quarterly* 11.4 (December 1994), 561–582.

Chiland, Elijah, and *Curbed* Staff. "The Ultimate 'Back to the Future' Filming Locations Map," *Curbed*, March 31, 2020. https://la.curbed.com/maps/back-to-the-future-filming-locations.

Chino Hills Incorporation Committee (CHIC). "Preserving the Future of Chino Hills ... through Incorporation." Brochure (ca. 1990).

"Chino Hills Project Under Construction." *Los Angeles Times*, October 2, 1976, H4.

Choctaw, William. Oral history interview conducted by James Zarsadiaz, Covina, CA, March 14, 2012.

Chowkwanyun, Merlin, and Jordan Segall. "The Rise of the Majority-Asian Suburb." *City Lab*, August 24, 2012.

"Citation Opens Phase 10 at Country Hills." *Los Angeles Times*, December 15, 1985, L3.

"Citizens Group Files Second Lawsuit over Proposed NFL Stadium." *Daily Breeze*, August 8, 2009.

Citrin, Jack, and Isaac William Martin (eds.). *After the Tax Revolt: California's Proposition 13 Turns 30*. Berkeley, CA: Institute of Governmental Studies Press, 2009.

City of Chino Hills, CA. "Transcript: Celebrating 25 Years of Excellence: 2016 State of the City of Chino Hills, Mayor Art Bennett." June 9, 2016.

City of Diamond Bar, CA. City Council Minutes, June 16, 1998.

———. "Council Member Wen Chang," City of Diamond Bar biography, February 2008.

———. Ordinance No. 2, November 3, 1998, February 15, 2005.

———. Planning Commission Minutes, August, 19, 1997.

City of Diamond Bar and Diamond Bar Historical Society. *Images of America: Diamond Bar*. Charleston, SC: Arcadia Publishing, 2014.

City of Industry, CA. "Facts about the City." http://www.cityofindustry.org/about -industry/facts-about-the-city.

City of Monterey Park, CA. City of Monterey Park Sample Ballot and Voter Information Pamphlet, April 8, 1986. https://www.montereypark.ca.gov /DocumentCenter/View/8187/19860408-April-8-1986-General-Municipal -Election?bidId.

City of Pomona, CA. *Phillips Ranch Specific Area Plan and Environmental Impact Report*, November 10 and December 6, 1976.

———. *Report on Phillips Ranch* (ca. 1978).

City of Walnut, CA. Municipal Code, 25-258: Purpose of article.

———. Ordinance No. 437, Article XXV: Signs, Sec. 25-260. July 9, 1986.

———. Ordinance No. 561, Sec. 1. January 12, 1994.

———. "City of Walnut, 2013–2021 Housing Element." February 2014. http:// www.hcd.ca.gov/community-development/housing-element/docs/walnut_5th _adopted021114.pdf.

City of Walnut and the Walnut Historical Society. *Images of America: Walnut*. Charleston, SC: Arcadia Publishing, 2012.

"Cityhood Proponents to Hold Country Rally." *Highlander*, September 14, 1983.

Clabaugh, Jeff. "Loudoun 'Agri-hood,' Willowsford, among Top in the Nation." WTOP, January 12, 2018. https://wtop.com/business-finance/2018/01/loudon -agri-hood-willsford-among-top-in-the-nation/slide/1/.

Clifford, Frank, and Anne C. Roark, "Racial Lines in County Blur but Could Return Population." *Los Angeles Times*, May 6, 1991, 1.

Cohen, Lizabeth. *A Consumers' Republic: The Politics of Mass Consumption in Postwar America*. New York: Vintage, 2008.

"Come One! Come All! To Cityhood Rally!" *Diamond Bar Windmill*, July 1983, 7.

"Concept 80." Brochure. Boise Cascade Residential Community (ca. 1979).

"Construction Can Suit Chinese Tradition, Lore." *San Gabriel Valley Tribune*, January 17, 1988, C8–C9.

"Construction of Controversial Rowland Heights Buddhist Temple Under Way." *Los Angeles Daily News*, February 6, 2011.

Cook, Orlene. "Letters to the Editor: Raping Mountains." *San Gabriel Valley Tribune*, April 23, 1988, B5.

"Cooks' Walks: Rowland Heights, Far Eastern Frontier." *Los Angeles Times*, June 4, 1992, H1.

Cottle, Elissa. "Candidate Says No to Cityhood." *Progress Bulletin*, August 25, 1986, 11.

———. "Cityhood Is Issue in Diamond Bar." *Progress Bulletin: Pomona*, February 3, 1986, 11.

"Country Atmosphere Appeals to Residents at Countrywood." *Los Angeles Times*, April 12, 1975, OC40.

"Country Atmosphere Showcase: The Ranch in Carbon Canyon." *Los Angeles Times*, May 18, 1985, O52.

"The Country: Comforts of Costly Homes amid Rugged Terrain." *Los Angeles Times*, June 26, 1980, SG1.

"Country Living Comes Naturally: With a Heritage of Haciendas and Hospitality." *Highlander Community Newspaper*, July 31, 1974, 1.

"Country Living: Diamond Bar Residents Were Asked about Their Community. Has the Promise of Country Living Been Fulfilled?" *Highlander Community News*, November 2, 1983, A-26, A-37.

"Country Park Villas on Phillips Ranch site." *Los Angeles Times*, December 4, 1982, M2.

County of Los Angeles, CA. "Incorporated Cities: Cities within the County of Los Angeles," 2010, http://file.lacounty.gov/SDSInter/lac/1043530_09-10CitiesAlpha.pdf.

———. "Hacienda Heights Community General Plan Part 1." County of Los Angeles Department of Regional Planning, July 1978.

County of Los Angeles Sheriff's Department. Office Correspondence from Eddie Leung (Deputy, Walnut/San Dimas Regional Station) to Larry L. Waldie (Captain, Walnut/San Dimas Regional Station), "Subject: Translation of News Articles from *Chinese Daily News*," August 20, 1995.

County of San Bernardino, CA. *1982 Chino Hills Specific Plan*.

Cristobal, Bella. Oral history interview conducted by James Zarsadiaz, Walnut, CA, March 16, 2015.

Culver, Lawrence. *The Frontier of Leisure: Southern California and the Shaping of Modern America*. Oxford: Oxford University Press, 2010.

Davis, Mike. *City of Quartz: Excavating the Future in Los Angeles.* New York: Verso, 1990.

Dear, Michael J. *From Chicago to L.A.: Making Sense of Urban Theory.* Thousand Oaks, CA: Sage, 2002.

———. "Understanding and Overcoming the NIMBY Syndrome." *Journal of American Planning Association* 58.3 (1992), 288–300.

Deckrow, Andre Kobayashi. "A Community Erased: Japanese Americans in El Monte and the San Gabriel Valley." KCET, September 29, 2014.

Denkmann, Libby. "Four Lessons from the Southern California House Seats Republicans Reclaimed in 2020." *LAist*, December 3, 2020.

DeLyser, Dydia. *Ramona Memories: Tourism and the Shaping of Southern California.* Minneapolis: University of Minnesota Press, 2005.

"Diamond Bar." Promotional brochure. Transamerica Corporation (ca. 1970).

"Diamond Bar . . . A Unique City in the Making." Brochure (ca. 1966).

"Diamond Bar Country." Brochure. The Diamond Bar Development Corporation (ca. 1980), 15.

"Diamond Bar Country Estates." Brochure. Diamond Bar Country Estates (ca. 1970).

"Diamond Bar Ends Century-Old Isolation." *Southern California New Homes: Map Guide to New Housing,* April/May/June 1970.

"Diamond Bar Homeowners Association." Advertisement. *Diamond Bar Windmill,* ca. 1980.

Diamond Bar Sister City, Inc. Information website, August 8, 1997, http://www .citivu.com/db/sistercity/.

Display Ad 97: "Your Best Home Value Is from a Quality Builder." *Los Angeles Times,* January 9, 1977, I3.

Display Ad 107 (no title). *Los Angeles Times,* November 18, 1979, G9.

Display Ad 145 (no title). *Los Angeles Times,* February 5, 1983, J9.

Display Ad 174, "Phillips Ranch: A Master Planned Community of Westmor Development Co.," *Los Angeles Times,* November 1, 1979, K4.

Display Ad 250, "Bring the Family to Snow Creek: Discover the Lifestyle to Last a Lifetime." *Los Angeles Times,* September 22, 1985, H13.

Display Ad 273, "River Run by Shea Homes." *Los Angeles Times,* May 18, 1986, I18.

Display Ad 335, "Five Things This Expert Looks for in a New Home." *Los Angeles Times,* December 7, 1985, S13.

Display Ad 368, "Two Elegant Neighborhoods, One Exceptional Community." *Los Angeles Times,* June 27, 1987, SG-B17.

Donna. Comments on online discussion board on "Rowland Heights' Cityhood Nears Reality." *San Gabriel Valley Tribune,* October 12, 2008.

Downing, Andrew Jackson. *The Architecture of Country Houses.* New York: D. Appleton & Co., 1850.

Drum, Kevin. "Happy 35th Birthday, Tax Revolt! Thanks for Destroying California." *Mother Jones,* June 7, 2013.

Dunn, Shawn. Oral history interview conducted by James Zarsadiaz, Walnut, CA, July 14, 2016.

Elliott, Farley. "Din Tai Fung's Original US Location in Arcadia to Close after 20 Years." *L.A. Eater*, June 10, 2020.

Engdahl, Derek. "Another Ganeshan Speaks Out." *The Windmill*, October 1982, 30.

Evans, Heidi. "'Slow Growth' Emerges as Key Issue in Local Politics." *Los Angeles Times,* November 2, 1986.

Fang, Jennifer Y. "To Cultivate Our Children to Be of East and West: Contesting Ethnic Heritage Language in Suburban Chinese Schools." *Journal of American Ethnic History* 34.2 (Winter 2015), 54–82.

"Filipino Family Has Timberline Home in Walnut, Fraternity Ties." *Los Angeles Times*, February 10, 1990, OCAA43.

Findlay, John M. *Magic Lands: Western Cityscapes and American Culture After 1940.* Berkeley: University of California Press, 1992.

"First 27 Lyon Co. Timberline Homes in Walnut Sell Out in 3 Hours." *Los Angeles Times*, February 7, 1988, DOC11.

Fishman, Robert F. "American Suburbs/English Suburbs: A Transatlantic Comparison." *Journal of Urban History* 13.3 (May 1987).

———. *Bourgeois Utopias: The Rise and Fall of Suburbia.* New York: Basic, 1989.

Foerstel, Ron. "New Year's Message: Our Past Is Not Our Potential." *Diamond Bar Windmill* 7.1 (January 1981), 13.

———. "An Open Letter to Diamond Bar Residents." *Diamond Bar Windmill* 7.12 (December 1981), 4–5.

Fogelson, Robert M. *Fragmented Metropolis: Los Angeles, 1850–1930.* Berkeley: University of California Press, 1967.

Fong, Timothy. *The First Suburban Chinatown: The Remaking of Monterey Park, California.* Philadelphia: Temple University Press, 1994.

Forbing, John. Oral history interview conducted by James Zarsadiaz, Diamond Bar, CA, December 19, 2011.

———. "President's Thoughts." *Diamond Bar Windmill*, January 1980, 6.

Foremost Foods Corporation. Information Page. http://foremostfoods.com/pages /866365/index.htm.

Formisano, Ronald. *Boston against Busing: Race, Class, and Ethnicity in the 1960s and 1970s.* Chapel Hill: University of North Carolina Press, 2004.

Frank, Ann. "Phillips Ranch Project Nears." *Los Angeles Times*, September 6, 1964.

Fruto, Richard Reyes. "Mr. Kim Goes to Washington." *Korea Times*, November 12, 1992.

Fuchs, Chris. "There Hasn't Been a Korean American in Congress since 1999. Come November, There Could Be 4." NBC News, August 28, 2018.

Fulton, William. *The Reluctant Metropolis: The Politics of Urban Growth in Los Angeles.* Baltimore: Johns Hopkins University Press, 2001.

Gans, Herbert. *The Levittowners: Ways of Life and Politics in a New Suburban Community.* New York: Columbia University Press, 1967.

Garcia, Dan, and Dan Shapiro. "Heed the 'Have-Nots' on the Slow-Growth Issue." *Los Angeles Times*, September 8, 1987.

Garcia, Matt. *A World of Its Own: Race, Labor, and Citrus in the Making of Greater Los Angeles, 1900–1970.* Chapel Hill: University of North Carolina Press, 2002.

Garner, Scott. "Neighborhood Spotlight: Hacienda Heights' Suburban Living Sprouted Where Orchards Once Grew," *Los Angeles Times,* November 30, 2018.

———. "Neighborhood Spotlight: Rowland Heights, an Eastern Suburban Getaway." *Los Angeles Times,* January 20, 2017.

Garreau, Joel. *Edge City: Life on the New Frontier.* New York: Anchor, 1991.

Garrett, Diana. Diamond Bar Incorporation '88 Committee mailer. March 1, 1988.

George, Paul S. "Passage to the New Eden: Tourism in Miami from Flagler through Everest G. Sewell." *The Florida Historical Quarterly* 59.4 (April 1981), 440–463.

Girardot, Frank. "Local GOP Delegation to Outnumber Those of 8 States." *Diamond Bar Highlander,* July 18, 1996, 12.

Goss, Kristin A. "Volunteering and the Long Civic Generation." *Nonprofit and Voluntary Sector Quarterly* 28.4 (December 1999), 378–415.

Gonzalez, Jerry. *In Search of the Mexican Beverly Hills: Latino Suburbanization in Postwar Los Angeles.* New Brunswick, NJ: Rutgers University Press, 2017.

"Great Divide Defines Race in 59th Assembly District." *Daily News,* February 19, 2006. https://www.dailynews.com/2006/02/19/great-divide-defines-race-in -59th-assembly-district/.

Greenhut, Steven. "California GOP's Final Death Throes." *The American Spectator,* December 1, 2016. https://spectator.org/california-gops-final-death-throes/.

Greenwalt, Frank. "Plan for Heights Wins Panel OK." *San Gabriel Valley Tribune,* July 7, 1978.

Gregory, James N. "The Okie Impact on California, 1939–1989." *California History* (Fall 1989), 74–85.

Gregory, John. "Sleepy Chino Hills Stirring to Boom Talk." *Los Angeles Times,* July 20, 1973, OC1.

"Guide to the Country Villages of Diamond Bar." Brochure (ca. 1970).

Ha, Simon. Oral history interview conducted by James Zarsadiaz, Diamond Bar, CA, August 11, 2017.

Haberman, Clyde. "The California Ballot Measure That Inspired a Tax Revolt." *New York Times,* October 16, 2016.

Hadar, Leon. "The GOP's Asian-American Fiasco: How Republicans Alienated a Once-Allied Bloc of Voters." *American Conservative.* November 9, 2012, http:// www.theamericanconservative.com/articles/the-gops-asian-american-fiasco/.

Haggerty, Judy Chen. Oral history interview conducted by James Zarsadiaz, Walnut, CA, June 23, 2016.

Hamilton, Denise. "Chart Houses: Taking Steps to Design Homes With Harmony." *Los Angeles Times,* May 18, 1995, SG1.

———. "Developers Trying to Make Asian Buyers Feel at Home in Southland." *Los Angeles Times,* June 17, 1995, 1.

———. "Gang Wars Bring Sorrow to School Turf." *Los Angeles Times,* October 25, 1990, SGJ1.

———. "In From the Sidelines: Asian-American Community Begins to Flex Its Political Muscle." *Los Angeles Times*, November 8, 1992.

———. "99 and Counting: Roger Chen's Chain of Ranch Markets Is Growing by Leaps and Bounds." *Los Angeles Times*, April 27, 1997, 1.

———. "Parents Seek School District Switch." *Los Angeles Times*, May 17, 1990, 1.

———. "A Patchwork of Ethnicity, Decade Sees Large Increase in Foreign-Born Population in Many Cities." *Los Angeles Times*, October 25, 1992, 1.

Hannon, Kerry. "For Panda Express Owners, It's about Family." *New York Times*, March 22, 2018.

Harris, Diane. *Little White Houses: How the Postwar Home Constructed Race in America*. Minneapolis: University of Minnesota Press, 2013.

Hartman, Donna M., and Andrew Golub. "The Social Construction of the Crack Epidemic in the Print Media." *Journal of Psychoactive Drugs* 31.4 (October–December 1999), 423–433.

Harvey, David. *A Brief History of Neoliberalism*. New York: Oxford University Press, 2005.

Hayden, Dolores. *Building Suburbia: Green Fields and Urban Growth, 1820–2000*. New York: Vintage, 2003.

Hayoun, Massour. "This Is America's Best Chinese Food," *Anthony Bourdain's Parts Unknown*, April 4, 2017. https://explorepartsunknown.com/koreatown-la/san-gabriel-valley-chinese-food/.

Healy, Brian. "Town and Country: New Urbanism." *CBS Sunday Morning*, May 20, 2007. https://www.youtube.com/watch?v=LRrl7LwNUtw.

Henry, Jason. "Industry NFL Stadium Proposal Overshadowed by Inglewood, Carson." *Pasadena Star News*, February 26, 2015.

Hirano, Steve. "Election: Long List of Candidates but Not Many Issues." *Los Angeles Times*, October 25, 1992.

———. "For Church Design, Future Is in Doubt." *Los Angeles Times*, May 28, 1992, 1.

———. "Fund-Raiser by City Council Candidate Draws Criticism." *Los Angeles Times*, September 24, 1992, 3.

———. "7 Political Newcomers Seek Council Seat Elections." *Los Angeles Times*, August 13, 1992, 7.

Hirt, Sonia A. *Zoned in the USA: The Origins and Implications of American Land-Use Regulation*. Ithaca, NY: Cornell University Press, 2019.

Hise, Greg. *Magnetic Los Angeles: Planning the Twentieth-Century Metropolis*. Baltimore: Johns Hopkins University Press, 1997.

"Historic Ranch to Be Big Community." *Los Angeles Times*, November 15, 1964, O1.

Ho, Catherine. "Rowland Heights Tries Again for Cityhood." *Los Angeles Times*, January 8, 2009.

Ho, Maggie. Oral history interview conducted by James Zarsadiaz, Diamond Bar, CA, August 11, 2017.

Hoder, Randye. "A Passion for Asian Foods." *Los Angeles Times*, June 6, 1991, SEJ4.

Hofer, Don. "Teacher Lauds Acts by 'Remarkable Students.'" *Los Angeles Times*, April 22, 1990.

"Homeowner Unit to Push Civic Affairs." *Los Angeles Times*, November 17, 1972, SG6.

"Homes Located on Quarter-Acre Lots." *Los Angeles Times*, March 14, 1981, SG-A30.

Honer, Elizabeth G. "Letters to the Editor: Written to the Incorporation '88 Committee." *Diamond Bar Windmill*, September 1988, 22.

"Horcher Announces Candidacy." *Diamond Bar Windmill*, September 1983, 46.

Horton, John. *The Politics of Diversity: Immigration, Resistance, and Change in Monterey Park, California.* Philadelphia: Temple University Press, 1995.

HoSang, Daniel. *Racial Propositions: Ballot Initiatives and the Making of Postwar California.* Berkeley: University of California Press, 2010.

Howard, John. "Where Are They Now? Former State Senator Frank Hill." *Capitol Weekly*, March 9, 2006. https://capitolweekly.net/where-are-they-now-former -state-senator-frank-hill/.

Hsia, Chen-Li. Oral history interview conducted by James Zarsadiaz, Rowland Heights, CA, April 3, 2012.

Hsu, Madeline Y. *The Good Immigrants: How the Yellow Peril Became the Model Minority.* Princeton, NJ: Princeton University Press, 2017.

Hung, Yu-Ju. "Chinese Americans and Cityhood Movement in Hacienda Heights in 2003." *Chinese Studies* 4 (2003), 95–109.

———. "Transnational and Local-Focus Ethnic Networks: The Development of Two Types of Chinese Social Organizations in the San Gabriel Valley." *Southern California Quarterly* 98.2 (Summer 2016), 194–229.

"Incorporation Petitions." Advertisement. *Diamond Bar Windmill* 8.7 (July 1982), 21.

Jackson, Helen Hunt. *Ramona.* New York: Little Brown, 1884.

Jackson, Kenneth. *Crabgrass Frontier: The Suburbanization of the United States.* New York: Oxford University Press, 1985.

Johns, Al. "Walnut Valley, Bypassed Many Times, at Threshold of Boom." *Los Angeles Times*, July 23, 1961, 11.

Johnson, Cathy (pseudonym). Oral history interview conducted by James Zarsadiaz, Rowland Heights, CA, February 26, 2012.

Johnson, Dave (pseudonym). Oral history interview conducted by James Zarsadiaz, Rowland Heights, CA, February 26, 2012.

Johnson, Donna. "City May Be Moving into The Country." *San Gabriel Valley Tribune*, June 21, 1987.

Kalita, S. Mitra. *Suburban Sahibs: Three Immigrant Families and Their Passage from India to America* New Brunswick, NJ: Rutgers University Press, 2003.

Kang, K. Connie, and David Pierson, "Asian Population Surges in County." *Los Angeles Times*, February 12, 2004.

Kathol, Pam. "The Beginnings of Incorporation." *Diamond Bar Windmill* 7.6 (June 1981), 10.

Katz, Jesse. "Gangs Fail to Sideline Game 2nd Time Around." *Los Angeles Times*, September 29, 1990.

———. Oral history interview conducted by James Zarsadiaz via telephone, March 22, 2018.

Katz, Jesse, and Mitch Polin. "Nogales Football Set to Resume after Gang Fears Canceled Game." *Los Angeles Times*, September 28, 1990, B1.

Kelley, Daryl. "San Gabriel Valley Growth Roars On: 200,000 Residents Added Since 1980." *Los Angeles Times*, February 19, 1989, 1.

Kelley, Susan, and Marsha Bracco. Letter to Rowland Unified School District. June 1, 1989.

Kelly, Barbara M. *Expanding the American Dream: Building and Rebuilding Levittown*. Albany: State University of New York Press, 1993.

Khalid, Asma, and Michel Martin. "The Shifting Allegiances of Asian-American Voters." NPR, October 9, 2016.

Kidd-Hewitt, David. "Crime and the Media: A Criminological Perspective." In *Criminology: A Reader*, edited by Yvonne Jewkes and Gayle Letherby. New York: Sage, 2002.

Kim, Claire Jean. "The Racial Triangulation of Asian Americans." *Politics and Society* 27.1 (March 1999), 105–138.

Kim, Jessica M. *Imperial Metropolis: Los Angeles, Mexico, and the Borderlands of American Empire, 1865–1941*. Chapel Hill: University of North Carolina Press, 2019.

Kim, Victoria, and Frank Shyong. "'Maternity Tourism' Raids Target California Operations Catering to Chinese." *Los Angeles Times*, March 3, 2015.

Kinchen, David M. "Stock of Unsold Homes Drops Dramatically." *Los Angeles Times*, April 2, 1989, H2.

King, Rob, Spencer Olin, and Mark Poster (eds.). *Postsuburban California: The Transformation of Orange County since World War II*. Berkeley: University of California Press, 1991.

Klein, Karen E. "Learning Art of Selling to Asian Buyers." *Los Angeles Times*, April 20, 1997.

Knoll, Corina. "Feeling Bullied by Stadium Project." *Los Angeles Times*, October 24, 2009.

———. "Zen Center Is Suing Walnut, Alleging Religious Discrimination." *Los Angeles Times*, September 25, 2011.

Knox, Paul. *Metroburbia, USA*. New Brunswick, NJ: Rutgers University Press, 2006.

Kolberg, Stephanie. "Crafting the Good Life in Irvine." In *City Dreams, Country Schemes: Community and Identity in the American West*, edited by Kathleen A. Brosnan and Amy L. Scott. Reno: University of Nevada Press, 2013.

Kopytoff, Verne G. "Homes Near Los Angeles Heed Asians' Preferences." *New York Times*, August 27, 1995, R7.

Krieger, Alex. *City on a Hill: Urban Idealism in America from the Puritans to the Present*. Cambridge, MA: The Belknap Press of Harvard University Press, 2019.

Kruse, Kevin. *White Flight: Atlanta and the Making of Modern Conservatism*. Princeton, NJ: Princeton University Press, 2007.

Kuan, Ivy. Oral history interview conducted by James Zarsadiaz, Walnut, CA, June 24, 2016.

Kwak, Nancy. *A World of Homeowners: American Power and the Politics of Housing Aid*. Chicago: University of Chicago Press, 2015.

"Laband Village." Advertisement. *San Gabriel Valley Tribune*, June 3, 1990.

Lagatree, Kirsten M. "The Power of Place: Ancient Chinese Art of *Feng Shui* Helps Believers Determine If Placement of Home Ensures Prosperity." *Los Angeles Times*, July 18, 1993, K1.

Lai, Ginger. "Diamond Bar Making History..." *Highlander Community News*, November 2, 1983, 2.

———. "New Mayor Returns to City Hall Again and Again and Again." *Highlander Community News*, April 29, 1981, 1.

Landsbaum, Mark. "Diamond Bar Council Has Votes but No City." *Los Angeles Times*, November 10, 1983, SG1.

———. "Houses Sprout in E. Valley: Area Booms to Dismay of Some Already There." *Los Angeles Times*, November 26, 1978, SG1.

———. "Residents Sue Developer of 'The Country.'" *Los Angeles Times*, August 2, 1979, SG1.

Lane, Barbara Miller. *Houses for a New World: Builders and Buyers in American Suburbs, 1945–1965*. Princeton, NJ: Princeton University Press, 2015.

Langdon, Philip. *A Better Place to Live: Reshaping the American Suburb*. New York: Harper Perennial, 1994.

"Large Crowds of Homeseekers Flock to Family Tree in Walnut." *Los Angeles Times*, March 24, 1985, J18.

Lassiter, Matthew. *The Silent Majority: Suburban Politics in the Sunbelt South*. Princeton, NJ: Princeton University Press, 2006.

———. "The Suburban Origins of 'Color-Blind' Conservatism: Middle-Class Consciousness in the Charlotte Busing Crisis." *Journal of Urban History* 30.4 (May 2004), 549–582.

———. "Suburban Strategies: The Volatile Center in Postwar American Politics." In *The Suburb Reader*, edited by Becky Nicolaides and Andy Wiese. New York: Routledge, 2006.

Lawson, Gary. "Opening of Street to Spell Gridlock in Diamond Bar." *Los Angeles Times*, August 26, 1990, 3.

Lee, Robert G. *Orientals: Asian Americans in Popular Culture*. Philadelphia: Temple University Press, 1999.

Lee, Susan. "Susan Lee: Coldwell Banker." *The Windmill*, April 1999, back cover.

———. "Susan Lee: Coldwell Banker." *The Windmill*, September 1998, back cover.

———. "Susan Lee: Prudential." *The Windmill*, October 1991, 55.

Leibman, Ted, and Bruce Cain. "Mapping California Voters." *Los Angeles Times*, October 19, 1986.

Leibowitz, Ed. "The Real Reason Sriracha Has to Stay in Southern California." *Los Angeles Magazine*, July 21, 2014.

"Letter to the Editor." *The Highlander*, ca. May 31, 1989.

Lew, Karen. "GOP San Gabriel Valley Candidate Hails Rising Asian Population." *Asian Week*, June 3, 1988, 18.

"Lewis Homes Offers 2 Projects in One Master-Planned Community." *Los Angeles Times*, February 11, 1989, SG12.

Lewis, Mike. Oral history interview conducted by James Zarsadiaz, West Covina, CA, October 5, 2011.

Lexington. "Are White Americans Unusually Individualistic?" *Economist*, March 20, 2013, http://www.economist.com/blogs/lexington/2013/03/asian-american-vote.

Li, Wei. *Ethnoburb: The New Ethnic Community in Urban America*. Honolulu: University of Hawaii Press, 2008.

———. "Spatial Transformation of an Urban Ethnic Community: From Chinatown to Ethnoburb in Los Angeles." In *From Urban Enclave to Ethnic Suburb*, edited by Wei Li, 74-94. Honolulu: University of Hawaii Press, 2006.

Libman, Gary. "A Question of Basic Rights? Zoning: Designers and Religious Leaders Are Asking If the City Council Went Too Far by Restricting the Size and Design of a Mosque in Granada Hills Neighborhood," *Los Angeles Times*, September 19, 1990, 1

Lim, Joaquin. Oral history interview conducted via telephone by James Zarsadiaz, February 18, 2015.

Limerick, Patricia. *The Legacy of Conquest: The Unbroken Past of the American West*. New York: W.W. Norton & Company, 1987.

Lin, Sara. "An Ethnic Shift Is In Store." *Los Angeles Times*, April 12, 2007.

Little, Jo, and Ruth Panelli. "Gender Research in Rural Geography." *Gender, Place and Culture: A Journal of Feminist Geography* 10.3 (September 2003), 281–289.

Lo, Bill (pseudonym). Email correspondence with James Zarsadiaz, May 26, 2002.

———. Email correspondence with James Zarsadiaz, September 15, 2002.

"Local Buddhist Priest Home Fire-Bombed." *Los Angeles Times*, July 3, 1989, 1.

Los Angeles Almanac. "Historical General Population, City & County of Los Angeles, 1850 to 2010." http://www.laalmanac.com/population/po02.php.

Low, Setha. *Behind the Gates: Life, Security, and the Pursuit of Happiness in Fortress America*. New York: Routledge, 2003.

Lowe, Michael. "Letter to the Editor." *Diamond Bar Windmill*, February 1989, 15–16.

Ludwig, Ashley. "Family Fair Celebration Planned in Walnut." *Diamond Bar Patch*, October 2, 2019. https://patch.com/california/diamondbar-walnut/family-fair-celebration-planned-walnut.

Lui, Mary Ting Yi. *The Chinatown Trunk Mystery: Murder, Miscegenation, and Other Dangerous Encounters in Turn-of-the-Century New York City*. Princeton, NJ: Princeton University Press, 2007.

Lung-Amam, Willow. "That 'Monster House' Is My Home: The Social and Cultural Politics of Design Reviews and Regulations." *Journal of Urban Design* 18.2 (April 2013), 220–241.

———. *Trespassers? Asian Americans and the Battle for Suburbia*. Berkeley: University of California Press, 2017.

Ma, Sheila (pseudonym). Oral history interview conducted by James Zarsadiaz, Rowland Heights, CA, October 7, 2011.

Malnic, Eric. "Article on Inner-City Criminals Criticized; Times Accused of Maligning Blacks in Story on Raids in Suburbs." *Los Angeles Times*, July 20, 1981, OC-A1.

Maney, Gregory M., and Margaret Abraham. "Whose Backyard? Boundary Making in NIMBY Opposition to Immigrant Services." *Social Justice* 35.4 (2008–2009), 66–82.

"Mapping California Voters." *Los Angeles Times*, October 19, 1986, 28.

Markazi, Arash. "Holes in Industry NFL Stadium Plan." ESPN, October 11, 2011.

Marsh, Pamela. "MRF One Year Later: The Fight Goes On." *Walnut Valley Independent*, June 15, 1995, 8.

Martin, Isaac William. *The Permanent Tax Revolt: How the Property Tax Transformed American Politics.* Stanford, CA: Stanford University Press, 2008.

Martinez, Michael A. "Battle over MRF Escalates." *Walnut Valley Independent*, July 20, 1994, 4.

Masters, Nathan. "How the Town of Sherman Became the City of West Hollywood." KCET, December 1, 2011.

May, Elaine Tyler. *Homeward Bound: American Families in the Cold War Era.* New York: Basic Books, 1988.

McGirr, Lisa. *Suburban Warriors: The Origins of the New American Right.* Princeton, NJ: Princeton University Press, 2001.

McLain, Jennifer. "Leftovers from City Hall: Rowland Heights and Cityhood." *San Gabriel Valley Tribune*, December 27, 2007.

McLellan, Dennis. "Robert Gouty, 73; Political Advisor to GOP Candidates." *Los Angeles Times*, October 21, 2001.

"Meadow Ridge in Phillips Ranch Offers Best Neighborhoods." *Los Angeles Times*, May 21, 1983, J41.

Medina, Jennifer. "New Suburban Dream Born of Asia and Southern California." *New York Times*, April 28, 2013.

Messner, Rebecca (dir.). *Olmsted and America's Urban Parks.* Film. PBS (2011).

"Metropolitan Plan Wins No Support in Valley Districts." *Los Angeles Times*, November 16, 1978, SG1.

Meyer, Richard E., and Mike Goodman. "Marauders from Inner City Prey on L.A.'s Suburbs." *Los Angeles Times*, July 12, 1981, A1.

Miller, Jack. "Religion in the Philippines," Asia Society. https://asiasociety.org /education/religion-philippines.

Miller, Jeffrey. "Diamond Bar Ready to Settle Dispute over Traffic Impasse." *Los Angeles Times*, July 16, 1989.

———. "Growth Foes in Chino Hills, Diamond Bar Forge Alliance." *Los Angeles Times*, December 18, 1988, SG1.

———. "Little City of Walnut Breaks Out of Shell." *Los Angeles Times*, June 26, 1986, SG1.

———. "Plan to Extend Road Drives Diamond Bar into Uproar." *Los Angeles Times*, December 1, 1988, SG1.

———. "Pomona Mayor Hints at Annexation If Diamond Bar Fails to Incorporate." *Los Angeles Times*, September 27, 1987.

———. "Protests Derail Cityhood Drive in Diamond Bar." *Los Angeles Times*, August 4, 1988.

———. "Study Predicts Traffic Jam in Grand Avenue Extension." *Los Angeles Times*, January 15, 1989.

———. "Schabarum Draws Line on Road Extension." *Los Angeles Times*, February 25, 1989.

"Models Near Completion at Sun Country." *Los Angeles Times*, May 19, 1984, P22.

Mollenkopf, John Hull. "School Is Out: The Case of New York City." In *The City, Revisited: Urban Theory from Chicago, Los Angeles, and New York*, edited by Dennis R. Judd and Dick Simpson, 169–185. Minneapolis: University of Minnesota Press, 2011.

Monboit, George. "Neoliberalism—the Ideology at the Root of all Our Problems." *Guardian*, April 15, 2016.

Moon, Louise. "Inside Asia's Pressure-Cooker Exam System: Which Region Has It the Worst?" *South China Morning Post*, June 9, 2018.

Mozingo, Joe. "In Orange County, Land of Reinvention, Even Its Conservative Politics Is Changing." *Los Angeles Times*, November 5, 2018.

Nelson, Lee. "Drive Reaches Goal." *Highlander*, January 13, 1988.

———. "Exclusive Neighborhood Adds New Wrinkle to Cityhood Controversy." *Diamond Bar-Phillips Ranch Highlander*, June 24, 1987.

———. "Red Herrings, Fish Tales Cloud Cityhood Issue." *Diamond Bar-Phillips Ranch Highlander*, September 16, 1987.

Newton, Edmund. "After Years of Unchecked Growth Developers Encounter New Opposition." *Los Angeles Times*, March 19, 1987, 1.

———. "Anglo Enclave Becomes an Ethnic Patchwork." *Los Angeles Times*, March 3, 1991, 1.

———. "Buddhist Temple Emerges from a Suburb." *Los Angeles Times*, January 17, 1988, AOC19.

———. "East Settling into West: Buddhists Near End of Battles over Temple." *Los Angeles Times*, January 10, 1988, B1.

———. "No-Growth Rebellion Grips a Once-Quiet City." *Los Angeles Times*, June 21, 1987, SG1.

———. "Pete Schabarum: The Veteran County Supervisor May Be the San Gabriel Valley's Most Powerful Politician, and He's Used to Getting Results." *Los Angeles Times*, July 19, 1987.

Ni, Ching-Ching. "Rowland Heights Fears Being Annexed Away." *Los Angeles Times*, October 12, 2009.

Nicolaides. Becky. *My Blue Heaven: Life and Politics in the Working-Class Suburbs of Los Angeles, 1920–1965*. Chicago: University of Chicago Press, 2002.

Nicolaides, Becky, and Andrew Wiese (eds.). *The Suburb Reader*. New York: Routledge, 2006.

Nicolaides, Becky, and James Zarsadiaz. "Design Assimilation in Suburbia: Asian Americans, Built Landscapes, and Suburban Advantage in Los Angeles's San Gabriel Valley since 1970." *Journal of Urban History* 43.2 (March 2017), 332–371.

Ochoa, Gilda. *Becoming Neighbors in a Mexican American Community: Power, Conflict, and Solidarity*. Austin: University of Texas Press, 2004.

O'Connor, Anne-Marie. "Learning to Look Past Race." *Los Angeles Times*, August 25, 1999, VC-A1.

Okihiro, Gary Y. *Margins and Mainstreams: Asians in American History and Culture*. Seattle: University of Washington Press, 1994.

Olivo, Antonio. "Democrats Reflect a New Face of San Gabriel Valley." *Los Angeles Times*, March 4, 2000.

Ong, Aihwa. *Flexible Citizenship: The Cultural Logics of Transnationality*. Durham, NC: Duke University Press, 1999.

Osajima, Keith. "Asian Americans as the Model Minority: An Analysis of the Popular Press Image in the 1960s and 1980s." In *Reflections on Shattered Windows: Promises and Prospects for Asian American Studies*, edited by Gary Y. Okihiro, Shirley Hune, Arthur Hansen, and John Liu. Pullman: Washington State University Press, 1988.

O'Sullivan, Arthur, Terri A. Sexton, and Steven M. Sheffrin. *Property Taxes and Tax Revolts: The Legacy of Proposition 13*. Cambridge: Cambridge University Press, 1995.

"Overview of an 8,000-Acre Planned Community: Diamond Bar." Transamerica Corporation (ca. 1975).

Padoongpatt, Tanachai Mark. "'A Landmark for Sun Valley': Wat Thai of Los Angeles and Thai Suburban Culture in 1980s San Fernando Valley." *Journal of American Ethnic History* 34.2 (Winter 2015), 83–114.

"The Palm Plan at Family Tree Homes Has Two Spacious Levels." *Los Angeles Times*, September 29, 1985, I20.

Palmer, Arthur. "Forced Busing." *Diamond Bar Windmill*, March 1979, 1.

Pan, Philip P. "Temple Finding Acceptance in Neighborhood." *Los Angeles Times*, July 29, 1993.

Park, Lisa Sun-Hee. *Consuming Citizenship: Children of Asian Immigrant Entrepreneurs*. Stanford, CA: Stanford University Press, 2005.

Perry, Tony. "Outspent Fong Seeks Donations from Asian Americans." *Los Angeles Times*, April 15, 1998, VYA3.

"Petition Drive—November 7, Blitz." Letter to Incorporation '88 Committee. October 26, 1987.

Philip, Daniel. "Letter to the Editor: Walnut: Retirement of City Manager Holmes." *Los Angeles Times*, March 23, 1995.

"Phillips Ranch." Advertising supplement. *Los Angeles Times/Los Angeles Herald Examiner/San Gabriel Valley Tribune/Santa Ana Register* (ca. 1979).

"Phillips Ranch: A Master Planned Community of Westmor Development Co." Westmor Development Co. (ca. early 1980s).

"Phillips Ranch: Project Has Something for Everyone." *Los Angeles Times*, September 15, 1979, OC-B44.

"Phillips Ranch Projects Have Many Options." *Los Angeles Times*, July 14, 1984, J1.

"Phillips Ranch: Rural Setting with Something for Everyone." *Los Angeles Times*, December 22, 1979, OC-D1.

Pido, Eric. "The Performance of Property: Suburban Homeownership as a Claim to Citizenship for Filipinos in Daly City." *Journal of Asian American Studies* 15.1 (February 2012), 69–104.

Pierson, David. "Cityhood Vote Divides Hacienda Heights." *Los Angeles Times*, June 1, 2003.

———. "Close to L.A. but Closer to Beijing." *Los Angeles Times*, June 19, 2008.

———. "Hacienda Heights Wonders: Now What?" *Los Angeles Times*, June 5, 2003.

Plunk, Lydia. "'A Meadow I Used to Know Every Inch Of.'" *Diamond Bar Patch*, May 31, 2011. https://patch.com/california/diamondbar-walnut/a-meadow-i-used-to-know-every-inch-of.

———. "Origins of the Ranch Festival." *Diamond Bar Patch*, August 10, 2011. https://patch.com/california/diamondbar-walnut/origins-of-the-ranch-festival.

"Pomona Comes of Age in Deadly Way." *Los Angeles Times*, October 29, 1989, SG-J1.

Porterfield, Jason. *Tattoos and Secret Societies*. New York: Rosen Publishing, 2009.

"Presenting Diamond Bar: A Planned City." Quinton Engineers, Ltd. (ca. early 1960s).

"Prop. 187 Approved in California." *Migration News at UC Davis*, December 1994. http://migration.ucdavis.edu/mn/more.php?id=492_0_2_0.

Pulido, Laura. *Black, Brown, Yellow and Left: Radical Activism in Los Angeles*. Berkeley: University of California Press, 2006.

Pulido, Laura, Laura Barraclough, and Wendy Cheng (eds.). *A People's Guide to Los Angeles*. Berkeley: University of California Press, 2012.

Putnam, Robert D. *Bowling Alone: The Collapse and Revival of American Community*. New York: Simon & Schuster, 2000.

"Quiet, Small-Town Ambiance Found at Snow Creek." *Los Angeles Times*, December 6, 1987, OC-E9.

Quintana, Craig. "Phillips Ranch Has Buyers Lining Up for Homes That Aren't Built Yet." *Los Angeles Times*, March 2, 1989.

Rainie, Lee, Scott Keeter, and Andrew Perrin. "Trust and Distrust in America." Pew Research Center, July 22, 2019. https://www.pewresearch.org/politics/2019/07/22/trust-and-distrust-in-america/.

Ramakrishnan, Karthick. "How Asian Americans Became Democrats." *The American Prospect*, July 26, 2016.

Ramakrishnan, Karthick, Janelle Wong, Taeku Lee, and Jennifer Lee. "Asian American Voices in the 2016 Election." National Asian American Survey. http://naasurvey.com/wp-content/uploads/2016/10/NAAS2016-Oct5-report.pdf.

Ramos, George. "From 'Chicano Beverly Hills' to Street Vendor." *Los Angeles Times*, February 22, 1993.

Rasmussen, Cecilia. "Community Profile: Walnut." *Los Angeles Times*, November 22, 1996, 2.

"Red Carpet: Elegant Properties, Inc." *The Windmill*, January 1993, 44.

Red Ribbon. "About Us: Our Sweet Story." http://www.redribbonbakeshop.us/.

Reft, Ryan. "Redefining Asian America: Japanese Americans, Gardena, and the Making of a Transnational Suburb." KCET, August 22, 2014.

Reich, Kenneth. "Conservatives Fight It Out: Heavy Reagan Vote May Push Dreier Over Lloyd," *Los Angeles Times*, October 20, 1980, C1.

Reinhold, Robert. "In the Middle of L.A.'s Gang Wars." *New York Times Magazine*, May 22, 1988.

Reynolds, Dave. "MRF Update." *The Windmill*, August 1994, 20.

Richardson, Bill (pseudonym). Oral history interview conducted by James Zarsadiaz, Hacienda Heights, CA, October 13, 2011.

Richardson, Laura (pseudonym). Oral history interview conducted by James Zarsadiaz, Hacienda Heights, CA, October 13, 2011.

Roberts, Sam. "In Shift, 40% of Immigrants Move Directly to Suburbs." *New York Times*, October 17, 2007.

Roderick, Kevin. "The Times Poll: Most in L.A. Pleased but Fear Crime." *Los Angeles Times*, March 25, 1985, SD3.

Rome, Adam. *The Bulldozer in the Countryside: Suburban Sprawl and the Rise of American Environmentalism.* Cambridge: Cambridge University Press, 2001.

Romney, Lee. "Chinese Americans Make Political Strides." *Los Angeles Times*, November 28, 1993.

——. "Recall, Slow Growth Highlight Local Races." *Los Angeles Times*, November 4, 1993, SGJ1.

——. "26-Acre Mall Approved Over Protest of Committee." *Los Angeles Times*, August 29, 1993.

Rowland Heights Buckboard Days. "History." https://buckboarddaysparade.org /history/.

"Rowland Heights Housing Plan Denied." *Inland Valley Daily Tribune*, November 6, 2010.

"Rowland Heights: Teen Shot While Standing on High School Ball Field." *Los Angeles Times*, February 18, 1993.

Rowland Unified School District. RUSD School Board minutes, item 432A. March 30, 1989.

——. RUSD School Board minutes, item 65A. September 6, 1990.

——. Stanley G. Oswalt Academy School Accountability Report Card. http:// www.rowlandschools.org/ourpages/auto/2014/1/21/52855677/2013%20SARC %20Stanley%20G_%20Oswalt%20Academy.pdf.

Rudeee. Comments on online discussion board on "Rowland Heights' Cityhood Nears Reality." *San Gabriel Valley Tribune*, October 12, 2008.

Ruggio, Linda. "Letters to the Editor: Don't Shut English Speakers Out!" *Walnut Times Magazine*, June 15, 1994, 6.

Sahagún, Louis. "East L.A., 1968: 'Walkout!' The Day High School Students Helped Ignite the Chicano Power Movement." *Los Angeles Times*, March 1, 2018.

Saito, Leland. *Race and Politics: Asian Americans, Latinos, and Whites in a Los Angeles Suburb.* Urbana: University of Illinois Press, 1998.

San Gabriel Valley Economic Partnership and Cal Poly Pomona College of Business Administration. *2019 San Gabriel Valley Economic Forecast Summit*. Los Angeles County Economic Development Corporation, San Gabriel Valley Economic Partnership, April 4, 2019. https://laedc.org/wp-content/uploads/2019/04/2019 _SGV_Econ_Summit_final_w_appendices.pdf.

"San Gabriel Valley: Reward Offered in Bombing at School." *Los Angeles Times*, November 7, 1995.

Sandul, Paul J. P. *California Dreaming: Boosterism, Memory, and Rural Suburbs in the Golden State*. Morgantown: West Virginia University Press, 2014.

Schmid, Carol. *The Politics of Language: Conflict, Identity, and Cultural Pluralism in Comparative Perspective*. New York: Oxford University Press, 2001.

Schoner, Carl. Oral history interview conducted by James Zarsadiaz, Diamond Bar, CA, June 22, 2018.

———. *Suburban Samurai: The Asian Invasion of the San Gabriel Valley*. Self-published, 2006.

———. *When We Were Cowboys*. Self-published, 2009.

Schwarz, Benjamin, and Christina Schwarz. "Going All Out for Chinese." *Atlantic*, January 1999.

Shabsin, Martee. "Martee Shabsin, Prudential California Realty Ad." *The Windmill*, April 1995, 11.

Shah, Nayan. *Contagious Divides: Epidemics and Race in San Francisco's Chinatown*. Berkeley: University of California Press, 2001.

Shea Homes. "The Estates at Snow Creek." Advertisement. *Los Angeles Times*, January 11, 1987, H5.

Shyong, Frank. "Monterey Park Sign Ordinance Debate Recalls '80s Ethnic Controversy." *Los Angeles Times*, August 3, 2013.

Siao, Grace Wai-Tse. "Asians Join Bush in Victory." *Asian Week*, November 11, 1988, 1.

———. "Korean Council Candidate Offers Multilingual Hot Line: Jay Kim Vows to Pay for Phone Service and Translation." *Asian Week*, February 16, 1990, 13.

Simon, Richard. "Antonovich Faces Little Opposition: 5th District Usually Elects Conservative." *Los Angeles Times*, March 18, 1984, SG1.

Singer, Audrey, Susan W. Hardwick, and Caroline B. Brettell. *Twenty-First Century Gateways: Immigrant Incorporation in Suburban America*. Washington, DC: Brookings Institution Press, 2008.

"Single-Family Homes in Hacienda Heights Open." *Los Angeles Times*, October 16, 1983, G23.

Sister Cities International. Sister City Membership Directory 2012. https://www .sistercities.org/sites/default/files/SCI%20MEMBER%20DIRECTORY%202012.

"Slowing of Growth in Walnut Pledge by New Councilmen." *Los Angeles Times*, April 16, 1972, SG-A1.

Smith, Henry Nash. *Virgin Land: The American West as Symbol and Myth*. Cambridge, MA: Harvard University Press, 1970.

Smith, Neil. "New City, New Frontier: The Lower East Side as Wild, Wild West." In *Variations on a Theme Park: The New American City and the End of Public Space*, edited by Michael Sorkin, 61–93. New York: Hill and Wang, 1992.

Smith, Sharon (pseudonym). Oral history interview conducted by James Zarsadiaz, Diamond Bar, CA, March 15, 2012.

Soja, Edward. "Los Angeles: City of the Future?" BBC/Open University (1991). You-Tube. https://www.youtube.com/watch?time_continue=16&v=pkYIwlcjCOI.

———. *Third Space: Journeys to Los Angeles and Other Real-and-Imagined Places*. Malden, MA: Blackwell, 1996.

"Some in Chino Hills Nervous about Ethnic Shift Exemplified by Asian Supermarket." *Press-Enterprise*, February 7, 2007.

Sorkin, Michael (ed.). *Variations on a Theme Park: The New American City and the End of Public Space*. New York: Hill and Wang, 1992.

South El Monte Arts Posse. "¡La Lucha Continua! Gloria Arellanas and the Making of a Chicano Movement in El Monte and Beyond." Tropics of Meta, UCLA Chicano Studies Research Center, January 22, 2015, https://www.chicano.ucla.edu/files/news/TropicsofMeta_LaLuchaContinua_12215.pdf.

Spiegel, Claire, and K. Connie Kang. "The Fast, Rocky Rise of Jay Kim." *Los Angeles Times*, October 27, 1993.

"Spotlight: L.A., San Bernardino County Officials to Open Grand Avenue, Chino Hills Parkway Sept. 1." *Los Angeles Times*, May 27, 1990.

Staley, Jayne. "Letter to the Editor." *Highlander*, ca. 1989.

Stamm, Maggi. "Who Let the Committee Define Issues?" *San Gabriel Valley Tribune*, September 5, 1987.

Starr, Kevin. *Americans and the California Dream, 1850–1915*. New York: Oxford University Press, 1973.

———. *The Dream Endures: California Enters the 1940s*. New York: Oxford University Press, 1997.

Stewart, Janice (pseudonym). Oral history interview conducted by James Zarsadiaz, Diamond Bar, CA, March 7, 2012.

Stilgoe, John R. *Borderland: Origins of the American Suburb*. New Haven, CT: Yale University Press, 2012 (1988).

Storrer, William Allin. *The Frank Lloyd Wright Companion*. Chicago: University of Chicago Press, 1994.

Sugrue, Thomas J. "Crabgrass-Roots Politics: Race, Rights, and the Reaction against Liberalism in the Urban North, 1940–1964." *Journal of American History* 82.2 (September 1995), 551–578.

———. *The Origins of the Urban Crisis: Race and Inequality in Postwar Detroit*. Princeton, NJ: Princeton University Press, 1996.

———. "Race, Rights, and the Reaction against Liberalism." *Journal of American History* 82.2 (September 1995), 557.

Sullivan, Deborah. "Walnut: City Manager Retires, Prompts Uproar over Ethnic Tensions." *Los Angeles Times*, February 23, 1995.

Takaki, Ronald. *Strangers from a Different Shore: A History of Asian Americans*. Boston: Little, Brown and Company, 1989.

Tan, Caroline. "Proposal for 'English Only' Council Meetings Leads to Civil Rights Questions." NBC News, July 14, 2012.

Tanaka, Rodney. "Bilingual Store Signs a Challenge." *Whittier Daily News*, January 4, 2003.

———. "Sign Regulation Urged." *San Gabriel Valley Tribune*, September 25, 2000, 1.

Taylor, Mechelle. "Another Ganeshan Speaks Out." *The Windmill* 9.1 (January 1983), 23.

Tchen, John Kuo Wei. *New York before Chinatown: Orientalism and the Shaping of American Culture, 1776–1882*. Baltimore: Johns Hopkins University Press, 2001.

Teaford, Jon C. *City and Suburb: The Political Fragmentation of Metropolitan America, 1850–1970*. Baltimore: Johns Hopkins University Press, 1979.

———. "Dividing the Metropolis: The Political History of Suburban Incorporation in the United States." In *The Routledge Companion to the Suburbs*, edited by Bernadette Hanlon and Thomas J. Vicino. New York: Routledge, 2019.

———. *The Metropolitan Revolution: The Rise of Post-Urban America*. New York: Columbia University Press, 2006.

"This Is the Right Time for Cityhood." *Diamond Bar Windmill*, February 1989, 4.

Thompson, Jon F. "Religious Leader Appeals for Better Understanding of Buddhism, Temple." *San Gabriel Valley Tribune*, February 3, 1988, B1.

Thompson, Sandra (pseudonym). Oral history interview conducted by James Zarsadiaz, Walnut, CA, March 7, 2012.

"3 Students Hurt in Pipe Bomb Explosion at La Puente School." *Los Angeles Times*, October 31, 1995.

Thurman, Jim. "85c Bakery-Café Opens in Hacienda Heights." *L.A. Weekly*, August 15, 2011.

Tongson, Karen. *Relocations: Queer Suburban Imaginaries*. New York: New York University Press, 2011.

"Torres, Molina Woo Ballot Losers: Elections." *Los Angeles Times*, January 24, 1991, SBB1.

Torres, Vicki. "Shooting Leads to Tighter School Security: Violence: Access to Nogales High School Is Restricted. Male Victim, 17, Is in Fair Condition." *Los Angeles Times*, February 18, 1993.

"Tribal History," Gabrielino-Tongva Tribe. http://www.gabrielinotribe.org/historical-sites-1/.

Trinidad, Elson. "L.A. County Is the Capital of Asian America." KCET, September 27, 2013. https://www.kcet.org/socal-focus/la-county-is-the-capital-of-asian-america.

Tsang, Audrey. "Audrey Tsang: Re/Max." *The Windmill*, April 1999, 23.

United Nations. "Five Things You Should Know Now about the COVID-19 Pandemic." March 16, 2020. https://news.un.org/en/story/2020/03/1059261.

US Bureau of the Census, 1980, 1990, 2000, 2010. https://data.census.gov/cedsci/.

US Congress. "California Forty-First District." In *Official Congressional Directory,*
   1997–1998: 105th Congress. Washington, DC: United States Government Printing
   Office.
———. "Jay C. Kim." US House of Representatives History, Art & Archives. https://
   history.house.gov/People/Detail/16304.
Untitled promotional piece. *Diamond Bar Windmill,* October 1982, 37.
Viehe, Fred W. "Black Gold Suburbs: The Influence of the Extractive Industry on
   the Suburbanization of Los Angeles, 1890–1930." *Journal of Urban History* 8.1
   (November 1981), 3–26.
"Village Oaks Offers Affordability and a Rural Lifestyle." *Los Angeles Times,* Novem-
   ber 1, 1986, P10.
"The Villages at Diamond Bar." Brochure. McCombs Corporation (ca. 1980).
Villanova, Joel. "Diamond Bar Watching Nearby Development." *Diamond Bar-
   Phillips Ranch Highlander,* April 8, 1987.
———. "High School Heads Horcher's MAC Goals." *Highlander,* February 4,
   1987, A3.
Villanueva, Nick (pseudonym). Oral history interview conducted by James Zarsa-
   diaz, Riverside, CA, October 12, 2011.
"A Visit to Diamond Bar's Long Lost Sister City." *Diamond Bar Patch,* July 15, 2011,
   https://patch.com/california/diamondbar-walnut/a-visit-to-diamond-bars-long
   -lost-sister-city.
Walker, Jill. "Surge of Hispanic Gangs Seen in Los Angeles." *Washington Post,* May
   29, 1990.
Wallace, Renee. "Anti-cityhood Group Forms in Diamond Bar." *Diamond Bar-
   Phillips Ranch Highlander,* January 18, 1989.
"Walnut Council, Residents Oppose Proposed NFL Stadium." *Daily Breeze,* Sep-
   tember 25, 2008.
Wang, Oliver. "San Gabriel Valley Goes Viral: The Fung Bros Rep the 626." KCET,
   May 7, 2012.
Ward, Mike. "Development Is Year's Hottest Issue." *Los Angeles Times,* December 31,
   1989, J1.
———. "Diamond Bar Mayor Would Be First Korean-American Elected to Congress
   If He Defeats Democrat Bob Baker in November." *Los Angeles Times,* June 21,
   1992.
———. "GOP Seen as Tough to Beat in New Assembly Districts." *Los Angeles Times,*
   August 30, 1992, SGJ1.
———. "Homeowners United to Counter Rise in Crime." *Los Angeles Times,*
   August 4, 1974, SG6.
———. "Incumbents Face Soft Opposition in Race for Congress." *Los Angeles Times,*
   October 23, 1986, SG1.
———. "Local Elections: 8 in GOP Seek Hill's Seat; 2 Vie to Oust Moorhead 52nd
   Assembly District." *Los Angeles Times,* May 24, 1990, 1.
———. "Local Races a Lesson in Contradiction: Elections." *Los Angeles Times,*
   June 4, 1992, SGJ1.

———. "Pomona Votes No on Plan to Boost Tax by Half a Cent." *Los Angeles Times*, October 5, 1989, SG1.

———. "Rival to English Initiative Proposed." *Los Angeles Times*, November 10, 1985.

Watanabe, Teresa. "Chinese Take to U.S. Politics." *Los Angeles Times*, April 8, 2003, VYB1.

Wei, Helen (pseudonym). Oral history interview conducted by James Zarsadiaz, April 6, 2012, Diamond Bar, CA.

Williams, Darlene. "Hacienda Heights Cityhood Vote." *Los Angeles Times*, June 14, 1992.

Wilson, Jake B. "The Racialized Picket Line: White Workers and Racism in the Southern California Supermarket Strike." *Critical Sociology* 34.3 (April 2008), 349–367.

Winston, Hillary. "Letters to the Editor: Rape of the Valley." *San Gabriel Valley Tribune*, April 16, 1988, B5.

Winton, Richard. "Addressing Unlucky Street Numbers." *Los Angeles Times*, October 3, 1993, SG-J1.

———. "Asian Americans Flex Growing Political Muscle." *Los Angeles Times*, September 12, 2001, VC-B1.

Wong, Kayiu. "Republican Candidate John Cox Courts Chinese American Business Leaders in San Gabriel Valley." *San Gabriel Valley Tribune*, July 20, 2018.

Wong, Sarah (pseudonym). Oral history conducted by James Zarsadiaz, Walnut, CA, April 9, 2012.

Wu, Ellen. *The Color of Success: Asian Americans and the Origins of the Model Minority*. Princeton, NJ: Princeton University Press, 2015.

Yee, Christopher. "More Asian-Americans Live in San Gabriel Valley Than in 42 States, Report Says." *San Gabriel Valley Tribune*, February 22, 2018.

Zarsadiaz, James. "Elaine Chao Is Sticking by President Trump. That Shouldn't Be a Surprise." *Washington Post*, November 13, 2017.

———. "What Really Drew Asian Immigrants to the Suburbs?" *City Lab*, October 12, 2012.

———. "Why Gentrification Is So Hard to Stop." *City Lab*, February 17, 2014.

Zhou, Min. *Contemporary Chinese America: Immigration, Ethnicity, and Community Transformation*. Philadelphia: Temple University Press, 2009.

———. "'Parachute Kids' in Southern California: The Educational Experience of Chinese Children in Transnational Families." *Educational Policy* 12.6 (November 1998), 682–704.

Zirin, David. "Football in L.A." *Los Angeles Times*, October 29, 2009.

INDEX

Note: page numbers followed by *fig.*, *tab.*, and *map* indicate figures, tables, and maps.

anti-development (*continued*)
232n49; sexual violence rhetoric and,
159; suburb collaboration in, 158–59,
161–62; traffic concerns and, 160. *See
also* Slow Growth movement
Anti-Incorporation Committee (Diamond
Bar), 171–72
Arcadia: address changes in, 72; Asian
conservatism and, 138; Asian immigrants in, 68; competition for homes in,
66, 76; English as official language in,
217n70; English-signage laws, 110–11;
high-performing schools and, 40, 119;
pan-Asian American pride in, 190
Arciero & Sons, 230n38
*Asian American Business Group v. City of
Pomona*, 115, 219n94
Asian businesses: accusations of reverse
racism, 104–5, 108–9, 111; Asian disapproval of, 99–103; associations with
visual disorder, 108, 110, 113–15, 185;
bilingual signage and, 47, 103–4, 107–9,
111, *114fig.*, 115; country living rhetoric
and, 85, 100–101, 103–5, 108, 111–13;
design assimilation and, 104, 106–7, 111,
115; as discouragement of assimilation,
47, 103, 108–9, 111–13; East Valley and,
3, 99, 150; economic benefits of, 105, 107;
English-signage laws, 103–4, 107–11;
ethnoburbs and, 15; fears of Asian
takeover, 115; linking of Asian officials
with, 105; nativist rhetoric and, 99,
104–5; 99 Ranch Market and, 99–100,
102–6; opposition to, 85, 99–102, 106;
orientalist stereotypes of, 100–101, 104;
Pic 'N' Save stores, 105, 217n66; preference for invisibility, 101, 104, 107; racial
anxieties and, 100, 182–84; San Gabriel
Valley and, 3, 190–91, 240n9; social
controls and, 115; strip malls and, 40,
102, 111–12, *114fig.*; suburban conformity and, 109; traffic congestion and,
114; visibility of Asian culture, 112–13,
185. *See also* immigrant landscapes
Asian immigrants: accusations of cutthroat
academics, 121; accusations of reverse
racism, 182; assimilation and, 16–19, 80,
82–83, 111–12, 116; associations with

urbanism, 100; blame for traffic, 100;
class-based issues, 131–32; conservativism and, 6, 137–45, 224n65, 225n69,
227n93; country living suburbs and,
16–18, 53, 62, 65–68, 80–81, 116, 210n40;
cross-racial partnerships and, 117–18;
defining, 14–15; direct advertising to,
66, *67fig.*, 68, 74; discrimination and,
89, 97–98, 115–16, 136, 142–43; diverse
alliances and, 9, 14, 16; double standards
for, 6–7, 109; East Valley and, 1, 3, 38,
82, 197n1; ethnic and cultural practices,
6, 17; frontier nostalgia and, 6, 10, 17;
global capital and, 14, 65, 68, 73, 92, 137,
150, 156; homeownership and, 6, 65,
69–70, 79; impact on built environment, 9, 11, 17; as model minority, 6,
16–17, 80, 85, 89, 91, 116, 118, 120, 122,
131, 135, 145–46, 220n11, 226n88; "otherness" and, 82, 85, 145; political impact
of, 6, 9, 11, 13, 17–18, 131–32; postwar
American modernity and, 101–2; pressure to conform, 15–17, 19; racism and, 3,
16; Republican outreach to, 138–40,
226n88; self-segregating, 102; spaces of
belonging and, 82–83; testing cultures
and, 120; transgression of mainstream
customs and, 111–12; white color-
blindness and, 16. *See also* anti-Asianism
Asian Pacific American Legal Center of
Los Angeles (APALC), 111
Asian realtors, 40, 119, 126, 220n4
Asian suburbanites: address changes and,
72–73, 212n70; aesthetics of public
spaces and, 11, 102–3, 110–11; American
Dream and, 66, 79; anti-MRF activism,
132–35; anti-urbanism and, 69; assimilation and, 82–84, 117–18, 138; civic
engagement and, 142–44, 183; class
privileges of, 6, 12, 16–17, 19, 21, 101, 131,
145, 168; conformity and, 83, 85, 107,
109, 145–46; conservativism and, 137–
42, 191–92; country living and, 5, 84–85,
102, 111, 116, 142, 145, 190, 193–94;
critics of, 83–85; culturally specific
design elements, 70–73; design assimilation and, 84–85, 101; East Valley and,
3, 8, 10–11, 65–75, 82, 98, 188–89,

193–94; English Only advocacy, 107–8, 110–11; ethnoburbs and, 9, 200n32; *feng shui* homes and, 70–71; homeownership and, 70, 75, 101; invisibility of ethnic expression and, 6, 17, 85, 101, 111–12, 115–16; model minority narrative, 140–41; NIMBYism and, 84, 131, 223n55; political impact of, 81, 130, 184; proximity to privileges of whiteness and, 6, 83, 118; public schools and, 119–20, 124–28, 130–31, 220n4; quality of life concerns, 192–93; racial homogeneity and, 189–90; rhetorical strategies and, 86; rurality and, 77; school redistricting movements, 123–26, 128–31; Slow Growth movement and, 140; social controls and, 80, 84, 145; spatial regulation and, 84; transnationality and, 11, 68, 118, 190; upper-income, 6, 8, 11, 34, 65, 101–2, 130, 166, 188; urban residents and, 69; white anxiety and, 109, 165. *See also* country living suburbs

assimilation: Asian immigrants and, 3, 16–19, 80, 82–84, 102, 111–12, 116–18; Asian "otherness" and, 82, 85; conformity and, 47, 83; economic policies and, 138; English signage and, 108–9; ethnic retail discouragement of, 103; ethnoburbs and, 102; frontier imaginary and, 17; Hsi Lai Buddhist Temple and, 93; social controls and, 84; spaces of belonging and, 82–83. *See also* design assimilation

Azusa, 119

Bakersfield, 201n9
Baldassare, Mark, 149
Baldwin, Elias "Lucky," 22, 44
Baldwin Park, 110
Barraclough, Laura, 23, 33, 98
Barthes, Roland, 10
Bartholomae, William A., 27
Bartholomae Oil Corporation, 27
Beecher, Catharine, 23
Beiswanger, Mark, 71
Bell, 138
Benjamin, Rich, 174
Biden, Joe, 192

Blacks: association with urbanism, 152, 170, 183; country living suburbs and, 62, 64; East Valley and, 54–55, 119; negative stereotyping of, 85, 119, 121, 129, 152; political left and, 137; public schools and, 121–22, 124, 128–29, 130–31; rural heritage and, 55; white distancing from, 119
Blugrind, Larry, 104–5
Boceta, Rolland, 125
Bonelli Regional Park, 40
Bonilla-Silva, Eduardo, 5, 91
Bourdain, Anthony, 191
Bowler, John, 50, 53
Bowler, Patricia, 50, 53
Boxer, Barbara, 140
Boyle Heights, 54, 138
Bracco, Marsha, 124
Briesmeister, Wilfred, 87
Brookside Equestrian Center, 35, 94
Brown, Nadine, 156–57
Brown Power mobilization, 138
Brunner, Ingrid, 153
Buckley, William F., 56
Buddhism: campaigns to demystify, 89–91; concerns with foreignness, 88, 92; IBPS and, 86; opposition to traditional design of, 88–89; questions of legitimacy, 88; social conservatism and, 91. *See also* Hsi Lai Buddhist Temple
Buffington, Dan, 180, 231n39
built environment: Asian immigrant impact on, 9, 11, 17; color- and class-blind rhetoric, 179; culturally specific design elements, 73, 85–86, 88–89, 93, 95; design assimilation and, 84–85; disruption of country living, 17, 111–13; Euro-American design standards, 47, 84–85, 99, 104, 109, 111; invisible ethnic presence in, 48, 85, 115–16; non-English signage and, 103–4, 107–11, 115–16; public condemnation of shifting, 106; transformation in, 79; visibility of Asian culture, 103–4, 107–9, 112–13
Burbank, 25
Bush, George H. W., 137, 139
Bush, George W., 225n69
Bush, Laura, 139
Butterfield Ranch development, 205n72

transnationality and, 41; unsavory reputation of, 39–40; village-based identities in, 39–40; white flight from, 236n39

Chino Hills in Traffic, Chino Hills Against Traffic (CHITCHAT), 162, 232n58

Chino Hills Parkway, 163

Chino Valley, 38–39

CHITCHAT. *See* Chino Hills in Traffic, Chino Hills Against Traffic (CHITCHAT)

Choctaw, William, 63–65, 96–97, 125

Christiana Oil Corporation and Capital Company, 27

Chu, Betty Tom, 191

Cisneros, Gil, 192

citrus industry, 22, 41–42, 44

cityhood (incorporation): annexation threats, 180–81, 187; anti-Asianism and, 18, 166, 177–78, 182–87; anti-incorporation movement, 171–72, 175–77, 181–84; Asian support for, 166; Chino Hills and, 18, 25, 40, 112, 151, 162, 165, 187; civic autonomy and, 18, 113; class anxieties and, 165–66, 178, 180–81; conservative opposition to, 171–72, 234n26, 235n37; design assimilation and, 112, 185; Diamond Bar and, 18, 25, 79–80, 112, 151, 157–58, 162–63, 165, 167–77, 180–81, 186, 231n39, 234n16, 235n30; East Valley and, 25; fears of Asian influence in, 151; fears of higher taxes, 171, 174, 176, 235n37; grassroots movements for, 148; in greater Los Angeles, 187, 239n92; Hacienda Heights and, 151, 165, 181–84; increased regulation and, 171–72; LAFCO guidelines for, 169; local control and, 18, 113, 162, 165–69, 173–77; multiethnic alliances and, 183, 185, 238n70; nativist rhetoric and, 181, 185; Old Guard opposition to, 183–84; Pomona and, 206n90; protection of country living and, 18, 79, 148, 151, 166–67, 169–70, 172–73, 181, 186–87; protection of property values, 167, 170; quality of life concerns, 147–48, 162, 172–73, 180, 184; racial anxieties and, 165–66, 170, 174–75, 178, 180–86; as reaction to change, 148, 151, 165–67, 174–75, 181, 187; role of globalization in, 179–80; Rowland Heights and, 151, 165, 181, 184–86; Slow Growth movement promotion of, 162–63, 165; Walnut and, 25, 35, 112, 155; xenophobia and, 18, 181, 183–85; zoning laws and, 112

City of Industry: Asian businesses and, 40, 102, 112, 178; business zoning in, 132; development of, 34; ethnoburbs and, 103; land-use proposals in, 144; MRF plan in, 132–34; multilingual signage and, 115; NFL stadium proposal, 144, 192; Puente Hills Landfill and, 182; threat to annex Hacienda Heights, 180–81; threat to annex Walnut, 35; traffic congestion and, 114–15; transformation in built environment, 79

civic engagement: Asian activists and, 141–44, 182–83, 238n70; Asian homeowners and, 144, 183; homeowners associations (HOAs) and, 168; increase in, 227n98; local control and, 169; personalization of politics and, 149; white residents and, 183

Claremont, 22

class and classism: affluent Asians and, 6, 16, 65, 102, 118, 178; Asian built environment and, 9, 80, 102–3, 112, 115; country living rhetoric and, 5, 50, 151, 159, 164; incorporation arguments and, 165–66, 178, 180–81; multiethnic alliances and, 17, 81, 141, 145; Old Guard and, 54; political activism and, 131–32; rhetorical devices and, 179; school redistricting movements, 119, 121, 123–26; suburbia and, 6, 8–9, 24, 35, 43–44, 58, 80, 82

Clinton, Bill, 137, 139

Coachella Valley, 41

Cofer, Maurice, 147, 154, 159

color-blindness: country living ideal and, 5; multiculturalist rhetoric and, 19, 86, 104, 108, 189; racial harmony beliefs, 108; rhetorical devices and, 5, 16, 19, 55, 64, 86, 94, 104, 179, 183; white suburbanites and, 16, 179

Compton, 183

Concerned Citizens for Diamond Bar Traffic Control (CCDBTC), 162–63, 232n58

conservativism: anti-communism and, 138; anti-government rhetoric and, 56, 168, 171, 173, 180, 235n37; anti-incorporation, 171–72, 234n26, 235n37; Asian immigrants and, 6, 16, 118, 132, 135–44, 191–92; East Valley and, 58, 101, 117–18, 136–41, 145, 179–80, 191–92, 226n86; Hsi Lai Buddhists and, 91; meritocracy ideals and, 55–56; neoliberal economic policy and, 137, 180; Old Guard and, 54, 135–37, 143, 145, 192; protection of country living and, 159, 162–63, 191; racial anxieties and, 148; social issues and, 91, 137; suburbia and, 65, 192; Sunbelt and, 56, 140; tax revolts and, 160, 168, 171, 235n37. *See also* Republican Party

Cook, Orlene, 159

Corona, 161

Coto de Caza, 8

Cotten, William, 229n7

Country Estates Homeowners Association (CEHA), 204n52

country living: American Dream and, 21, 55, 64; Asian assimilation and, 16–18, 111; Asian investment in, 134; class and race in, 5–6; concerns with end of, 18, 147–48, 152, 164, 169–70, 193; disassociations of Asian culture with, 100–101, 107; East Valley and, 2, 4–5, 10, 15, 17–21, 48–49; master-planned communities and, 4, 20, 26, *27fig.*, 28–29, 53; mythology of, 5, 19; as political tool against change, 6, 85–86, 91–93, 95–99; spatial regulation for, 29; weaponization of term, 7; Western agrarianism and, 4, 10, 16; whiteness and, 5–6, 16, 23, 151. *See also* anti-development; Asian suburbanites; country living motivations; country living suburbs; rurality

country living motivations: affordability and, 54, 57–58, 66; anti-urbanism and, 56, 58, 60, 69, 75–76, 81; Asian immigrant families, 19, 65–75; bucolic settings and, 57, 75, 77; commuting to Los Angeles, 60, 76; conservativism and, 58, 62, 65; culturally specific design elements, 70–73; escape from modernity and, 49, 55; family life and, 49, 53, 57–58, 64–66, 78; *feng shui* homes and, 70–73; freedom and, 49, 57–58; frontier nostalgia and, 54, 58; gated communities and, 62; high-performing schools and, 58, 60, 74–75, 77, 119, 123, 220n4; homeownership and, 50, 65, 69–70, 75, 79; luxury homes and, 58; meritocracy and, 55–56, 64, 75, 146; middle-class lifestyle and, 58, 60–62, 65, 69; modern amenities in, 60, 62, 65, 69; natural surroundings and, 53, 55, 62, 73–75; open space and, 60–61; plain-folk Americanism and, 57; popular culture depictions, 74–76; proximity to privileges of whiteness and, 6, 83; race neutrality and, 16, 19, 68; racial and ethnic diversity, 64–65; remoteness and, 54–55; rustic lifestyles and, 55–57, 64–65, 77; safety and, 76; spatial regulation and, 61, 64, 73, 76, 79; traditionalism and, 49, 57, 61, 68–69

country living suburbs: aesthetic parameters of, 105, 112; anti-urbanism and, 38, 193; assimilation and, 16, 117; associations with refinement, 23, 85; civic engagement and, 5; class-based unity and, 34, 81, 112; conservativism and, 132, 141, 191; diverse alliances and, 6, 17, 195; escape from modernity in, 15, 21, 25, 49, 55; everyday urbanism and, 8; family life and, 37, *37fig.*, 38; feminized rhetoric and, 159; frontier nostalgia and, 5–8, 10, 15, 20–21, 49, 54, 164; Latinos and, 14, 62; low-density policies in, 48, 150, 152; minimization of Asian culture and, 48, 101, 111; multiethnic alliances and, 142; politics in, 117; property values in, 120, 133; protection of, 7, 15, 18, 54, 101, 131, 140, 142–43, 192; public schools and, 40, 58, 60, 65, 74–75, 118–23, 219n3, 220n4; racial exclusion and, 5–6; racial homogeneity and, 189–90; racial liberalism and, 19, 81; regional identity of, 26; urbanization and, 152–53; western rurality and, 5, 19, 24, 38, 53, 56, 79; white settler colonialism and, 135. *See also* Asian suburbanites

The Country neighborhood (Diamond Bar): CEHA and, 204n52; commodified rurality in, 30, 32–33; country living and, 30–34, 204n52; custom-built homes in, 30, *32fig., 33fig.*; Emerald Pointe project and, 231n39; equestrianism and, *31fig.*, 32–33, 204n52; frontier imaginary and, 32–33; HOA in, 175; incorporation support in, 175; spatial regulation in, 31–32

COVID-19 pandemic, 194, 241n22

Covina, 22, 34–35, 139

Cox, John, 191

Crabtree, Jim, 183

Crawford, Margaret, 8

Creekside neighborhood (Walnut), 123–25, 128, 154, 221n17

Cristobal, Bella, 75–76, 80

Culver, Lawrence, 213n91

Daley, Bill, 36

Dana, Deane, 112

Darling, James, 95, 97

Davis, Gray, 240n13

Davis, Mike, 7, 213n91

DBCC. *See* Diamond Bar Citizens for Cityhood (DBCC)

DBIA. *See* Diamond Bar Improvement Association (DBIA)

DBMAC. *See* Diamond Bar Municipal Advisory Committee (DBMAC)

Dear, Michael, 7, 205n67

Del Crest Homes, 46

Democratic Party, 137, 139, 179, 225n69

design assimilation: Asian businesses and, 104, 106, 111; Asian homeowners and, 84–85, 107; incorporation and, 112, 185; local officials and, 84, 101, 106

Diamond Bar, *4map*; address changes in, 72–73; affordable housing loopholes and, 231n38; agrarian identity and, 26, 53, 62, 79, 153–54, 172, 176, 202n21; anti-development in, 152–54, 157–59, 231n39; anti-incorporation movement, 171–72, 175–77; anti-MRF activism,

132–33; anti-urbanism and, 157–58, 170; Arabian horses and, 26–27, 203n31; Asian residents in, 62, 66, 68, 177, 190; Asian sister cities, 223n59; associations with refinement, 101; boundaries in, 172, 235n32; Chinese businesses in, 3; Community Plan, 172, 231n39; commuters and, 28, 44, 161–63; conservativism and, 56, 101; country living in, 2, 24, 26, *27fig.*, 28–34, 50, 53, 55–56, 61, 79–80, 152–53, 167, 173; developer-provided amenities, 230n38; domesticity and, 29; Emerald Pointe project, 230n38, 231n39; end of agriculture in, 28; English-signage laws, 108, 110; equestrianism and, 30, *31fig.*, 32–33, 57; frontier nostalgia and, 32–33, 79, 151; gendered rhetoric for, 29; General Plan for, 172; Grand Avenue extension opposition, 161–62, 172; HOAs in, 157, 167–69, 174, 202n22; incorporation and, 18, 25, 79–80, 112, 151, 157–58, 162–63, 165, 167–77, 180–81, 186, 231n39, 234n16, 235n30; Incorporation Petition Committee (IPC), 170; invisibility of Asian culture in, 48, 85; Los Angeles County governance and, 30, 203n48; master planning and, 1, 26–30, 33, 35, 46, 53, 110, 167, 170, 203n32; median household income, 1980–2010, *50tab.*; middle-class lifestyle and, 61–62, *63fig.*; natural surroundings and, 26, 62; pan-Asian American pride in, 190; Parks and Recreation Commission, 62; Planning Commission, 62; Pomona threat to annex, 178–80, 187; population growth in, 152; public schools and, 119–21, 128–30; quality of life concerns, 162, 172–73, 180; race/ethnicity in, *51tab., 52tab.*; regional grocery strike in, 138; rural ideal and, 28, 30–32, 62, 153; rural urbanism and, 34; school redistricting movements, 128–30; Self-Determination Committee, 169–70; senior housing in, 231n38; shopping and recreational options, 29–30; Slow Growth movement and, 30, 151, 157–58; spatial regulation in, 29, 31–32, 79; suburbanization of, 16; traffic congestion and, 160;

Diamond Bar (*continued*)
Transamerica and, 27, 29–30; urbaniza-
tion and, 30, 152–53, 161, 167, 172,
203n48; white flight from, 236n39. *See
also* The Country neighborhood
(Diamond Bar)
Diamond Bar Chinese Association
(DBCA), 134
Diamond Bar Citizens for Cityhood
(DBCC), 170
Diamond Bar Country Estates Association,
204n52
Diamond Bar Development Corporation, 30
Diamond Bar Homeowners Association
(DBHOA), 167–69, 174, 234n16
Diamond Bar Improvement Association
(DBIA), 174, 234n16
Diamond Bar Municipal Advisory Com-
mittee (DBMAC), 157–58, 169, 174,
230n38, 234n16
Diamond Bar Ranch, 26–27, 142, 167
Diamond Bar Republican Women
Federated, 62
Diamond Bar Windmill, 167, 174, 235n37
Diamond Ranch High School, 130
Diamond View Estates (Phillips Ranch),
42–43
Dole, Bob, 140, 226n86
domesticity, 29, 36
Downing, Andrew Jackson, 23
Dreier, David, 226n86
Dunn, Shawn, 20, 129

Earl, Robert, 42
East Los Angeles, 138, 208n1
East San Gabriel Valley, *4map*; agrarianism
and, 22, 34, 54–55, 80, 150, 153–54, 161;
American Dream and, 7; anti-
cosmopolitan suburbs in, 25; anti-
urbanism and, 49, 58, 81, 155;
Asianization of, 1, 3, 10–11, 38, 68–75,
82, 98, 109–10, 164, 166, 188–91, 197n1;
associations with refinement, 78, 101;
attractiveness to homeowners, 53–54,
58, 60; bucolic settings and, 57, 75, 77,
92; class in, 9, 19; community and
in-home amenities, 236n50; conservativism and, 58, 101, 117–18, 136–41, 145,

179–80, 191–92, 226n86; country living
in, 2, 4–5, 10, 16, 18–21, 25–26, 28,
48–49, 53, 158, 164, 193–95, 204n62;
cultural capital and, 190; demographic
changes in, 2–3, 99, 148, 152–53, 191;
desirability of, 151–52; economic expansion in, 54, 148; English-signage laws,
115; Eurocentric narratives in, 23; everyday urbanism and, 8; feminized rhetoric
and, 159; frontier nostalgia and, 2–4, 15,
20, 23, 48, 80; as idyllic place, 21, 24, 28,
53; invisibility of Asian culture in, 85;
master-planned communities and, 1, 8,
24–25, 28, 34; maternity tourism and,
193; modern lifestyle and, 69; mythical
California and, 24, 28, 165–66, 191; Old
Guard in, 134–35; oral history and,
12–15; pan-Asian American pride in,
190, 193–94; pastoralism and, 22; public
schools in, 118–19, 123–31; racial
anxieties and, 236n39; refinement and,
78, 80; rurality and, 53, 56, 79–80; rustic
lifestyles and, 28, 31, 48, 55–56; Slow
Growth movement and, 18, 80, 147–59;
small-town identity in, 22; social controls and, 34; suburbanization of, 3–5,
11, 16, 18, 22, 147–49; urban expansion
in, 150; white flight from, 174–75,
236n39; whiteness and, 135
East Valley. *See* East San Gabriel Valley
edge cities, 24–25, 202n18
Ellis, Shiuh-Ming, 192
El Monte, 138
Emerald Pointe (Diamond Bar), 230n38,
231n39
Encino, 60–61
Engdahl, Derek, 129
English Only movement, 107–10, 115,
217n70, 226n88
environmental movement, 159, 168
equestrianism: in Chino Hills, 40; in
Diamond Bar, 26–27, *31fig.*, 32–33, 35,
57, 203n31, 204n52; in Hacienda
Heights, 46; mandatory bridle trails
and, 206n76; in Rowland Heights, 46;
in Walnut, 35, 77, 206n76
ethnoburbs: Asian immigrant avoidance of,
80, 101–2; assimilation and, 102;

defining, 9, 15; San Gabriel Valley and, 101, 200n32; visibility of Asian culture, 103–4, 200n32; West Valley and, 72
everyday urbanism, 8

Fang, David, 183
feng shui homes, 70–73
Filipino immigrants: agrarianism and, 76; Catholicism and, 215n32; conformity and, 146; country living and, 17; East Valley and, 66, 85, 93–94; homeowner-ship and, 70; suburban lifestyle and, 3, 66–68, 75–76, 83. *See also* St. Lorenzo Ruiz Catholic Church
Findlay, John, 75, 202n18
Fish, Barbara, 238n70
Foerstel, Ronald, 157, 169
Fogelson, Robert, 7, 149
Fong, Matt, 140
Fong, Tim, 9
Forbing, John, 163, 167, 186
Fremont, 11
Fresno, 201n9
frontier imaginary, 3, 10, 21
frontier nostalgia: anti-urbanism and, 49; Asian immigrants and, 6, 10, 17; country living and, 5–8, 10, 15, 20–21, 49, 54, 58; cultural myths of, 48; East Valley and, 2–4, 15, 20, 23, 48, 80; Jeffersonian/Turnerian ideas and, 23; master-planned communities and, 22–23; mythology of, 15; protection of, 164; suburbs and, 25, 79; whiteness and, 3, 23, 33, 105, 116; white settler colonialism and, 33
Fuller, Anna, 88, 92
Fung Brothers, 190

Gabrielino peoples, 21
Gahon, Joven, 111
Garcia, Matthew, 22, 200n30
Gardena, 86
Garden Grove, 108
Garreau, Joel, 24, 202n18
Garrett, Diana, 173
Gartel-Fuerte Homeowners Association, 147
gated communities, 32, 62
gentleman farming, 23

Gingrich, Newt, 140
Glendale, 25
Glendora, 35, 138
Gold, Jonathan, 190
Goldwater, Barry, 56
Gonzalez, Jerry, 200n30
Gore, Al, 139, 225n69
Grand Avenue extension project, 160–64, 172
Gray, Charlie, 181

Ha, Bonnie, 78
Ha, Maggie, 78–79
Ha, Simon, 78–80
Hacienda Heights, *4map*; affluent families in, 58; agrarianism in, 46, 48, 204n62; agriculture and, 44; annexation threats, 180–81, 187; Asian immigrants in, 66, 68, 177–78; Asian strip malls in, 40, 102, 112; bucolic settings and, 45–46; CDPs and, 25; Chinese businesses in, 3; Chinese settlement in, 18, 45; Commu-nity General Plan, 45–46, 208n116; country living in, 53, 55, 204n62; Countrywood subdivision, 45; demands for modern amenities, 46; demographic changes in, 45; development in, 34, 44–46; equestrianism and, 46; ethno-burbs and, 15, 101, 103, 112, 178; family life in, 45; fear of Asian takeover, 182–84; gentleman farming and, 44, 207n111; incorporation and, 18, 151, 165, 181–84, 234n26; July 4th parade col-laboration, 142; lack of local control in, 46–48, 106; Los Angeles commuters and, 44, 55; median household income, 1980–2010, *50tab.*; Mexican Americans in, 45; nativist rhetoric and, 181–82; "old California" imagery, 23; opposition to Hsi Lai Buddhist Temple, 86–93; public schools and, 119–20; race/ethnicity in, *51tab.*, *52tab.*; regional grocery strike in, 138; remoteness and, 54; Slow Growth movement and, 151; suburbanization of, 16, 45; transformation in built environ-ment, 79; as unincorporated area, 25, 34, 44, 46–48, 178; visibility of Asian culture, 112–13; western rurality and,

Hacienda Heights (*continued*)
44; white flight from, 236n39. *See also*
Hsi Lai Buddhist Temple
Hacienda Heights Chinese Association,
142
Hacienda Heights Improvement Association (HHIA), 86–87, 89, 207n111
Haggerty, Judy Chen, 3, 101, 135–36, 184,
186, 192, 227n93
Hanna, Terrence, 68
Hannon, Michael, 86–87
Hart, Edwin, 44
Hart-Celler Act of 1965, 3, 11, 198n5
Hayakawa, S. I., 227n88
Healy, John, 90–91
Herrera, Art, 50
Herrera, Carol, 50, 128
HHIA. *See* Hacienda Heights Improvement Association (HHIA)
Highlander, 177
High Tor Homeowners Association,
214n17
Hill, Frank, 138
HOA. *See* homeowners associations
(HOAs)
Ho-Hilger, Mei Mei, 142–44, 227n93
Hollydale, 57
Holmes, Linda, 155–56
homeowners associations (HOAs): anti-development politics and, 154, 157, 162,
167; governing authority, 25, 168, 186;
growth of, 168; newsletters and, 235n37;
policing of space by, 24, 202n22; political activism and, 168–69
homeownership: American Dream and, 10,
21, 50, 69–70, 75, 79; Asian immigrants
and, 6, 65, 69–70, 79; citizenship and,
70; country living and, 16, 18–19, 48;
political impact and, 15–16; US international aid initiatives and, 69–70
Honer, Elizabeth G., 174–75
Honer, Stanley M., 174–75
Hong Kong Plaza, 113
Horcher, Paul, 140, 158, 163, 172–73
Horton, John, 9
Howard, Ev, 153
Hsia, Chen-Li, 122
Hsieh, Fred, 66

Hsi Lai Buddhist Temple, *87fig., 90fig.*;
anti-Asianism and, 182; assimilationist
behavior and, 93; attraction of outsiders
to, 86; changing attitudes about, 90–91;
Chinese immigrants and, 45, 86; country living rhetoric and, 91–93; criticism
of design, 87–88; Democratic fundraising at, 139; denial of racist opposition,
88, 91–92; Hacienda Heights opposition
to, 85–93; harassment of, 89, 215n18;
message of inclusion and, 89–91; minimizing of ethnic expression, 88–89, 93;
racist opposition to, 87–89; social
conservatism and, 91; support from
High Tor Homeowners Association,
214n17
Hsu, Norman, 141
Huff, Bob, 191
Huff, Mei Mei, 191
Huntington Park, 53, 56

IBPS. *See* International Buddhist Progress
Society (IBPS)
immigrant landscapes: associations with
visual disorder, 108; association with
urbanism, 88; as disruptive to country
living, 17, 98–99; race and, 99; racial
liberalism and, 105; spaces of belonging
and, 83; spatial regulation and, 106;
white anxiety and, 83, 99. *See also* Asian
businesses
incorporation. *See* cityhood
(incorporation)
Incorporation '88 Committee (Diamond
Bar), 172, 174–75
Incorporation Petition Committee (IPC),
170
Indian Springs (Rowland Heights), *59fig.*
Inland Empire, 8, 110, 137, 236n39
International Buddhist Progress Society
(IBPS), 86, 92
Irvine, 24, 202n18, 202n21, 206n79
Isett, Jack, 97

Japanese immigrants, 199n28
Jarvis, Howard, 168, 170
Jenkins, Kyen, 154
J.M. Peters Co., 68

country living, 187; racial liberalism and, 107; racism and, 6

municipal advisory councils (MACs), 234n16

National Velvet, 35

nativism, 85, 99, 104, 138, 156, 181, 185

New Taipei City, Taiwan, 223n59

Newton, Michael, 105

NIMBYism: Asian immigrants and, 131–32; defining, 214n2, 223n55; protectionism and, 205n67; in Walnut, 35; white discontent and, 84

99 Ranch Market, 99–100, 102–3, 105–6, *106fig.*

Nixon, Richard, 179

Norquist, Grover, 168

North Hollywood, 88

North Whittier Heights, 44, 207n111. *See also* Hacienda Heights

Norton-Perry, Gwenn, 104–5

Nyal, Ivan, 231n39

Ochoa, Gilda, 200n30

"old California" imagery, 22–24, 28, 201n12

Old Guard: anti-Asianism and, 136, 142–44; anti-development and, 94, 149, 154, 156, 159; anti-incorporation and, 183–84; anti-MRF activism, 134–35; anti-urbanism and, 54; Asian influence over, 17, 118; conservativism and, 54, 135–37, 143, 145, 192; frontier nostalgia and, 62, 77; local politics and, 135–36, 141–43, 145, 166; multiethnic alliances and, 17, 132–37, 142–44; opposition to 99 Ranch, 100; opposition to St. Lorenzo proposal, 94–97; preservation of country living and, 149, 159; tensions with Chinese community, 142; views on Asian neighbors, 134

Olmsted, Frederick Law, 23

oral history, 12–15

Orange County: anti-development in, 165; Asian immigrants in, 8, 110; Carbon Canyon land, 206n84; Chino Hills development and, 39, 206n84; competition for homes in, 119; conservativism and, 137–38; Greater Los Angeles and,

7; Irvine master-planning in, 202n18; large-scale development in, 150; open space in, 39; suburbanization of, 24

Pacheco, Bob, 144, 228n105

Pacific Plaza (Rowland Heights), 113, *113fig.*

Padoongpatt, Mark, 88

Palomares, Ygnacio, 22, 26

Palos Verdes, 7

Pao, William, 134

Papen, Phyllis, 163, 175, 180

Parts Unknown (Bourdain), 191

Pasadena, 25

pastoralism, 20, 22, 25, 30, 176

Peralta, Rudy, 109

Pereira, William, 24

Phillips, Louis, 22, 41, 206n92

Phillips Ranch, *4map*; citrus industry and, 41; City of Industry MRF plan and, 132; as country living neighborhood, 25, 41–43, *43fig.*, 53; Diamond View Estates, 42–43; frontier imaginary and, 42; Grand Avenue extension opposition, 162; livestock in, 26; Los Angeles commuters and, 44; master planning and, 34, 41–43; median household income, 1980–2010, *50tab.*; open space in, 41; promotion of agrarian heritage, 42, 202n21; promotion to upwardly mobile white families, 42–43; public schools and, 130; race/ethnicity in, *51tab.*, *52tab.*; rural ideal and, 41–42; rural whiteness and, 42–43; spatial regulation in, 79; suburban class consciousness and, 43; suburbanization of, 16, 161; white flight from, 236n39

Phongpharnich, Pachri (Pat), 89

Pic 'N' Save stores, 105, 217n66

Pico Rivera, 138

Pido, Eric, 70

Pluth, Sharon, 87, 91–92

politics: anti-MRF activism, 132–34; Asian challenge to white control, 132, 184–85; Asian conservatism and, 136–43, 191–92, 225n69, 226n88, 227n93; Asian immigrants and, 6, 136–37, 140–41, 192, 225n69; civic engagement and, 149; class-based unity and, 141; East Valley

Rowland, John A., III, 99
Rowland, John A., IV, 171
Rowland, Lavinia, 171–72, 176–77
Rowland Heights: agrarianism in, 48,
204n62; annexation threats, 187; anti-
development in, 158; anti-MRF activism, 134; Asian residents in, 3, 47, 62,
66, 102, 177, 185–86, 190; Asian strip
malls in, 40, 102, 110, 112, *114fig.*, 185–
86; Buckboard Days, 142; CDPs and,
25; class diversity in, 110; Coordinating
Council, 47; country living in, 46, 53,
57, 115, 204n62; demographic changes
in, 47; development in, 34, 44, 46–47;
English signage proponents in, 109, 115;
equestrianism and, 46; ethnoburbs and,
15, 101, 103, 105, 112, 178; Filipino immigrants in, 94; frontier nostalgia and, 46;
General Plan for, 47; HOAs in, 186;
incorporation and, 18, 151, 165, 181,
184–86; Indian Springs tract, *59fig.*; lack
of local control in, 46–48, 106; Los
Angeles commuters and, 44, 46; luxury
homes in, 47, 205n72; median household income, 1980–2010, *50tab.*; MRF
in, 224n62; multiethnic right-wing
alliances, 141; multilingual signage and,
114fig., 115; 99 Ranch Market and, 99;
opposition to condominiums and
apartments, 192; pan-Asian American
pride in, 190; parachute children and,
122; pro-incorporation forces, 114;
protection of pastoral environment in,
47; public schools and, 119–20, 123–27;
quality of life concerns, 184; race/
ethnicity in, *51tab.*, *52tab.*, 210n32,
222n26; regional grocery strike in, 138;
rurality and, 44, 46–47; suburbanization of, 16, 161; transformation in built
environment, 79; as unincorporated
area, 25, 34, 44, 47–48, 177, 186; visibility of Asian culture, 112–13, *113fig.*;
white-collar families in, 58; white flight
from, 236n39
Rowland Heights Advocates for Cityhood
(RHAC), 185
Rowland Heights Chinese Association, 3,
4map, 185

Rowland Heights Community Standards
District (RHCSD), 114
Rowland Heights Coordinating Council
(RHCC), 114, 185
Rowland Unified School District, 120,
123–27, 222n26
Rubottom, William "Uncle Billy," 26
Ruggio, Linda, 109
Rumpilla, Al, 176–77
rurality: American distrust of cities and, 23;
associations with refinement and
morality, 23; competing visions of,
235n35; disassociations of Asian culture
with, 100; East Valley and, 53, 56,
79–80; fears of end of, 21, 107; frontier
imaginary and, 10; local control and,
48; master-planned communities and,
28, 30–32, 38; preservation of, 46–47;
romance of Western, 5, 19, 38; suburbia
and, 48. *See also* country living; Western
rurality
rural land-use activism, 33–34
rural urbanism, 23

Saito, Leland, 9
San Bernardino County, *4map*; Chino
Hills development and, 38–39, 163;
Grand Avenue extension project, 160–
63; Greater Los Angeles and, 7; large-
scale development in, 150; traffic
congestion and, 160–61
San Dimas, 22, 34, 40, 226n86
San Fernando Valley: anti-development in,
165; Asian settlement in, 8; competing
visions of rurality in, 235n35; declining
reputation of, 61; demographic changes
in, 33–34; exclusionary politics in, 98;
gentleman farming and, 208n111;
politicization of mainstream issues,
232n49; post-war homes in, 60; rural
land-use activism, 33; rural urbanism
and, 23
San Gabriel: address changes in, 72–73;
Asian immigrants in, 78, 100, 119; dated
homes in, 79; high-performing schools
and, 119; racial politics and, 9; Slow
Growth movement and, 150
San Gabriel Mission, 21, 34

San Gabriel Valley: agriburbs in, 22; Asian businesses and, 190–91, 240n9; Asian conservatism and, 136–38; Asianization of, 1, 8, 66, 68, 82, 111, 188–91; Asian realtors and, 119; color- and class-blind rhetoric, 179; competing visions of rurality in, 173, 235n35; concerns with crime, 231n47; conservativism and, 137, 224n65; design and signage in, 115–16; English Only movement, 217n70; ethnoburbs and, 137, 200n32; *feng shui* homes, 70–71; indigenous Tongva in, 21; Latinx/Chicanx suburbanization in, 200n30; mythical California and, 191; neoliberal economic policy and, 180; politics in, 117; public schools and, 119; racial diversity in, 64; rural urbanism and, 23; settler colonialism in, 21–22; 626 nickname, 199n25; Slow Growth movement and, 150, 152; Spanish colonization and, 14, 21. *See also* East San Gabriel Valley; West San Gabriel Valley

San Gabriel Valley Tribune, 235n37
San Joaquin Valley, 201n9
San Marino, 66, 74, 110, 119, 138
Santa Clarita, 187, 239n92
Schabarum, Pete, 88, 112, 162, 214n17, 234n16
Schoner, Carl, 1–2, *2fig.*, 197n1, 197n2
school redistricting movements: anti-Asianism and, 121–22, 124; class anxieties and, 121, 123–26; desirability of Asian students, 120–22, 131; multiethnic alliances and, 124–26, 128, 130–31; parachute children and, 121–22; parental choice and, 125; property values and, 120, 122, 124–27; racial anxieties and, 119, 122–26, 128–30; regional boundary battles, 122–28, 131
Schwarz, Benjamin, 188–89
Schwarz, Christina, 188–89
Schwarzenegger, Arnold, 192
Scott, Allen, 7
Self-Determination Committee (Diamond Bar), 169–70
SGAEC. *See* Stop Grand Avenue Expressway Committee (SGAEC)
Shea Homes, 20, 25, 38, 68, 158, 205n72

Shilin, Taiwan, 223n59
Shindo, George, 156
Simon, Bill, 139
Simon, Cindy, 139
626 Night Market, 190
Slow Growth movement: anti-Asianism and, 18, 148, 150, 164; citizen coalitions, 162, 232n58; Diamond Bar and, 30, 157–58; East Valley and, 18, 80, 147, 149–59; ecological destruction rhetoric and, 159–60; Grand Avenue extension opposition, 160–62; low-density policies and, 150; partnerships between suburbs in, 158–59; personalization of politics and, 155–56; promotion of incorporation, 162–63, 165; protection of country living and, 18, 140, 147–48, 151, 158–60, 163–64; quality of life concerns, 147; as reaction to change, 151, 164–65, 187; resistance to multi-unit homes, 35; San Gabriel Valley and, 150, 152; traffic concerns and, 160; Walnut and, 35, 150–51, 155–56; West Valley and, 150–51
Smith, Drexel L., 96, 123
Smith, Glenda, 87
Smith, Henry Nash, 10
Smith, Ken, 61
Smith, Neil, 10
Smith, Sharon, 61–62, 65
Snow Creek neighborhood (Walnut): anti-MRF activism, 132; country living in, 20–21, 37, *37fig.*, 38; executive homes in, 36; family life in, 37–38; homeowners associations (HOAs), 154
social capital, 8, 11, 118
social controls, 4, 34, 80, 115, 145
Soja, Edward, 7, 202n18
Souplantation, 194
South Bay, 60, 86
Southern California: American Dream and, 7; country living and, 5, 23; economic expansion in, 54; everyday urbanism and, 8; impact of recessions on real estate, 65; incorporation and, 166; master-planned communities and, 22, 25, 206n79; Midwestern migration to, 53, 129, 209n18; Pacific Rim capital

in, 14, 68, 137, 150, 156; pan-Asian American pride in, 190; political fragmentation in, 149; popular culture depictions, 69, 74–76; promotion of pastoralism in, 20, 25; racial anxieties in, 58, 83, 107; regional voter characteristics in, 58; sprawl in, 20, 22, 24, 28; suburbanization of, 24–25, 28; sunshine narratives, 78, 81, 213n91

Southern California Association of Governments (SCAG), 150

South Gate, 44, 53, 56–57, 75

South Pasadena, 119

Spanish colonization, 14, 21

Sprague, Jannee, 152

sprawl, 24, 28, 147, 159, 168

Staley, Jayne, 177

Starr, Kevin, 213n91

Steel, Michelle Park, 240n13

Steel, Shawn, 240n13

Stewart, Elizabeth, 128–29

Stewart, Janice, 55–57, 110, 128–29

Stewart, Richard, 56–57

St. Lorenzo Ruiz Catholic Church, *94fig.*; anti-MRF activism, 134; compromised design of, 98; country living rhetoric and, 85–86, 93, 95–98; criticism of Filipino-centrism, 93–94; Filipino immigrants and, 93–94, 96–98; Walnut opposition to, 85–86, 93–99; white resistance to, 96–97

St. Martha Catholic Church, 93

Stokes, Donald, 171, 231n39

Stop Grand Avenue Expressway Committee (SGAEC), 162–63, 232n58

Su, Mary, 73, 227n93

Suburban Samurai (Schoner), 1, *2fig.*, 197n1

suburbia: address changes in, 72–73, 212n70; American Dream and, 10, 21, 79–80, 199n24; anxieties about transformation in, 148; Asian-friendly building design and, 68, 70–72; Black and Latino threat narratives, 152; citizenship and, 16; community and in-home amenities, 236n50; conservativism and, 137, 192; country living in, 5–8, 15–18, 24, 34, 53; country living motivations for, 49–50, 54–58, 60–66; demographic changes in, 148; domesticity and, 29, 36; East Valley and, 3–5, 11, 16, 18, 22, 147–49; as edge cities, 24–25, 202n18; environmental movement and, 159; ethnic diversity in, 60–62, 209n22; ethnoburbs and, 9, 15, 200n32; Euro-American design standards, 47, 82, 84–85, 99, 104, 109, 111, 115–16, 118; frontier nostalgia and, 21, 25; homeowner privileges and, 154, 164; homogeneity myths and, 8; impact on rural space, 39; Latinx/Chicanx, 15, 200n30; master-planned communities and, 22, 27–28, 34, 202n21; middle-class lifestyle and, 61, 65, 80, 82, 102, 119, 151, 166, 179; myths of, 5, 9–10, 15, 19, 148, 193–94; pastoralism and, 20, 30; racial diversity in, 62–64, 209n22; racial liberalism and, 19, 81; remoteness and, 54; as reproduction of other locales, 7–8; rurality and, 5, 16, 19, 48; spaces of belonging and, 83; spatial regulation in, 61, 64; Sunbelt and, 45, 202n18; urbanized, 24; vertical growth and, 25; western Americana narratives in, 20–21, 23, 25; whiteness and, 16–17, 19, 23, 82–84, 118, 166, 174. *See also* Asian suburbanites; ethnoburbs

Sugrue, Tom, 137

Sunbelt: color- and class-blind rhetoric, 179; conservativism and, 56, 140, 237n57; decentralized government in, 149; homeowners associations (HOAs) and, 168; master-planned communities and, 202n18; metropolitan, 7, 24; populism and, 143; suburban politics, 237n57; suburbs and, 24, 45

Sykes, Tom, 62

Takaki, Ronald, 14

Taylor, Elizabeth, 35

Taylor, Mechelle, 129

Taylor, Roy, 88

Teaford, Jon, 149, 166

Temple City, 150

Tennant, Forest, 110

Thompson, Larry, 60

Thompson, Sandra, 60–61, 65, 108

open space in, 35–36, 61, 75, 204n65; opposition to St. Lorenzo Ruiz Catholic Church, 85–86, 93–99; Pacific Rim capital in, 156; Parks and Recreation Commission, 64; Planning Commission, 64, 94–96, 228n105; population growth in, 152; promotion of agrarian heritage, 36, 150, 202n21; property values in, 120; public schools and, 119–21, 123–28, 220n4; quality of life concerns, 192; race/ethnicity in, *51tab.*, *52tab.*, 63–65, 156, 210n32; rural authenticity and, 48, 154; rural-themed subdivisions in, 35–38; rural urbanism and, 37; school redistricting movements, 123–28, 130, 223n42; Slow Growth movement and, 35, 150–51, 155–56; Snow Creek neighborhood, 20–21, 36–37, *37fig.*, 38, 132, 154; spatial regulation in, 64, 79, 156–57; suburbanization of, 16, 161; Three Oaks, 228n2; Timberline neighborhood, 36, 66–67; tract homes in, *155fig.*; Walnut Hills project, 147, 154, 156, 164, 228n2; white-collar families in, 58, 60–61; white flight from, 236n39. *See also* Snow Creek neighborhood (Walnut); St. Lorenzo Ruiz Catholic Church

Walnut Area Residents for Change (WARF), 222n24

Walnut Family Festival, 142

Walnut Hills Development Company, 156

Walnut Hills project, 147, 154, 156, 164, 228n2

Walnut Times Magazine, 156

Walnut Valley Unified School District (WVUSD), 120, 123–26, 128, 220n4, 222n26

waste management, 132–34. *See also* Material Recovery Facility (MRF)

Wat Thai Buddhist Temple, 88

Watts, 208n1

Wedell, Donna, 91

Wei, Helen, 101, 111

Welch, Bud, 90

Wentworth, June, 95, 150

Wentworth, William, 149–50

Werner, Gary, 163

West Covina: annexation of Walnut, 35; Asian strip malls in, 40; City of Industry MRF plan and, 132; class diversity in, 119; competition for homes in, 75; development of, 34; English-signage laws, 110–11; Filipino immigrants in, 93–94; public schools and, 123–24; race/ethnicity in, 119

Western rurality: Asian assimilation and, 112; concerns with end of, 107; country living and, 5, 19, 38, 65, 193; protection of, 93; suburban lifestyle and, 5; threat of Asian families to, 47, 100

West Hollywood, 187, 239n92

Westminster, 108

West San Gabriel Valley: anti-Asianism in, 100, 150; Asian stores in, 150; Asian suburbanization in, 11, 100, 150; Chinese immigrants and, 8–9, 66, 68, 72, 199n17; pan-Asian American pride in, 190; political left and, 138

When We Were Cowboys (Schoner), 1, 197n2

white-Asian conflict: Hsi Lai Buddhist Temple and, 86–91; incorporation movement and, 18; postwar suburbia and, 6; public schools and, 121, 221n13; resistance to Asian settlement, 9, 14–15; resistance to ethnic change, 91; transnationality and, 11

white flight, 43, 119

whiteness: country living and, 5–6, 16, 23, 151; frontier imaginary and, 3, 23, 33, 105, 116; privileges of, 14, 17, 83, 145; rural land-use activism and, 33–34; suburbia and, 16–17, 19, 23, 82–84, 118, 166

whites: acceptance of Asian immigrants, 15–16, 118, 142, 144; alliances with Asian residents, 142; backlash against civil rights, 179, 237n57; color- and class-blind rhetoric, 16, 179; country living and, 5–6; cross-racial partnerships and, 117–18, 143–44; defining, 14; frontier imaginary and, 3, 10; perceptions of Asian consumers, 224n68; social controls and, 145

Founded in 1893,
UNIVERSITY OF CALIFORNIA PRESS
publishes bold, progressive books and journals
on topics in the arts, humanities, social sciences,
and natural sciences—with a focus on social
justice issues—that inspire thought and action
among readers worldwide.

The UC PRESS FOUNDATION
raises funds to uphold the press's vital role
as an independent, nonprofit publisher, and
receives philanthropic support from a wide
range of individuals and institutions—and from
committed readers like you. To learn more, visit
ucpress.edu/supportus.